Scottish Nationalism

Scottish Nationalism

*History, Ideology and
the Question of Independence*

Richard Finlay

BLOOMSBURY ACADEMIC
LONDON • NEW YORK • OXFORD • NEW DELHI • SYDNEY

BLOOMSBURY ACADEMIC
Bloomsbury Publishing Plc
50 Bedford Square, London, WC1B 3DP, UK
1385 Broadway, New York, NY 10018, USA
29 Earlsfort Terrace, Dublin 2, Ireland

BLOOMSBURY, BLOOMSBURY ACADEMIC and the Diana logo are
trademarks of Bloomsbury Publishing Plc

First published in Great Britain 2022
This paperback edition published 2023

Copyright © Richard Finlay, 2022

Richard Finlay has asserted his right under the Copyright, Designs and
Patents Act, 1988, to be identified as Author of this work.

For legal purposes the Acknowledgements on p. vii constitute an
extension of this copyright page.

Cover image © LNER poster by Doris Zinkeisen, 1898–1991

All rights reserved. No part of this publication may be reproduced or transmitted
in any form or by any means, electronic or mechanical, including photocopying,
recording, or any information storage or retrieval system, without prior permission
in writing from the publishers.

Bloomsbury Publishing Plc does not have any control over, or responsibility for, any
third-party websites referred to or in this book. All internet addresses given in this
book were correct at the time of going to press. The author and publisher regret any
inconvenience caused if addresses have changed or sites have ceased to exist, but
can accept no responsibility for any such changes.

A catalogue record for this book is available from the British Library.

Library of Congress Cataloging-in-Publication Data

Names: Finlay, Richard J., author.
Title: Scottish nationalism : history, ideology and the question of
independence / Richard Finlay.
Description: London ; New York : Bloomsbury Academic, 2022. |
Includes bibliographical references and index. | Contents: List of figures–
Acknowledgements–List of abbreviations–Introduction–The historic nation–
Nationalism–Three constitutionalism–Home rule and unionism–
Ideology: left, right and the state–Conclusion–Bibliography–Index.
Identifiers: LCCN 2021054360 (print) | LCCN 2021054361 (ebook) |
ISBN 9781350278103 (hardback) | ISBN 9781350278134 (paperback) |
ISBN 9781350278127 (pdf) | ISBN 9781350278110 (epub)
Subjects: LCSH: Self-determination, National–Scotland–History–21st century. |
Scotland–Politics and government–21st century. | Nationalism–Scotland–History. |
Scottish National Party. | Scotland–History–Autonomy and independence movements. |
Scotland–Relations–Great Britain. | Great Britain–Relations–Scotland.
Classification: LCC DA828 .F56 2022 (print) | LCC DA828 (ebook) |
DDC 20.5409411–dc23/eng/20211123
LC record available at https://lccn.loc.gov/2021054360
LC ebook record available at https://lccn.loc.gov/2021054361

ISBN: HB: 978-1-3502-7810-3
PB: 978-1-3502-7813-4
ePDF: 978-1-3502-7812-7
eBook: 978-1-3502-7811-0

Typeset by Newgen KnowledgeWorks Pvt. Ltd., Chennai, India

To find out more about our authors and books visit www.bloomsbury.com
and sign up for our newsletters.

Contents

List of figures	vi
Acknowledgements	vii
List of abbreviations	viii
Introduction	1
1 The historic nation	23
2 Nationalism	55
3 Constitutionalism	89
4 Home rule and unionism	121
5 Ideology: Left, right and the state	157
Conclusion	191
Notes	195
Select bibliography	237
Index	245

Figures

1 By-election poster (1928) from the National Party of Scotland invoking the spirit of William Wallace   24
2 This photograph shows all those who attended the SNP Conference (1956) at the Allan Water Hotel, Bridge of Allan   56
3 SNP Election Committee, 1964   90
4 The National Party of Scotland at the Glasgow University election for rector (1928) when Compton Mackenzie was narrowly defeated by the prime minister Stanley Baldwin   122
5 Cartoon from the *Scots Independent* (1935) illustrating the point that government policies work to the advantage of England against Scotland   158

Acknowledgements

My colleagues and friends at the University of Strathclyde have provided a solid base of support over the years, and I owe them an incredible debt of gratitude. Evan Stewart discussed the ideas contained in this book at length and helped me to considerably sharpen my argument. Thanks also to Alastair and May. Ewen Cameron helped widen my knowledge on specific aspects of the history of the Scottish National Party (SNP) and Steve Slater on wider aspects of 19th century British politics. Abigail Lane and Emily Drewe from Bloomsbury Academic Press have been the very models of professionalism and efficiency. My thanks also to two anonymous referees who helped sharpen up the focus of the book. The following have helped in more tangential ways: Kate, Stevie and Leon Love, Thomas and Kaleigh Conroy, Sue Livingstone, Robert and Janette Finlay, Andi and Andy Curley, Rachel Robbins and Gordon Craig. The book is dedicated to Jack with lots of love.

Stirling, 14 June 2021

Abbreviations

BL	British Library
NLS	National Library of Scotland
NPS	National Party of Scotland
SHRA	Scottish Home Rule Association
SNC	Scottish National Congress
SNL	Scots National League
SNP	Scottish National Party
SRO	Scottish Records Office

Introduction

> *But the problem is whether there's vitality enough left to feed the nation with the courage and endurance to assert those sovereign rights. So much of our Nationalist propaganda has been concentrated on telling people that if we managed our own affairs we should manage them more profitably, but there's no vision of true independence inspiring such an argument. When you press that kind of Nationalist you'll find that he is using a municipal drain-pipe as a telescope for the future. His Scottish Parliament is hardly more than a glorified County Council. He's not prepared to sacrifice half a crown, much less imperil his own livelihood. And if he's not prepared to face material loss. He's right to be canny. I believe that the kind of independence a few of us dream of would involve ten and perhaps twenty years of hardship and bitter self-denial.*
>
> – Mackenzie, *The North Wind of Love*, vol. I, 15

The author of *Whisky Galore*, the founder of *Gramophone* magazine and a former British intelligence officer, Compton Mackenzie stated it starkly in a way that few would find politically expedient, that Scottish independence was a matter of principle that went beyond pound and pence. It was a fundamental point of political conviction, and the evolution of the reasoning behind it is the subject of this book. Any hope that the referendum of 2014 would settle the constitutional relationship between Scotland and England now looks forlorn. As the journalist Alex Massie describes it, the national movement is like a wave of zombies. No matter how many times unionism defeats it, Scottish independence will keep coming back and, unlike the defenders of the status quo, it only has to win once to secure victory.[1] The objective of the Union is now reduced to survival. At the time of writing, opinion polls have shown those who support independence at consistently around 50 per cent, but the demographic breakdown makes unhappy reading for those content with the constitutional status quo. Put bluntly, the Union in Scotland is maintained by the elderly with younger people more in favour of independence, although it may be the case that as voters become older their scepticism increases as to the wisdom of constitutional change.[2] It is safe to say, however, that a clear majority of people in Scotland have at some time or another believed in Scottish independence, and almost two-thirds believe that Scotland will become independent at some point in the future. The omens for the Union do not look good. Furthermore, the electoral landscape of Scotland has been transformed with the Scottish National Party (SNP) having established a political hegemony that has been unprecedented for almost a century.[3] One would have go back to the time before the First World War when the Liberals held fifty-eight out of seventy-two Westminster parliamentary constituencies with 54 per cent of the vote to witness the extraordinary dominance enjoyed by a single political party in Scotland and that was in the days before universal suffrage. The SNP has been in government in Edinburgh since 2007 and has won a majority of Scottish Westminster seats in the last three general elections, which, according to Margaret Thatcher, would have been a mandate for independence.[4] In addition to the impact of Brexit on the constitutional future of Northern Ireland, there are very real questions as to whether the British state will survive long into the twenty-first century. If Scotland becomes independent, the United Kingdom ceases to exist because, technically, in 1707 the two separate kingdoms of Scotland and England united to create Great Britain – neither Wales nor Northern Ireland are kingdoms – so no Scotland means no Britain and no United Kingdom. Needless to say, the ending of the British state would probably have a number of international ramifications in terms of maintaining Great Power status.

The speed and rapidity of the changes that could bring about unprecedented constitutional change on the British mainland would not have been anticipated several decades ago. Few could have suspected that the survival of the United Kingdom of Great Britain and Northern Ireland would be in doubt. For a long time the Scottish national movement was considered a marginal force in both Scottish and British politics, but it has now assumed a major contemporary significance. As things and ideas that matter to us in the present by default matter in the past, the historical significance of the Scottish national movement has correspondingly increased because of its current relevance. Almost one hundred years ago, the idea that Scotland should become a modern, independent nation state came into being, and that vision has sustained several generations of political activists until the present one is now within touching distance of that goal. Contrary to what many expected at the time, the inane ramblings and fantastical imaginations of a small number of political misfits have matured over time to become the accepted political wisdom of possibly the majority in Scotland. Irrespective of what the future holds, the fact that the political landscape of Scotland, and to a lesser extent Britain, has been shaped by their ideas now for several decades has assured them of a place in the history books.[5]

The objective of this study is straightforward: it is to give those pioneers their place in a history book. It will chart and explore the development of what might be described as the philosophical kernel of Scottish nationalism. That is to say the fundamental political principles around which the Scottish national movement has built and continues to build its argument for independence.[6] In the rough and tumble of contemporary political debate, a lot of the basic philosophical assumptions are either forgotten or simply assumed without any close examination or discussion. As will hopefully be shown, the idea of Scottish independence is based on a number of intellectual building blocks which provide the platform from which the proposition can be launched into the political arena. In the next two paragraphs the basic intellectual architecture that holds up the argument for Scottish independence will be described in order to provide a route map of where the book intends to go. A Scottish nationalist is someone who believes that Scotland is a nation and as a nation it should exercise its right to self-determination. History is important because it shows that Scotland was one of the first nations in Europe and had most of the usual hallmarks associated with nationhood. The union with England altered what would have been the normal historical trajectory into modern statehood. Independence would therefore correct this historical anomaly and set Scottish history back on its normal track. Scottish nationalists are nationalists because they believe in the primacy of the nation as a political unit and that statehood is the natural condition for nations. This is a quite narrow and specific definition of nationalism, and although this political philosophy has a lot of unpleasant ideological baggage associated with it, those who believe in Scottish independence have had to engage with the wider intellectual ramifications of articulating such a clear territorial identification as the foundation of their political philosophy. As we shall see, some have thought long and hard about the issues of nationalism and some have not. Although Scottish nationalists may believe that the union with England in 1707 was a mistake or that it was achieved by fraudulent means, the fact remains that most accept that by the constitutional and diplomatic standards of the day, it was legal. Unlike other nationalists in different parts of the world where independence is associated with ideas of national liberation, Scottish nationalists recognized the legality of the British state and, as such, believe that it can only be undone by legal and constitutional methods. Although there were a very small number of hotheads, Scottish nationalism, unlike many other nationalisms, has a core philosophic commitment to attain its political aims by peaceful, legal and constitutional means.

Scottish political culture, by and large, has accepted that Scotland is a nation, and the principal division that now exists centres around whether that nationhood can only be expressed through independence or whether it can be accommodated within the Union. The campaign for the creation of a Scottish parliament within a devolved constitutional settlement, although still maintaining the British state, has always used the language of Scottish nationality to make its claims. Scotland ought to have a parliament because it was a nation, not because it was a more effective administrative unit. Unsurprisingly, there is a considerable intellectual overlap between the arguments for a devolved settlement and independence, with many in the latter camp believing that the former was a crucial first step towards the latter. Many Unionists also believed this, and hence their opposition to any form of constitutional change, which, it was argued, will inevitably lead to a terminus of independence. Unionists also accept that Scotland is a nation, but as will be argued in this book, the nature of Unionist nationality is a complex one and does not quite match the idea that the Union is an Anglo-Scottish partnership as many see Britain as *the nation*. Scotland's nationality is largely historic and the relationship is a hierarchical one with being British at the apex. How this squares with normal definitions of nationhood is, to say the least, problematic and hence the reason why nationalists reject the basic proposition of unionism as being incompatible with ideas pertaining to national dignity. This has been countered by arguing that the Union is a partnership and not one of dominance. Finally, Scottish independence is a policy, not an ideology. It is a single issue in a world of politics dominated by bodies of ideas that are usually located on the left–right axis of political ideology. Most political movements evolve a bundle of ideas to support their particular cause or interest, and the Scottish national movement was no exception. Given that the dominant political discourse over the twentieth century was that between left and right, no political movement could escape this basic fact of life. Furthermore, nationalism was an ideology associated with the right because it promoted the primacy of the nation above that of class, and left-wing critics argued that this was simply a ruse of the establishment and elites to deflect attention away from the social inequities associated with the development of capitalism. Paradoxically, most members of the national movement since its inception have tended to belong to the left, and intellectually reconciling the primacy of the nation with the social iniquities within the nation has been a major intellectual undertaking. For some the circle can be squared by making the case that independence will make for a fairer society, which involves engaging with the wider ideological dimensions of the left/right dichotomy. But also, by its very definition, the national movement, theoretically at least, has to champion the rights and well-being of all in the nation and construct an appeal that is *supra* class and sectional interests, and this restrains the scope of its ideological engagement on the conventional left–right axis. This marks it out from other parties in the conventional world of politics that can use social class to establish a solid electoral constituency. In short, an intellectual mix of history, the idea of nationalism, constructing a constitutional road to independence in the world of Scottish politics while navigating the complexities of the left–right ideological axis in the period from the 1920s to the 1950s, all contributed to the making of a coherent body of ideas – or ideology – around which the quest for Scottish independence was formed. It will be argued that this philosophical core lies at the heart of the national movement, and all other policies and ideas orbit around this centre. This is not to say that the philosophy of Scottish nationalism was complete and its intellectual journey had come to an end but rather that the foundations of its subsequent development had been laid.

It can be said with a fair degree of confidence that the constitutional question has been a dominant theme in Scottish politics from the mid-1970s when the SNP made its first substantial electoral breakthrough, and while there has been an ebb and flow in terms of its significance, the point remains that of all the issues, it has had the greatest longevity and it shows no signs of disappearing. Since 2011 a majority of members of the Scottish parliament in Holyrood have been in favour of independence. In 2014 a referendum on Scottish independence showed that 45 per cent of the Scottish electorate voted to end the Union, which was a much tighter result than had been predicted, and at every subsequent general election, the SNP has won a comfortable majority of Scottish seats. The nationalist genie is out the bottle and reluctant to go back in again. At the British level, the 'Scottish Question' has been around for the same length of time as the 'Irish Question' was in the late nineteenth and early twentieth centuries. It is always difficult to discern historical trends when in the middle of them. When historians in England in the late nineteenth century charted the rise of the British Empire, they began with the Anglo-Scottish Union in 1707 as marking the beginning of the *Expansion of England*.[7] More recently, there has been the tendency to see that process in complete reversal. Scottish independence and the reunification of Ireland are now presented as part of the 'contraction of England' back to the position it had during the seventeenth century.⁸ Interestingly, one of the first scholarly discussions of Scottish and Welsh nationalism was made by Sir Reginald Coupland, the Beit Professor of Imperial History at Oxford in 1954. He was interested in the development of nationalism in the empire, especially in the white dominions, and did not believe that it was an intrinsically bad thing but rather a natural growth of political development:

> The word 'nationalism' has acquired in our time a sinister implication, but in this book it will be used to mean no more than an active consciousness of nationality and a devotion to the national interest. Nationalism in this sense is virtually identical to patriotism. Its morality depends on whether the national interest is rightly or wrongly understood.⁹

Coupland was especially interested in the relationship between nationalism and the state and whether national identity would survive without some form of political representation. While he did not believe that a dominion-style parliament would work for both Scotland and Wales, he did show a lot of sympathy for some form of federal relationship.¹⁰ Although Scottish independence has gained a wider degree of intellectual currency in the contemporary world as it has been tied in with the question of Brexit and the debate about British global decline and an existential crisis of identity,¹¹ it is not the intention of this study to attempt to address this question. Having said that, it will acknowledge, when appropriate, if matters have a bearing on the issue of the British imperial experience.

Scottish nationalism, Scottish national identity and Scottish independence have generated a growing body of scholarly literature, and recent publications by Scott Hames, Ben Jackson, Malcolm Petrie and Naomi Lloyd-Jones demonstrate a continuing interest in the topic.¹² Early studies of the movement in the 1960s and 1970s conflated the campaigns for home rule and independence and stretched the origins of the growth of Scottish nationalism as a political movement back into the mid-nineteenth century.¹³ Groups such as the National Association for the Vindication of Scottish Rights, which was formed in 1853 and complained about the treatment of Scotland in the Union but did not campaign for any constitutional realignment, were bundled together to create the idea of a continuity of nationalist tradition.¹⁴ Other than a fairly superficial similarity in terms of concern as to Scotland's place in the Union, there is little that would warrant any justification to view this and other ginger groups as direct forerunners of the modern nationalist movement. The focus on the campaign for home rule in the late nineteenth century and first half of the twentieth century as having a relationship to modern Scottish nationalism is more comprehensible in that it was always understood that home rule was a constitutional change that had a degree of overlap with independence, both in terms of creating a form of state apparatus and having a number of adherents who belonged to both camps. The use of the term 'self-government' further obfuscated the issue in that it was frequently used to describe the form of government that existed in the so-called white dominions of the empire, and those who believed in home rule and those who believed in independence were quite happy using the term and reading into it whatever they wanted to see. Where this book takes a different approach from previous studies is that it tightly focuses on a specific period in time and on those who advocated independence, that is, the creation of a separate Scottish state.

The works that have been done on the SNP have tended to concentrate on the organizational development, including its many secessionist and splinter movements, its institutional apparatus and the emergence of political strategies to engage with the process of contesting elections.[15] They have also examined the development of the party from a chronological perspective which does tend to magnify the significance of by-elections, general elections, party conferences and the like, and this does not help in elucidating the intellectual development of the movement. At this point, it is important to mention that most scholarly discussions of the nationalist movement in Scotland have come from political scientists who have contributed greatly to our understanding of the development of the SNP and the significance of Scottish independence in the contemporary world.[16] Of particular note is James Mitchell, who has always displayed great sensitivity to the historical context. He has produced a number of pioneering studies that have had a major impact on the study of both Scottish politics and Scottish history. His study of unionism brought back into focus the idea that Scottish Conservatism had always a much more nuanced understanding of the Union than their English colleagues. Unionism was not unitarianism.[17] Mitchell also made a significant contribution by examining the various strategies that have been employed historically in the endeavour to achieve self-government which examined pressure group tactics, cross-party campaigns, local plebiscites and dedicated organizations and political parties. The rationale behind the take up and success of each of the strategies provided an in-depth comparative study of the different methods used in the quest for constitutional change.[18] A steady output of articles and chapters altered, added and augmented our understanding of the development of the SNP and, more often than not, provided timely corrections to popular assumptions that had no substantive basis in fact. The idea that the SNP veered sharply to the left in the 1980s, for example, was effectively debunked by a close examination of policy development.[19] The first detailed examination of the party membership and its process of modernization and professionalization leading to its breakthrough in the early twenty-first century added to a substantial body of scholarly achievement.[20] Finally, a wider discussion that sets the issue of Scottish politics and its constitutional dimension in a panoramic historical perspective gives us our best bird's eye view of the long-term development of Scottish nationalism.[21]

While Mitchell has had an eye firmly fixed on the historical dimension, the same cannot always be said for some of his colleagues. One issue, which is a perfectly reasonable and understandable one, is that the study of political science is concerned with the contemporary world and as such has a focus on policies and developments that are concerned with the here and now. From the historian's perspective, the close discussion of specific aspects of policy, political strategy, opinion poll changes, power shifts, reshuffles and the like is often quickly overtaken by events.[22] Perhaps the best and rather unfortunate example of the short life of political science studies is by the eminent scholar (and distinguished historian) Iain McLean whose article on the 'Rise and Fall of the SNP' was published in 1970, just as the SNP began to rise again.[23] What this book hopes to achieve by examining the establishment of its core philosophic principles that are located firmly in the past is something that will outlast the vagaries of policy changes and shifts in contemporary opinion but at the same time still have a relevance to the present day because it discusses the stripped-down essentials of what gives a Scottish nationalist their political identity. Although these ideas, principles and values evolved over three-quarters of a century ago, they still have a contemporary validity. Scottish nationalists today still believe that they belong to a nation that has its authenticity demonstrated by history and that as a nation it should exercise its right to self-determination by constitutional means and do so while engaging with the wider political debate regarding devolution and unionism and navigate this within the framework of the left–right ideological axis. Contemporary debates on environmentalism, gender, educational policy, economic strategy and the other concerns of the reality of daily political engagement come on top of the intellectual foundations that were established many decades ago.

At this point in the discussion it is necessary to provide clear and precise definitions in our use of terminology.[24] The words 'nationalist' and 'nationalism' encompass a wide range of meanings that traverse an extensive distance in terms of both geography and chronology. Ho Chi Minh, the leader of North Vietnam during the 1950s and 1960s, and Lajos Kossuth, the figurehead of the Hungarian Revolution of 1848, can both be described as nationalists, but they have little intellectual or ideological affinity. We shall discuss some of these problems of definition in Chapter 2, but a conventional use of the word 'nationalist' is to describe someone who seeks to gain political independence from a larger political structure. Those who argued for Irish independence from Britain, Polish independence from Germany and Russia, Czech independence from the Austro-Hungarian Empire and Greek independence from the Ottoman Empire were known as nationalists. They wanted to align their nationality with independent statehood. In Scottish history, there has been a tendency to use the term 'Scottish nationalism' in relation to unionism to make the case that Scottish identity is perfectly compatible with British identity and, indeed, could reinforce it.[25] While this is undoubtedly true, the term 'Unionist nationalism' is problematic and inappropriate because it clearly makes no tautological sense in that a Unionist by definition is opposed to Scottish independence, and as far as most of the rest of the world is concerned, the word 'nationalist' is used to describe someone who strives for political independence.[26] This is a contradiction in the same way that a capitalist socialist or a liberal authoritarian is. Another confusion in Scottish history and politics is to talk about a small 'n' nationalism, which refers to Scottish identity and an affinity with the idea that Scotland is a nation. It is usually used when describing the movement for the creation of a devolved Scottish parliament, but again, as most of the world would understand it, this is not nationalism as conventionally defined.[27] Perhaps the weakest dimension from a methodological perspective of using the term 'nationalist' for those who do not support Scottish independence is that neither Unionist nationalists nor small 'n' nationalists actually described themselves thus. As such terms are applied retrospectively, there is a danger of anachronism in the sense that these labels would not be recognized by the historical actors themselves, and it therefore again begs the question whether it is appropriate to use the term 'nationalist' in any other context that does not stand for political independence. Although there are complications with home rulers which will be discussed in Chapter 4, throughout the book the terms 'Scottish nationalist' and 'Scottish nationalism' are used solely in the context of the endeavour to acquire (or as they would put it themselves, reacquire) independent, sovereign statehood. And to reinforce the previous point, Scottish nationalists always used this term to describe themselves and were described as such by their political opponents.

The term 'ideology' has had bad press, and it has become associated with the extreme left or the extreme right. It is usually used to describe a political perspective that is dogmatic and unbending and is often associated with the mindset of totalitarian regimes. The term 'ideologue' now has a pejorative ring to it. In reality, ideology means nothing more than a system of ideas or ideals associated with a political movement or point of view. Liberalism, for example, is an ideology, and in the absence of any other suitable term, the word ideology will be applied to the body of political thought that evolved around the Scottish national movement.[28] In politics, the relationship with ideas is a complex one. For some social theorists and historians, rather than shaping society and political movements, ideology is more a consequence of social and economic change rather than the cause of it. This view would hold that the upsurge in support for independence is not a consequence of the ideas and thoughts that are discussed in this book coming to some sort of germination, but rather it is a result of social, economic and cultural change which has created a favourable environment for those ideas to take hold. The chicken comes before the egg. Having said that, without those ideas in the first place, there would be nothing to take advantage of the favourable circumstance. The egg comes before the chicken.[29] In any case, the ideas under discussion emerged at a time when there was little likelihood of a nationalist electoral breakthrough and the prospect of an independent Scotland seemed a dim and distant possibility. The political ideas of the nationalists movement at this time were undoubtedly shaped by the wider socio-economic, cultural and political background – all ideas are – but this was distinctly a minority view and one that did not in any meaningful way represent a socio-economic movement such as a radicalized working class or a marginalized middle class or a rejected segment of society. In that way the ideas have a currency of their own and are very much the product of their own distinctive environment of the world of Scottish nationalism in the mid-twentieth century.

Given what has been said, it might be a legitimate question to ask why these ideas matter. In the world of politics, ideas, or rather more accurately ideology, is of fundamental importance because it is the one thing that can confer legitimacy on a political movement, especially if the values that are being espoused are presented as being motivated from a moral point of principle and not narrow self-interest. In his study of eighteenth-century politics, Harry Dickinson made the point eloquently:

> Those historians who stress that political agents are primarily engaged in efforts to justify and legitimate their political actions thereby imply that these explanations have a chance of being believed and approved by others. Those political agents who seek to legitimate their actions may be endeavouring to disguise their self-interested desire for power, but they clearly hope that either their audience will be misled into believing their protestations that they are acting out of principle

or that the audience will realize that it is in their own interests to support these actions and label them as principled. In other words, either the audience genuinely believe in certain principles, or it wishes to register approval of what these agents are trying to do and, for its own self-image, prefers to describe these agents as men of principle. In either case, men are recognising that there are actions which the age is prepared to admire or condemn. Legitimation is only possible if a society makes it clear which actions it will deplore as being self-interested and which it will admire as being 'principled'.[30]

In short, no political principles, no legitimacy. The adherence to a particular ideology is the fundamental point of identification with a political movement, and, theoretically at least, all who belong to that movement must profess an affinity with these ideas. It may seem like a fairly logical and straightforward thing to say, but when we think of all the reasons why people enter the world of politics, we can see why ideas are vital to legitimacy. There is the apocryphal story of Captain Walter Elliot, who would go on to become a Conservative Scottish secretary of state in 1936. At the end of the First World War he received a telegram asking to stand as a parliamentary candidate in Lanark to which he replied that he would be delighted and added as an afterthought, for which party?[31] Many enter politics because it is seen to be part of a family tradition, for others it is due to a sense of public service, many for self-centred reasons, some because they like politics as a career and then, finally, a number because they believe in the ideology and principles of the movement. One of the reasons why the ideas of any political movement at its inception matter is that they are produced almost exclusively by people who believe in these principles because with none of the trappings of political or electoral success, only the dedicated and committed are involved. Those ideas and values then become the benchmark of political adherence, and membership is possible only through acceptance of this ideology.

The evolution of ideas, values and policies is a process that can be reconstructed by looking at the correspondence of prominent figures in the movement who are often more candid in private letters as to the motivation, rationale and aspirations that lie behind public pronouncements. The National Library of Scotland houses an extensive collection of the private papers and correspondence of the key figures who were involved in the movement until the mid-1960s, and these have been consulted. The various nationalist journals are also a useful forum for the circulation of ideas, and there has been a long tradition of public debate that has taken place in these open forums. In particular, the *Scots Independent* which was established in 1926 has been, quite often to the annoyance of the SNP leadership, a place where ideas, speculations, pronouncements and arguments have been aired. By examining the accumulations of written pieces on particular topics, it is possible to see the emergence of broad areas of agreement, as well as the sharp contours of disputation. Nationalist pamphlets, texts and memoires are further sources of information, and the fact that the movement was in the main led by middle-class activists meant that there was always a steady literary output which is of great use to the historian. The Scottish national movement has had a strong connection with the artistic world, and their ideas and writings have been the focus of literary scholars. Hugh MacDiarmid and Neil Gunn, in particular, have been subject to numerous studies and their intellectual worlds explored and discussed.[32] One problem with the attention that the literary movement has received from scholars is that quite often the primary focus is on their artistic endeavour, with politics rendered to secondary consideration. Furthermore, such figures tended to be marginal in terms of the movement, and their public profile tends to exaggerate the weight that their ideas carried among the rank-and-file nationalists. As far as possible, parallels, comparisons and contrasts with nationalist movements in Europe will be made to provide a broader context and wider discussion of the issues.

Having said all that, one of the major problems in reconstructing the process of building an ideology or a political philosophy is that there can be many different interpretations of what is meant by a particular policy or for that matter ideology. The objective of the SNP for most of its history was 'self-government' for Scotland. For some this meant political independence in a sovereign state, for others it was a devolved parliament working within either the British state or functioning within a British imperial framework like the self-governing dominion nations. Furthermore, for yet others it was a process that would start out as a devolved parliament but then evolve into an independent state if that was what the people of Scotland wanted. For some the principle of what the nature of a future Scottish government would be was the priority, for others it was the principle that the people should decide what form of government was best. And while the national movement was, in the main, focused on a single issue, the reality was that it was unlikely to garner much political success if that was the only thing in its political programme. British political history in the nineteenth and early twentieth centuries was littered with the remains of various single-issue campaigning groups who largely worked by applying pressure on the established parties. From the Anti-Vivisection League to the church disestablishmentarians, there were a variety of organizations that did their best to cajole, persuade and sometimes threaten the main parties to implement the policy that formed their raison d'etre.[33] This was the method favoured by those in support of Scottish home rule or self-government in the late nineteenth and early twentieth centuries. After the First World War the main focus of their expectations was on the Labour Party and by the latter part of the 1920s there was a growing consensus that this strategy was unlikely to succeed. The only way to bring about Scottish self-government was to form a specific political party for that purpose which would contest elections to achieve this goal.[34] As soon as this happened, it ceased to be a single-issue pressure group that only needed the one policy and became a political movement that would need a stronger and more robust ideological apparatus to support its electoral endeavours.

Although there was always a rationale for the creation of a Scottish parliament and many of those arguments could simply be carried over into the new organization, the formation of a tailor-made political party rather than relying on the existing ones was a step change in terms of political priorities. Why that should be the case now required a much greater and in-depth elucidation. The idea that as a nation Scotland required its own state apparatus is a much larger philosophic proposition, especially in the changed international circumstances following the First World War where new ideas regarding nationhood and statehood were in circulation.[35] These new ideas and new expectations would have to be engaged with and the reasons why the nation should become the primary unit of political organization required considerably more detailed arguments to back it up. The equation of statehood and nationhood needed a reassessment of ideas pertaining to Scottish nationality and an explanation as to why the current constitutional arrangement was no longer effective. In the changed world after the Great War, there were many new nations, especially in Central and Eastern Europe.[36] At the Paris Peace Summit in 1919 where the new boundaries of European nations were drawn up, the increasingly independent new nations of the 'white dominions' made up part of the British delegation but not the old 'mother' nation of Scotland.[37] Ireland had asserted its nationality against the might of the British Empire by force of arms.[38] While the Scots clearly conceived of themselves as a nation, it was a nation without most of the features required for recognition by other nations. Statehood, government and the acknowledgement by other states through international and diplomatic protocol were increasingly seen as necessary to demonstrate the legitimacy of Scottish nationhood. The Scotland of the nineteenth century where nations were contained within multinational entities such as the Austro-Hungarian, Russian and Ottoman empires suddenly found itself in the twentieth century where nations were states and vice versa. It was a new age of international recognition and aspiration with multinational entities such as the League of Nations and growing international agreements on trade, regulation and the like.[39] For a number, Scottish nationality had been left behind and needed to be brought into the modern world by having its own government and state apparatus. This also chimed in with the notion of the right of all nations to self-determination and the emphasis on democratic representation. One major difference between the pre–First World War world of devolution and home rule all round was that it had to a large extent jumped from a British domestic context into an international one. Even the British group of nations, as the white-dominated dominions were called, became increasingly internationalized after the war as Canada, Australia, New Zealand and South Africa each began to become more independent in foreign policy.[40]

So how would Scottish nationalists demonstrate that Scotland was a 'real' nation just like all those others that had sprung into life in the period after the First World War? Perhaps the most direct and simplest way was to turn to history, and this forms the basis of the first chapter. All nations construct narratives about their origin and development, and as the nineteenth-century French historian Ernest Renan pointed out in his seminal lecture *Qu'est-ce qu'une nation?*, this was just as much about collective forgetting as collective remembering.[41] On the face of it, there did not seem to be an issue. What would become the Kingdom of Scotland is traditionally dated from the mid-ninth century when Cinaed mac Ailpin (Kenneth MacAlpin) united the Scots and Picts, and this was among the first nations to emerge in Europe.[42] The kingdom expanded to include all of what would become Scotland, it fought off repeated attempts at English invasion and colonization, it had its own church, its own laws, its own administration and formed international treaties with other countries, and its monarchy married into the other royal houses in Europe, including the English Tudors. As a consequence of this, the Scottish king ascended to the crown of England in 1603, but the two kingdoms remained separate legal and constitutional entities. For a Scottish nationalist, the problems started in 1707 when the Scottish and English political elites formed a political union between the two kingdoms, or perhaps the proper way to view this is a union between two early modern states. Up to this point, Scottish historical development was like any other established nation in Europe. Although the Union of 1707 maintained the survival of the Scottish systems of law and education and guaranteed the status of the Presbyterian Church as an established national church, the loss of its parliament and the integration into the English political system meant that it did not continue with the normal development associated with other countries which would emerge as 'nation states' in the nineteenth century.[43]

Just as the nations that emerged as nation states in the eighteenth and nineteenth centuries had their own historical narratives, so too did those nations that aspired to statehood and national liberation. The would-be nations of Europe of the nineteenth and twentieth centuries constructed their historical accounts with a clear ideological imperative to demonstrate that the quest for freedom from colonizing and invading larger nations was the dominant historical theme.[44] As can be seen from the broad outline of Scottish history above, a narrative that culminated with a quest for freedom from occupation and colonization was going to be problematic. Firstly, invasion had been successfully resisted until 1707. Secondly, although Scotland ceased to be an independent nation in 1707, this was done through negotiation and not force. Thirdly, and most problematically, what was eradicated in 1707 was statehood and not nationhood. Most Scots still believed that they were a nation, even without having their own separate state. For most European nationalist movements, history became an important ideological prop, but in the Scottish case this was problematic, and Chapter 1 explores why it proved impossible to refashion Scottish history into a conventional nationalist account of resistance to colonization. Furthermore, while not necessarily promoting a colonialist interpretation of the Scottish past, it was always going to be difficult for nationalists to construct a radically different vision of the Scottish past because there was a large degree of historical consensus with a Unionist reading of history. Both nationalists and Unionists accept that it was important that Scotland maintained its independence until the Union of 1707, and the fact that it was able to resist conquest by one of the most powerful European kingdoms was a source of great pride for all. Nationalists argued that history was fine until the Union, which was a mistake, and Unionists argued that independence was a necessary prerequisite for the Union. Unlike Ireland and Wales, Scotland was not conquered, something that both nationalists and Unionists agreed was important to their political vision of the past. Fourthly, the reasons for the acquiescence in the Union and the experience of the period after 1707 created its own problems as we shall see. While the interwar era was one associated with decline, the eighteenth and nineteenth centuries were ones of great Scottish achievements. The national movement could trumpet the inventiveness and ingenuity of the Scots as evidence of their ability for self-government, but to do so would show that the Union worked. A negative reading, on the other hand, could dent national self-confidence. The difficulties of navigating the complexities and contradictions of the Scottish past, it will be argued, meant that the national movement did not evolve an ideological history in the same way that we see with other nationalist movements who used the historical experience as one of the sharpest weapons in their intellectual armoury. As Scottish nationalists found out, the Scottish past was wobbly and unwieldy.

If Scottish history offered little ideological succour for the national movement, then the subject of Chapter 2 – nationalism – was even more problematic. As a political force, nationalism has probably been the most destructive phenomenon to afflict the world, and the ideology comes with a lot of unpleasant and damaging baggage. Needless to say, the movement has always been wary of its association with nationalism, and (apart from Glasgow University students) the word was avoided in the title of the various political organizations, all of them opting for the less problematic and arguably more ideologically neutral 'national'.[45] The term 'nationalism' is hopelessly imprecise because there are a number of variants of the phenomenon which range from the liberal to the extreme in terms of their attitudes to those who do and those who do not belong to their perception of the nation. Each of these types of nationalism theoretically can manifest itself with its own unique characteristics in all the different nations in the world. This is not to say that there are not significant similarities.[46] Although many are uncomfortable with the description 'nationalist' and would rather not use the term, it is an appropriate label for the following reasons.[47] Firstly, the terms 'nationalism' and 'nationalist' are the ones most commonly used to describe those who seek political independence for a nation from a larger territorial entity. Secondly, there is the semantic one that those who stress the primacy of the Scottish nation as a political unit must be Scottish nationalists and espouse Scottish nationalism. That, however, does not mean that they endorse the full panoply of the excesses of nationalism that was evidenced throughout history. As we shall see in Chapter 2, the easiest way to avoid the association with the ills of nationalism was to argue that it was simply a means to an end. Nationalism was purely expedient or instrumental in that once independence was achieved, it ceased to serve any function. The idea that the goal of Scottish independence was simply the best way to remove nuclear weapons or establish a more left-wing or fairer society has frequently been used as a way to blunt the ideological dimension of nationalism. Although the expedient dimension of Scottish independence has been a key feature of much of the nationalist message, it cannot completely be disassociated from the national dimension because it is specifically limited to Scotland. Fundamentally, it is the fact that Scotland is a nation that enables such expedient arguments to be made, so it does not completely escape from the shadow of nationalism.

As is argued in Chapter 2, many made the case that nationalism was neither an inherently good or bad thing and that it was an organic part of human political development. Rather, it was the uses that nationalism was put to that was the problem. Tapping into a tradition of European 'Liberal' nationalism or what we today would call 'civic nationalism', the case was made that the nation was the natural unit of government in the world and that to deny it to Scotland would leave it somewhat incomplete. Nationalism was the basis of internationalism because without the former, the latter could not exist. All nations had the right to self-determination, and an outward-looking and democratic nationalism did not threaten anyone. This line of argument was bolstered by a focus on small nations, and many made the claim that large nations were artificial creations, bureaucratic and impersonal, in which the citizen has no genuine connection to the state and in these circumstances, militarism and imperialism were able to flourish. Small nations, it was claimed, were inherently peaceful because they did not have the capacity to threaten or subdue other countries. The use of the small nation as a way to disassociate from the problems of nationalism, however, came under sustained intellectual assault from both the left and right in interwar Britain. Small nations created instability and competition among the great powers as the larger would always endeavour to absorb the smaller, and this would pull Britain into conflict in Europe as the 1919 Settlement was a source of great contention. 'How horrible, fantastic, incredible it is that we should be digging trenches and trying on gas masks here because of a quarrel in a far-away country between people of whom we know nothing,' opined Neville Chamberlain of the Sudeten crisis in 1938.[48] The small nations that created instability in Europe were caused and created by nationalism, it was claimed, and the danger of continental commitments meant that the empire was left exposed. Here too, according to right-wing critics, the greatest danger was colonial nationalism that sought to bring about the end of British rule, especially in India.[49] The left was equally hostile. The unbound admiration for the Soviet Union convinced many that absorption of small nations into a bigger state's administrative and economic infrastructure made more sense, especially in order to defend socialism from external threats. At a less intellectual level, it was used to justify Soviet expansion into the Baltic states and Eastern Europe during and after the Second World War.[50] In spite of these issues, Scottish nationalists used small nations, especially those in Scandinavia and Western Europe as a template of aspiration and a practical demonstration of what could be achieved. A trend was established that has continued until today where favourable statistics and facts from small independent states can be mined and used in comparison with current conditions in Scotland to show similar small countries enjoy better health, prosperity, economic fortunes and less poverty. It was a convenient and effective way to bring to life potential futures in an independent Scotland.

As Ian Kershaw points out, the book *The Crowd: A Study of the Popular Mind* (1895) by Gustave le Bon underwent forty-five reprints and seventeen translations, and it had a profound influence on the discussion of nationalism because it argued that the emotional urges of the crowd would overwhelm the rationality of the individual.[51] The use of emotion as a means to whip up the masses through nationalism was seen as its most dangerous and destructive quality. Nationalism was not the politics of the rational, and with that in mind, there was perhaps a tendency by the leadership of the national movement to overcompensate by being dull, careful, precise and prone to the use of statistics and facts in making arguments. For a number, especially those on the artistic side of the movement, the emotional dynamic of nationalism was one that they engaged with. While there was talk of a 'national reawakening' and a 'spiritual revival', especially during the 1930s, many felt a deep sense of unease because it echoed the growth of extremism in mainland Europe. Others, however, sought to explore the non-materialist and non-rational dimension of nationalism because they believed an emotional engagement with the nation was a fundamental and vital aspect of the phenomenon. That ethereal quality is one that has been neglected in discussion because politics is dominated by an assumption that it ought to be dictated by reason alone. Perhaps those thoughts and ideas by a small number of artists offer an intriguing insight into what might be a wider, if unspoken and neglected, aspect of nationalism.

Chapter 3 deals with one of the most important and significant aspects of the national movement in Scotland: its legalist and non-violent nature. The Irish campaign for self-government and the subsequent revolution cast a long shadow in Scottish nationalist circles with some taking it as an inspiration, but most believed it served as a warning. From the outset, it was recognized that a revolutionary path to independence was not one that was likely to garner much support from the public, and Scottish nationalists, unlike many of their counterparts in other parts of the world, were remarkably sanguine in accepting that their fellow countrymen and women were unlikely to take up arms for the cause, let alone die for it. A legal and constitutional path to independence required a clear line of argument to sustain its acceptance among members and followers and also to circumvent potential hotheads. As will be argued, this involved an in-depth discussion as to the nature of the British state that was formed as a result of the Anglo-Scottish Union in 1707. Most nationalists argued that the treaty that was negotiated in 1707 was a flawed one which contained a host of inconsistencies and created an unbalanced constitutional arrangement. Whatever the reasons for the passing of the treaty and whatever problems associated with it, in spite of vociferous denunciations and condemnations of its consequences, most accepted that it was lawful and binding. Although a minority refused to recognize the legality of the British state, most accepted it, and if Scotland entered into a union with England by legal and constitutional means, then, so the argument went, it would have to use legal and constitutional means to leave. As we shall see, the Union settlement had one major problem. Although an international treaty between two sovereign states, its terms and conditions were not believed to be binding on the future Westminster parliament and as such, theoretically at least, the road to independence could be blocked by the British parliament which had an inbuilt English parliamentary majority. After all, this was what had stopped the enactment of Irish home rule because although a majority of Irish members of parliament (MPs) had supported the policy since the 1870s, Westminster had consistently blocked the way until 1911. Furthermore, even when the home rule bill was passed, the parliaments in London still claimed the right to decide the constitutional future of Ireland because sovereignty resided in Westminster.[52] For Scottish nationalists, this meant the construction of an alternative constitutional tradition that would challenge the idea that Westminster had the right to decide on whether Scotland could become independent or not.

The Union created a sort of constitutional and legal cul de sac because it removed any idea that England could govern by right of conquest, but by the same token, it also removed any Scottish notion of the right of resistance because there had been no English occupation. Furthermore, there was no specific and independent mechanism created to provide a constitutional oversight of how the Union worked in practice. Paradoxically, the treaty created a constitutional entity that could ignore or rip up the very treaty that created it. Scottish history demonstrated a clear constitutional imperative that conferred the right of resistance to tyranny, and this could be articulated all the way back to the Declaration of Arbroath in 1320.[53] Nationalists set their face against constructing a tradition of revolt in the way that Irish nationalists did, and, in any case, it would have been difficult to do so because the last popular rising in Scotland was in 1820. There was no real evidence of popular hostility to the Union in the nineteenth century that would come anywhere near matching that of Ireland. Furthermore, the use of the idea of the Solemn League and Covenant by Ulster unionists in 1912 clearly demonstrated that the raw material was there to construct a quite robust and extralegal line of argument in support of the idea of Scottish popular sovereignty, but this was not a road which many Scottish nationalists would wish to travel.[54] Such ideas were pointless unless it could be demonstrated that the will of the people demanded constitutional reform or independence and that could only be shown to exist through the ballot box. The idea of the sovereignty of the people was one that gradually evolved through the 1920s and 1930s in nationalists circles, and it emerged in response to the idea that the sovereignty of Westminster was absolute. It was also a vital element in wedding the movement to a constitutional and legal route to independence through the ballot box because until it could be proved ineffective, armed resistance would remain off the table.

The construction of a distinctive Scottish constitutional tradition was a significant element in bringing in a component of conditionality in the relationship with the British state. The importance of having a separate system of law was fundamental in reinforcing nationalist arguments because it gave a firm legal basis to the idea of a Scottish nation. Again, this was a major difference with a lot of other nationalist groups in Europe in that a Scottish nationalist could geographically point to where Scotland began and England ended. The messy ethnic intertwining that marks out a lot of the questions of nationality and statehood in twentieth-century Europe has not been an issue because Scotland is clearly defined in terms of its territorial extent by law.[55] Scotland was more than a historical and cultural construct; it was a legal entity and demonstrated that, whatever else may be claimed, the Union of 1707 was not an incorporating one. Violations of the Union were used repeatedly to demonstrate the constitutional incoherence of the British state and that Scottish rights that had been guaranteed had no formal protection under the existing political system. The constitutional twilight zone of the Union allowed for the development of a distinctive Scottish tradition which placed sovereignty in the people which was traced back to the Declaration of Arbroath with its assertion of the contractual nature of kingship:

> Yet if he (King Robert) should give up what he has begun, seeking to make us or our Kingdom subject to the King of England or the English, we should exert ourselves at once to drive him out as our enemy and a subverter of his own right and ours and make some other man who was well able to defend us our King.

The Deposition of Mary Stuart, the signing of the National Covenant in 1638 and the Claim of Right which set out the reasons for the lawful deposition of James VII in 1689 were all incorporated into a narrative that showed that the sovereign will of the Scottish people had a legal and historical force behind it. The sparseness of the Union Treaty and its incomplete nature meant that there were intellectual gaps that nationalists could exploit.[56] As we shall see, perhaps the greatest nationalist triumph was in getting their Unionist opponents to agree that sovereignty did reside with the

Scottish people and that they, if they so desired, have the right to leave the Union and become an independent nation. Having established the major constitutional principles underlying the debate on Scottish independence, all that was required was to work out the mechanics of the process.

Chapter 4 explores the wider intellectual world of Scottish nationalism by examining its relationship with its Scottish constitutional siblings, namely home rule or devolution and unionism. Along with nationalism, these three political philosophies have come to establish a symbiotic relationship within the Scottish body politic over the course of the twentieth and early twenty-first centuries. The reason for examining them is that it helps to enable a wider perspective of the national movement and provides a clearer sense of the intellectual context. The issue of devolution and home rule with nationalism is a complex one, and Chapter 4 starts by examining the contemporary divide because devolution has often been presented as a way of shoring up the United Kingdom rather than dismantling it. Devolution is an administrative reform of government that may have a political or democratic input, but its raison d'etre has always been greater government efficiency and accountability. Home rule, because this was the phrase first used in relation to Ireland, carries the baggage of an association with nationalism because the principle argument used in support of it is that Scotland is a nation with its own peculiar needs, but they can be satisfied with a limited form of democratic government without the need to have complete independence. It has always had this schizophrenic quality, and this has been reinforced by the fact that some see it as a way to stop nationalism by providing a half-way house between the Union and independence and some see it as a way of making the transition to independence easier by setting up a lot of the government infrastructure that would be required by a sovereign state. For this reason many nationalists have always supported devolution because it is a 'stepping stone' to independence and obviates the problems associated with building up a state apparatus from scratch. Scotland used to be described as a 'stateless nation' before the advent of devolution, now it would be more accurate to describe it as a 'semi-state nation'.[57]

The historian's perspective helps to clarify why there has been this degree of conflation between home rule and independence. The term used both by home rulers and those who believed in independence as their preferred constitutional outcome was, more often than not, 'self-government'. While there was an expedient reason for both the home rule and the independence camps to use this term in order to maximize potential support, the phrase has its origins within the wider constitutional development in the British Empire, especially in relation to the 'white' dominions. In the British world of the nineteenth century, the first local parliaments were established in Canada, Australia, New Zealand and South Africa and over time came to accrue more and more powers.[58] When the Irish nationalist Charles Parnell made his statement that 'no-one has the right to fix the boundaries of the forward march of a nation', he was clearly alluding to the idea that devolution, home rule or self-government was a process and not a fixed constitutional event.[59] This is how many have understood the process of devolution in the past. Although there have been arguments in favour of devolution that have endeavoured to disassociate it from being a sop to national identity, in the main most of the reasons advanced for the creation of a Scottish parliament have been in essence more or less the same as that advanced for independence. The notion that the sovereignty of the Scottish people entitles them to have the form of government that they see as most appropriate to their needs works just as well for independence as it does for devolution or home rule. And within this proposition, there is an important caveat, namely that as a matter of democracy, it is a decision left up to the Scottish people as to how far they want to travel on their constitutional journey. As we shall see, for some the creation of a Scottish parliament, no matter its precise constitutional position, would provide an effective forum for the people of Scotland to exercise their sovereign rights to self-determination. If they wanted to stay within the United Kingdom, that was up to them; likewise, they could opt for independence should they so desire. Although the current debate between devolutionists that want to maintain the existing British constitutional settlement and those that argue for independence looks like a fundamental divide in the Scottish political firmament, it actually masks a considerable amount of mutual agreement. Most concur with some form of Scottish national political representation, most accept that the constitutional settlement is for the Scots to decide themselves and most affirm that it is their sovereign right to do so. Although not always trumpeted, on a point of principle it has been agreed that Scotland *can* be an independent nation and the real question under debate is *should* Scotland be an independent nation.

Just as there have been bonds of affinity between home rulers and nationalists, there are equally solid connections between unionism and Conservatism, and indeed, for most of the twentieth century given the Tory aversion to home rule, that relationship has been especially strong to such an extent that the terms 'Unionist' and 'Conservative' were often coterminous.[60] On the face of it, the idea of Scottish unionism is a relatively simple one, which is that the Scottish nation and English nation formed a political union in 1707 but kept their nationalities intact within the newly created British state. In other words, unionism is not unitarism and acknowledges the distinctive national dimension of Scotland. As Chapter 4 argues, although a seductively framed philosophy that seemingly encompasses Scottishness and Britishness without any sense of conflict or contradiction, there are a number of intellectual sleights of hand that tend to escape notice. Firstly, we might adapt Gwyn William's question and ask when was Scottish unionism?[61] There is the issue of retrospectively applying ideas of present-day unionism on the past when it is quite clear that a number of Unionists did not endorse or understand the idea of unionism as it has subsequently been set out and that there has been a significant element that has understood the relationship as being one of assimilation. As John Roebuck, the English Radical MP for Sheffield, explained in 1857:

> I know I am saying that which to Irish ears is grating and harsh, but recollect that we have before our eyes the example of a country united with England under far different circumstances from those in which Ireland was united – namely, Scotland. Now, Dublin is at present no further from London than Edinburgh, but at the time when Scotland was united with England, Edinburgh was in reality three weeks' journey from London, and then no Viceroy was placed in Scotland. See the change effected by the electric telegraph and the railways – Dublin is brought

within eleven or twelve hours' communication with London. Compare that with the three weeks' journey to Edinburgh when Scotland was made an integral part of England. Let not, then, any Irish Gentleman suppose that I mean anything offensive. What I mean is that Ireland should be part of England – really a part, and I think I may appeal to my own political career to show that I do not want to impose on Ireland anything which England does not bear. I want an equal law for Irishmen and Englishmen. I do not want the distinction of Irishmen to exist. Cork ought to be like York. There ought to be no difference between the great county of York and the great county of Cork, except that one is somewhat more distant from London than the other; but to tell me that there is any difficulty in governing Ireland in consequence of its distance, is to tell me that our forefathers were unable to govern Scotland. Now, is that true? Has not the union of Scotland with England been of the greatest benefit to both countries, and more especially to the former country?[62]

In 1932, the Unionist MP for Paisley J. P. Maclay worried how Scottish aspirations and sentiments could be reconciled while remaining an 'integral part of England'.[63] It might be unionism, but not as we now know it. Secondly, there is the issue that is seldom addressed which is the way that Britain provides an alternative national identity for Scots and that Scottish identity is not really different from that of an English region. The British state has evolved in the mind of many Scots into a nation and has all the hallmarks that we would associate with national identity.[64] The fact that Britain is a bigger and more powerful nation has ensured that even if we accept the idea of a dual identity, the larger one is dominant, and this has been stipulated to such an extent that any notion of a partnership is quickly dispelled. Thirdly, there is the intellectual coherence of unionism at a British level. Unionism in Northern Ireland is very different from that in Scotland, and while there are English Unionists, as an intellectual creed, it is non-existent. Finally, there is the rather basic point that unionism is a kind of flimsy intellectual decoration designed to give Conservatism in Scotland a more distinctive dimension. Modern Scottish unionism was an outgrowth of the Irish issue, and the unionism being promoted was that of Ireland. As a political philosophy, British Conservatism has always had a strong focus on localism and local identity and has firmly set its face against any form of constitutional change.[65] In its essential elements, it is hard to see what is fundamentally different between Conservatism and unionism. The Labour movement, on the other hand, has always had a tradition of supporting home rule, and while it may have ebbed and flowed, there was always a segment that supported some form of devolution.[66]

For many, then and now, the issue of Scottish self-government or independence is one that is so important that it trumps all other political concerns and on its own it has sufficient political weight to require no further intellectual apparatus to sustain or promote it. As will be discussed in Chapter 5, this was a forlorn hope, and the 1920s witnessed the end of the attempt to use the mainstream political parties as a vehicle for the creation of a Scottish parliament. It became apparent to proponents that in order to boost the appeal of Scottish self-government, it would be necessary to illustrate the concrete differences that the establishment of a Scottish parliament would make to the lives of ordinary voters. There was also a more fundamental reason for engaging with practical politics. As the primary goal of the Scottish national movement was for the creation of a Scottish state, there would need to be some explanation as to what that state would do and why this would be an improvement. While many hoped and believed that the promotion of the national cause would elevate the issue above the division of the left–right axis of ideology which dominated politics in the twentieth century, one fundamental difficulty was that expectations on the role of the state was one of the key barometers of that divide. Given that politics was largely based around perceptions of class interests and that this formed the main electoral constituencies, it was incumbent on the national movement to decide how it could either surmount this or whether it would appeal to one side or the other. As we shall see, the argument oscillated between the two points of view.

Although the membership of the national movement tended more to the left than the right, the imperative of being a national movement that could appeal beyond the class divide limited the degree of engagement with the ideological axis, and one way in which the issue of left and right could be avoided was to focus on what was described as Westminster mismanagement. Unfair treatment in terms of taxation and public expenditure, the pursuit of policies that favoured England rather than Scotland and a litany of other biased interventions had a twofold objective. The first was to give the movement credibility by showing that it had a handle on the substantive social and economic issues of the day, and the second was to show how independence on its own without any interventions in favour of either the left or right would lead to a material improvement. Needless to say, this was a considerable restraint on policy development. A move to greater self-sufficiency to fill the gap left by Westminster inefficiency, it was believed, would appeal to both consumers and producers, left and right, employees and employers. Also, the movement placed more focus on agriculture and rural society because this would bring Scotland in line with other small Western European nations and also because it was a field that both Labour and the Conservatives left unfurrowed.

A major issue that faced the movement in terms of its engagement with practical politics is that an endeavour to try and steer a neutral ideological line between the left and right was to push it into the middle ground. In the period after 1945, with the new post-war political consensus that stressed the role of the state in terms of its responsibility to provide for the socio-economic well-being of the citizen from the cradle to the grave, the centre ground was a crowded place as Conservatives and Labour vied with one another to poach any potential voters from the political overlap. Politics was more about management than policy, and it was difficult for the SNP to come up with anything distinctive and original of its own. Furthermore, the thrust of post-war policy was greater use of state intervention and one issue facing the national movement was that this would increase both the presence and importance of the very state in Scotland that they hoped to leave. This created a sort of catch-22 situation, because, as a centrist party, it could not campaign against the growth of state activity as this was part and parcel of the norm throughout Western Europe, especially in those countries that were held up as a model for an independent Scotland to follow. Not surprisingly, the SNP put a lot of emphasis on local democracy as a way to counteract the influence of the growth of the bureaucratic big state.[67]

Finally, the movement sought to marry up particular policies that could be presented as being part of a Scottish political tradition. As we have already mentioned, the focus on the agrarian economy and rural society was not that different from other centrist political movements in Western Europe, and probably a facet in this line of thinking was to bring the socio-economic profile of Scotland in line with other similar nations. The need to be distinctive pushed many to advocate for the Douglas Credit scheme in the interwar period largely because it was seen as independent of big business and the trade unions and thus a supra-class policy. Douglas was a Canadian engineer who wanted to regulate the economy by providing more money in the form of credit to workers in order to increase purchasing power.[68] Moreover, it was not advocated by either the Conservatives or the Labour which made it distinctive. In the post-war era, the suspicion of British state intervention led to a greater emphasis on the rights of the individual and a more circumspect view of the idea of collectivism. In that sense they were more like the Scandinavians whose version of social democracy placed a heavy emphasis on the rights of private property and social solidarity that is based on what the state can do for the individual. As will be argued, a number of these ideas have a strong echo of the New Liberalism which existed in Scottish political culture in the pre-1914 era in which state intervention was regarded as justified in order for the individual to be able to realize his or her talents and make the most of their abilities which was the classic notion of individualist liberalism. Without a minimum education and a minimum guarantee of economic and social well-being, traditional notions of Liberal freedoms are meaningless.[69]

We can untangle the intellectual threads that were woven together in the early days of the Scottish national movement to create the body of philosophy that would sustain the SNP as it matured and developed as a political party. By examining how history, nationalism, constitutionalism, the ideas of home rule and unionism and the relationship of independence to the left–right ideological axis were bundled together, we can see how it led to the emergence of a coherent political world view. It need not be said, but given the partisan nature of contemporary Scottish politics surrounding the question of independence at the moment, this book will probably be mined for selective quotes that will be taken out of the wider context to score some pettifogging point. The period under review was one in which ideas of race, ethnicity, gender and other issues were radically different from our own, and any attempt to portray them as otherwise would be intellectually dishonest. In this respect, the Scottish national movement was not substantially different from the political world in which it emerged. The intellectual apparatus that evolved in this era was one needed to sustain an independent nationalist political party. This is the focus of the book, and it is argued that this came into existence largely in the period before the 1960s. All subsequent ideas, values, ideals and policies revolve around this kernel, even though many of those compositional elements no longer carry the weight that they once did and have receded into the intellectual background. This book is a gentle reminder of that history.

1

The historic nation

To the Irish all History is Applied History, and the past is simply a convenient quarry which provides ammunition to use against enemies in the present. They have little interest in it for its own sake, so when we say that the Irish are too much influenced by the past, we really mean they are too much influenced by Irish History, which is a different matter. That is the History they learn at their mother's knee, in schools, books and plays, on radio and television, in songs and ballads.
   – Stewart, *The Narrow Ground: The Roots of Conflict in Ulster*, 16

As Tony Stewart points out above, history can be, and often is, used to serve ideological purposes. All nationalist movements have used history as a political weapon to justify their aims and ambition because of its malleability to project and promote ideological objectives. The chapter starts off by looking at the relationship between history and nationalism and some of the peculiarities caused by the strange historical trajectory experienced by the Scottish nation which was independent up until the Union with England in 1707. So for most of its thousand odd years of history, Scotland was an independent national entity. The Union, however, meant that the Scottish historical experience was not that of a small nation that matured into statehood, such as the Netherlands, which was the historical trajectory that nationalists argued it should have had. Nor was it a history where the nation was absorbed by conquest by a larger and more powerful neighbour, such as Latvia or Ireland. Because of this it was difficult to construct a typical nationalist narrative of a quest for freedom from colonial oppression, although some did try. The Union of 1707 was a political settlement that absorbed much nationalist intellectual energy in explaining why a supposed freedom-loving nation, which had a proud record of rebuffing English endeavours at conquest, ended up surrendering its independence without a fight. All of which posed a real intellectual conundrum that was difficult to resolve. This chapter will explore the contradictions and complexities of why history has not provided the Scottish movement with the same ideological props enjoyed by other European nationalists and why the Scottish past has not had the central position in the quest for independence that we might expect.

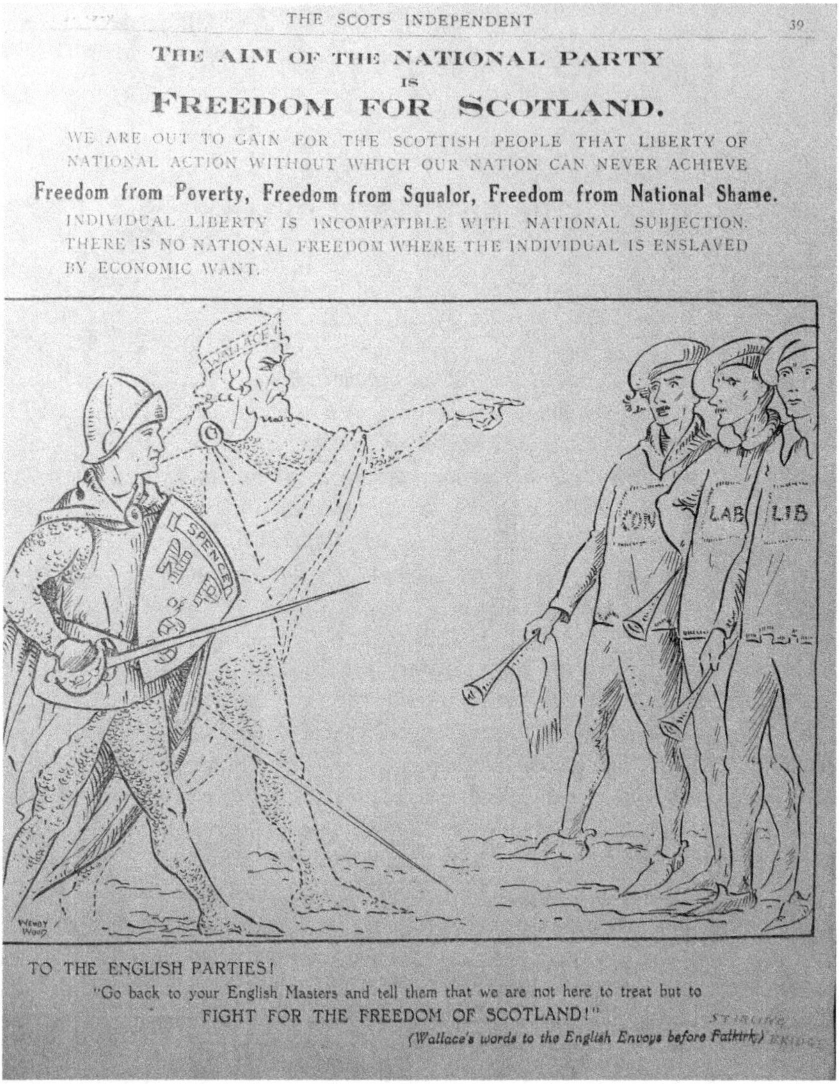

Figure 1 By-election poster (1928) from the National Party of Scotland invoking the spirit of William Wallace (Source: *Scots Independent*).

History and ideology

Scottish nationalists have two considerable advantages in their quest for independence compared to other nationalist movements in Europe. Firstly, Scotland is a clearly defined territory because of its legal system – one can point exactly where England ends and Scotland begins – and this has meant that there is no dispute regarding its border. Indeed, the border with England has hardly changed over the past thousand years or so, and in spite of the warfare of the medieval period, it is one of the most stable in European history.[1] As such, Scottish nationalism has not had the problems associated with irredentist nationalism in which the 'people' have been separated into other nations or states and a key focus has been to bring them all together. This separation of peoples and ethnicities was one of the major problems with the Versailles Settlement after the First World War as the construction of new nation states did not always geographically align with nationalities.[2] While the issue of the right of self-determination of nations was recognized in the post-war treaty and seen as a way of reducing conflict in the future, arguably the Versailles Settlement created as many problems as it solved.[3] The legal and territorial rigidity of the definition of 'Scotland the place' has meant that ethnic and racial ideas have not risen to prominence as a means to compensate for the lack of precision in a geographical definition of Scotland and the people therein. The fact that the Anglo-Scottish border has been fairly static has massively helped to reinforce this clear territorial identification in terms of national identity. It has also meant that there has not been a politics of reclamation in which lost territory has been a rallying call for nationalists. The partition of Ireland in 1922 is an example close to home where disputed territory has been a driver of nationalist claims.[4] Another point worth emphasizing is that there has been little in the way of an English influx into the Scottish borderlands, unlike Wales which has experienced extensive English migration into its eastern regions which has helped dilute Welsh identity in that area.[5] In spite of recent claims that there is a 'borderlands' identity which encompasses the Anglo-Scottish border, the reality is that cultural identity remains distinctive on either side.[6]

A second major advantage for those who promote Scottish independence is that they are advocating a polity that has not only existed before but existed for a long time. As many have pointed out, Scotland has been an independent nation for most of its long history since its inception as a kingdom in the 840s. Indeed, it was among the first recognizable nations in Europe.[7] As Robert Bartlett pointed out, there were only fifteen established crowns in Europe by 1350, one of which was the Scottish one.[8] Although definitions about the meanings of nations and states are complex in the medieval and early modern eras, the fact remains that Scotland was once a nation that had the full panoply of powers and institutions that was normal for a medieval and early modern state, and this history is the foundational bedrock for all arguments about reacquiring Scottish statehood. Put simply, that which once existed can exist once again. Before the Union of 1707, Scotland was an early modern state that had its own monarchy, parliament, army, navy, law and church and had been recognized by other nations as an independent entity by diplomatic protocol and treaties. Having established many of the fundamentals of statehood gave Scottish nationality a maturity, and because the Union was not a conquest which would normally entail an attempt at eradication or assimilation, its nationhood was not extinguished, and indeed, it was preserved both through its institutions and arguably more importantly through its historical memories. It is somewhat axiomatic and therefore tends to be understated, but the idea of the 'nation' is fundamental to the existence of most states as the 'state' and 'nation' are seen as coterminous, the former being an outgrowth of the latter. To be a nation state demands first a nation, and it is Scotland's history which most clearly defines it as a nation. Crudely put, after the formation of the Scottish nation in the ninth century, it held off subsequent repeated English attempts at conquest and absorption, and this became the dominant theme in Scottish history. A narrative emerged that stressed its fundamental difference to that of its southern neighbour. Scottish architecture, relations with the European mainland and culture, for example, developed in a markedly different way from England, and up until the Reformation, an alliance with France against the English was a key component of Scottish foreign and diplomatic policy.[9] Even the emergence of a common bond of Protestantism and the experience of having a shared monarch did not eliminate this sense of difference which was encouraged on both sides of the border.[10] For nationalists, the Union of 1707 with England was an aberration in the sense that it interrupted the normal development of the nation into a modern state and that independence would correct this historical anomaly. To coin a phrase, it would put Scotland back on the right historical track. So for Scottish nationalism to evolve as a coherent ideology, it was necessary firstly to make an intellectual case that history clearly demonstrated that Scotland was indeed a nation destined for a sustainable statehood, and secondly, that this historical trajectory was bounced off course in the past, but it could be rectified in the present and future. History matters for Scottish nationalists because for them, the course of history or destiny will not be complete until independence has been attained. Consequently, history serves an important ideological function in accounting for the failure to sustain statehood in 1707, but also crucially demonstrates that the sinews of national development were and are strong enough for the resumption of political independence in the future.

So far, there has been little that has been said that could not be applied to most European nationalist movements regarding the fundamental importance of history.[11] This is because it is only through a historical explanation that one can account for the absence of statehood. In most histories of small nations, the reason for the absence of statehood is usually attributed to the imperial aspirations of larger neighbouring countries that have used conquest as a means of territorial aggrandisement and subsequently subverted any demands for independence by the use of superior power. A classic example of this phenomenon is the way in which Irish nationalists constructed a historical account of the nation that explained the connection between Ireland and the mainland as a result of English or Anglo-Saxon imperialism and that the struggle to be free from this domination was the defining characteristic of Irish history.[12] Similarities are also apparent in the Polish quest for independence which was sandwiched between Prussian/German and Russian imperial ambitions.[13] The ethnic and national tensions within the Austro-Hungarian Empire and its subsequent break-up gave rise to one of the earliest studies in the field of nationalism.[14] Although many of the different nationalist accounts of the drive for independence in Europe have similarities, including the tendency to create or highlight what is often seen as a unique or distinctive historical path – *Sonderweg*, to use the German word – how nationalists construct historical meaning is an important part of their belief system, and to make sense of it, it is necessary to reconstruct such accounts for it provides many of the key points of ideological reference. Because it is such a large topic and its primary function is to serve doctrinal needs, what will be discussed below is necessarily a pared-down version of the nationalist reading of the past. Also, what is being attempted here is an endeavour to outline the main contours of this understanding of Scottish history because there are probably as many versions of the Scottish past as there are Scottish nationalists. Also, there are some hefty disagreements. For some, history is not a major preoccupation; for others, there will be a tendency to highlight some historical interpretations rather than others and sometimes there will be radically different interpretations of the same phenomenon. To illustrate the point, for some nationalists John Knox was a liberator who freed the nation from Catholic superstition, and it shows the nation's inherent desire for freedom.[15] For others, he was an agent of capitalism and Anglo-Saxon imperialism that paved the way for English subjugation[16] and for many, someone best avoided because he brings to the surface sectarian tensions that weaken the national movement by highlighting religious divisions within Scotland.[17] In short, history and historical events are rarely unproblematic. Forging, in the sense of hammering out and creating, a nationalist history that explains and justifies the cause of Scottish statehood in the present was, and is, one of the key ideological functions of the nationalist movement because even though few discuss it, all nationalists accept without qualification that Scotland is a nation and that its historic destiny is independence. History matters, but its relationship to nationalist ideology is by no means straightforward.

Scottish nationalist ideology has had to work with the body of historical material that had been built up in the nineteenth century before the movement emerged in the 1920s.[18] In the main there was a Unionist slant running through most Scottish historiography which tended to point towards the inevitability of the creation of the British state, but at the same time, there was a considerable amount of what might be described as 'patriotic' literature which cast the work of Scots and Scotland in a favourable light. By and large, this was mainly a roll-call of the great and good and the many achievements made for the benefit of humanity, science and progress and a contribution to the success of the British Empire.[19] What marks out the Scottish historical experience as different from the European norm is an essential part of the Unionist narrative which stresses Scottish independence up until the Union with England in 1707. This means that there is considerable room for a form of historical consensus with disagreement confined to the period in the seventeenth and early eighteenth centuries and beyond. Both nationalists and Unionists accept that an independent nationhood was the norm in Scottish history until at least the Union of the Crowns in 1603 with any differences usually centred on emphasis. Unionists tend to focus on similarities that point the way forward to the Union in the future, such as the shared Protestantism of the Reformation, with those of a nationalist proclivity pointing out the essential distinctiveness of the Scottish experience and would emphasize that whereas the Reformation was imposed from above in England, it came from below by popular demand in Scotland.[20]

There was an intellectual dilemma, however, with the nationalist engagement with the Scottish past in the post-Union period. Many popular accounts of Scottish history in the nineteenth century made great play of the qualities, character and, above all, the intelligence of the Scots, and these tended to be viewed favourably by nationalists as they cast the attributes of the Scottish people in a positive light. Such qualities would obviously make for a successful independent nation. Yet, if such things were true, as many Scots believed, and statehood was the natural condition for nations, why had they not maintained or reattained independence? It was an awkward conundrum. Either the Scots were not as nationally endowed as they thought or else they had consciously set their face against independence and statehood.[21] Also, the lack of independence did not seem to prohibit the emergence of all those fine qualities that many waxed lyrically over in terms of scientific achievement, martial prowess, entrepreneurship and all the other factors associated with the stereotypical 'Scots on the Make' in the nineteenth century.[22] The inherent contradictions in such an interpretation were not appealing for nationalists, and although there was a downturn in Scottish economic fortunes after the First World War, it was not readily apparent in the 1920s that this was a long-term trend. The issue facing the nationalist historian was how to turn this body of patriotic literature towards making the expedient case for independence while maintaining the positive qualities and achievements of the post-Union age. The fact that Scotland had produced some of the most distinguished thinkers during the Enlightenment of the eighteenth century and excelled in industrial and technological invention and innovation during the nineteenth century would tend to negate the argument for the need for independence as clearly the Union did not inhibit or prevent progress. Alternatively, dismissing the positive capabilities of the Scots and downplaying their national proclivities, achievements and abilities would arguably undermine the very principle of having an independent Scotland. To claim that the Scots were not as intelligent as they liked to think they were and easy prey to flattery and manipulation might make for clear intellectual coherence but was unlikely to garner much support among the Scottish populace. If Scottish history was a relatively straightforward account of repeated English colonization, the ideological task would be a simple one; Scottish resistance to English imperialism would be the dominant theme. But even at its most elementary level, the contours of Scottish history are too numerous and convoluted to be crammed into such a simplistic mould. Political activists have to work with an educated public and pre-existing historical discourses and accounts. Ideology will only have use if it has some element of believability, and while there were endeavours to construct a model of English colonialization of Scotland that was similar to the Irish experience, as we shall see, it gained little purchase. There was the issue of credibility as English invasions were few and far between and with the possible exception of Fort George, few symbols of English occupation existed. Furthermore, there was a consensus among Unionists and nationalists that the Union of 1707 was concluded between two *independent* nations, and while there may have been bribery and corruption, there was no coercion. For Unionists and nationalists the fact that Scotland was not conquered helped explain the different historical trajectory from Ireland, in which Anglo-Irish relations were characterized by bad blood and the resentment of conquest.[23] The Union, it was argued, came about after a sufficient time had elapsed for Scottish nationality to establish itself, and this was preserved in 1707. According to Thomas Carlyle the fact that Scotland held off English invasion in the medieval era meant that the Union with England would not be on 'tyrannous unfair terms'.[24]

At this point it is worth pointing out the remarkable overlap that exists between nationalist and Unionist readings of the Scottish past and the considerable areas of consensus that have existed between the two. Up until comparatively recently, the Unionist reading of Scottish history has been fairly positive, and it is only with the emergence of nationalism in the 1960s that it became more pessimistic. In particular, this negativity has manifested itself most noticeably in the debate surrounding the Union of 1707 in which the argument was made that it happened because Scotland was a failed state that was bankrupted by the Darien Scheme. This became an established orthodoxy and according to one historian, 'The Scots did not go into Union simply because they were poor and saw no other way of riches, but because they were poor and rapidly getting poorer.'[25] The 'narrative of the failed state' has cast a long shadow over current political discourse even though it is fraught with a number of methodological problems. Firstly, short-term financial crises were the norm in early modern states. Britain and France both nearly went bankrupt in 1720.[26] Secondly, although Darien may have cost Scotland a quarter of its liquid capital, the post-Union regime greatly increased taxation and tariff collection by 45 per cent, which suggests that there was still a healthy amount of income.[27] Furthermore, between 15 and 20 per cent of all its revenue went south, which begs the question of how such an impoverished nation could find this extra money. Using Roy Campbell's figures, the Scots requited back to the Treasury in London more than the equivalent which was the £400,000 used to compensate the Scottish investors for the loss of Darien by 1720.[28] As Allan Macinnes points out, the Scottish elite were effectively bribed with their own future taxes, demonstrating that the Scots' reputation for financial probity was some way off in the future.[29] Moreover, there has been very little discussion as to what value £400,000 had in 1707, and the following figures will perhaps provide a better idea of the financial context. In 1706 alone, for example, the subsidies paid to English allies were: £34,000 for the Palatines, £43,000 for the Saxons, Bothman Dragoons got £9,000 all of which was paid from the yearly Supply raised in Westminster and in direct subsidies £494,000 for the allies; £500,000 augmentation for the Duke of Savoy and a further £100,000 for Savoy's special services and £22,000 for the Hessians.[30] In comparative terms, the Union with Scotland was not expensive. Tom Devine's more nuanced argument claims that the Union in terms of its economic dimension presented both opportunities and risks, and the key thing that explains post-Union development was how the Scots reacted to these.[31] Furthermore, by drawing attention to Ireland, it is possible to argue that the Union, or more accurately the relationship with England, far from being an economic saviour was just as capable of producing underdevelopment and stagnation.[32] Whether intentional or not, the narrative that Scotland entered into the Union with England in 1707 because it failed as a state is one that is heavily laden with ideological presumptions and purposes.

Contrast contemporary negativity with Lord Rosebery's account of 1871 in which, while acknowledging Scottish poverty, he handles the issue of Scottish pride with considerable sensitivity and argues that the Union was in many ways a paradox because Anglo-Scottish hostility was the very reasons for its passing. The antagonism had reached the point that there would have to be a Union or there would be two permanently armed camps north and south of the border with 'Scotland to be a nation of soldiers'.[33] In accounts of most other eras, however, there was not much of a difference between the conventional historical narrative and that told by nationalists. Take the example of William Wallace, who could be cast as a Scottish patriot who held back English conquest and assimilation and thus paved the way for Union in 1707.[34] Unionists and nationalists agree on the story of Wallace, but what distinguishes them might be described as either the Unionist or nationalist turn in Scottish history. For Unionists Wallace guaranteed that Scotland would remain independent until the time was right for a merger with England in 1707; thus he can be cast as a Unionist because without him Scotland would have been conquered and there would not have been the negotiated Treaty in 1707. For nationalists, the Union can be portrayed as a betrayal of Wallace's legacy because he was, first and foremost, a champion of Scottish independence. As we shall see, the nationalist turn in Scottish history was an important factor in providing the ideology that would justify the reacquisition of statehood lost in 1707.

Colonialism?

For a number of Scottish nationalists in the 1920s, the example of Ireland was most influential because the movement came into being at the time of the Irish Revolution. The Irish nationalist account of history leant heavily on a religious and ethnic binary model that neatly encapsulated the Anglo-Irish relationship as a division between Saxons and Celts, Catholics and Protestants, natives and foreigners. The story of Ireland was cast as one in which Saxon invaders had repeatedly tried to colonize the country and that 'real' Irish were both 'Celtic' and Catholic, while Unionists who tended to be protestant and 'Teutonic' were portrayed as alien. Not surprisingly, Irish nationalists endeavoured as far as possible to show that Ireland was fundamentally different from England, and this was a large part behind the programme of Sinn Fein's cultural activities which in the early twentieth century sought to re-establish the Gaelic language and heritage.[35] Such racialized ideas were part and parcel of the European idea of nationality at this time. For Scotland a 'faith and fatherland' programme had the danger that it could just as easily highlight the similarities with England as the differences because Protestantism and Anglo-Saxon ethnicity could be reflected into a considerable part of Scottish history.[36] Also, there was an alternative to revolution in the form of the long-running issue of self-government based on devolution which was not as radical as independence and had been firmly established in the 'white dominions' of the British Empire.[37] For many of a more moderate disposition this was the route that Ireland should have taken, and they argued that the Irish nationalists' cause had been hijacked by extremists and that this had no bearing on Scottish self-government.[38] The baleful influence of Irish republicans in the United States was blamed for Ireland following the American model of revolution and revolt.[39] Not surprisingly, in the period following the Irish War of Independence and Civil War (1918–22), Scottish nationalists were polarized in their attitudes as to whether Ireland would act as an aspirational model for Scotland to follow or was instead a dire warning.

One group of Scottish nationalists lifted most of their ideology straight from their Irish counterparts and sought to explain the Scottish relationship with England as a similar one to Ireland based around notions of colonialism and race. For this group, whose ideas had their origins in notions of pan-Celticism in the early twentieth century, Scotland was also a Celtic victim of Anglo-Saxon imperialism. The foremost proponent of such ideas was the Jacobite-inclined aristocrat and Gaelic activist Ruaraidh Erskine of Mar.[40] Celtic fundamentalists believed that ideas of race and ethnicity formed the core of Scottish identity and constructed their own peculiar version of Scottish history that drew heavily on Irish nationalist readings of the past and was clearly inspired by the political programme of Sinn Fein.[41] It was the first attempt at a modern nationalist historiography that had statehood, as opposed to self-government or home rule, as an objective:

> We in Scotland have much to learn from Ireland ... we are much more than ten years behind her. First, we must find our national consciousness, and, blushing from its discovery, we must set ourselves to build up our nationality from the foundation. The foundation – the bedrock of our Celtic origin – is already awaiting the builders, and the cornerstone – our inimitable Gaelic language of Scotland, the only national language of Scotland – is already in the hands of the hewers. All is ready to start; we have only to will, then lift our tools, and, starting where Wallace left off set to work to build for ourselves the noble edifice of our nationality.[42]

In this vision, the Scots belonged to the Celtic race, but over time due to English and 'Anglo-Scots' (Scottish collaborators) influences, their Celtic identity had been diluted and forgotten and independence would only happen once the Scots had re-engaged with their Celtic heritage or gained – to coin an inelegant phrase – Celtic consciousness. According to the poet and writer Christopher Murray Grieve who is better known by his pen name, Hugh MacDiarmid:

> A sense of continuity and tradition can only be recovered by 'connecting up' again with our lost Gaelic culture. This is the background to which we must return if we are ever to re-establish a Scottish classical culture. Without realising our relationship however disguised linguistically, political or otherwise, to the Gaelic traditions, we will be unable to rise to major forms.[43]

The Celtic consciousness of the Scots could be reinforced, according to Ruaraidh Erskine of Mar, by seeking 'to strengthen our relations with the race conscious Irish in Scotland'.[44] For a number of early nationalists, myth and belief were the key ingredients required for a successful nationalist movement, and this could justify bending and distorting the facts for the greater political good:

> Our effort must be concerned with the awakening of the national consciousness in life, in Scottish customs, in literature, in all those things that will make for a distinctive Scottish individuality ... Scotland is at present suffering from an inferiority complex. She must out-soar that. Statistics will never give her wings.

She must re-discover her ancient spirit through contemplation of her vanished excellence.[45]

Just as the Scots were classed as Celtic, the English were classed as Saxons who 'came to the shore of Britain from Germany ... and spread their "Kultur" in the approved manner by outrage, torture and death'.[46] Not surprisingly, Celticists focused a lot of attention on the decline of the Gaelic language and highlighted the assault on the Gaeltacht from both the British and the 'anglicized' government of James VI who was castigated for the plantation policy in Ulster in the early 1600s as it denuded the Scots of an important cultural wellspring. It was a deliberate policy to break the Gaels into two distinct communities. James was an easy target for demonization as his ambition for the English throne was portrayed as a cultural betrayal. His genocidal campaign against the MacGregor clan was explained as a sort of displaced hatred against his Gaelic-speaking tutor George Buchanan who tried to instil in the young king the notion of 'Celtic democracy', and once ensconced on the English throne, his tyrannical temperament was not subject to any Scottish checks. The Union of the Crowns in 1603 assumed a significant place in all nationalist readings of the past as it clearly marked a step change in Anglo-Scottish integration. According to this vision of history, English imperial aspirations would be satisfied through subterfuge and collaboration with traitors.[47]

For the Celticists, the Union of the Crowns marked the beginning of a campaign that would 'de-Celticize' Scotland and reduce the Gaelic-speaking population to a rump. This was part of James's plan to secure his position on the English throne and assimilate his northern subjects under the guise of 'Great Britain', which was a cloak for English imperialism. According to a Scottish supporter of Irish independence and Gaelic enthusiast William Gillies:

> James, the wisest fool in Christendom, left Scotland with a sigh of relief. Free of turbulent barons and truculent preachers, he could rule his northern kingdom by a stroke of the pen: Scotland would become in his own words, 'but as Cumberland or Northumberland, and those other remote and northern shires'. It was with enthusiasm that James came to adopt the traditional English policy and to share the hope of England's rulers, from Edward I to Cardinal Wolsey, for the complete subjugation of Scotland.[48]

This explanation meant that nationalists could still incorporate the story of Scottish resistance to English military conquest because as Scotland and the Scots were a nation just like any other, it was only natural to national dignity that they should fight for independence. Scotland had not surrendered its sovereignty on the battlefield, nor was it taken away from them by feat of arms. Building on the quasi-republican tradition that already existed in Scottish history regarding the duplicitous nature of the monarchy and aristocracy, the explanation used to account for Scottish racial subjection was English trickery which knew how to manipulate the ambitious and self-serving nature of the Scottish elite. It was their own version of the 'stab in the back' school of historical explanation:

> What England was not able to wrest from Scotland on the battlefield, she set about attaining by chicanery and political intrigue ... the absorption of Scotland through a Union of the Crowns ... political intrigues which extended over a generation and culminated in the 'Treaty of Union'.[49]

This form of trickery and manipulation culminated in 1707 when the Scots were hoodwinked into giving away their parliament. A key revision pushed by nationalists in the early 1920s concerned the legitimacy of the Treaty of Union, and the well-known accusations of bribery and corruption, together with popular opposition to it, were used to claim that it should never have happened. A phrase that was frequently used to describe the 1707 Treaty was the 'pretended Union'. The Scots National League, which was the most hard-line of the organizations that came before the Scottish National Party (SNP), was very emphatic about the Union of 1707:

> The Parliament of Westminster has not, and has never had, any right to legislate for Scotland. The pretended 'Union' was passed by a combination of force and bribery, against the wishes of the overwhelming majority of the Scottish people, of all politics and all creeds. The people of Scotland were not consulted at this time; at no time have they ever given formal assent to this 'Union'. An Act of Parliament passed in the manner of the Act of Union, has no moral or constitutional validity. As the Act of Union is itself illegal, it follows that the Acts of the Westminster Parliament in relation to Scotland are also illegal, unless at any future time they be confirmed by the vote of an independent Scottish Parliament.[50]

In effect, such a historical reading refused to recognize the legality of the British state. This in turn opened the way to legitimize an opt-out from the existing political structures and possibly sanction the use of extra-parliamentary political activity and forms of direct action. It should be stressed that the organizational capacity of the League meant that there was very little likelihood of a revolt or uprising and, in many respects, the purity of the programme was a means of both distinguishing themselves and cutting themselves off from other legitimist pressure groups. This hard-line view, however, limited the options available for political strategy:

> In the days since the pretended Union of 1707, three methods have been brought forward for the improvement in the political status of our country ... If the Union be null and void as we believe, obviously the Union Parliament has no right to legislate for Scotland, and we must not make ourselves parties to illegality by sending men to that Parliament.[51]

This was a political cul de sac which meant abstaining from the established political process without offering an alternative strategy.

Accordingly the Union could be undone by three methods. The first was rebellion or rising as had been attempted by the Jacobites in the immediate aftermath of the Union in 1715 and 1745. The Celticists had, however, a distinct disadvantage compared to the Irish in that there was no long-standing tradition of Scottish revolt to compare to the Irish risings or rebellions since Henry II's invasion of the twelfth century that could be appropriated into a narrative of continuous native resistance to imperialist control. Because Scotland was an independent nation prior to 1603 or 1707, the Scottish Celticists did not have the same stock of centuries to drawn on to construct a plausible tradition of anti-colonial resistance. It was further complicated because the one tradition of revolt that they could draw on was the Covenanting idea of the seventeenth century when there was popular resistance to the Stuart monarchy in defence of the Scottish Kirk.[52] This was associated very closely with Presbyterianism, however, and had been successfully mobilized by Ulster Unionists in their Solemn League and Covenant of 1912 in opposition to Irish home rule.[53] For a group that sought to emulate the Irish route to independence, this was an awkward part of Scottish history. The Jacobite movement, because it was in support of the Stuart monarchy, was equally problematic given the support for republicanism. The failure of the 1715 and 1745 risings which had their roots in the Highlands, however, it was argued, gave the green light for an 'Anglo-Saxon' assault on the Gaeltacht which sought to remove the people from their 'racial roots' and disassociate them from their culture and nationality:

> The papers of the period bear this out and Wolfe writing before the day of the battle [Culloden] says 'I assure you as few prisoners were taken of the Highlanders as possible'. Ten years after, in 1755, Wolfe again writes urging the necessity of massacring Cluny and the MacPhersons, and outlines a scheme where this could be effected by a heavy hand without mercy. So far we have dealt with those who opposed the power of England; we have just space to mention those who succumbed to that power and were foolish enough to help to place the fetters upon others. The devastation of the glens, the disarmament of the clans, and the degradation in the loss of the national garb were forced on the Scots who had helped the Hanoverian as well as upon those who opposed that foreign yoke … So much for the inception of our glorious history of our Highland Regiments who have fought for England in every quarter of the globe, and gained for themselves a soldier's death on the field or in the workhouse, or at best an assisted passage to one of England's colonies.[54]

A second possible method was to use the existing political structures to send members of parliament (MPs) to Westminster to agitate for some form of self-government; however, there was considerable scepticism as to how it could overcome the inbuilt English majority. The lessons of the Parnellite Irish Home Rule Party were cited to show the limitations of such a policy.[55] Also, there was an assumption that England wanted to keep Scotland under its control. The third way to resist was taken from Sinn Fein which was for the elected MPs to refuse to take their seats in Westminster and reconvene in a makeshift parliament in Edinburgh. It was described as the Carnwath system after the Scottish Jacobite George Lockhart of Carnwath who proposed something similar in the aftermath of the Union.[56]

As we shall see, a central part of the explanation for the loss of political independence was the role of collaborators and an aristocratic elite which did not put the nation's interests first. Just as the Irish had to contend with the Anglo-Irish, the Scottish national interests were subverted by 'Anglo-Scots'. The following description of Scottish parliamentarians reinforced the idea that the parcel of rogues who were bought and sold for English gold had not changed much over the ages:

> To this [Westminster] the miserable body of sycophantic time-servers and place seekers, who have been humble enough, and timid enough, and anti-national enough to get to St. Stephen's, have largely contributed to, so that today it is as true as when Lecky [the nineteenth-century Irish historian] wrote this scathing indictment of the political representation of Scotland. He says that the Scots are 'one of the very few instances in History of a nation whose political representation was so grossly defective as not merely to distort, but absolutely conceal its opinions'. And again 'Scotland was habitually looked upon as the most servile and corrupt portion of the British Empire' ... Their presence there emphasises the fact that they have turned their back on the principles for which the heroes of Scotland fought, and that they swallow the fraudulent Treaty, secretly signed in the cellar of 177 High Street, Edinburgh, with all the degradation it entails, while by the oath they swear on entering the English Parliament they acknowledge the King of a foreign race, who rules only 'England and the dominions thereunto pertaining'.[57]

While the Hanoverians were easy to cast as foreigners, the Scots had an altogether greater difficulty compared to the Irish in presenting their own fifth column as foreign. Although the 'Old English' had largely gone native, the Anglo-Irish elite in the modern era could be traced back to settlers who had come from England and Scotland, particularly during the seventeenth century. In language, religion and origin the Irish Protestant Ascendancy was different from the majority of the population and as such the ruling Irish elite could be presented as 'foreign'. This was especially the case following the dispossession of Catholics during and after the Civil War, and this process was intensified after the reconquest of Ireland in 1690.[58] This was not possible in the Scottish case as James VI or the Duke of Argyll, for example, could not really be cast as anything other than Scottish. For the construction of a nationalist historiography or *national mythos* the absence of alien scapegoats was a considerable disadvantage as it meant acknowledging that a considerable part of the ruling body politic was corrupt and working against the Scottish national interest.

As part of this myth of the de-Celticization of Scotland, great efforts were made to maximize the Gaelic-speaking area in the past with claims that it stretched all the way down to the borders. The idea that Scotland could be split into a Highland Celtic race and an Anglo-Saxon lowland race was rejected because 'the lowlander is in the main the descendent of Celtic ancestors ... What actually happened in the lowlands was not a displacement of the Celtic people but a very gradual displacement, spread over many hundred years, of the Celtic languages'.[59] For some, the explanation for de-Celticization was to be found in feudalism. Crudely put, the argument went as follows: The Irish Celtic culture was stronger than its Scottish counterpart at the time of the Anglo-Norman conquest and was able to absorb the invaders, whereas in Southern Scotland, the Celtic roots were cast off. There was a trade-off, however, in that although the

Scots lost their Celtic cultural homogeneity, the Anglo-Norman influences meant that they were better able to stave off English invasion than their Irish counterparts. H. C. MacNeacail was able to integrate a new interpretative standard into the conventional works of Scottish history:

> It is important to note that this feudal Scotland, for centuries after Bannockburn, had to contend with an enemy whose attempts on her independence hardly ever ceased. England was that enemy. Pledged to respect Scottish independence as England was, she yet systematically disregarded her obligations. By one means or another she endeavoured to compass the downfall of Scotland. Let Andrew Lang [1905] tell of the methods employed. 'The English idea' he says 'from Flodden Field to Fotheringay, had one steady purpose, to foster factions in Scotland by every form of deliberate perfidy ... by money and lies to purchase traitors, to hire stabbers, to breed mischief, to subsidise rebels, to break up all honest national union, to sow suspicion, to debauch loyalty ... The great power of England, baffled a hundred times in her old pretensions of supremacy, defeated in open field, or faced with tireless resolution, sank to the cowardly daggers, or the base intrigues of such weak causes as are worked by priests and women.' A damning indictment indeed.[60]

Again, there was a conspiracy to minimize the influence of Celtic culture in Scottish history, and Unionists such as Sir Walter Scott were blamed for introducing ideas of 'racial' divisions in the past as this divided the Scots against themselves. It was claimed that Scott 'has coloured for four generations of Scots their whole vision of Scotland. He was the principal agent in imposing on his countrymen that "inferiority complex" that distinguishes Scotland among the nations'.[61] The tokenism associated with the 'Highland Cult' for its failure to promote the Gaelic language and the fact that its main proponents were 'firm believers in the political subordination and enthusiastic supporters of the political eclipse of the Gael, his land and his language' made them easy targets and, furthermore, 'to divide and conquer is an old and effective method … but I do not think history records any nation on which this masterpiece of rascality has been practised with more success than the Scots'.[62] Having lost their Celtic 'racial' identity, the Scots, it was argued, were manipulated into the service of the British Empire and encouraged to regard their Celtic brothers and sisters in Ireland with antipathy. For some this was similar to a person who had lost their memory, and it was argued that if the Scots could regain consciousness of their Celtic heritage, they would demand independence:

> I know Scotland well from the Tweed to John o' Groats – few know it as well – and I fearlessly assert that Scottish Celts hate Anglo-Saxon Teutonic rule as heartily as their brethren in Ireland. It was an ill day for the Celtic people when the German Georges and their German Jew supporters got their grip on Alba, Erin and England. We must unite again, clear them out and re-establish our noble Celtic ideals in place of the Teutonic 'Kulture' [sic] and its military despotism now ruling or trying to rule, our nations.[63]

Undoubtedly, the principal attraction of the Celtic model of nationalist historiography was its polarity and the lack of any ambiguity or grey areas. By reducing the issue to one of race, Celt or Saxon, it was designed to polarize the issue and push Scotland into the same orbit as Ireland, and if the interpretation of Scottish history could be made to do the same in relation to Saxon imperialism against the Celt, then it might follow that the outcome would be the same in terms of stirring up the desire for independence.

The Wallace myth was by the early 1920s fairly well established and did not require much work to turn him into a Republican hero. The title 'Great Liberator' was an echo of the sobriquet awarded to Daniel O'Connell who led the Irish Repeal movement in the first half of the nineteenth century.[64] Poems and plays often had Wallace in the company of Washington, William Tell and other historical luminaries. Wallace was also handy because he could be used to form a link to the emergent Labour and socialist movement which was changing the Scottish political landscape in the period after the First World War.[65] For republican nationalists, Wallace was a much more appropriate symbol of the fight for Scottish independence because he was easier to ideologically mould for contemporary purposes than King Robert the Bruce:

> Five times at least Bruce perjured himself over sacred relics to be Edward's man, and five times he crawled back and was forgiven … Bruce having come to the conclusion that the throne of Scotland was perhaps after all on a par with his 28 manors in Yorkshire … Wallace, Protector of Scotland and leader of her army on behalf of and by consent of the community built from below on the democratic basis of the peoples' will … Let us go forth then … when the grasp of England and its commercialism and its imperialism have been shattered once and for all, that there will be no need to remind a Bruce of his duty as our far-seeing ancestors did in 1320 [the Declaration of Arbroath]. The community will be the ruling power, and on the same and stable foundations of Celtic culture and Celtic communism from which Wallace drew his inspiration, we who share his convictions and speak his tongue will use both to work out freedom for our beloved land.[66]

For a nationalist movement that was intent on following the example of Irish republicanism, Wallace as a 'man of the people' was altogether more appealing than a monarch. For some, Bannockburn was portrayed only as a partial success because of the role of Robert the Bruce who, as a member of the aristocracy and a landowner, had a vested interest in maintaining the existing feudal system:

> A far-sighted patriotism would have restored the Celtic polity, a polity far more progressive and enlightened than its feudal supplanter. Bruce not only maintained feudalism, he strengthened it. He gave grants of land to his baronial and knightly followers, mostly Anglo-Normans, mainly turncoats like himself, some of them turning even at the last moment. The 'common people', the Celtic backbone of Scotland whose indomitable patriotism had given him the crown, got nothing.[67]

Although never quite able to cast the Scottish aristocracy as 'alien' in the way that the nobility of Ireland were portrayed as being of English and therefore of a different ethnicity, the Scottish elite occupied the prime position in the demonology of nationalist villainy. Carlyle's quip about the Scottish aristocracy as a pack of hyenas was frequently recited, and the republican theme could be strengthened by utilizing historical works from the Labour Movement, most notably Thomas Johnston's *Our Noble Families* (1909).[68] Nationalists were able to build on a pre-existing historiography which portrayed the aristocracy in a negative light as consistently subverting the national interest for their own personal gain. The Liberal hegemony that was established in the mid-nineteenth century utilized a basic aristocratic/monarchy versus the people dichotomy which could give Scottish history a republican slant. The Wallace story, the conflict between John Knox and Mary Queen of Scots, the Covenanters' persecution by the Stuarts and the belated recognition of Robert Burns could be utilized to promote the myth of an inherently democratic and egalitarian Scotland.[69] The Lad O' Pairts myth in which a boy (never a girl) uses the education system to realize and release their talents and rise in society was a common theme for nineteenth-century Scots, although it was never quite pursued to its intellectually logical destination of republicanism.[70] The deposition of Mary Queen of Scots was used by nationalists to demonstrate the historical utility of the concept of the sovereignty of the people, although Celticists were ambiguous about the Reformation as it marked a period of common Protestantism between Scotland and England, while Ireland remained Catholic. The association between Protestantism and the rise of capitalism was also a further source of ambiguity and one that would gain fairly widespread intellectual currency as republicans sought to shore up their left-wing credentials:

> The feudal system was essentially autocratic in some of its manifestations. The Celtic system, on the other hand, has considerable pretensions to be styled democratic, as compared with its rival … its moral inferior. The natural course of the Celtic state is in the direction of a republic, not in that of a monarchy.[71]

The idea of republicanism was also influenced by the ideas of the Clydeside revolutionary John Maclean because in the febrile politics of the post-war era the revolutionary Marxist had come to the conclusion that Scottish nationalism could be used, as was demonstrated by Irish nationalism, to undermine the British state and in so doing prevent the next stage of capitalist development in which the two greatest imperial powers, Great Britain and the United States, would slug it out for world domination.[72] This association with the left was an important factor in reinforcing republicanism and the fact that the Crown was symbolic of the British state and 'the executive force which drives the political and military machinery of England's capitalist system'.[73]

Although it has tended to be downplayed in recent times, the Irish War of Independence was a seminal moment for the development of nationalist ideology in Scotland and the advocacy of political independence. Its legacy, however, was ambivalent. On the one hand, it supplied a successful model of how to achieve independence from Britain, but on the other, it was based on violent revolution that would come with a high cost. Ultimately it would polarize Scottish nationalist opinion and the constitutionalists who would advocate using the existing political machinery of contesting elections would win out, but in the early 1920s it galvanized a small number to wholeheartedly support their Irish compatriots. The campaign to disrupt armament shipments and supplies to the British military in Ireland was portrayed as an act of Celtic solidarity.[74] By the time of the Treaty in 1922, the military activity had stopped and the need to propagandize against British activity in Ireland ended. Maclean had died in November 1923 as his constant campaigning took its toll. The left had hardened its opposition to nationalism as per instructions from the Comintern in 1919 and future revolutionary activity would be at a British level only.[75] Ireland left an intellectual mark on the development of Scottish nationalist political thought, but its violent associations meant that increasingly constitutional and legal arguments would predominate, which shunned notions of direct action. As far as understanding the Scottish past was concerned, it was becoming more and more of a stretch to say that the only way in which independence could be achieved was through revolution. Some Celticists did make allusions to secret London organizations that had a role in undermining Scottish national sentiment and there were some heavily racist outburst against English immigration which was viewed as colonialist:

> Insidious and increasing, the English peril has recently taken on alarming proportions, as the English cities have to get rid of their surplus undesirables, weaklings unfit for the rougher life of the colonies, and from these elements Scotland gets her new citizens ... The character and neighbourhood in which the English reside has undergone a complete alteration. The shops in the district have been taken over by glib tradesmen, who not only supply the strangers, but by assiduous hat-touching and the sycophantic manners peculiar to the lesser Saxon, have secured the patronage of many Scots people; so that the business of the native tradesmen languishes.[76]

In the Celticist model of Scottish history there was a tendency to ascribe the lack of nationalism in Scotland to colonialism from England and although the Irish model was a key inspiration, this was not without considerable intellectual difficulties. How to map the particulars of the Irish situation on to the peculiarities of the Scots was a real challenge. In addition to the problems of not having a tradition of revolt, the prospect of a violent revolution was unlikely to garner success because there was clearly no popular appetite among the Scots for an armed uprising. Indeed, it was argued that goading by the British state into a pre-emptive rising was something to be avoided at all costs: 'All the other associations which are out to overturn English rule and capitalism and militarism, its twin supporters, are not going to oblige with an Amritsar, nor even with a Peterloo.'[77] In the case of Lewis Spence, the leader of the Scottish National Movement, he did not yet 'advocate taking up the rifle, because that is a course I feel would hardly appeal to the majority of our fellow countrymen – although it is the method I would personally prefer', it was possible to accommodate his personal braggadocio with political reality.[78]

A major problem for the Celtic fundamentalists was that while they could tinker around some of the edges of the established version of Scottish history, the complete Celticization of the Scottish past was a hard sell. For most people, the notion of an ethnic or racial homogeneity did not accord with the orthodox view of Scottish history.

More or less from the outset of the Celticist model of Scottish history there was a vocal opposition from within the ranks of Scottish nationalism. Most commonly, this was to posit an ethnic/racial plurality within the early Scottish kingdom and reject the idea of an exclusively Celtic nation.[79] Indeed, surprisingly up until the 1960s and 1970s, it was not uncommon for this crude form of racial and ethnic notions to be used in the account of the early formation of the kingdom, with the implication being that a lack of homogeneity meant that Scotland somehow lacked a crucial ingredient in its national make-up.[80] Despite this peculiarity, for our purposes, the thing to note is that conventional wisdom held (and still holds) that Scots, Picts, Britons, Saxons and Vikings were the key ingredients in the early Scottish melting pot. Indeed, one of the key criticisms made by the Celticists was the idea that the Celtic contribution was undermined, but this shows that the established view held that the Scottish realm was made up of a variety of peoples which did not fit with the Celtic/Teutonic dichotomy. The theme of Highland/Lowland division which was likewise denounced as a false division was balanced by frequent reference to the mixing of Highland and Lowland heritage – or to use the contemporary phrase – blood. Robert Burns, David Livingstone and others were celebrated for having this peculiar mix in which, following the prejudices of the day, attributed certain characteristics to one side or the other.[81] The rejection of the legitimacy of the Union of 1707 and thus the British state almost led to a revolutionary position by default. The Celticist reading of history was problematic because a strong racial and imperialist model, as was the case in the Ireland, vindicated a revolutionary road to independence. For moderate Scottish nationalists, this was unlikely to work because it would not garner support and attain its objective. Furthermore, it lacked intellectual credibility as there was an inability to construct a tradition of risings and rebellions as the Irish nationalists had done in which Easter 1916 could be placed as the latest in a long line of attempts to throw off the yoke of English imperialism. In copying the Irish nationalist reading of the historical relationship with England, Scottish Celticists, no matter the issue of intellectual credibility, painted themselves into a corner in which there was more or less a compulsion to follow a revolutionary nationalist strategy.

Perhaps the most significant blow to the Celticists' model came from Art O'Brien, the leader of the Irish Self-Determination League of Great Britain, who, while endorsing Scottish independence and nationalism, pointed out that the Scots and the Irish had very different historical experiences:

> In later [historical] developments, there are many points of dissimilarity, possibly due to the fact that that whilst Ireland has developed agriculturally, Scotland has tended to develop more on industrial lines. Those are fields of thought capable of boundless arguments; but, it is a fact that Scotland has to a very great extent, accepted the Union with England, whereas Ireland never ceased, in one way or another, to contest it. Now that the Scots people begin again to realise the disadvantages of Union, it is more difficult for them to break down the obstacles which they have largely themselves built in the path of the reassertion of their national independence. In Ireland we have had our experiences, lessons that may serve to guide Scottish nationalists in their struggle; but the differences in

national atmosphere between the two countries, as indicated in this article, are fundamental to the consideration of any national policy for Scotland. They could only be disregarded at grave risk to the success of such a policy. The period of evolution of a Scots national movement must, according to normal laws, be longer than it was in the case of Ireland.[82]

Clearly, the understanding and version of Scottish history that was utilized was important in determining the responses to the strategy of independence. While the Celticist model was problematic primarily because of its association with revolution and violence, the gradualist and constitutionalist road to independence also had its share of historical difficulties. The legitimacy of the Union of 1707 was a thorny issue and one that was by no means uncontroversial in that to vigorously denounce it as an illegal and unconstitutional act, which many thought it was, might lead one to question the very legitimacy of the current British state. Theoretically, this could encourage nationalists to break the law by not paying taxes, filling in census forms and other acts of civil disobedience. At the same time by not engaging in civil disobedience, was one tacitly acknowledging the legitimacy of the British state? Nationalists could use their understanding of history to construct a model which while not recognizing the British state de jure, recognized it de facto. This may seem a pedantic point, but it is one that goes to the heart of the nationalist aspiration for independence in that the British state must be tolerated until the goal of self-determination is achieved. These constitutional issues will be discussed in greater length in Chapter 3, but it is important to flag them up at this point in our discussion. Recognizing the practical political existence of the British state, if not its legality, also meant that a version of Scottish history could be constructed that limited the narrative of English coercion so as to encourage a constitutionalist and legalist approach to achieving independence. This historiography also had the advantage that it did not require the substantial rewriting that the Celticists model demanded and could dovetail itself as far as possible with the existing body of historical understanding. In this model, history could be used to demonstrate that the Scots had all the qualities required for good self-government. It could also be used to show that within the Union, Scottish self-interest was not best served because the bigger nation invariably put its own needs first. History could be trawled to show that Scotland got a raw deal from the Union. Finally, history could be used to instil greater national self-awareness and confidence in the people and address the deficit in cultural knowledge which moderates acknowledged along with fundamentalists, that existed in Scottish society. The cause of the deficit could take on a spectrum of blameworthy individuals and groups.

Union

The Union of 1707 occupies a large part in the development of a nationalist historiography because it was the formal end of the Scottish state.[83] The Union of the Crowns may have been an important step on this path, but it was both reversible and limited as the Civil Wars and the Revolutions of 1688/90 demonstrated the boundaries of Anglo-Scottish integration within the regnal union. Furthermore, royalists could be reassured that independence in the contemporary world did not mean the end of the regnal union as was demonstrated by the self-governing dominions in the empire that still retained the monarch as the head of state.[84] The year 1707, however, marked a different phase in the 'absorption' of Scotland into England because it abolished the Scottish parliament and in so doing removed the effective mechanism that would ensure the development of the modern nation state. Whether nationalists liked it or not, the Union was by the standards of the time a legal and constitutional act that witnessed the absorption of Scotland's political life into that of England. Although the Union was not popular with the Scots at the time, it was difficult for nationalists to retrospectively claim it illegitimate because it went against contemporary public opinion. Some could and did claim that it violated the Scottish constitution as enshrined in the 1689 *Claim of Right* and argued that Scotland still retained the 'rights of a nation':

> Scotland is one of the most ancient states in Europe. Scotland and England are two nations with different histories, laws, religions and methods of government. Scotland has fought over three hundred field battles with England to guard her sovereign rights. The Scottish people never at any time surrendered these.[85]

Although Whig constitutional nationalists such as Fletcher of Saltoun were lauded for their opposition to the Union at the time of its negotiation, there was the awkward issue of the Jacobites who were the most staunchly anti-Unionist and offered the most realistic prospect for overturning the Union.[86] For those of a republican perspective, this created a problem in that while they would have abolished the parliamentary union, the regnal union would remain intact. And few could be unaware that the reclamation of the *English* throne was the key Jacobite objective in which Scotland and the Scottish Crown were used as a convenient stepping stone. Furthermore, those most influenced by Irish history, and the ones most likely to argue that the Union had no legal basis, had to deal with the fact that Jacobitism had been stripped out of the Irish past because of its association with the monarchy by republicans.[87] Even for those who accepted a more traditional account of the Scottish past, a common historical perception of the Jacobites was as authoritarian tyrants who ground down Presbyterian democracy. Jacobites could not accept the fundamental nationalist claim that sovereignty resided with the people and not the Crown. The issue of Catholicism and religious divisions made them fairly useless as raw material from which to construct a tradition of revolt in a country that saw itself as overwhelmingly protestant in the first half of the twentieth century.[88] The problems of using or extolling Jacobite resistance to the Union put paid to creating a legitimate tradition of revolt as the risings in 1715 and 1745 could not be used as a demonstration of popular opposition. In any case, there was no serious resistance to the Union after that. Furthermore, the powerfully engrained idea that the treaty had been a voluntary agreement effectively pushed the nationalist movement into a constitutional and legal channel for the attainment of independence. Apart from the practical consideration that any notion of violence was unlikely to garner popular support, the proposition remained that what had been made by the law could only be undone by the law. And to do that, one required political power.

The Union raised a number of awkward issues for nationalists. The easiest historical explanation would be one that eschewed history altogether and said that the Union of 1707 was a good thing at the time but its course had now run and that it was time for the two nations to go their own separate ways. Variants of this argument were used by some devolutionists who argued that a constitutional model constructed in the eighteenth century was out of date and needed modification to take account of the needs of democracy.[89] The injustices of the current union arrangement need not lead to its abolition but rather its modification, and while nationalists were happy to accept the step closer to independence that devolution would bring, the possibility of a reformed union accepted in principle that the union was a good thing which was clearly an anathema to many nationalists. At its most elemental form, the projection of the fundamentals flaws of the Union backward in time was a way to reinforce the idea that the Union was inherently a bad thing and not salvable. The Union at its inception would come to represent all that was problematic with the Scottish political elite and could be utilized as a way to demonstrate what was the recurring problems in the Anglo-Scottish relationship and why independence was the only viable solution. Furthermore, the historical view of the Union was a sort of barometer for the intensity of nationalist perspective, and judgements on the Union ranged from moderately favourable and understanding to unremitting hostility. Crudely put, the prevailing view of the Union at any one time was a good indication of the strength of nationalist sentiment in that the more uncompromising in regard to an absolute commitment to independence, the greater the tendency to see the Union as a dastardly deed.[90]

For all nationalists, the bedrock of the importance of the Union is that it was the mechanism by which England was able to control Scotland. While many nationalists conceded that there were benefits of the Union, such as securing the succession, bringing an end to Anglo-Scottish enmity, removing the threat of Catholic Jacobite tyranny, freedom of trade and laying the foundation for the development of the British Empire, these were incidental by-products of the main objective which was to ensure that an independent Scotland did not threaten English interests. Even a relatively benign view of the negotiations had to come to the conclusion that the result was not satisfactory or there would be no need for some form of change towards self-government. The numerical superiority of England, be that in politics, population or economics, ensured that it could never be a partnership of equals and also guaranteed that English interests would predominate. This was especially the case because 'the present political parties are dominated by, and their policies controlled by, English majorities'.[91] Furthermore, it was easy to present the Union as being the culmination of long-standing English aspirations to control Scotland which stretched back to the reign of Edward I.[92] While the Union could be and was presented as a form of modus vivendi in which cooperation replaced conflict and that the compensations for the loss of independence made it a sort of bargain, for nationalists the loss of self-determination was a deal too far. In essence the Union was the barrier that could separate nationalists from devolutionists in that the former wanted it abolished and the latter wanted it amended or updated. Yet, in both respective cases, there was an agreement that in its historical form it was no longer valid, and this consensus helped mask a quite fundamental division. This was further reinforced in that both groups believed there was a utility in maximizing support, even though they had different long-term objectives.[93]

From a Unionists perspective the treaty can be sold as a sensible accommodation, but for nationalists there is the problem of how to explain why the nation sold its sovereignty so cheaply. How could the same nation which produced the famous lines from the Declaration of Arbroath, 'It is in truth not for glory nor riches, nor honours that we are fighting, but for freedom – for that alone which no honest man gives up but with life itself'. be 'bought and sold for English gold'? The answer of course was 'the parcel of rogues' identified by Robert Burns that constituted the elite of Scotland, but then again, this was the same elite that 'so long as one hundred of us remain alive, never will we be brought on any condition under English rule'. Truth be told, history could be awkward. Conventional wisdom held that the real value of the Union was that it was only reached after the Scots had proved their valour and had not been conquered.[94] Apart from the boost to self-esteem of not being conquered, and indeed some Scots liked to recount the number of times the English had been conquered,[95] there is an important but neglected point in that up until comparatively recently, it was widely held that conquest conferred the right to rule. So the Union in a way was a recognition by England that it had no right to rule Scotland except by constitutional agreement.[96] That ability to remain free until 1707 was enough to ensure that there was mutual respect between the two countries which would put previous enmity behind them and go on to create the British state. This explained the Scottish enthusiastic engagement in the British state and Empire, whereas the Irish never got over the conquest and was always a surly and uncooperative participant in the Union. As the Liberal MP for Kilmarnock Alexander Shaw put it with tongue firmly in cheek:

> The whole history of Scotland differs from the history of Ireland. Scotland is not a conquered country. It was not Scotland that was annexed to England but it was Scotland which annexed England, and the results were most disastrous, because our very distinguished line of Stuart kings in the person of James VI. came here. That very fine and distinguished line of monarchs came south to England and became corrupted – *corruptio optimi pessima*. Unfortunately, you had to cut off his son's head.[97]

In popular accounts of Scottish history, Britain and the empire was a larger stage upon which to act out their national characteristics, and the clearest evidence of this was usually the roll call of Scots who had become prime minister.[98] That Unionist myth had largely been formed in the nineteenth century at a time when Scottish achievement was rampant, but by the twentieth century the sheen was beginning to wear, especially in light of the economic problems after the First World War.[99] In the 1920s, the idea of English indifference and the subverting of Scottish interests to the benefit of the southern neighbour was a frequent nationalist complaint in contemporary politics. Not surprisingly this was reflected back in time into the nationalist interpretation of the how the Union came into existence. Accordingly the elites in Scotland were prepared to sell out their birthright for economic gain, and the English elite knew that they could be bought. Although the bribery and corruption dimension of the passing of the Treaty of Union had been around since the days of Burns, nationalists sought to reinforce this and make it the main feature of the story. 'Bribery and corruption secured its [the Union] passage through the Scottish Parliament. Financial drugging and doping on England's part secured a majority.'[100] In doing so, they were emphasizing the long-standing corruption of the Scottish political elite. As always, much of historiography is about emphasis, and by stressing the role of the perfidious Scottish aristocracy, nationalists were able to present the Union as certainly unjust, if not illegal:

> Scotland entered the Union upon equal and honourable terms, but in drawing up the details of the Act, her statesmen blundered badly. An ambiguous clause which never should have been allowed to pass, gave excuse later to allow appeals from the Court of Session to the House of Lords; a grossly disproportionate number of members was allocated to Scotland – by her population she should have had 85, she got only 45; worst of all no independent tribunal was set up to interpret and enforce the Act. And when the English in later years, repeatedly and dishonestly violated it both in letter and spirit, Scotland had no means of redress ... for the fulfilment of the engagement she had to trust to England's honour; the honour of a country that is an admirable trustee for barbarous and backward races, but incapable of fair dealing with other civilized peoples.[101]

By utilizing a quasi-republican trend in Scottish history, the nationalists were able to present the Union as the culmination of a tradition of treachery and duplicity by the Scottish aristocracy dating back to the betrayal of Wallace, but it also questioned the sustainability of the Union by showing that there were incompatibilities in blending the separate political traditions of Scotland and England.

For some more moderately disposed nationalists, the duplicity of the Scottish aristocracy could be ignored or downplayed if the problem could be represented as one in which the noble aspirations of the Union to overcome the differences of Scotland and England simply could not be achieved because of ingrained national differences that would only show up once the agreement was reached and after which the numerical superiority and power of the English would determine the way the Union would develop to Scotland's disadvantage. This was a way to square the circle of how a vibrant nation could lose its independence:

> Scotland, alone, I believe, amongst European nations has never been conquered by the sword. That is a fact in which we all take a legitimate pride. Yet, few of us realize its implications, though to these can be traced the profound psychological differences between the Scottish and English nations and this too, explains the profound dissatisfaction (often erroneously referred to as 'sentiment') the sense, indeed of violation that the Scots feel at the gradual subordination of his traditions and institutions to those of England since the Parliamentary Union of 1707. For our Scottish institutions – Army, Church, Parliament, Educational System and the rest – are those of a nation of free men and express imperfectly, no doubt, the will of the nation, the *communitas,* as it is called in early writings, whereas the institutions of England are those of a nation subordinated to a powerful ruling

caste – those in fact imposed on the Anglo-Saxon commonality by their Norman conquerors. And although England, like other fundamentally feudal countries, is moving towards democracy, the basic difference persist today.[102]

In essence, the nationalist conundrum was how to explain why Scotland had all the qualities associated with a nation state but allowed itself to be dominated by England and why those national characteristics did not result in the fruition of independence. The intellectual gymnastics involved in squaring this conundrum sometimes produced the outlandish claim that the Scots were too freedom loving for their own good and ideas relating to Celticism resurfaced in notions associated with 'Clannism' which was represented as more egalitarianism than feudalism:

> History indicates that the genius of the Scottish people was working towards nationalism based on a federation of the clans, and that the movement was jolted out of its natural course by the alien introduction of Norman Feudalism. Feudalism is based on Tyranny and could only be imposed on a conquered or subdued nation. It was a short cut to national unity of a sort. England was conquered and feudalised from coast to coast and coerced into a reverence for 'law and order'. Scotland was never conquered and never thoroughly feudalised. Feudalism and 'Clanism' have jostled with each other down the ages, and, worse still in men's minds. Scotland has gained by retaining its unconquered and unsubdued spirit, but has lost by associating independence with disorganisation.[103]

Although not universally accepted by all nationalists, the Scottish elites and aristocracy more often than not were portrayed as the historical villains, rather than the English or the English elite, and this bad leadership was the cause of Scotland remaining in the Union.

The nationalist reading of Scottish history after the Union operated on two levels. On the one hand, there was a spirited account which showed off the Scots and their natural abilities, but on the other, there was frequent reference to how the Scots had been unjustly and unfairly treated as a result of the existing political arrangement with England. As we have discussed, nationalists would add a particular gloss or emphasis to specific aspects of Scottish history, but it is also important to remember that the promotion of Scottish history and culture in and of itself, shorn of political purpose, was a nationalist aspiration on the basis that a familiarity with Scotland's past would lead to the questioning of the current political status quo and ultimately support for independence. Although certain 'distortions' of Scottish history could cause ire, the core ideological premise of the nationalist is that an objective understanding of Scottish history, culture and contemporary affairs would logically lead to support for independence. The endeavours of the Celticists to reconstruct a narrative of Scottish history was a project that remained fairly marginal, and, in reality, the majority of the nationalists interpretation of Scottish history was based on a historiography that developed during the Union and, apart from the occasional difference of emphasis, was remarkably similar to the ideas that were in wider circulation in Scottish society in the 1920s and 1930s.

In a separate chapter we will discuss the ways in which nationalists could make common cause with devolutionists as an expedient step in the right direction towards independence, but the Union was also a common source of discontent. As the foundational document of the British state, frequent reference was made to its violations, and for nationalists this could be used to show that it was redundant and for devolutionists is could show that the Anglo-Scottish relationship needed to be reformed. The original form of the Union, incorporation, it was argued, 'has been a failure … After two centuries of formal Union, there is no uniformity in legislation. Is it not reasonable that Scotland should herself shape and pass those purely Scottish laws?'[104] Matters came to the fore in 1929 because the reform of Scottish local government in which the Royal burghs were to be abolished was the first time in the era of modern politics that there was a clear case of a breach of the terms of the Union.[105] For John MacCormick, the leader of Glasgow University Nationalist Association and a law student, the issue was one he would return to in the early 1950s regarding the coronation numeral of Elizabeth, namely the English legal doctrine of parliamentary sovereignty:

> The view that the Treaty of Union is not binding on Parliament depends on the English doctrine of the absolute supremacy or sovereignty of Parliament. It is forgotten that that doctrine was never held in Scottish constitutional law before the Union. And we are told that so far as the constitution is concerned, Scotland must accept the dictates of English law.[106]

The issue for MacCormick and others was that although the treaty was an agreement between two sovereign nations, once it was enacted, the principle of *English* parliamentary sovereignty rendered it null and void. The Union, as had been demonstrated more or less since its inception, was not binding on parliament. According to another critic, because the treaty failed to provide a constitutional safeguard,

> the omission of such a safeguard to the interests of Scotland as the provision of an independent tribunal would have been, in the absence of a Parliament in Scotland, had this, among other consequences, that it led Englishmen to regard Scotland as no longer a nation, but a dependency of England … That conviction still prevails among Englishmen. England to them is Great Britain, and they constantly speak of it as such. They have even gone the length of inserting the name England instead of Great Britain in a treaty with a foreign country. As regarding Scotland as on an equality with an English county, we have frequent examples of that … It implies that Scotland has ceased to be a nation and is a province, or county, or what you will, of England. Had the Scottish Parliament been retained, or were it once more restored, it would be a much needed bulwark of Scottish nationality, against this insidious tendency to ignore it.[107]

So the historical violations of the Union could be used to demonstrate that the Anglo-Scottish relationship was not a partnership of equals and that the Scots held an inferior position. Furthermore, although the treaty could be used to show that the Scots were not a conquered people, it did not guarantee their national dignity and rights. Indeed, one of the reasons why the Union featured so prominently in nationalist accounts of the past was the belief that ignorance about the treaty led many Scots to assume that their history was the same as England's or that the nation was of little consequence before 1707. Furthermore, this was amplified by English attitudes: 'In a broadcast lecture, Professor Trevelyan said at the Union, Scotland became merged in England. Not, mark you, that Scotland and England became merged in Great Britain, but that Scotland became merged in England. That is history as it is taught at Cambridge University.'[108] It was claimed that Unionists 'lose no opportunity to belittle the importance of Scotland in status and prestige among the European nations in pre-Union times'.[109] For others, the Unionist bias meant that for the period after the Union 'Scotland is lost in the Empire, a condition which, no doubt, is very gratifying to the shades of early imperialists as Edward I, the murderer of Wallace, and other arch enemies of Scotland'.[110]

For both devolutionists and nationalists, the iniquities and the Anglo-Scottish relationship since 1707 could be cited to demonstrate that the relationship needed reform or sundered. For devolutionists the fact that most of the original articles related to economic factors was used to make the claim that there was no need to abolish the Scottish parliament in 1707 and a federal system would have secured the same original objectives.[111] The sordid facts surrounding bribery and corruption which were often presented as the reasons behind the passage of the Union in 1707 need not deflect from the wider need to secure an Anglo-Scottish or British constitutional arrangement, and the episode of the Union neatly illustrates the fact that while devolutionists and nationalists could share the same historical explanation regarding an episode in the Scottish past, it did not necessarily mean that they shared the same political objective. History mattered to nationalists for the simple reason that many believed that a wider and more in-depth knowledge of the nation's past inevitably led to the conclusion that independence was desirable and necessary. In many respects it was almost an article of faith among many nationalists that if only the population was more aware and knowledgeable about the Scottish past, then there would be a greater sympathy with the nationalist cause. Hence, for many, the reason for so much antipathy towards the question of independence was that Scots did not know enough about their own history which was neglected in schools and that the solution was for a greater emphasis on Scottish history in the education system. The treatment of Scottish historical records and the funding of the National Library of Scotland compared to its English equivalents was cited as evidence of the lack of respect held in Scottish society for its past. The formation of the Saltire Society in 1936 was part of an effort to promote a greater understanding of Scottish history and culture.[112]

Post Union

A strong factor running through nationalist accounts of the past was an almost counterfactual demonstration to show how successful the Scots would be if they were an independent nation. The roll call of inventors, scientists, artists and the great and good were trotted out to show that the nation had no shortage of producing talent and, indeed, overproduced and over-contributed to the sum of British greatness: 'To discover comparable achievement by so small a nation in so short a time we should need to go back from the time of James Mackenzie [the eighteenth-century author of *A Man of Feeling*] to the Age of Pericles.'[113] As one critic caustically remarked, the Scots have 'imprinted their mark on the planet in almost every sphere of action and thought, except self-government. Since 1707, the Scots have skilfully practised the Nelson touch by turning their blind eye to the fact that they are in a subordinate position'.[114] It was frequently asked how the Scots could not govern themselves when so many of the British prime ministers had been Scots? Nationalists co-opted the existing Scottish historiography and pushed the patriotic dimension which emphasized the important role Scots played in making a contribution to Britain and used it to make the political point that the nation had all the natural abilities required to make independence work. The obvious danger with this strategy was quite simple in that if the Union was so good at showcasing the successful qualities of the Scots, why change? Also, if the Union and empire offered a much bigger stage and greater opportunities, why should a Scot be content to lead four million souls when at the zenith of the imperial heyday this covered a quarter of the planet's inhabitants as Florence Horsburgh, the Tory MP for Dundee, argued:

> I would remind hon. Members that in the old days we heard a great deal of walls that were built in the north of England to keep away from England certain tribes of the north. Walls were built and were found to be of no use. Further walls were built, but still the population of the north scaled them. I believe that whatever wall or barrier people tried to put up, we of the Scottish race would scale it. It is not merely a case of being fit to govern themselves. We think we are fit to govern all the world. I would ask those who advocate this scheme of Home Rule if they are willing to see Members who sit for Scottish constituencies shut out from Cabinet rank in the Imperial Parliament? Are they willing to give up for ever the idea that a Member for a Scottish constituency can be Prime Minister of Great Britain? I for one am not willing to give up that idea. Are they willing to shut out Scotsmen and Scotswomen from taking the biggest positions arising from being able to do the largest amount of work not only for Britain but for the British Empire? If they are willing to do that, then we will say that they have lost their Scottish characteristics.[115]

Having demonstrated that throughout their history the Scots had shown more than enough talent and ability to govern themselves, there was the awkward issue of explaining why this situation was no longer acceptable.

Devolutionists could make the case that self-government would not limit the opportunities in the British state and empire and that the Scots could enjoy the best of both worlds. For nationalists, this involved the construction of a narrative that had to show that what may have been good for individual Scots and the wider imperial apparatus was in fact bad for Scottish society. This had a particular resonance in the interwar period as many of the Unionists certainties could no longer be taken for granted as the nation faced significant economic challenges.[116] The advent of mass democracy and class-based political realignment also radically changed commonplace assumptions. One area where nationalists could take what was seen as a positive in the past and make it negative in the contemporary world was emigration. Over the course of the latter part of the nineteenth and early twentieth centuries a narrative had emerged in Scottish society about the natural 'elasticity' of the Scots and how they made splendid migrants as they were imbued with the characteristics of entrepreneurship, intelligence, education, a work ethic and an ability to adapt to new and challenging circumstances. The activities of the Scots overseas became something that Scots at home could celebrate because it showed off their supposed national characteristics which all agreed were very praiseworthy indeed.[117] This was especially the case in an intellectual atmosphere which was profoundly shaped by social Darwinist assumptions about 'racial' characteristics. At its most extreme in the interwar era, nationalists took much of that narrative and altered its primary conclusion by appealing to eugenicist notions that the best elements of the 'race' were being dispatched overseas and thus denuding the quality of 'race' at home.[118] Such notions were given extra potency by highlighting population decline in both the Highlands and rural Scotland, and indeed, a central claim was that instead of supporting ex-servicemen to emigrate to the white dominions, that money should instead be spent on schemes of land resettlement in the countryside and in the Highlands.[119]

The debate is interesting in that it clearly demonstrates that many nationalists were not impervious to arguments of race and 'racial hygiene', but it also shows that rural and Highland Scotland occupied a place of greater cultural or spiritual importance than the industrial lowlands. Part of the explanation is to be found in a common European nostalgia for rural life and anti-industrialism which was especially heightened during the economic turmoil of the 1920s and 1930s when faith in industrial capitalism was stretched to breaking point.[120] Also, it could be that rural and Highland Scotland was more easily thought of as being Scottish whereas the urban conurbations seemed more British or cosmopolitan. Having said all that, Scottish nationalists are no different from other European nationalists who all seem to idealize the rural idyllic as the key emblem of national identity. The correlation between emigration and rural decline was one that energized many nationalists in the period up to the 1970s, and ideas of race were never far from the surface.[121] Also, it is worth pointing out that for some, immigration was seen as a threat to national identity with a number of individuals identified as nationalists being prolific in their outpourings of the 'Irish Menace to Scottish nationality'.[122]

For nationalists, the history of the Union was one in which there were successes in the eighteenth and nineteenth centuries, but by the interwar era, this was drying up. To put it crudely, it was a story of the Union having passed its sell-by date. This meant that the positives of the past could be contrasted with the negatives of the present. One such example can be drawn from economic history. The period after the Union witnessed a golden era of economic growth and expansion as Scotland emerged as a technological leader in heavy industry. Scottish engineering and shipbuilding together with a history of invention was cited as evidence of the basic ability of the Scots to have a successful economy. The changed economic circumstances of the interwar era brought a much greater sense of pessimism as the economy stagnated.

In most of the nationalists polemics of the interwar years that dealt with the economy, technological decline and industrial collapse were laid squarely at the feet of the Union because it was an ineffective mechanism of government. The growing divergence within the British economy in which a prosperous south was contrasted with decline in the north was cited as a practical consequence of the neglect of Scottish interests under the Union. The fact that success had been achieved in the past was used to make the claim that current failure was not inevitable. The contrast of past successes with present failures became a simplistic, but effective use of history to make a political point in the present. In many respects, it could hardly be otherwise as the narrative of Scottish history since the inception of the modern nationalist movement after the First World War is that the Union is, in some way or another, failing the Scottish people and that its most obvious manifestation was in the economy.[123]

Another aspect to note in nationalists historiography is the approach to shared aspects of history with the rest of the United Kingdom and in particular the issue of the British Empire. In one sense it could be used to promote the story of Scottish virtues and intrepid endeavour, but, at the same time, it also raised awkward questions as to the relationship with England in the sense that were the Scots junior partners or, more negatively, a subservient arm of their imperial masters.[124] This dichotomy was captured by the American radical Henry George in a speech in Glasgow in 1884:

> Those Scottish highlanders have been an ideal people with the aristocracy. They fight like lions abroad, and they have been taken abroad at the dictate of the very power which has oppressed them, to rob and plunder, and kill other people; but they are tame as sheep at home ... alongside a Scottish lion you ought to put a Scottish sheep.[125]

Within the nationalist movement, the role of the Scots in the empire was a barometer of left- and right-wing tendencies. For right-wingers, a central aspect of the argument for self-government was that Scotland was a mother nation of the empire and as such should be accorded the status of being able to rule itself rather than have the status associated with dominion nations. For some the fact that the Scots had been successful pioneers, explorers, entrepreneurs and colonial governor generals was cited as evidence that there was enough talent in Scotland to make the case for governing themselves. Others used the imperial dimension to illustrate perfidious Albion as holding back Scottish freedom. For some, the British Empire was simply the story of the English exploiting the Scots' fighting ability for their own benefits:

> Has not England built up her great Empire at the point of Scottish bayonets? Have innocent Highland crofters ever hesitated to defend England against an invasion of equally innocent Boer farmers, when Jewish gold and diamonds were at stake? Has there ever been a private scrap anywhere on earth but the Scot has 'joined in'? Is there a Crown or Republic in Europe which has not been established without the presence of a kilt? Can there be a spot on the map which bears not the impress of a Scottish brogue. Have not the Scots helped many

people to become nations? Are not Scotsmen to be found at the top in every civilised and uncivilised country in the world?[126]

Whatever the perspective, the empire was used by both imperialists and anti-imperialists to make the case for Scottish independence.[127]

As was mentioned earlier, Scottish nationalists believe that a good knowledge of the nation's past will make people conducive to the idea of independence and that to some extent the reluctance to back the idea of self-government was due to people not having confidence in the nation; this was explained by a lot of historical ignorance. So nationalists have been vociferous in promoting Scottish history and advocating its compulsory teaching in schools. Its absence from the curriculum in schools was blamed for this state of affairs. According to one critic, a textbook then in use had

> a list 'people in our story', which is given to assist the Scottish child to understand his country's history, we are not surprised to find that of the 32 names mentioned over half are non-Scots ... In this list we find Samuel Pepys, Titus Oates, Judge Jeffreys, Walter Raleigh, John Bunyan and others ... whose connection to Scotland's story is not quite clear.[128]

Throughout the twentieth century, nationalists have promoted Scottish commemoration of significant events, with the life of Wallace and the Battle of Bannockburn being among the most high profile because of their association with the cause of independence. An attempt to promote 6 April as Independence Day after the Declaration of Arbroath in 1320 never really got off the ground.[129] As we have seen, the medieval period, because it is before the Union, was fairly unproblematic and both Wallace and Bruce were icons that appealed beyond the nationalist spectrum, although the attempt to co-opt them to the cause of independence has been criticized by Unionists. What has been striking, however, is that what were important events in the Scottish Victorian calendar of commemoration such as the Reformation, the National Covenant and the Revolution of 1690 have been omitted, largely, it can be assumed, on account of the potential to raise religious divisions.

For many nationalists the issue of historical ignorance was compounded by a form of cultural imperialism in which English history was presented as that covering the whole island. Nationalists were able to build on a backlog of historical grievances in the nineteenth century in which English insensitivity to the Scottish past was the cause of considerable consternation. Lord Rosebery often played to the public gallery on the importance of Scottish history,[130] and there was a persistent grumbling about the use of the words 'England' and 'English' to describe Britain and British,[131] the use of the numeral VIII in the coronation of King Edward which took no account of the fact that there had never been a king of that name in Scotland meant that the offending number was pointedly omitted in Scottish loyal addresses,[132] and other historical indignities were all seized upon to show that the Scots had their own separate history and resented the assumption that they had been swallowed up by a Greater English history.[133] It was argued that a widespread public knowledge and understanding of the history of Scotland was an essential cultural prerequisite for independence and that the greater dissemination of Scottish history was likely to create more converts. In and of itself, such activities need not necessarily indicate hostility to the Union but rather a desire to see that Scottish history was properly observed. For nationalists, such widespread insensitivity to the Scottish past was indicative of a wider tendency within the Union that Scotland was treated unfairly and not given proper respect. The accession of Queen Elizabeth was another occasion when widespread English indifference incurred public opprobrium.[134]

Conclusion

In 1931, Hugh MacDiarmid elaborated on and modified the idea of Gregory Smith that there was a 'Caledonian Antisyzygy' in which conflicting polarities existed within the one entity, and this was a marked feature of Scottish literature and thought, best exemplified in Robert Louis Stevenson's *Jekyll and Hyde*. MacDiarmid's essay was an intellectually rambling affair that added little to Smith's original observation, but it became a form of rallying cry for the Scottish cultural renaissance of the interwar era and its influence carried on into the post-war era, most notably in the ideas of Tom Nairn.[135] The duality of the nationalist engagement with post-Union history has been its most striking feature. As we have seen, the question as to whether Scotland was a colony or not occupied a considerable intellectual space in the early days of the nationalist movement. Its subsequent re-emergence in the form of 'internal colonialism' simply reinforced the non-ethnic variant of reading the Scottish past as the Celtic fringe did not constitute all of Scotland and that the Lowlands had a different historical experience from the Highlands.[136] The desire to trawl the Scottish past for concrete evidence of the nation's capacity for self-government while at the same time purporting that the existing constitutional arrangement was an inhibitor of 'national genius' meant that reading the Scottish past pulled in two separate directions: one positive and the other negative. Furthermore, there was a considerable overlap with traditional Unionist accounts as, intellectually, the two drew from the same sources. Scottish success can show the capacity for self-government and can also be used to show that the Union works. Equally, Scottish failure can be used to make the case against self-government but also to demonstrate that the Union is failing. The inability to produce a radically divergent nationalist history has to a large extent been compensated by a growing Unionist suspicion of Scottish history per se and the unfounded assumption that a wider public engagement with the Scottish past would lead to an endorsement of independence.[137] Undoubtedly many nationalists believed and still believe this to be the case; the problem has been the Unionists tendency to uncritically accept this. Furthermore, the growth in academic history with its various sub-specialisms in economic, social, cultural and gender history has had an impact in blunting a crude political and ideological focus of history.[138] In particular the dominance of labour historiography in which class was the primary mechanism by which the past was interpreted cast a long shadow over the post-war era as it chimed in with contemporary political expectations of the Scots as being a left-leaning people. This, rather than a Unionist or nationalist narrative, became the dominant interpretation that reached its zenith with the advent of Thatcherism in the 1980s. Indeed, it was the twisting of this leftist-leaning paradigm into one in which class was increasingly conflated with nation that marked a turning towards something of a neo-nationalist historical explanation.[139] Again, the use of class and the traditional location within the left–right political spectrum meant that in spite of its nationalist overtones it could be used by devolutionists in the Labour Party to make the case for Scottish home rule in that class acted as a sort of antidote to nationalism. Although the SNP would leave the Scottish Constitutional Convention which laid down the blueprint for the establishment of a Scottish parliament in the 1990s, the arguments used by devolutionists in relation to the sovereignty of the people and the right of the Scottish people to choose a form of government best suited to their needs were identical to the ones used by the nationalists to justify independence, which were mainly drawn from a Scottish constitutional tradition.[140]

2

Nationalism

A closer examination of a number of randomly selected studies of the concepts of nations and nationalism reveals that each author interprets these terms quite differently. This is accompanied by efforts to be original, which have reached a global scale, with regard not only to interpretations and definitions but also to the creation of new terminology. The basic difficulty lies in attempting to analyse modern social and cultural processes by making use of a term that emerged in the Middle Ages and has been used continually until modern times. Although the common root of the term 'nation' was the Latin natio, its transfer or translation into different languages took place under a variety of circumstances, both political and social, thus giving it rather divergent meanings.
– Hroch, *European Nations: Explaining Their Formation*, 3

In this chapter we examine the arm's-length relationship that the Scottish national movement has had with nationalism, and as Hroch points out above, the issues associated with the elasticity of the concept prevent easy and clearly defined definitions. The term 'nationalism' remains a complex and difficult issue because of the negative connotations that it has acquired over the course of the twentieth century. In essence, this chapter explores the various techniques, explanations and justifications that have evolved to explain why Scotland as a nation should be regarded as a political unit that has primacy over all other considerations. The bedrock of the engagement with nationalism was to demonstrate that the Scottish variant was shorn of the worst aspects and excesses that had scarred the human experience in the twentieth century. Scottish independence as a means to an end or a better society has been a prominent feature as has the explanation that there are civic and liberal forms of the phenomenon. Furthermore, the promotion of a national dimension in Scottish politics has been a second pillar of nationalist strategy as the more that the Scots see themselves as a nation, so the argument goes, the more inclined they will be towards independence. The difference between small and large nations was another important aspect of the debate and was used to disassociate Scottish nationalism from aggressive and chauvinistic imperialism which was believed to be a consequence of the artificial construction of nationalism in large states where communal bonds of affinity were impossible because of the scale and size of the territorial extent of places such as the

Figure 2 This photograph shows all those who attended the SNP Conference (1956) at the Allan Water Hotel, Bridge of Allan (Source: *Scots Independent*).

Front row: George Leask, Bruce Watson, Arthur Donaldson, Tom Gibson, Fiona Smart, Helen McIntosh, Olive Bruce, Vi Donaldson.

Second row: Murdoch Young, Ian Howard, Olive Halliday, Robert McIntyre, Angus MacIntosh, David Rollo.

Third row: Willie Gillespie, Russell Hill, James Halliday, John Frew, Andy Bruce (London), John Smart, Bobby Stevenson, unknown.

Fourth row: Mr Nicolson, unknown, Mr McIntosh, unknown, Ian Smith, Eoin Grant, Hugh Watson.

Back row: Robin Leask, John Gilchrist, unknown, Joanne Watson, unknown.

Soviet Union, Germany, Britain and France. Furthermore, it was claimed that the small nation was a natural product of human social interaction. The chapter ends with a discussion on the importance of landscape and the sentimental engagement with territory because it is one that tends to be ignored as it involves the taboo subject of emotion in politics.

Instrumentalism, liberalism and ethnicity

Throughout the history of the Scottish National Party (SNP) it has been common to represent the party as having little in the way of an ideology and holding an ambivalent relationship with the concept of nationalism. Although sometimes caricatured as a Fascist political organization that espoused the cause of nationalism as an end in itself, the party has relentlessly portrayed itself as a liberal and progressive movement.[1]

Most of the time, the discourse that has emerged has been in the conventional political language of left and right, and above all, the SNP was primarily a means to an end. Nationalism was simply a mechanism to achieve independence which was not promoted as an end in itself but as a way to bring about a different kind of society. The idea of nationalism for expedient or instrumental purposes has a long historical pedigree within the movement, and in the main, the principal argument was that independence was always about securing a better form of government and the socio-economic, cultural and political benefits that would accrue from this. For a number of leaders, such as Robert McIntyre, pragmatism was the central pillar of their political philosophy and that ideology of any type was best treated with a large degree of suspicion.[2] For some, the SNP would cease to exist as a distinct political party once independence was achieved and that it would splinter into left- and right-wing segments that would champion political interests based on the conventional ideological axis.[3]

This has caused problems because while the party has had to operate in the real world of conventional left-right politics, which means taking a stand on certain issues, a number of purists have insisted that such issues should be decided once independence has been achieved. According to Roland Muirhead too much policy and focus on specific issues would exacerbate divisions, and 'if I had my own way, I would have no constitution, but simply the object stated [self-government] and leave the body to develop policy as it goes along'.[4] Such a narrow political programme would not help the party's electoral prospects because the voter, not unreasonably, might expect to be told where the SNP stands on most of the pressing issues of the day.[5] To some extent, this could be sidestepped by arguing that independence was about national liberation from the bonds of the British state which, it was claimed, prevented the Scots from having a better society or rather a society more suited to their needs and aspirations. This could be framed to include a moral dimension, and after the First World War the following statement would become a standard theme in making the case for independence or self-government:

> Self-determination is one of the watchwords of the New Europe and the New Age. It expresses concisely the essential demand of every nation conscious of its nationhood. Every nation worthy of the name demands the power to shape its own destiny in freedom, to determine the lines of its own national progress, to mould its own national life. The soul of the nation insists on free and complete self-expression.[6]

This freedom to do things is the fundamental pillar upon which all subsequent arguments about having independence to promote particular political policies and visions rest. So, as we shall see, even the eschewal of an ideological nationalism, which instrumental nationalists advocate, still requires a conception of the 'nation' at the heart of the argument.[7] This 'expedient' nationalism is characterized by statements that proclaim that an independent Scotland would better serve social justice or some such other conventional political objective, and a whole host of aspirations have been tied to the mast of independence, ranging from the removal of nuclear weapons from

Scottish soil to the ending of Conservative governments. In many respects, 'expedient' nationalism allows its proponents to sidestep the thorny issue of nationalism and all the troublesome ideological baggage that the idea contains, especially the difficult subjects of exclusivity and notions of national superiority that have been such a hallmark of nationalism in other places and at other times. In short, the idea of nationalism is reduced from a core ideological belief to one of a simple function in order to attain worthwhile and, more often than not, more liberal, progressive and tolerant goals.

It is easy to see why there is an awkward relationship with the philosophy of nationalism, especially since the end of the Second World War, because there is a near universal consensus that it has been the most destructive political idea of the twentieth century.[8] Nationalism, in the sense of believing in a nation's superiority to others or the promotion of the 'national' interest against all other aspects of domestic policy, continues to have bad press as it is associated with illiberal, intolerant and authoritarian views in which the 'national' interest is used as a means to divert the populace from problems at home.[9] Furthermore, nationalism is presented as profoundly irrational and draws its strength from appeals to raw, unthinking emotion, especially among segments of the less-educated and less-informed elements of the population.[10] The use of nationalism as a tool to whip up popular sentiment against foreigners and immigrants is a key factor in explaining populism as a political force.[11] More than anything, it is the association of nationalism with the destructive forces of Nazism and Fascism during the Second World War that has put the philosophy beyond the pale for most liberal-minded people. As a political philosophy nationalism is the politics of cultural despair that offers nothing in the way of a positive message.[12] A major problem for those who espouse nationalism as a means to achieve an independent statehood is that it is often considered by political and social scientists as being the same phenomenon that wreaks havoc when it has access to the full panoply of state power, especially a large and powerful state apparatus which persecutes and dominates those that it considers enemies of the nation, be that domestic or foreign.[13] The distinction between pre- and post-state nationalism is not one that is readily appreciated or understood.[14]

Historically, a fundamental pillar in the intellectual construction of nationalism has been notions of 'race' or ethnicity in the sense that, in its most extreme form, membership of the nation is determined by a supposed biological heritage or kinship.[15] The conflation of 'race' with nation was used throughout Europe in the late nineteenth and twentieth centuries to exclude those people who happened to be in a nationally defined territory but were nevertheless deemed not to be part of it. It could also be used to make the claim that people of the same ethnicity or race in other nations ought to be reunited with the 'mother' country. The most obvious example of this is how the Nazis used 'race' to claim that Jews were not part of the 'Aryan' nation of Germany and justify the expansion of a Greater Germany to include ethnic Germans in other nations such as the Sudatenland in Czechoslovakia.[16] An example closer to home, which conveniently gets forgotten about, is the application of racial terms in the nationalist/Unionist debate in Ireland which also dovetailed with religious divisions.[17] Although nationalists and Unionists in Ireland paid lip-service to the idea of inclusivity, the reality of much of the debate was characterized by a nationalist view that held that the true Irish were 'Celtic' and Catholic as opposed to the incomers who were Anglo-Saxon and

Protestant and thus alien.[18] Similarly, unionism sharpened to focus on the protection of a geographically specific group of people in the north who had a shared ancestry with those on the mainland who saw themselves as British and not Irish. Pockets of this debate still survive to this day.[19] The ethnic nationalism that followed in the wake of the collapse of Yugoslavia and the rise of the far-right in Europe following the economic crash in 2008 confirmed nationalism as a dangerous and exclusive ideology. Not surprisingly, nationalists in Scotland have fallen over themselves to disassociate their values and beliefs from nationalism as commonly understood in the world today and have even rebranded themselves as belonging to the 'independence movement'. From time to time, there is debate as to whether to drop the 'National' in the 'Scottish National Party'.[20]

There is, however, a danger of throwing out the national baby with the nationalist bathwater. As we shall see, many Scottish nationalists have been at pains to demonstrate that not all nationalisms are alike and that, indeed, there are benign variants of the phenomenon that have socially progressive features. Drawing on a nineteenth-century font of what has been described as 'liberal nationalism' in which movements of national liberation were seen as a means for European peoples to break the dominance of aristocratic feudalism and create political structures based on progress and enlightenment, an alternative form to the usual notion of authoritarianism and chauvinism was possible.[21] This 'liberal nationalism' was much in evidence in nineteenth-century Scotland as Scots supported a number of nationalist causes ranging from Kossuth in Hungary to Garibaldi in Italy, with some taking part in the Italian Risorgimento.[22] Irish nationalism was not supported because of its association with Catholicism which, it was argued, would lead to papal domination and reactionary government. In the twentieth century, the intellectual construction of civic nationalism, which confers national status based on residency, has emerged as an antidote to its ethnic variant, and this has been a marked feature in Scotland, especially since the 1980s as a mechanism to mobilize Scottish society in opposition to the Thatcherite onslaught against the social democrat institutions of the post-war Welfare State. This notion of civic nationalism was based around the idea of civil society and widely interpreted as being a major factor in the Scottish rejection of Thatcherite policies and ethics.[23] It is worth pointing out that throughout Europe, civic nationalism has always existed in conjunction with ethnic nationalism, but it has not received the same attention from historians and political scientists as its more virulent counterpart. An example of civic nationalism can be seen in Pearce's Proclamation of the Irish Republic during the Easter Rising, and it is a good elucidation of the principles:

> The Irish Republic is entitled to, and hereby claims, the allegiance of every Irishman and Irishwoman. The Republic guarantees religious and civil liberty, equal rights and equal opportunities to all its citizens, and declares its resolve to pursue the happiness and prosperity of the whole nation and of all its parts, cherishing all of the children of the nation equally, and oblivious of the differences carefully fostered by an alien Government, which have divided a minority from the majority in the past.[24]

As a nationalism that can be portrayed as not really being a nationalism in the normal sense in which it is commonly understood, civic nationalism was used to promote and legitimate the idea of home rule or devolution in Scotland at the end of the twentieth century. The demand for a Scottish parliament was commonly portrayed as emblematic of a society that was more left leaning, and this was reinforced by the growing divergence between Scottish and English electoral behaviour where the Conservative Party which formed the British government was reduced to an electoral rump north of the border.[25] The idea that civil society was the key driver for constitutional change was important because it would be pushed by the non-nationalist left and centre political parties. Furthermore, the dividing line between civil society and civic nationalism was conveniently blurred.[26] In the 1980s, the emergence of civic nationalism in response to a Conservative government that had little popular support among the Scottish electorate was explained as a reaction by Scotland's distinctive civil society to the imposition of unpopular policies which went against the grain of a greater collectivist sense of society than was the case in England.[27] Certainly this approach allowed a number of significant difficulties to be sidestepped as residence was used as the qualification necessary for inclusion in Scottish society, and by emphasizing society as a whole rather than individuals or Scots, the issue of ethnicity did not matter. Culture and identity were subsumed under a broad political category whose primary focus was on its difference with England and most usually within the familiar ideological axis of left and right. Yet, almost unnoticed is the fact that the ideas used by devolutionists to justify the creation of a Scottish parliament as 'representing the form of government, best suited to the needs of the Scottish people' and legitimized by the notion that sovereignty resides in the Scottish people were identical to the arguments used by nationalists for independence.

While civic nationalism has been a predominant theme in the ideology of Scottish nationalism, ethnicity has also played a part. Indeed, whether we like it or not and whatever reservations we may have about it as a political concept, by definition, ethnicity has to be at the bedrock of all European nationalist ideology. The reason for this is simple in that nationalism requires first a nation and the definition of what constitutes a nation is largely based on a shared historical experience. This then becomes the story of the ancestors of the country, and it is around this core of a common cultural and historical experience that the ideology of nationalism is constructed. Thereafter, ethnicity need not be so central, but in extreme forms of nationalism it remains pivotal mainly as a way of defining who are, and who are not, members of the nation. That said, in and of itself, ethnicity is not necessarily a bad thing. Notions of ethnicity are used by émigré communities around the world to help maintain a sense of their identity, and the Scottish diaspora is a very good example of the celebration of ethnic identity.[28] When used by émigré groups, celebrating ethnicity becomes a way of reinforcing multicultural identity because it then is one of many different ethnicities. It does become problematic, however, if it is used domestically by the *dominant* ethnic group to reinforce an idea of national identity because it is exclusive and at odds with civic nationalism.

The issue of ethnicity does not have quite the same purchase in Scottish nationalism as elsewhere. As was mentioned in Chapter 1, the legal definition of the territory of Scotland has meant that the need to construct the nation out of the settlement of ethnically defined Scottish people has not been necessary. Simply put, Scotland existed on one side of a legally defined boundary which was situated in an area, unlike Wales, that was not prone to an influx of immigrants.[29] Historically, the Anglo-Scottish border remained sharp and reinforced cultural and national identities on either side.[30] A second reason why ethnicity has had little purchase in Scotland is that the nation regarded itself as a mongrel creation. According to Peter Hume Brown writing in the late nineteenth century, 'Of these four nations, the Picts and the Britons had been settled there from a period which has not been ascertained; while the Scots and the Angles were comparatively new-comers. From the union of these four peoples, the Scottish nation was to emerge, though blended with other elements that appreciably affected its character and destiny.'[31] The ethnic mix of the Scots was a constant refrain in Scottish history during the era when ethnic nationalism was most virulent in Europe.[32] The Picts, the Scots, the Britons and the Vikings had all left their mark, and even in the 1970s this largely ethnic and racial interpretation of the creation of the Scottish nation was regularly recited. The difference between ethnic and racial ideas of nationality is that the former is based on ideas of culture while the latter is constructed around ideas of biology or 'blood'.[33] The ethnically diverse nature of early Scottish history has even been used as an argument against both independence and home rule on the grounds that no purely ethnic Scottish nation exists and that the Highland/Lowland divide was a major factor in claiming that the Scots did not have the ability to rule themselves.[34] There were frequent insinuations that Scottish national aspirations were somehow fake or false; according to the Scottish Tory Sir Robert Horne: 'I do not profess any less passion for my native land than those candidates for Parliament who in the Lowlands of Scotland go to their meetings in a kilt to the playing of bagpipes.'[35] While the debate about race and ethnicity has ebbed and flowed since the eighteenth century, many saw the mixture as a source of strength, especially in the nineteenth and early twentieth centuries.[36] For a number of nationalists the 'Scottish amalgam' was something to be promoted:

> I maintain that Scotland has in herself these two aspects of genius, strongly enough characterised and differentiated to allow them to fuse and to condition each other without confusion or conflict. Indeed such a fusion is wanted for fertility, for lasting fruit. Highland imagination and Lowland steadiness, Highland daring and Lowland grip. The best promise for the future of Scotland's art lies in the marriage of those two.[37]

This emphasis on the 'mongrel nation' also explains why the notion of Scotland as a Celtic nation, in the same way as Ireland and Wales have been portrayed, was always going to be problematic. Indeed, a number of Scottish historians in the late nineteenth and early twentieth centuries argued that it was a largely a Lowland army of ethnic Teutons that defeated the English at Bannockburn with the Celts of the Highlands playing little or no role in maintaining Scottish independence. Needless to say, this was disputed.[38]

Undoubtedly the very bad press that nationalism per se has received as an ideology following the Second World War and its continued association with racism and chauvinism have meant that there has been a general reluctance to discuss the meaning of Scottish nationalism as an ideology or as a set of beliefs and instead the focus has been on its more pragmatic and functionary side. The one form of nationalism which has had an intellectual legitimacy in the twentieth century is that associated with anti-colonialism and anti-imperialism. In the main, this has been most prevalent with the campaign to end European imperialism following the Second World War, and while Irish nationalism has had a strong anti-colonial intellectual seam running through it, it has been less well established in the Scottish case, although as we have seen there have been several attempts to offer such an interpretation.[39] The division of nationalism into a black-and-white paradigm in which it is used for either oppression or liberation has not helped the Scottish movement both because of the difficulty of constructing a clearly delineated model in which it was conquered and oppressed like the Irish, and also because of its European background which shares a lot of the common intellectual heritage as the oppressing kind. A cursory glance at the activities of Scots within British imperialism gives rise to the notion that far from being colonized, the Scots were colonizers.[40] Furthermore, the dominance of Marxist thinking on Third World anti-colonialism laid more stress on liberation from capitalist imperialism than national liberation, and indeed, many argued that nationalism itself was a Western intellectual construct which was created by the imperialists as a means to divide and conquer.[41] That said, forms of colonialist models of interpretation were used particularly in relation to the Highlands which were argued to have undergone a form of internal colonialism.[42]

The nation and the state

The modern movement that was dedicated to the re-establishment of Scottish statehood was born during the 1920s and developed in an intellectual environment in which nationalism was seen as an up-and-coming ideology in Europe between the wars.[43] This was also before its worst manifestations had appeared, and though aspects are obvious with hindsight, the predominant belief was that nationalism, if not benign, was an almost natural political force.[44] Perhaps the most significant thing to point out in the era after the First World War was that the idea of the nation, as it was generally understood in Scotland, was transformed by international events. In the first place, there was the impact of the Versailles Peace Conference that created new nation states and that statehood was the 'natural' condition of nations. The peace treaty put a great deal of emphasis on the correlation between nations and states and enshrined this in a European context in the widely used phrase 'All nations have the right of self-determination'.[45] Versailles was significant in two ways. Firstly, it went against the conventional wisdom that existed before 1914 in that the greater would absorb the smaller by breaking up the European parts of the Ottoman, Austro-Hungarian and German Empires into their 'national' constituents and according them statehood.[46] Secondly, it conflated notions of the nation with the state and made many in Scotland think about nationality in those terms. In the era of the League of Nations, Scotland had no official existence. It was absent from the peace talks, and a number of individuals were caught out by all sorts of trivial and mundane examples which seemed to question the legitimacy of Scottish nationhood. One example was a League of Nations pamphlet for schools which featured all the countries of the world by showing children dressed in their national costumes, and in spite of being a very conspicuous piece of national attire, the kilt was missing.[47] Scotland was excluded from the almanacs designed to teach children about the many nations (some of them new), and this especially jarred given that it focused on simplistic facts such as the capital city or the national costume or the national musical instrument or figures of national literature and so on. The problem that Scotland faced as a stateless nation was that it seemed to have more of the 'characters and requirements' of a nation than many of the new ones. The paradigm that statehood was now a universally recognized criterion for nationhood was one that caught out many Scots in the post-Versailles era.

For a number of people, the Scottish claim to national self-determination was greater than that of many of the new nations coming into existence:

> In some of the countries for which independence has been claimed there are people of widely different races and tongues, and there will be many difficulties in the application of the principle of self-government. But in its application to Scotland no such difficulties can or will arise. Scotland is unconquered and unconquerable, a free and independent nation, and co-equal partner with England in the Union. Its history is one long record of determined struggle against tyranny and oppression, and no nation has made greater sacrifices in the cause of freedom. Many are the attempts to impose upon Scottish law and customs contrary to the people's will, but neither in the domain of politics or religion have these attempts succeeded, and the pages of Scottish History are glorious with the names of the heroes and martyrs who shed their blood on behalf of Liberty and Independence.[48]

It is hard not to conclude that with so much public attention, domestically and internationally, focused on the emerging new nations of Europe a number of Scots were chagrined that this process was by-passing their own special claims to having a distinctive 'national' story. Furthermore, because nations required statehood in order to garner international recognition and legitimacy, especially with the growth of supra-national agencies and bodies, the fact that Scotland was excluded from the League of Nations, for example, was one that many could not understand. Bluntly put, Scotland did not meet the requirements now necessary for the legal acceptance of what was required to be a nation. For whatever reason, the intellectual climate now held that a nation could not be regarded as such unless it had its political independence. Furthermore, the fact that the new Dominion nations of the British Empire were represented at the peace conference but not one of the 'mother nations' came as a shock to many, who struggled to see how Scotland could be excluded but new countries like South Africa, Australia, Canada and New Zealand were included in the British delegation:

> Scotland is an older and greater nation than any of the overseas Dominions, great as these are. Indeed. They have been to a large extent built up by the enterprise

of her sons and daughters. Scotland has a national contribution to make to the world that entitles her to separate representation on the Assembly of the League of Nations on the same footing as Canada, Australia, South Africa – and Ireland. A League of Nations that excludes the Scottish nation, with its long and splendid history and its immeasurable service to the world, is an imperfect instrument of international progress.[49]

A petition calling for Scottish representation at Versailles, for example, included the following prominent figures from the Labour Party: Tom Johnston, David Kirkwood, Neil MacLean, James Maxton, Manny Shinwell and Alexander Willkie (all of whom would be future members of parliament (MPs)).[50] As will be discussed in Chapter 4, at this time the lines between home rule, self-government and independence were quite blurry, and many who described themselves as home rulers did envision devolution with a foreign policy dimension. The breakaway of Ireland (or most of it) from the United Kingdom and possibly its empire seemed to confirm that this was the era in which small nations could reassert their claims to national independence.[51] This quite fundamental change in perception of what constituted a nation was also reinforced by the fact that many Scots believed Scotland was every bit as much a nation as Ireland:

> Her national case for home rule is as strong as Ireland's. Scotland is a nation, with her own national characteristics, temperament, point of view, her own systems of law and judicial procedure, her own peculiar social conditions, and her own system of administration.[52]

Many of the old nineteenth-century Scottish assumptions regarding the idea of nationhood that had existed comfortably within the Union clearly no longer held up to the new expectation that nations ought to have full control of their political destiny.

It is worth exploring the ideas Scottish nationalists held at the inception of the movement as they deal with what was meant by 'nationalism' in a fairly honest way, certainly more directly given subsequent difficulties associated with the meaning of nationalism. In short, by looking at the origins of the movement we can garner an insight into what was meant by nationalism and see it in its essential form. It was seen as a natural political evolution that required no special pleading or apologies. According to Erskine of Marr:

> Every sane scheme of internationalism implies and entails nationalism; and that being so, why should Scotsmen surrender their nationality and sink their national identity in that of another nation … But until national frontiers shall be entirely obliterated, race abolished, nationality prohibited, national culture proscribed, and, lastly, but by no means least, some common language evolved which shall take the place of the existing national tongues, the fool is not the man who wishes to restore her independence to Scotland.[53]

A word of caution needs to be expressed at this moment. We have to avoid the danger of presentism where we read our own contemporary notions and definitions into the past and essentially remove early-twentieth-century ideas from their proper historical context.[54] While we may use terms such as 'ethnic nationalism' or 'civic nationalism', it is important to remember that this is not how contemporaries would have understood them even though, in essence, this is what they were. While many were aware of the variety of forms of nationalism, the language and terms used to describe this phenomenon were different to those that we would use today. Although nationalism had been associated with the misery of the First World War and was seen as the intellectual property of the political right, Scottish nationalists could and did follow the Irish notion that small-nation nationalism was different from big-nation nationalism in that because it lacked the capacity to coerce or force its will on other nations, it was not a threat to world peace. This was especially the case following the Versailles Peace Treaty:

> The day of small nations has only really come. The League of Nations has given to small nations a place more important than they ever had in days of old. They now count in world policy, as they always counted in world culture. There is a real place and function in the world for small nations, small holdings and small business, as well as for large nations and farms and businesses. Scotland as a self-governing nation would be an integral part of the biggest world combination of all, the League of Nations.[55]

As will be discussed below, Scottish nationalism made a virtue of small nations and argued that in and of themselves, they made the world a safer place and as such were a blessing for humankind. For that reason alone, it was considered legitimate and in a different category from big-nation nationalism which was often conflated with imperialism.

The commitment to Scottish statehood was the basic qualification to become a nationalist, but even at the outset, there was ambivalence with regard to nationalism in that the term does not appear in the name of the Scottish National Party or in its forerunners. Semantically, anything pertaining to 'national' is 'nationalist', but the fact that the latter word has been avoided shows that many were aware of its problematic connotations. The use of the word 'national' denoted a commitment to promote the 'national' interest of Scotland as a distinct cultural and territorial entity which, it could be claimed, was overshadowed or undervalued by being within the British state which was politically dominated by parties that operated on a British basis. This was a crucial way to distinguish the movement from the British parties which, it was argued, would always put the interests of England first because it dominated the political representation of the British state through its numerical superiority. There was an intellectual overlap here with devolutionists who advocated home rule for the same reason, because both accepted that there were distinct national interests for each of the component nations of the United Kingdom:

> The present centralized system of government is undemocratic. Each of the nations is liable to have its national opinion on its own affairs outvoted by the representatives of the other nations. England may have advanced legislation

on purely English questions imposed upon her against her will by the votes of Scotland and Wales. More often Scotland has to submit to having her desire for progressive Scottish legislation over-ridden by a Conservative majority of English members.[56]

The creation of a separate party was also a clear statement that Scottish independence could come only from an organization set up for that purpose, because it was assumed that the British parties had a vested interest in keeping Scotland a part of the British state and that this would effectively relegate Scottish interests behind that of England: 'The present party system, which is essentially irrelevant to the interest and well-being of Scotland, is not only hindering her progress, but actually contributing to her decline.'[57] The failure to deliver home rule for both Scotland and Ireland was used to buttress the argument that Scottish independence or self-government would never come from the British parties which regarded Scotland, like Ireland, as a form of possession. As the stalwart champion of Scottish home rule, Roland Muirhead claimed: 'So long as Scots political organisations are controlled by the English party concerns in London, there is practically no hope for Scottish self-government being made a primary issue at the general election.'[58] A number of arguments ranging from economic factors to the vested interests of particular political parties that relied on Scottish MPs to buttress their numbers were used to reinforce the notion that England would not let Scotland go and it would become an article of faith that the objective of Scottish independence was contrary to the interests of the British state. Only complete control of all the levers of government would enable Scotland to attain its true potential, and this insistence on having total political power is what separated nationalists from devolutionists:

> Nothing effective for Scotland will ever happen in Scotland itself until this London tyranny is broken and Scotland has its capital and control within its own borders. That is the nationalist policy and demand. At the above mentioned meeting [home rulers] Scotland was only the 'North' or 'the other side of the border'. That is the mentality of the Union.[59]

Although nationalists would always claim that the 'national' interest was best served by independence, it was possible that Scottish national interests could still be served and protected within the Union. Usually this was driven by pragmatic and short-term considerations, such as preventing the closure of a factory or improving some facet of the quality of Scottish life, such as health. In the 1930s, this was especially pronounced as a result of the economic impact of the Great Crash and a widespread perception that Scotland was being badly treated compared to the 'south'. As an editorial in the *Scotsman* put it, 'Scottish conditions, both industrial and administrative, present their own problems but continuance of the fundamentally false policy of centralising everything on London will, sooner or later, finish Scotland as a nation and reduce her to a mere province of England.'[60] This has meant that the movement could operate a two-pronged strategy by looking to do the best for the nation as a distinct entity within the Union which did not necessarily mean independence first, although this in itself did not inhibit the promotion of the case for independence as the first prong of the strategy.

The promotion of Scottish economic interests within a wider British framework, such as the creation of factories as opposed to warehouses and proposing the construction of hydroelectric schemes for the Highlands during the Second World War, chimed in with a wider Scottish political consensus which argued that Westminster paid insufficient attention to Scotland and that more needed to be done to improve the economy of the Highlands to help retain population and improve standards of living.[61] This strategy of acting as a vanguard of the national interest could put pressure on the existing political parties and helped to give nationalism a political currency that acted independently of independence, to use an inelegant phrase. Although the promotion of a 'national' interest was largely a pragmatic response to events as they happened, in most cases it could also be used to make the case for independence. The reform of local government in 1929 which abolished the Royal Burghs, for example, was a case in point where the nationalists claimed that independence would have guaranteed their survival. As Lewis Spence put it somewhat hyperbolically, 'The Nationalist party is the only battering-ram capable of breaking down these modern examples of Anglo-Norman tyranny.'[62] The automatic defence of any perceived Scottish 'national' interest also meant that it could put itself at the head of a tradition that sought to safeguard Scottish interests from English and British encroachments, even if that meant promoting what was ultimately a recognizably British interest such as the campaign to save the Argyll and Sutherland Highlanders regiment from being disbanded in the 1960s.[63]

The Scottish 'national dimension' was also reinforced by the fact that the party was territorially limited in its electoral ambitions to Scotland and operated a policy that members could not belong to other British political parties. This gave the SNP a unique selling point in that it was the only political party that had an exclusive interest in Scotland. This separation from the other British political parties was an important part of nationalist identity, as was its commitment to securing self-government by winning a majority of the Scottish parliamentary seats which, it was claimed, would constitute a mandate to begin the process of opening up negotiations with the British government for independence. Central to this strategy was the objective to reinforce the notion of Scotland as a distinctive and clearly defined national entity in a political sense. While it may be argued that over the course of the twentieth century as a whole, nationalist parties in Scotland had only limited electoral success, but in one crucial respect this did not matter, as its mere existence helped reinforce the notion of a distinctive national dimension in Scottish politics. In one sense while ostensibly acting as a political party, it also performed a function as a pressure group to promote the idea of Scotland as having its own distinctive political agenda.[64]

It is important to point out that the nationalists of the early twentieth century did not start this process of formulating the idea that there was a distinctive Scottish 'national' interest, but they were able to pick up the threads from previous campaigns and give it more direction. From the time of the Union onwards there has been a haphazard stream of activity designed to promote or preserve Scotland's 'national' interests, especially when it appeared they were under threat. In the nineteenth century this could range from the trite, such as the flying of the wrong flags on state occasions, to the more serious fact that only two days were set aside at Westminster for parliamentary debate on Scottish legislation.[65] In the twentieth century, the National

Party promoted itself as the guardian of Scottish interests. Quite simply, this could involve any matter in which there was a competition between Scotland and England, such as the location of a government agency or the winning of a contract to a firm in which Scottish society as a whole would benefit. It also meant highlighting perceived injustices such as the awarding of the design of the new Scottish Office building to an English architectural firm.[66] Often, the numerical superiority of English MPs in the House of Commons gave rise to complaints that Scottish national interests were not given due regard or were being neglected, but it was not necessarily the case that independence was required to solve this. A constant refrain was the lack of attention that Scotland received within the House of Commons because of 'imperial congestion', and this was something that Unionists were forced to agree with.[67] Devolution would tackle these issues and help promote the 'national' interest. As will be explored in Chapter 4, there was considerable intellectual and political overlap between those committed to independence and those in favour of devolution, and the term 'nationalist' has often been used to describe people who were devolutionists rather than supporters of independence. Furthermore, given that the British Empire was in existence for a large part of the twentieth century, many formulated their ideas of self-government in relation to the position of the 'white' dominion nations. For example, the booklet on Home Rule which had over ninety thousand copies distributed argued that Scotland should have a parliament that would give it the same constitutional status as Ireland, and this would mean becoming a Dominion nation within the British Empire and also a member of the League of Nations because 'there can be no complete League without one of the world's oldest, most virile and most progressive nation, the sturdy, democratic folk of the little northern land'.[68] While many of the demarcation lines between devolutionist and nationalist would be firmed up over the course of the twentieth century, it is important to note that they were often quite confused, especially in the interwar period.

Although nationalists liked to identify with what was perceived to be the 'national interest', it is important to point out that they did not have a monopoly on this. The idea of a Scottish 'national interest' is a contested one because for Unionists it is best served by the Union and for nationalists it is independence. And for both groups, the idea of Scotland is the fundamental intellectual underpinning for both political philosophies. It is not without its complexities, however. The relationship between Scottish nationalism and independence is not quite as straightforward as it seems. Theoretically it would be possible to have an independence movement and party and eschew any notions of nationalism, although this would be very difficult. For example, left-handed people might demand their own state, but this would only be practical if they were in the same place or territory. This sense of place or territory is a fundamental prerequisite of nationalism and gives geographical reality to the nation. This notion of what political theorists call a 'bounded territory' is fundamental in the construction of a nationalist vision because it allows the building of traditions over time within a confined area.[69] In a historical sense, one needs the 'national' dimension as a basis for independence because without it there is no underlying rationale that gives meaning and purpose to the utility of political independence in a separate state. The normal political 'cleavages' of class, gender, ideology and so forth cannot simply be extracted from society and placed in a confined space. This is reinforced by a clear notion of territory because states have borders to define the extent of their jurisdiction. And if there is a distinctive culture and history in this defined territorial space, so much the better. So, unsurprisingly, Scottish nationalists have sought to reinforce the notion of a Scottish national dimension, and the more prominent and clearly defined Scotland is as a nation, it is assumed, the more easy it is to make the case for independence. Hence, the pursuit of a 'national' interest, even if it does not directly bear on the question of independence, nevertheless, reinforces the notion of a distinctive national entity, and the greater the sense of a national entity, the more solid is the bedrock for the intellectual case for independence.

The 'right of national self-determination' is the starting point of the ideology of Scottish nationalism. As Scotland is a nation, it follows that as a nation it should assert its right to govern itself as many others have done over the course of the twentieth century. A nation that does not govern itself was, and is, regarded as an unnatural state of affairs, and for many Scottish nationalists there was, and is, incomprehension as to why Scots should not wish to govern themselves. The logical assumption following on from this is that if Scots are not governing themselves then they are being governed by another country. The argument underlying this assumption is based on arithmetic in that under the current constitutional arrangement, there is an inbuilt English majority that the Scots cannot overturn:

> Of the shoddy futilities and the shams of English policies we have had more than enough. Scotland's first and supreme need is not English applications of Toryism, Liberalism or socialism, but absolute freedom from the blighting influences of Westminster and its works.[70]

Therefore, if there is a clash between Scottish and English interests, the English will always win out on account of their numerical superiority. The same argument is applied to British political parties, and this dominance by the English majority in the Conservative, Labour and Liberal parties was one of the core reasons for the establishment of a separate Scottish political party to fight for the cause of independence in the interwar era.

> Scotland in theory has her due representation at Westminster. In actual practice she would fare as well with none at all as with her present representatives. Whatever their party, they are so immersed in English politics and so much at the beck and call of their English leaders that while they pay occasional lip service to their own country, they dare not raise a hand to help her. They allowed the Scottish Local Government Act to be passed in the face of opposition of almost every local authority in Scotland. They tolerated the closure of Rosyth and the consequent victimisation of Dunfermline, a flagrant injustice to Scotland in order to keep English shipwrights and Admiralty contractors in employment. When the Moray Firth fishermen have their lines and nets cut to pieces by foreign trawlers, our Scottish MPs cannot persuade the so called 'British' government to move a finger on behalf of the merest injustice. They protested against the application to

Scotland of the new transitional benefit arrangements, but when the government cracked its whip, they immediately withdrew their opposition. These are but four examples of the complete futility of Scotland continuing to hope that her interests can be protected by her present 'party' representatives in London.[71]

Again, underlying the logic of this argument is a central ideological kernel that there is a definable Scottish national interest which is distinctive and different from a British or English national interest. This basic assumption that all nations should have statehood in order to promote their national interests is a foundation stone of nationalist ideology. It is natural for nations to be states, and indeed, nations that are not states can be damaged or held back from attaining their aspirations and realizing their potential. R. B. Cunninghame-Graham summed up the frustration felt by many nationalists in a speech in June 1930:

> There is something that appeals to me as a Scotsman, there is something to stir one's heart, something to make one feel that we are representatives of a distinct nationality – a nationality severed from all other nationalities and as different from our friends in England as we are from the German, the French, the Russians or any other nationality. The British Empire today has become a confederation of varying states ... And I ask you is Scotland inferior to any one of these nationalities? I ask you as Scottish men and women whether it is not an injustice that cries to heaven and a sin against political science that the one nationality – the oldest of those that I have mentioned, and older perhaps than England itself, as a separate state – should be subservient to them, a mere appendage to the predominant partner, a mere county of England such as Yorkshire.[72]

One point that tends to be overlooked is that because of the changes that followed the First World War and the promotion of new nations and statehood on the international scene, a significant number of Scots believed that the current constitutional arrangement in the United Kingdom somehow meant that the national dignity of the nation was slighted. The acquisition of statehood meant that many nations had stolen a march on the Scots, and it was almost as if Scotland had been relegated in terms of its national status.

Justifications

As an ideology, nationalism is essential for those political activists in stateless nations who want to achieve independence and become states because it requires first and foremost a recognition of the nation as the primary political entity which surpasses in importance what might be described as the day-to-day ideology of the left and the right. The fundamentality of the nation in political discourse is what makes a nationalist a nationalist, be that a seeker of independence or not, and this central tenet of political perspective is what distinguishes nationalists from non-nationalists. By simple dint of logic, therefore, because of the centrality of the nation, those who seek

Scottish political independence are nationalists. That is not to say that they must come with all the associated ideological baggage, but with no nationalism there is no nation and if there is no nation, there can be no independence. Having said all that, many commentators on nationalism have an ideological blind spot in that as the nation remains the basic political unit, nationalism is associated only with those groups that wish to alter the existing political boundaries, but those who operate within the existing structures somehow are exempt from any association with nationalism.[73] For example, the leader of Belgium will pursue policies that can be described as being in the national interest, but it does not make them a nationalist. Delineating the legitimate boundaries of nationalism as a political philosophy has always been problematic for Scottish nationalists especially given that the ideology has had so many negative connotations. Nationalism as a political philosophy could be legitimized by employing a number of intellectual devices. Firstly, it could be understood as necessary only until Scotland became independent, after which it had no further purpose. This, it has been argued, gets around the harmful effects because its existence is tied to a specific objective and has an inbuilt sell-by date after which it becomes redundant.[74] Secondly, there was a defence of nationalism, or perhaps better expressed as an *apoligetica*, that made the claim that there were many virtues in nationalism and, furthermore, that the most commonly associated evils were actually related to imperialism, which was a deviant form of nationalism. Thirdly, there is a qualitative difference between big-nation nationalism and small-nation nationalism, and most of the evils associated with the ideology are to be found in the former. By their very nature, small independent states were unable to threaten international peace, and, it was argued, the more the number of small nations the better chance of diminishing the prospect of war. This was a widely held interpretation for most of the twentieth century and was mainly a western European perspective, but in more recent times it has been demonstrated that small nations are not immune from the worst excesses of nationalist chauvinism. Small nations also acted as exemplars of what an independent Scotland could look like. Finally, there have been efforts to articulate a defence of nationalism based on the notion that it serves a 'spiritual' purpose. Mazzini's notion that a nation is a living task whose purpose is to make a contribution to the welfare of the international community is one that has found an echo among many writers in Scotland in the era before the Second World War.[75]

The expedient nature of nationalism has been the vision most powerfully articulated by members of the SNP, and its currency has operated to such an extent that many have claimed to not be nationalists in the conventional sense of the word. That argument, however, can mask a deeper ideological imperative that holds that nationalism can bridge the conventional divisions and cleavages in society. The 'means to an end argument' could act as a catch all that could net both the right and the left without the need to compromise because these issues were only to be settled once independence had been achieved. By agreeing on the principle and only the principle of independence, it was believed by some that the ideological divisions of left and right would be parked until the objective was achieved. That belief required a lot of faith in the ability of independence on its own to act as a unifier and in reality almost veered towards a mystical conception of nationalism. After all, one of the points of conventional nationalism was that it would obviate the traditional social divisions between left and right. As the novelist Neil Gunn put it:

> Division has been Scotland's arch fiend and has always stood on 'doctrinal purity' ... At any rate by this time we should have learned from our history that if ever we are going to achieve a national aim it can only be by a major harmony that refuses to be wrecked by a minority discord. Now I maintain that this major harmony can be achieved only on a basis of broad principle and will inevitably be wrecked by an over early definition of detail or machinery underlying the principle.[76]

Needless to say, that such unifying principles were never clearly defined beyond the idea of independence, which it was argued, was a good thing in itself. Most of the proponents of this 'non-political' approach failed to appreciate that this argument had much of the same hallmarks associated with conventional ideals of nationalism that called for national unity and the like, even though the quest for independence was seen as an objective that could be divorced from nationalism. The idea that independence would be electorally attractive on its own would be plagued by the demands and practices of conventional politics which made it difficult for single issues to work for a conventional political party. Indeed, the issue was truncated into the point that it was more expedient to get the other conventional parties to endorse the principle through non-party pressure group tactics.[77] The reality, however, is that over the course of the twentieth century, a nationalist consensus settled around the belief that as a political philosophy, Scottish nationalism had to adopt the trappings associated with conventional parties in order to broaden its electoral appeal. A philosophy that centred on independence as a pragmatic means to an end could equally be used to justify an exclusive approach based around socio-economic policies that could be tied to the left/right spectrum. Usually this was associated with the argument that independence was necessary in order to pursue particular policies which were either obstructed or blocked by Westminster. In part, as will be discussed later, much of this was driven by the fact that to compete in the political marketplace for voters' loyalty, the SNP had to adopt a wide range of policies that offered comparison to the competition.[78]

All that said, however, nationalism as an ideology which centres on the basic principle that all nations should exercise self-determination because it is a good thing to do has been at the core of the beliefs of the Scottish nationalist movement. For many, because nationalism would lead to independence, it was both a moral and a natural phenomenon. Indeed, nationalism has had a positive articulation that is quite different from the traditional negative variant which is presented as offering no progressive qualities. In other words, there has been an intellectual tradition which sees nationalism as a political force for good in this world, although it has to carefully engage with the conventional ideological difficulties associated with supporting nationalism which evolved in the wake of both the Great War and the rise of Fascism. Philosophically speaking this has not been easy, and its sheer difficulty tends to deter many from acknowledging and defending its positive features and makes the expedient version more popular as it does not involve any of the complexities of argument to distinguish between different strands of an ideology that has uniformly had a pretty bad press. That said, there is an inescapable truth, squaring support for national self-determination with nationalism is a sine qua non – no nationalism, no nation, no self-determination. As Andrew Dewar Gibb put it, 'A nationalist is simply a man who is conscious of his people as a nation and who would shape his people's policy in accordance with that belief.'[79] For Gibb and others, nationalism could be bad or it could be good:

> In a world which recognises and sanctions the existence of independent states, to say of a man or a group of men that they are evil because of they are conscious of the rights and virtues of their own people and would shape their actions accordingly is sheer irrelevance. Such a policy cannot with any show of reason be condemned as evil until its aims and its methods are known. It would be equally absurd to praise or condemn on the score of internationalism before it was known what measures that policy was leading. It is therefore dishonest to use the word 'nationalist' and 'nationalism' as connoting evil. The words in themselves are neutral; that is, they point to something which is good or bad according to the use which is made of it.[80]

So that while the predominant intellectual trend in the Western world was for a negative engagement with nationalist ideology, Scottish nationalists had to work in the opposite direction to construct a positive reading.

The starting point for this case was that the nation was a natural evolution and that the negative associations with nationalism such as militarism, chauvinism and the like were the result of aberrations. For many Scottish nationalists, the worst features of nationalist excess were associated with imperialism and that it should be this, rather than nationalism, which should be condemned. According to Robert Muirhead:

> Wars as a rule are due to imperialism, not to nationalism, to the attempt of some states to dominate others or hold in subjugation a people which it feels itself to be a nation with the right to govern itself. In the history of our own land we find that for hundreds of years Scotland waged no wars except those arising from the persisting attempts of the rulers of England to bring Scotland under subjection.[81]

Nations that had a healthy relationship with nationalism – however that was construed – did not threaten the peace and were good neighbours. A civic pride, a joy in national achievements and even the desire to be better than one's neighbours in terms of economic performance and social infrastructure did not necessarily lead to chauvinism. Indeed, a friendly international competition could lead to all-round improvements, it was claimed, and could act as an inspiration to others. The individuality of the nation was, according to the literary critic William Bell, a natural social evolution:

> Those that assert that nationalism is the main source of all the discordant conditions in the world at large seem to ignore a host of other contributory causes. Whether for good or evil, social evolution has achieved an array of vastly different peoples, each of which is endeavouring to express itself through the medium of its own

national genius. Just as the alphabet is the basis for expressing the numerous great literatures of the ages, so are the separate peoples the alphabetic units through which are expressed the mighty notes of national character. It is not a vaguely international outlook that should be cultivated, but rather a cosmic vision on the part of all nationals already evolved.[82]

Nationalists cited numerous authorities to back up the idea that the nation was a natural social evolution, and in and of itself, this phenomenon was a harmless part of human development. The Gladstone Professor of Political Theory at Oxford W. G. S. Adams was approvingly quoted: 'We cannot really define Nationalism save as a growth due to association of a community in history … where there is the true seed of nationalism, there is something very indestructible, which may lie dormant for a long period of time, but which slowly and surely emerges into new life.'[83] While Albert Einstein is best known for his quote that 'nationalism is an infantile disease. It is the measles of mankind' was another whose words were used to deflect criticism:

> Internationalism does not mean the surrender of individuality. There is no reason why a nation or a race should not preserve its traditions … I can see no wrong in enlightened patriotism, in love of country or race. But patriotism is no excuse for any group of men to assail its neighbours or to impress its point of view upon others by fore and sword. I believe in self-determination for nations and individuals.[84]

Such ideas formed the basis of the common refrain that to be a true internationalist one had first to be a nationalist and that without nations, internationalism was meaningless. It was a basic point but one that nationalists had to constantly reinforce.

Scottish nationalists tapped into a nineteenth-century civic notion of nationalism associated with the ideas of Cavour, Mazzini and Garibaldi in which patriotism and civic responsibility in one's own nation led to respect for other nations and was thus the true basis of international cooperation.[85] According to Archie Lamont writing at the end of the Second World War:

> Internationalism which implies the subjugation of so many jealousies and fears will not be obtained by its imposition from without upon this or that people. It can only be obtained by the quickening of conscience of each nation and by the reformation of national life from within. It is the highest aim of integral nationalism to effect a complete reorientation of national outlook to get rid of the desire of one nation to impose its will upon another, to exploit the resources of another, or to disparage the civilization and intellectual achievements of another.[86]

An appreciation of the particular qualities and attributes of one's own nation was essential to see the same qualities in other nations. Without being a nationalist in the true sense of the word, it was argued, one could not be an inter*nationalist*. This strictly etymological approach to the issue was a basic intellectual building block in the defence of Scottish nationalism. Nationalism was presented as having an affinity with the national community, and in an idealized way it was a common bond that could hold society together. At various times it was used as an antidote to the centralizing tendencies of socialism and the impersonal forces of capitalism.

Parallels were drawn between the uniqueness of the nation within the international community and the individual within society. Both personal freedom and national distinctiveness was in danger of being crushed by the ideologies associated with the impersonal transnationalism on both the left and right; be that communism, fascism or capitalism. For Compton Mackenzie, nationalism was about 'preserving the fag end of individuality' in an age that was removing all the distinctive qualities associated with the nation and the person: 'by preserving national characteristics, it was possible to preserve the characters of individuals and prevent the sinking into the faceless masses'.[87] Hugh MacDiarmid argued that 'Celtic' notions would help maintain Scottish national individuality in an increasingly standardized world:

> It will be easy to show that in accordance with the principles of the ancient Gaelic Commonwealth; that it supersedes the economic differences of Conservatism and Liberalism on the one hand and Socialism on the other; and it effectively challenges the standardisation and robotisation of humanity towards which international capitalism is now tending, and towards which international socialism would only more quicken us. It affords a means for the retention and revival of the individual and national values, Mr. Ramsay Macdonald [leader of the Labour Party] deplores the decadence of old centres like Edinburgh, but is afraid that the attraction of London is too great. But has he ever tried to find a means of overcoming this cursed Metropolitism, and the soulless Cosmopolitanism to which it in turn is tributary?[88]

Indeed, nations, especially small ones, were thought to be an antidote to the centralizing tendencies that were evident during the twentieth century. Furthermore, the ideologies of Fascism, communism and capitalism projected a vision of 'mass man' – impersonalized and dehumanized – and for some Scottish nationalists, their nationalism, although it may look backwards to the past, was a way of maintaining the importance of individuality and personal liberty. According to Christine Orr:

> I believe in nationalism because I love differences – human, colourful and interesting because I hate a shoddy cosmopolitan sameness ... I neither hate nor despise the points in which English outlook, character and customs differ from ours. I repudiate all desire to abuse or sneer at them.[89]

The internationalist dimension in which nations were the basic building blocks of the international order has been a consistent feature of nationalist thought, and its intellectual development can be traced through the specific periodization associated with aspects of internationalization or a pan-national dimension. Simply put, if the international order was the natural way of things, then the absence of the Scottish nation to take its place alongside the other nations was a wrong that had to be righted. Many Scots believed, for example, that Scotland had more of the attributes of a nation than Ireland and the Dominion Nations of the British Empire, and as such, it was argued that Scotland should take it international place, just as the Irish had done:

> Scottish nationalism in the largest sense of the term means the revival and reconstruction of Scottish national life in every aspect and every direction, the restoration of Scotland to an independent place in the world as a cultural, economic and political unit. This is impossible without complete and unrestricted self-government, not less than that enjoyed by the Irish Free State and the great Dominions beyond the sea.[90]

In other words, it would be *natural* for Scotland to take its place among the other nations, and the ability to contrast and compare with others added weight to this argument.

The idea that statehood should be the natural condition for Scotland was reinforced in the twentieth century as it was a period in which new nation states were constantly emerging. For many, this was a global phenomenon that should include Scotland. The early-twentieth-century home rule movement and the pre–Second World War SNP located a self-governing Scotland within the intellectual parameters of the British Empire. The evolution of self-government and nationhood within the 'white dominions' was held up as a natural development and seemed to validate the idea of the nation as the fundamental unit of political organization. For many in Scotland, the forces of nationhood and self-government which were having an impact on the dominions was also at work in the home nations of the United Kingdom. After all, Canada, Australia, New Zealand and South Africa were not only self-governing but also adopted federal structures of government, and in the period before the First World War there was an expectation that this form of imperial government would emerge in the home nations with 'home rule all round' in which each of the constituent nations of the United Kingdom would have their own parliaments.[91] This expectation that nations and self-government went together was reinforced after 1918 by the establishment of the League of Nations and its principle of the right of nations to self-determination. This was especially the case following the Versailles Settlement which witnessed the emergence of small nation states throughout east and central Europe. As the empire lost it centrality in British political thought it was replaced by a focus on the potential for pan-Europeanism which would act as an intellectual counterweight to British imperialism.[92] George and Mary Dott are good exemplars of the idea that nationalists could form the basis of greater international cooperation by their attendance at the Hague Conference in 1948 in which ideas about future European collective political integration were aired.[93] This marked the beginning of the nationalist association of independence in Europe that would eventually culminate in Jim Sillars's exposition of the intellectual case for membership of the European Union.[94] The creation of the United Nations and its charter was another source of legitimization for nationalist aspirations towards independence, popularly given expression that Scotland had to take its place in the alphabetical list of nations between Saudi Arabia and Sweden.[95] The growing list of independent nations after 1945, in particular as a result of decolonization, was cited as evidence of the nation state as the natural evolution of politics. Undoubtedly, the international location, be that in the British Empire, the League of Nations, the European Union or the United Nations, has been an intellectual counterpoint to accusations of isolationism and parochialism. Also, it was a way of reinforcing the notion that nations by definition ought to be states.

Small nations

The exemplar of other small nations in Europe was a critical part of the argument in favour of Scottish independence and one that could be used to show that not all nationalisms were dangerous or harmful. The success of small nations in Europe could be used as a beacon of hope for Scottish nationalists to emulate. The debate regarding the efficacy of small nations was one that Scottish nationalists engaged with as it was by no means universally accepted that they were a good thing for the peace of the world. Certainly in the nineteenth century and for much of the twentieth century there was a popular belief in circles associated with international politics that the smaller would be swallowed up by the larger and that small nations were an inconvenience and a source of international instability.[96] Certainly they were a byword in the Foreign Office for decline, and the phrase 'doing a Holland' was frequently used with a note of derision.[97] There were, however, a few defenders of the small nation, most notably the historian H. A. L. Fisher who argued that the guarantee of the security for the small nation was a good barometer of the state of civilization.[98] Intellectually, this went against the grain of conventional thought. In the context of the British Islands, the 'Expansion of England' to incorporate Scotland and Ireland was seen as a natural progression in which the greater swallowed up the lesser.[99] Such ideas fitted in with the predominantly social Darwinist interpretation that was applied to history and international relations as exemplified by the description of the Ottoman Empire as the 'sick man' of Europe.[100] In the period post Versailles, the small nations could be recast as more normal, and the accretion of the Austro-Hungarian Empire, for example, was more the aberration than the norm, and hence the reason why it fell apart.

The intellectual acceptance of small nations in a European context, however, did not last long, especially in Britain where old ideals reasserted themselves. According to one critic, the growth of nationalism was the prelude to a new Dark Ages:

> If this theory so popular today among the small nations were to be embraced in its entirety, and the nation state accepted as the final perfect type of human political organisation, there would be an end of all talk of a world-state, and ultimately the peace of mankind is bound up with the realisation of that ideal. A policy of Poland for the Poles, France for the French, Wales for the Welsh, if carried to its logical conclusion would be the inauguration of a new dark age, with more intense national rivalries and bitter hatred than anything seen before.[101]

In the interwar period and after, Scottish nationalists had to operate in an intellectual climate in which small nations were increasingly perceived as a problem and a source of growing instability. In Britain, for different reasons, both the left and the right were not sympathetic to the idea of independent small nations. For appeasers and imperialists, they were the cause of division and ethnic tensions. In Europe, the 'Sudeten' problem and the irredentist nationalism sparked by the Versailles Settlement reversed much of the received wisdom about the creation of new states after 1918, and indeed, for those after a quiet international life, it seemed to create more problems than it solved.[102] The growth of nationalism in the empire was seen as another problem that threatened and weakened the unity of the British people. In imperial circles, nationalism was a 'problem'.[103] Any initial socialist flirtations with nationalism following the Great War were soon abandoned as the idea was categorized as bourgeois false consciousness.[104] Furthermore, the interwar expansion of the Soviet Union was held up as an advance for socialism by many intellectuals on the left and the absorption of the small Baltic states explained as the onwards march of progress.[105] The Soviet war effort absolved its pre-war expansion, and the left worked assiduously to construct an intellectual case for the removal of small nations that lacked the wherewithal to defend themselves and were better off under Soviet protection.[106] According to the Labour Party thinker and historian G. D. H. Cole, writing in 1942:

> The idea of nationality as a basis for independent statehood is obsolete. Economic development, including the development of the economic arts of war, has destroyed it finally. The independence of small states, and indeed of all states, save the largest and richest in developed resources, is impractical now that a mechanised army and air force belonging to a great state can simply sweep aside all the resistance they can offer. The upmost 'independence' any small state can hope for in the future is a false independence, behind which lies complete domination by a greater neighbour. That, or existence on mere sufferance, or as a buffer between greater neighbours, almost certain to become a battleground if those neighbours fall out.[107]

The consolidation of resources and the rationalization of state apparatus and administration made for more scientific and effective socialism while ethnic diversity was acknowledged through language rather than nationality.[108] Furthermore, the English left had a traditional disdain for what they described as Celtic nationalism. According to George Orwell:

> But Celtic nationalism is not the same as Anglophobia. Its motive force is a belief in the past and future greatness of the Celtic peoples and it has a strong tinge of racialism. The Celt is supposed to be spiritually superior to the Saxon – simpler more creative, less vulgar, less snobbish etc. – but the usual power hunger is there under the surface. One symptom of it is the delusion that Eire, Scotland or even Wales could preserve its independence unaided and owes nothing to British protection. Among writers, good examples of this school of thought are Hugh MacDiarmid, and Sean O'Casey. No modern Irish writer, even of the stature of Yeats or Joyce, is completely free from traces of nationalism.[109]

Nor, so it would seem, was Orwell. In the period during and after the Second World War, the intellectual tide was moving against small nations in Europe and the dictum that big was beautiful was reinforced by the growth of transnational organizations, especially during the Cold War when it was argued that it was increasingly difficult to survive economically and militarily without the protection of bigger states. According to Arthur Turner, a historian writing on the issue of Scottish home rule in post-war era, the prospect for an independent Scotland was bleak:

> Recent history is littered with the wrecks of the policy of national self-determination. The states of Eastern Europe which came into existence in 1919 on the simultaneous, and unique, disappearance of the German, Austrian, and Russian empires, lived but twenty years, and to-day none of them, save perhaps Yugoslavia, preserves its independence. The course of the Second World War showed clearly that small states existed only on sufferance. In the world as it is to-day it may well be argued that even France and the United Kingdom are too small to be effective units. The still smaller states are, therefore, while viable, extremely vulnerable. The lesson to be drawn is surely that, while an independent Scotland could, no doubt, exist. Its existence would necessarily be precarious.[110]

To counteract this trend, nationalists claimed that small nations were a bulwark for democracy because they were of a size that the population could connect to the state in a meaningful way. Larger states, it was argued, were amalgams and thus a source for conflict and instability. Impersonal and bureaucratic large states did not foster a meaningful bond with the population, it was claimed, and this was a factor in encouraging the state and its allies to propagate baser forms of attachment associated with chauvinism:

> There is an essential bond between the national independence of the small state and democracy – just as there is a connection between the big imperial state and that levelling down of human beings which one associates with a vast exporting belligerent factory civilisation. Democracy necessarily depends on the healthy functioning of a national conscience and will, and the Big States, as a result of too much casuistry and opportunism in their propaganda, both internal and external, about their excellence and benevolence, seem scarcely to know the difference between right and wrong.[111]

Large states swamped individuality, and this connection between nationalism and individualism, while at first sight a seemingly contradictory notion, was an important factor in justifying Scottish independence. The existence of nations was taken as a natural development from humanity's sociability and an expression of individualism. Individuals banded together to protect their kith and kin and in common with many Europeans in the interwar period, Compton Mackenzie traced this back to the Ancient Greeks whose city state democracies were held to be the origins of European nations and individualism which was contrasted with what was described as the 'Asiatic Horde'.[112] The repulsion of Darius at Salamis, Mackenzie argued, was the moment that individuality coalesced in defence of freedom to form nations.[113] For nationalists, this development followed a natural course and marked an emotional attachment to a given territory. Geographical boundaries separated different people who over time took on distinctive characteristics. The significant point that Scottish nationalists chose to emphasize was that geographical limitations made nations small and that the ability to express individualism and have a distinct emotional attachment to a given piece of land was *naturally* limited by distance. Therefore, so the argument goes, nations were naturally small and that big nations were artificial creations made up of amalgams of smaller nations and the emotional attachment was one that was artificially created: 'The Austro-Hungarian and Ottoman Empires proved less durable that their constituent nationalities, precisely because they were bureaucratic and inspired by no generous sentiments.'[114]

The power of this emotional attachment was such that even though small nations were absorbed and swallowed up by larger expansionist nations, the national sentiment and the desire for nationhood refused to die away. Again, this was something useful for Scottish nationalists because the resurgence and survival of small nation states in Europe could be held up as an exemplar for Scotland and show that amalgamation and union were not necessarily binding for all time. Poland was a frequently cited example of the indestructability of national sentiment, and the re-emergence of the Baltic states along with the creation of Romania, Czechoslovakia and Yugoslavia in the period following the First World War showed that empires tended to decline more than nations.[115] If other peoples could reclaim their sovereignty, so too could Scotland. The continuity of national sentiment in even more oppressive environments than Scotland was cited as evidence of its natural tendency towards survival. The suppression of language, culture, history and the like was something that nationalists could point to and make the claim that Scottish national sentiment would be more vibrant if it was not being held back by the actions of the British state and establishment:

> The denial of our nationality, the indifference to its claims to be cherished, revelled in, cultivated, compose a problem which is no less real than those of our slums and overcrowding ... no nation, permitting itself to be cut off from its past, and failing to advance and maintain its tradition, has yet succeeded in warding off the material hardships, consequences of its spiritual poverty ... Two centuries of government from England have given the stimulus to the process of denationalisation. Today our sense of nationality is widely so degraded as to be content with vague, often inaccurate, memories of the past.[116]

There was a twofold advantage in the claim that the current national sentiment was only in embryonic form because firstly it could be used as an excuse for current political weakness, but secondly it held out the promise that once awakened it would take on greater political potency. Compton Mackenzie claimed that the desire for nationality was almost like a genetic quality in that it could lie dormant until the correct conditions materialized for its awakening. In this way, nationalists were like a nation's safety mechanism for survival during periods of occupation, union or assimilation, and numbers did not matter because all it required was a few to hold the faith. Furthermore, it could not be rushed:

> Speaking for myself, I should prefer to see the victory of Scottish nationalism come more slowly than quickly, because I should dread a parliament in Scotland until the existing divisions in opinion had been so completely discredited that no man would dare offer himself for election without first purifying himself of the taint which clings to every existing political party ... We must look ahead ... We must not sell our faith for a discount for cash. A Scottish parliament to manage Scottish affairs means in the minds of our opponents ... the kind of parochial Home Rule they contemplate. To my mind it would be better to wait for thirty years and die at the end of it with every dream unfulfilled than accept such a parody of a nation's life.[117]

Small nations worked at two levels for Scottish nationalists. Firstly, they demonstrated that independence was possible and that size was no impediment. Secondly, they could be mined for favourable and positive examples with which to make the case for independence in the first place. By focusing on small western European nations it was possible to claim that they were inherently more efficient, socially cohesive and had more effective government than larger nations by comparing a range of socio-economic indicators.[118] As exemplars, they were useful in making claims about what Scotland could achieve, but more crucially, they were used to advance the proposition that the nationalism of small European nations was distinctive and different from that of larger nations in which chauvinism and expansionism threatened peace. Small-nation nationalism could be cast as virtuous in that it acted as a block on big-nation nationalist expansionism. After all, small nations did not have the strength and military capacity to threaten their neighbours, and indeed, the promotion of Scottish nationalism was cited as a way of making the world safer and lessening the likelihood of war by adding to the sum of peaceful nations in the world, and for many, there was an element that by breaking up Britain, a blow was struck at an imperialist and aggressive power. This argument was advanced by the Marxist John Maclean in the aftermath of the First World War; he believed that imperialism was the inevitable outcome of capitalism and the Great War was the result of the European powers turning on themselves after carving up the world for their empires.[119] Maclean claimed that the two big capitalist powers that survived the war would eventually turn on themselves and that the United States and Britain would ultimately go to war with each other.[120] He also believed that Irish and Scottish nationalism could prevent this by striking a blow at the heart of the British imperial system. This was very much a trope in nationalist philosophy that big nations had an inbuilt tendency towards imperialism because of the consolidation of economic power and the military advantages that this entailed. Furthermore, the centralized bureaucracy of a powerful state apparatus meant that democracy was in danger of being overwhelmed. According to the Soviet apologist E. H. Carr:

> The wielding of unlimited economic power by a multiplicity of small national units is incompatible with civilisation ... Once the crabbing and confining effects

of small national markets, small national political systems and even small national cultures come to be felt as restrictions on a larger freedom, the days of the small independent national state, the embodiment of the ideals of 1919, are over.[121]

The fact that as a nation Scotland was small meant that it was unlikely to invade, conquer or molest anyone, and intellectually, this could thus diffuse the main claim against nationalism which was the danger it brought to international relations and world peace through its promotion of militarism and expansionist policies. Small nations, it was argued, escaped from this most damning indictment of nationalism. For some, particularly when it involved nuclear weapons based at Faslane, Scottish independence could be promoted as part of a wider campaign for nuclear disarmament. The argument could be turned on its head and the claim made that if small nations were not safe, then there was something wrong with the international order.[122]

Small nations, particularly in Western Europe, were also useful because they could be held up as a prosperous model to follow and be used to show potentially what an independent Scotland could look like. Also, they could be used as a mirror to highlight areas where Scotland was failing or not improving at a sufficient rate. From the 1920s onwards, most socio-economic indicators and statistics ranging from infant mortality to per capita income were more favourable in the Nordic and Benelux nations and such comparisons were used to make the case that the Union was holding back Scottish socio-economic progress.[123] For example, the Scottish population failed to grow as fast as that of the other small northern European nations, and had it kept the same pace, it would currently be in the region of eight million rather than five. In the interwar era, Scottish infant mortality rates remained stubbornly high, while falling sharply in the Benelux countries. At its most extreme, it could be claimed that the Union was warping, or had warped, Scotland's natural economic development and that the industrial phase of its history as part of the British state was somehow a mistake and Scotland should have a similar socio-economic profile to the Nordic nations. Also, as there were quite a lot of small European nations, by dint of intellectual sleight of hand, it was fairly common to cherry pick the best statistic and almost create a mythical top-performing small nation which meant that on any range of statistics it was always possible to find a better achievement. Other small nations could also be used to model alternative socio-economic structures. Quite often this was utilized in relation to the agricultural sector and in particular the Highlands in which small-scale farming could be used as a form of economic regeneration and as a way to compensate for industrial decline. Right up to the present day, a key intellectual plank of the nationalist case has been the comparative underperformance of Scotland compared to European small nations.[124]

The focus on small nations definitely pushed a bias towards a rural Scotland largely because most of the successful small nations in Western Europe had fairly extensive agrarian economies.[125] It should also be noted that this was a theme that emerged in independent Ireland with decidedly unfavourable results.[126] Scottish nationalists were not alone in stressing that the heart of the nation or its spiritual embodiment was to be found in the countryside. This was common throughout Europe, largely as a result of the loss of faith in industrial capitalism associated with the depression of the interwar era. In any case, industrialization and urbanization seemed to produce the same results, largely problems, irrespective of geography, and the middle classes throughout Europe engaged in a sort of false nostalgia in which the countryside seemed to contain the residue of national characteristics. Folklore, literature, imagery and iconography and national costumes were all located in mythical representations of the past located in the countryside. Given that this was the area in which the greatest repository of national symbolism was located it is not surprising that it should be where the national movement focused much of its attention on. Furthermore, this was reinforced by some of the peculiar problems experienced by the agrarian sector, not just in Scotland but throughout Europe in the interwar era as prices collapsed because of the international slump.[127]

The land

An important feature of nationalist discourse was a strong identification with the territory and landscape of Scotland. For many, the scenery of Scotland had a mystical quality which reinforced a spiritual bond with the nation. Although Scotland was and is a mainly urban society, the fact that such a large proportion of its land mass was unoccupied and deserted may have encouraged a tendency to equate the land and the nation as one and the same. Certainly this is not an unusual feature compared to other nationalist movements where the territory and landscape takes on a disproportionate amount of cultural importance.[128] Not surprisingly the relationship between the land and the people was one that assumed great political significance.[129] Landownership also had a powerful symbolic political influence, and it remained a surprisingly dominant issue in politics north of the border in the twentieth century. Landownership and its association with the residue of feudalism were used to expose the inequities of the existing system, and by implication the problem was placed at the door of the Union. Scotland's landowning class was the traditional villains of the peace in the Scottish radical demonology, and nationalists used this skilfully to project the power held by the landowning class and all its associated inequities as being a problem that could only be solved through self-government, given the influence the landowners had in the British political system.[130] The issue of landownership was a fairly easy and graphic way in which to illustrate the disproportionate amount of land that was held in a few private hands, and the illustration of the vast swathes of territory held by the great families made a fairly unambiguous statement about inequality. The figures on landownership 'beat the Spanish and Irish figures into a cocked hat. They show that Scotland is a far more backward, feudal and landlord-ridden than Spain or Ireland'.[131] Furthermore, it illustrated the antiquated nature of ownership in Scotland and the survival of feudalism as in most other countries landownership was more evenly distributed, especially in Scandinavia.[132]

Landownership also linked into that other reservoir of symbolism: the Highlands. The injustices of the Clearances were incorporated into the narrative of both the villainy of feudalism and were illustrative of an injustice done to the Scottish people. As a repository of national sentiment and especially as the home of the Gaelic language, the assault of feudalism on the Highlands was interpreted as an attack on the essence of Scotland itself and the continued depopulation of the Gaeltacht, the abuse of landowning, which left land derelict, and the land-raiding activities in the interwar era provided a clear sense of continuity:

> Hundreds of thousands of acres gone to waste, hundreds of thousands of our virile native peasantry forced to emigrate, and hundreds of thousands of acres in our own, our native landed owned by people, either alien in race or, what is worse, renegades alien in sympathy to their kin. Alien capitalists with ample funds, for selfish personal gratification have been, and are prepared in the name of "society" to pay uneconomic prices for the land of the Scot ... Is it the intention to encompass the ultimate expropriation of the Scottish peasantry, and their decline to the status of landless serf entirely at the mercy of the alien?[133]

Small-scale crofting could be presented as a distinctive Scottish form of agriculture, and the denial of land to potential crofters was seen as a uniquely Scottish problem. Furthermore, it tapped into the residue of folk memory surrounding the land agitation that affected both Scotland and Ireland in the late nineteenth century.[134] With mass unemployment in the interwar era, many advocated small-scale farming as a solution and decried the amount of money that was spent on 'resettling' people in the empire which would lead to further population decline. In 1931, Scotland recorded an actual drop in population which was in stark contrast to most other small European nations and was seen as evidence of national decline.[135] More effective use of the land and policies that were population retentive would only come through the mechanism of independence or self-government. As was noted in Chapter 1, the decline of Gaelic was widely held as part of a cynical ploy to eradicate Scotland of its most distinctive national characteristic and pave the way for assimilation into England. The image of the downtrodden peasant evicted by the callous British landowners was a trope that many continued to return to.

In the period before the Second World War many made reference to an almost mystical dimension of nationalism and described the emergence of the new political movement as part of a 'spiritual awakening'. According to Compton Mackenzie Scottish nationalism was similar to the experience of religious conversion:

> We now alive in Scotland are offered the grace of sharing in the rebirth of a nation. That mysterious gift of Divine life which is continually being granted to individuals has hitherto eluded the analysis of any psychologist. We are familiar with the phenomenon of religious conversion ... Among the characteristics of all genuine conversions are the subject's suddenly heightened sense of ordinary life and an immensely wider perception of its richness. In a single instant of revelation he is made aware of the immortal substance of things; but his secret remains incommunicable ... I have seen the phenomenon of conversion among those who have awakened to a sudden comprehension of what true nationalism is. They are changed by some mystical experience, and in loving their country, they love their fellow country-men.[136]

The renaissance in culture and literature was included as part of this phenomenon of spiritual awakening. Needless to say, after the war this aspect of nationalism was dropped from political discourse largely as it was a common feature of Nazi and Fascist arguments about nationalism. The emotional dynamic of nationalism was nevertheless an important factor that many in the interwar period felt was worth highlighting. What was meant by this spiritual dimension was never properly elucidated and elaborated, largely because, no doubt, many believed it was self-evident. It was:

> A new appeal to the old deep-rooted faith of a nation, to the ideals of nationhood and a call to spiritual progress and nobility of purpose. It is on the burning patriotic core of every perfervid Scottish heart that nationalism should make its strongest call, rouse the high hopes and lofty ideals. And to that call, the whole nation should rally, as the world may rally to this movement ... we shall someday stand at the bar of the future, shall have to answer for Scotland. Let the answer be the fine one, the story be the noble one, of men who in an age of materialism, in a chaotic mockery of civilisation, saw an ideal above them and would not let it go.[137]

Such lofty sounding ideals could be dismissed as empty rhetoric with little or no meaning, but it is worth trying to reconstruct what nationalists were driving at. Some believe that this spiritual dimension would complement the socio-economic benefits of independence and for some it was all encompassing: 'Scottish nationalism is an urge towards national self-expression in every sphere of human life. Scotland is seeking to make her contribution to the world's life in many ways and to speak her distinctive message in different media.'[138] This universal notion of national self-expression, although always ill-defined, was one that many writers and activists described as being a fundamental motivating factor in their own commitment to the national cause.

The mythical or spiritual dimension of nationalism was clearly an important feature of the movement that many in the interwar era acknowledged, although the largely Presbyterian leadership of the SNP always tended to downplay this as it sought to portray itself as an organization devoted to hard-headed and practical politics. Furthermore, the role of emotion in politics was seen in a particularly bad light following the Second World War when it was portrayed as the fundamental component of Nazism and Fascism. Politics, it was argued, should only be about reason and rationality and associations with spirituality and emotionalism was to be avoided. Yet, nationalism has almost by definition a spiritual and emotional engagement, even though there may be a great reluctance to talk about this. A number of nationalist novelists reinforced the close association between the nation and territory by focusing on Scotland as a sense of place that had a strong emotional bond that connected the person with the environment, more often than not with a strong rural or Highland identification. The novels of Neil Gunn, for example, had this particular quality that emphasized the significance of landscape and the physical setting of the novel with a tendency towards a mythical past.[139] In MacDiarmid's *Drunk Man Looks at the Thistle* (1926), the protagonists is only able to engage in any emotional meaning with Scotland in a state of intoxication that allows a stream of consciousness to explore issues relating to national identity.[140] Arguably, the most thorough exploration of the relationship between nationalism and emotional attachment is to be found in the work of Compton Mackenzie, who has not received the attention from historians and literary critics that he perhaps ought to. This was for a number of reasons. He was English and a member of the establishment which set him at odds with the bulk of members of the nationalist movement. Furthermore, he was a Catholic, and his reputation was built mainly on his comic novels which perhaps has led him to be taken less seriously. Mackenzie explored the philosophy of nationalism in his magnum opus published in eight volumes called *The Four Winds of Love* written between 1937 and 1945.[141]

Some of the more difficult and awkward aspects of nationalism are tackled by Mackenzie in a fairly honest way, and he does not shy away from its emotional dimension. The novel is centred on the fictional playwright John Ogilvie who may or may not be a semi-autobiographical representation of the author himself. Along the way, the big themes of the twentieth century, such as the rise of totalitarianism, the development of international capitalism, revolutionary socialism and the like, are tackled and thrown into the mix. The main character's interest in nationalism is sparked at school in London when Fitz, who will become his best friend, becomes converted to the cause of Irish nationalism. It is in this awakening that Ogilvie sees the chance of a form of spiritual fulfilment and an antidote to the materialism associated with the new emerging ideologies of the twentieth century. Ogilvie undertakes a spiritual journey to his ancient homeland and reconnects with Scotland, and this establishes what can only be described as a sort of mystical bond between him and his new-found country. In treading the ancestral lands of the Ogilvie clan, he becomes informed of his ancestors' support for the Jacobite cause and 'feels' a presence. This mystical bond is one that is constantly reinforced throughout the story and what Mackenzie does is highlight the strong emotional attachment that exists between the nation and the nationalist, and it is this power of feeling and sentiment that are often absent in the rationalist equation in discussions on modern politics. Mackenzie's power as an author is not to provide answers to the questions that are thrown up by examining the interplay between emotion, spirituality and politics but rather to alert the reader to its presence and leave the observer to draw their own conclusions. Mackenzie is well aware of the complexities and issues that emerge and does not shy away from some of its more awkward facets. He expresses admiration for Fascism in Italy which he believes gave the Italians a better sense of themselves but denounces Nazism because of the nature of the 'German' character. Logical it isn't. The way in which this spiritual manifestation of the nation will materialize and how it will evolve in a democratic context are recognized as problematic and what the character Ogilvie advocates is the establishment of a dictatorship in order to avoid all the squabbles and divisions that would accomplish the process of creating Scotland anew. What marks out Mackenzie is his willingness to acknowledge the importance of emotion and spirituality in the construction of a nationalist world view and philosophy, when for most, these are issues best avoided or ignored. By arguing that the emotional and spiritual engagement with the nation is a critical and important facet of nationalist philosophy, Mackenzie makes the case that it should not be ignored or brushed under the carpet because, perhaps, therein lies a greater danger.

Conclusion

In recent times, the nature of Scottish nationalism has been noted for being progressive, liberal and outward looking in contrast to the traditional, inward-looking, intolerant and reactionary vision with which most versions of nationalism have been associated.[142] The fact that Scottish nationalists have been forced to debate the meaning of nationalism throughout the twentieth century from both a minority position and one with which the issue has had a universally bad press has meant that there has been a consistent and constant endeavour to disassociate the movement from its worst features and excesses. Undoubtedly that has been a major factor in ensuring its largely civic dimension. By stressing the expedient nature of Scottish independence, the issue of nationalism could largely be side-stepped. By differentiating between the various forms of nationalism, the liberal and civic version could be promoted and contrasted with the imperialist and chauvinistic versions. Furthermore, by arguing that the nationalism was simply the by-product of the fact that the nation was the natural unit of political organization meant that it was essentially morally neutral, but the uses that it could be put to were either bad or good and not an intrinsic feature of the phenomenon itself. The fact that the nation was widely accepted as the natural unit of political organization could be further used to make the case that because Scotland was not a nation state with its own government it was in an unnatural condition for an ancient and historic nation. The worst excesses of nationalism were in the main associated with imperialism and large nation states and by drawing comparisons to states that had a similar size of populations to Scotland, it was argued that small-state nationalism was altogether different species of the phenomenon that was benign and harmless to others. Other small nations were used to show what could be achieved through independence and held up as exemplars of the wisdom of independence as many of them had previously been in unions with larger states. Finally, while recognizing that an emotional attachment to the nation was a natural condition of nationalism, a number of writers and thinkers were able to draw attention to the need to acknowledge this often ignored and neglected dimension with all the awkward baggage that came with it. It was only by constantly engaging with and debating the problematic nature of nationalism that its worst effects could be avoided.

3

Constitutionalism

Continuity has been the dominant characteristic in the development of English government. Its institutions, though unprotected by the fundamental or organic laws which have safeguarded the 'rigid' constitutions of most other states, have preserved the same general appearance throughout their history, and have been regulated in their working by principles which can be regarded as constant. Crown and Parliaments, Council and great offices of state, courts with their judges and magistrates, have all retained, amid varying environments, many of the inherent attributes as well as much of the outward circumstance and dignity which were theirs in the medieval world of their origin. In no other European country is the constitution so largely a legacy from that remote but not unfamiliar age.
  – Keir, *The Constitutional History of Modern Britain*, 1

In spite of a Presbyterian Scottish father and a stint at Glasgow University, the master of Balliol College, Oxford, did not think the Anglo-Scottish Union was important, and it was only mentioned in passing in his *Constitutional History* in a very short section on 'Scotland, Ireland and Overseas Possessions'.[1] At the time, in the mid-twentieth century, this was the norm, and it was assumed that the English and British constitutions were one and the same thing. In this chapter, we will explore the development of constitutional ideas and legal routes to independence rather than the emergence of revolutionary means to obtain political objectives. Central to these arguments is the Treaty of Union because it was the mechanism which established the current constitutional arrangement. Above all else, if the British state was created by constitutional and legal means, then it could be undone by the same methods. The protection and promotion of a distinctive Scottish civil society based on its institutions was also seen as a means of reinforcing the legalist dimension of the national movement. The major dilemma facing those who advocate for independence is that while the Union did not confer upon England the right to rule Scotland, it did not readily point the way towards an escape route should it be desired because of the notion of parliamentary sovereignty which meant that any constitutional questions would be decided by an in-built English majority. As we shall see, this led to the piecemeal construction of a separate Scottish constitutional tradition in which sovereignty resides with the people. The creation of a higher constitutional entity than Westminster has introduced an element of conditionality in relation to the British

Figure 3 SNP Election Committee, 1964 (Source: *Scots Independent*).

Back row: W. McArthur, John Gibson, Gordon Wilson, Ian Macdonald, Alan Erasmusson.

Middle row: James McGinley, John Gair, Bruce Cockie, Anthony J. C. Kerr, David Stevenson, Douglas Drysdale, James Braid, Alex Bisset, William Wolfe.

Front row: Robert McIntyre, W. A. Milne, Rosemary Hall, Mrs Grieg, Mrs Goodsir, Mrs Connor, Arthur Donaldson, James Lees.

state. The chapter will conclude by pointing out that, paradoxically, nationalist electoral weakness at the end of the twentieth century meant that proponents of devolution and home rule increasingly felt it safe to use the nationalist argument of the sovereignty of the people as the mainstay to support their claim for the establishment of a Scottish parliament. The Conservative governments, like the Labour opposition, believed a nationalist electoral surge unlikely and countered arguments for a devolved Scottish parliament by saying that it was democratically the decision of the British government to make because it was a realignment of the Union. But, hoping to make life difficult for the Labour Party, many Conservatives argued that if the people of Scotland felt strongly about the issue, there was nothing to stop them voting for the Scottish National Party (SNP) and independence. The idea of the sovereignty of the Scottish people was pushed as much by Unionist politicians in the 1980s and 1990s, for their own reasons, as it was by the nationalist movement.

Legalism

One of the most notable features of the Scottish national movement, but one that rarely features in public discussion, is its non-violent nature and how this is in stark contrast to some other nationalist movements in the twentieth century.² It is something that is taken for granted, and the question is rarely put as to why this should be so. A quick glance at some nationalist organizations in Europe shows that violence and revolution were very much the norm, historically speaking.³ The Scottish national movement has had revolutionaries, but they have been few in number and of very little political significance.⁴ There have been acts of civil disobedience and, with the exception of blowing up a postbox that had an offending numeral after Queen Elizabeth in the early 1950s, they have been mainly non-violent.⁵ Above all else, two factors help explain this phenomenon. Firstly, as we have seen in our chapter on history, there is a grudging acceptance of the *historical fact* of the Union of 1707 as a legal entity. It may have been a bad thing or unjust or undemocratic, but, nevertheless, few would dispute that it was legal by the conventions of the time and had been concluded under the correct political protocols of the period. Also, the Union has the legal stamp of longevity in that it had existed for a substantial period of time and few have paid it serious attention because it was seldom challenged. Indeed, it was only in the late twentieth century that questions about reform or repeal of the Union became a serious political issue in Scotland. This was in stark contrast to the Irish Union which faced challenges more or less from its inception.⁶ It was the Irish home rule issue in the late nineteenth century which brought the matter of the Scottish Union to public notice and only then as a by-product of the interest in the Irish Union. We have to be wary of attributing present-day ideas onto people of the past, and it is important to remember that when the Liberal Unionists and the Conservatives in Scotland merged to form the Scottish Unionist Party in 1912, the Union that they promoted was the Irish one. The various Union Streets in Scotland are actually named after the Irish Union, and the first academic study of the Anglo-Scottish Union by James Mackinnon, published in 1896, hoped that 'this study may help to increase the knowledge of the reciprocal relations of England and Scotland these two centuries back which is the surest guarantee of mutual esteem and good fellowship in the future'.⁷ Mackinnon believed that not enough Scots were aware of their own Union and it was the Irish issue which had rescued it from 'the obscurity to which it had long been consigned'.⁸ The bicentenary of the Union in 1907 was a low-key event and apart from a number of articles in the *Glasgow Herald*, there was little to demonstrate major public awareness of the issue.⁹ Ironically, more than any other group in Scottish society, nationalists and home rulers have been the main proponents of increasing public awareness of the Anglo-Scottish Union.

The Treaty of Union denies any claims by England to govern Scotland by right of conquest. In the pre-Union era, English historians had made frequent dubious claims regarding the rights of the English Crown to Scotland, and some of these made reference to the idea of conquest in the dim and distant past.¹⁰ Although the idea of the right to govern by victory of force of arms is an old notion that many today will regard as morally repugnant, it should be remembered that much of the world throughout the twentieth century was governed by the right of conquest, and it was an internationally recognized legal entity until the end of the Second World War, although its legitimacy was clearly in decline in the court of international opinion after 1918.¹¹ The existence of European empires and the occupied countries of Europe during and following the Second World War demonstrated the political realities of military power and for many nationalist movements, state coercion was simply a fact of life. Although the United Nations established the principle of recognizing the rights of nations to 'territorial integrity', the Cold War realities which witnessed the occupation of Germany and Eastern Europe, and while the West, for example, refused to recognize the right of the Soviet Union to annex the Baltic States, the use of state power and coercion, whatever the legal technicalities, still carried a lot of weight.[12] Nearer to home, it is worth remembering that the claim of the English Crown to rule Ireland rested on the conquest of Henry II in the twelfth century and reconquest of Henry VIII in the sixteenth century.[13]

Conquest also entailed for many the right of resistance to take up arms against oppression through the use of force. Most nationalist movements constructed a history of resistance and revolt to legitimize armed insurrection, and the wartime activities of the resistance movement in Europe, albeit inadvertently, further justified the right to take up arms against invaders.[14] The absence of conquest, which may or may not confer legitimacy and the right to resist it, and the fact that there was a formal political union between Scotland and England meant that the normal preconditions for a revolutionary movement did not exist. From a European perspective, one of the striking features of the Anglo-Scottish Union is its longevity, and the fact is that political unions tended not to last on the mainland. The dismantling of dynastic and political unions has precedents in Scandinavia, the Iberian Peninsula and Eastern Europe, although they took place before the growth of nationalism in the nineteenth century. Therefore, given the longevity and constitutional nature of the Anglo-Scottish Union, it follows on that the dismantling of the British state or Scotland's extraction from it could and should be done by legal means. The philosopher H. J. Paton posed the pertinent question 'whether a nation entering into a free union was also free to leave it' with the heavy implication that on a matter of principle, it was, because otherwise it would not be a free union.[15] While there may have been universal agreement that the Scots could not be kept in the Union against their will, there was, however, no clear legal and constitutional mechanism for leaving. Working out how this could be done would absorb a lot of nationalist intellectual energy.

As the Irish demonstrated early in the twentieth century, leaving the Union was not as straightforward as it sounded because a majority of Irish Home Rule members of parliament (MPs) in Ireland and a majority of Sinn Fein MPs after 1918 could not compel the House of Commons to grant either Irish home rule or Irish independence, even though that was the clearly expressed wish of the majority of the Irish electorate.[16] Arguably the Irish Union was not really a free union in the sense that it was not between two sovereign states largely because Ireland was occupied during the 1798 Rising and Britain wielded a great deal of influence because of a constitutional entanglement between the two countries.[17] Although the Irish parliament increased its power in 1782 by a series of reforms designed to remove British constitutional limitations, it was never entirely clear whether the Irish parliament was truly independent of Westminster.[18] The situation in Scotland was different but similar because although the Union was a treaty between two sovereign states, the provision that law would be determined in future by the British parliament meant that England had and has an inbuilt numerical superiority in terms of the number of MPs that it elects and that – as we have seen on many occasions recently – the mechanism by which Scottish wishes are represented through the elections of MPs to Westminster can be ignored by the English majority, as had repeatedly happened to the Irish. Political party allegiance in the sense that British political parties operated in Scotland (but not Ireland) has helped to camouflage this basic arithmetical statement of fact, but at the end of the day, the Scots do not have a constitutional mechanism to overturn the sovereign will of parliament. English members would have to take part in Scottish affairs in Westminster as was pointed out in the late 1920s:

> English interference is, as a matter of fact, necessitated by the Standing Orders of the House. No vote is effective unless at least 100 members vote in favour. Thus, our 74 members, all in agreement, could march twenty times through the same division lobby without deciding anything, unless a certain number of English members saw fit to interfere.[19]

All of which takes us to our second factor in determining the constitutionalism of the nationalist movement in Scotland; a distinctive legal tradition and legal system. More than anything, this would provide the intellectual apparatus for a non-violent route out of the Union because it would enable the construction of a Scottish constitutional tradition that theoretically could supersede the legal authority of the Union.

The fundamental difficulty facing Scottish nationalists looking for a legal escape route from Westminster is the notion popularized by A. V. Dicey in the late nineteenth century that sovereignty resides in the British parliament and consequently with its English majority, irrespective of the wishes of the Scots or, for that matter, the Irish.[20] The issue has received little attention because the prospect of a majority of both Scots and Scottish parliamentarians wanting independence was, up until the past decade, seen as a very unlikely scenario. Irrespective of the issue of independence or self-government, however, the Anglo-Scottish political relationship had an in-built constitutional dimension because although the British state was a unitary one, it was nevertheless comprised of two distinct legal entities and jurisdictions. The issue of Scottish law was one that the British political system had to take into account, and up until the advent of devolution the role of the lord advocate as adviser to the British government on Scottish legal matters was clearly as much a constitutional role as it was political. This meant that the political relationship between Scotland and Westminster was of a quite fundamental difference than that between Westminster and the English regions. Although there was a tendency to follow Walter Bagehot in seeing the constitution as being based around English traditions and institutions, this was not always accepted in Scotland. In 1953, Lord Cooper, the lord president of the Court of Session, threw a constitutional spanner in the works:

> The principle of the unlimited sovereignty of Parliament is a distinctively English principle which has no counterpart in Scottish constitutional law. It derives its origin from Coke and Blackstone, and was widely popularised during the nineteenth century by Bagehot and Dicey, the latter having stated the doctrine

in its classic form in his *Law of the Constitution*. Considering that the Union legislation extinguished the Parliaments of Scotland and England and replaced them by a new Parliament, I have difficulty in seeing why it should have been supposed that the new Parliament of Great Britain must inherit all the peculiar characteristics of the English Parliament but none of the Scottish Parliament, as if all that happened in 1707 was that Scottish representatives were admitted to the Parliament of England. That is not what was done. Further, the Treaty and the associated legislation, by which the Parliament of Great Britain was brought into being as the successor of the separate Parliaments of Scotland and England, contain some clauses which expressly reserve to the Parliament of Great Britain powers of subsequent modification, and other clauses which either contain no such power or emphatically exclude subsequent alteration by declarations that the provision shall be fundamental and unalterable in all time coming, or declarations of a like effect. I have never been able to understand how it is possible to reconcile with elementary canons of construction the adoption by the English constitutional theorists of the same attitude to these markedly different types of provisions.[21]

So, theoretically, the principal mechanism that could be used to deny a Scottish exit from the Union was an English constitutional device. Although it was an understated observation, Lord Cooper did highlight what was the seeming intellectual incompatibility of the doctrine of parliamentary sovereignty with the wider constitutional ramifications of the Union of 1707.[22]

The Union

Our starting point for this discussion is that the Treaty of Union occupied an important role in the way that Scots perceived their constitutional position within the United Kingdom and their relationship with the larger and more influential English partner. Unlike Ireland where the Union ran into popular opposition from more or less its inception, the Scots had not demonstrated any real hostility to the Union following the Jacobite defeat in 1746 up until well into the twentieth century. Furthermore, many of the proponents in favour of home rule argued that it was a way of strengthening the Anglo-Scottish Union rather than undermining it.[23] The Union was an accepted, if not necessarily a conspicuous, part of Scottish political life. The treaty had a number of articles which guaranteed to protect Scottish interests in law, education and religion after the Union, but given that the Scots had signed up into a constitutional arrangement where the parliamentary sovereignty of Westminster was absolute, these protections and rights could be overturned by the parliament in London. As we shall see, the relationship between Scottish rights post-Union and the unlimited sovereignty enjoyed by Westminster was a bone of contention. At the time of the Union, the guarantee of these rights was absolutely critical in securing its passage, and there was a widespread expectation that they would be honoured. Without doubt, religion was the most contentious issue given that both countries had different ecclesiastical settlements which were jealously protected, and both the Scottish and the English Churches had a guaranteed position within each of their respective constitutional systems.[24] For the less powerful Scottish church there was a real fear that they would be swallowed up, and without the guarantees of the Act of Security which would preserve the Presbyterian settlement post-Union, there was little chance that the treaty would pass.[25]

The existence of two national churches within one state in which the king was head of one of them, but not the other, and where the upper chamber had English bishops sitting in it and could theoretically pass legislation that effected the Presbyterian settlement in Scotland demonstrated that the Union created a constitutional hotchpotch that lacked any semblance of a logical structure. This was especially the case in the House of Lords which had twenty-six bishops but only sixteen Scottish representative peers.[26] The use of patronage where landowners and the state could appoint minsters to certain parishes had been abolished in Scotland in 1690 as part of the Presbyterian settlement of the church. The treaty explicitly stipulated that it would not be reintroduced, but in 1712 the power of the aristocracy and of the state was increased in church affairs when patronage was reintroduced, as was tolerance for the Episcopalian Church which had effectively been banished in 1690. The Tory administration of the time was heavily Anglican in its ecclesiastical orientation, and the fact that Church of England bishops in the House of Lords were able to vote on Scottish church matters did not go unnoticed.[27] Given the gravity of ecclesiastical issues in securing the consent of the Church of Scotland for the Union, the fact that they could be so quickly overturned by the Westminster Parliament showed that the guarantees of the treaty were not worth the paper they were written on.

Many Scottish peers believed that if they were recreated as British peers they would be granted access to the House of Lords on their own right, and it would appear that many believed that would happen.[28] When the Duke of Hamilton was given his British title as the Duke of Brandon, he was still denied a seat in the Lords. This was widely interpreted as an insult to the honour of Scotland.[29] In 1713 a vote to dissolve the Union in the House of Lords narrowly failed to pass by four proxy votes, although the majority of the sixteen elected Scottish peers voted for the Union's dissolution.[30] Furthermore, the incident revealed how seriously English politicians took the issue because in 1707 the Whigs were most keen on the Union and the Tories were more sceptical with Lord Nottingham claiming that it violated the fundamental constitution of England.[31] In 1712, however, when the Tories were engaged in concluding the Treaty of Utrecht which would bring an end to the Spanish War of Succession, the Whigs, who were in favour of continuing the war, voted in favour of ending the Union as a way of embarrassing the government. It was a fairly graphic illustration that the Scots would always be at the mercy of the power of the English majority and whatever particular disposition motivated them.[32] The next violation of the articles of the Union would be the abolition of heritable jurisdictions in 1746 following the Jacobite Risings. A belief that Highland and particularly Jacobite landowners had too much power by having the ability to dispense justice that did not involve capital crimes was the main motivation. It was an act that few Scots in the circumstances of the time disapproved of as it was seen as a relic of bygone times and a bar to modernity.[33] There were no real violations of the treaty in the nineteenth century, although the issue of patronage in the Kirk would result in the 'Disruption' of 1843 when the church split in two with half walking out in protest at the failure to resolve the issue, especially when the House of Lords ruled that patronage was a form of property rights. The issue caused considerable resentment at Westminster's indifference to Scottish ecclesiastical sensitivities.[34] There were some minor infringements which were brought to public attention by groups such as the National Association for the Vindication of Scottish Rights in the 1850s.[35] By the eve of the First World War, the principal complaint was not so much about the Union as about the inability to accommodate growing Scottish demands within the existing parliamentary system.[36]

By the 1930s the Union had become a shorthand description of the existing constitutional relationship between England and Scotland. According to one critic:

> Our history in Scotland since the Union seems to be a record of local but ineffective protests against insults from the English parliament. Time and again we have seen the Treaty of Union that 'safeguard' of our national rights being wantonly ignored by the predominant partner: time and again we have declared that no proud nation can tolerate such national humiliation, but time and time again for all our vain protests, we have accepted breach of trust as a *fait accompli*.[37]

The young lawyer who wrote this, John M. MacCormick, who would become one of the leading lights of the nationalist movement, hit the nail on the head by identifying the issue that the Treaty of Union was not binding on the Westminster Parliament.[38] Hence the tendency to describe the treaty as nothing more than a 'scrap of paper' because potentially it had no constitutional weight or meaning. He further argued that as the Scots who signed the treaty thought that the safeguards would be binding on the future British parliament and because this was not so, as a legal contract it had been entered into on 'essential error' and as such was null and void: 'It appears therefore that legally there is no Treaty and no "Parliament of Great Britain". We in Scotland are submitting to the rule of a Parliament which properly has no jurisdiction over us.'[39] MacCormick identified the constitutional problem at the heart of the Union, although his natural moderate political disposition meant he never pushed it to its extreme.[40] Having signed away its sovereign parliament in 1707 to a new parliament in which English sovereignty would still reside because of its numerical superiority, how could it be reclaimed by constitutional means? Dr James Alston made the point that the fundamental problem with the Union was that when it was created, it was

> a striking and important omission that influenced profoundly the attitude the English adopted towards Scotland after the Union, with grave consequences to the interest and prestige of Scotland. I refer to the failure to make provisions for an independent tribunal, such as the Americans have in their Supreme Court, to which any interpretation of the Treaty or any breach of it by either country could be referred. The London parliament with its overwhelming English majority was left the sole judge of its own actions.[41]

An endeavour by the independent member for Dundee Edwin Scrymgeour to table a question in the Commons to the Lord Advocate asking whether 'there is any Court or Tribunal before which the question of the validity of that Act can be raised, argued and determined' if it contravened the Treaty of Union was rejected by the Speaker.[42] In short, Scotland had no constitutional safeguards and would always be at the mercy of an English majority in Westminster.

The constitutional and legal aspects of the Treaty of Union remained remarkably undeveloped in nationalist circles. The point made by Mackinnon that it was an international treaty between two sovereign parliaments and therefore should have been binding on the future British parliament was not clearly articulated.[43] Furthermore, the fact that the English parliament recognized the right of the Scottish parliament to pass the Act of Security in 1705 which effectively would see an independent Scottish foreign policy and different line of succession from England should negotiation between Scotland and England fail clearly demonstrates that there was no question as to the legal and constitutional independence of the Scottish state before the Union. This was a point made by the English Lord Treasurer at the time in the House of Lords who argued that the queen should not veto the act and that the only response the English could make would be through legal means which led to the passing of the Alien Act.[44] A trite point, but seldom mentioned, only sovereign nations conclude treaties with one another. It is worth noting that the British parliament did not recognize the sovereignty of Ireland in 1800 in the way that it recognized Scottish sovereignty at the time of the Anglo-Scottish union because Acts of Union passed in both the British and Irish parliaments were all that was needed to effect what was known at the time as the 'incorporation'. There was no treaty between Britain and Ireland.[45]

As was alluded to earlier by Lord Cooper, the Union was constitutionally incoherent. It was a makeshift deal constructed to solve a particular set of problems, which was described as the biggest political 'job' of the eighteenth century.[46] Whereas the Scots looked for rationality and structure in the future relationship, the English had a narrower perspective that focused on solving each problem and issue as it arose without much thought as to what the completed version would look like. For example, both the Scottish Claim of Right and the English Bill of Rights to this day remain on the statute book, even though the Union might be thought to be constitutionally incompatible with both. Certainly one English critic believed that Queen Anne had violated her Scottish Coronation Oath to uphold the Claim of Right by giving her assent to the Union.[47] It is worth pointing out that Lord John Somers, who was a Whig lawyer and someone who understood the ramifications of the Union in terms of its constitutional impact, believed that the treaty was only the first of a number of measures that would see the extension of English law into Scotland and 'cited Poland and Lithuania as unhappy examples of the perils of an imperfect union, where the advantages of general legislature were offset by their retention of their great offices of state and distinct diets'.[48] The first post-Union piece of legislation to deal with Scotland was an act 'for rendering the Union of the two Kingdoms more entire and complete' and showed that the treaty was only the first step in a process of wider integration and assimilation.[49] That said, Somers also acknowledged the highly expedient and contingent nature of the Union.[50] Also, at the time of the vote in the House of Lords to abolish the Union, many of the architects of the Union were happy to do so provided the succession could be guaranteed after the divorce.[51] So although the Union was described as an 'incorporating' or 'complete' Union at the time, the fact remains that this was more an aspiration than an established fact, and the failure to follow up with further legislation over the course of the eighteenth century meant it was largely unfinished as there was no further endeavours to align or extend law into Scotland, with the notable exception of 'treason'. The constitutional incoherence of the Union also explains the tendency of the main critics and theorists of the Westminster system of government such as Coke, Blackstone, Bagehot and Dicey to describe it as the English constitution.[52] A big part of the problem in seeing the limited constitutional implications of the Union has been the tendency in Scotland to only examine the issue from the Scottish perspective and frame the issue around the central question as to why the Scots agreed to it. The lack of an English historical perspective has meant that there has been an unbalanced view of its significance, especially in Scotland.[53] Furthermore, from a constitutional perspective, the fact that it was largely ignored in England because it was not deemed important enough was not on the radar of both Unionists and nationalists in Scotland who formed a consensus that it did.

The main culprits in promoting a limited constitutional and legal understanding of the Anglo-Scottish Union were Albert Venn Dicey and Robert Rait whose published work was the standard for most of the twentieth century, and its widespread acceptance no doubt coloured nationalist perspectives and helped to limit discussion.[54] Furthermore, the fact that the nationalist movement had made limited electoral progress before the 1960s meant that the issues of constitution and sovereignty, although important in themselves, were not seen as a political priority. The book by Dicey and Rait is a defence of the Union based on notions of far-seeing and wise statesmanship which is stronger on the historical background than the legal and constitutional issues which receive little or no attention. Rait was a historian who had a fairly negative view of his own country's parliamentary history, describing the pre-Union Scottish parliament as weak and ineffectual.[55] Dicey was a committed believer in the Irish Union and applied the notions of parliamentary sovereignty without considering that the Scottish case might be different and likened the treaty as a contract between two individuals rather than an international treaty. That said, both Dicey and Rait acknowledged that the Scottish parliament and hence the Scottish nation was a sovereign entity at the time of the Union. The English parliament was 'careful not to trench upon the independence of Scotland or the sovereignty of the Scottish Parliament. It does not contain a word which exceeds the admitted right of England to legislate so as to avert damage which might result to the country from Scottish laws'.[56] It was only in the 1970s that a more critical examination of the Union emerged, and then it was mainly in historical circles rather than legal ones.[57]

Although there was a reticence to expose the Union as a constitutional fig leaf, breaches of the treaty still triggered a knee-jerk reaction that was brought about by what was thought to be English indifference or arrogance, and the fact that the English were largely ignorant or apathetic about the issue meant that it was used as a way to reassert Scottish constitutional rights, though in reality, it was little more than point scoring. Much of it was arcane and old fashioned and dependent on the ire of middle-class Scotland. The plan to remove the Scottish Regalia to London for an exhibition at the time of Edward's Coronation in 1903 caused widespread indignation and the intervention of the Scottish secretary Lord Balfour of Burleigh.[58] Article 24 of the treaty prohibited the removal of the Scottish Crown from Scotland:

> The Crown, Sceptre, and Sword of State, the Records of Parliament, and all other Records, Rolls and Registers whatsoever, both public and private, general and particular, and Warrants thereof, continue to be kept as they are, within that Part of the united Kingdom now called Scotland; and that they shall so remain in all Time coming, notwithstanding of the Union.

One reason given why the Scots did not want to give up the Crown was a fear that it would be melted down, and they wanted it as insurance in case the Union failed.[59] It is a point that has largely gone unnoticed among historians, but it is surely significant given the Crown's historic importance as a symbol of sovereignty, especially given the controversy surrounding the publication by the English lawyer William Attwood of a pamphlet in 1704 which reasserted the old claims of Edward I that the English Crown had dominion over the Scottish Crown. This was robustly and convincingly rebutted by James Anderson in his pamphlet in 1705, *An Historical Essay Showing That the Crown of Scotland Is Independent and Imperial*. The Scottish Parliament accordingly rewarded Anderson, while ordering Attwood's book to be burned by the common hangman.[60] Given the associated significance of the Scottish Crown as a symbol of Scottish sovereignty and that this was well understood at the time, the fact that the Scots insisted on keeping hold of it is certainly something worth commenting on. Furthermore, the treaty in Article 2 sidesteps the issue that the English and Scottish Crowns are two separate legal entities, and although the notion of the 'Crown of Great Britain' had been used by Charles II, there is simply an assumption that there is now a Crown of Great Britain and that the Scots will accept the provisions of the 1701 English Act of Settlement which, through hereditary succession according to law, would pass to the Hanoverian line. At no point does the treaty stipulate that the Crowns of Scotland and England have been merged, although it may be implied, all of which raises awkward constitutional issues. The notion of parliamentary sovereignty is based on the idea of the 'Crown in Parliament', but that must surely be the English Crown and it begs the question, where does the Scottish Crown fit in all this? While the Scottish parliament may have been abolished in 1707, it is not at all clear that the Scottish Crown was, and this has important unresolved issues in regard to the question of Scottish sovereignty and what precisely was understood to have happened in 1707.

This failure to understand that the Union was a messy and incoherent constitutional arrangement led many to look for and interpret problems and anomalies as breaches and violations of the treaty. Both Edward's and Elizabeth's use of numerals (VII and II, respectively) ignored the Scottish royal line.[61] The abolition of the Royal Burghs in the Local Government Act of 1929, for example, brought forth a lot of business and middle-class support who pointed out that their abolition was a violation of the terms of the Treaty of Union.[62] The Union's preservation of the Presbyterian settlement hit the headlines in the 1950s with rumours that bishops were to be introduced into the Church of Scotland to pave the way for an Anglicization of the Scottish Church.[63] The appeal to the provisions of the Treaty of Union was a common response to a popular feeling that Scottish sensibilities were being ignored. For nationalists, this was evidence that the Union was a constitutional figment of the imagination that could be ignored at will and that the Union did not provide the guarantees and securities that were claimed by Unionists.

Civil society

For nationalists, and for that matter Unionists as well, the Union did leave behind the residue of civil society that was evidence of the existence of what was once a separate Scottish state and consequently defence of the ecclesiastical, legal and education systems was deemed an important way to promote the idea of a distinct Scottish nation. Historically, protection of the church was closely linked with national identity, and Presbyterianism was cited as evidence of the strong sense of individual liberty among Scots.

> The typical Scot – the Scots who has made the deepest impression on the world's mind – has been the man of independence and grit and self-reliance – the man who fears no man, who cringes before no superior, clerical or lay, the man who stands foursquare on the rock of his Christian manhood – the man o' independent mind who looks and laughs at tinsel show and riband star and a' that, the man whose integrity and honesty are above the favour of the great ones of the earth.[64]

It was also used to account for the love of learning and defence of freedom that were key characteristics of how Scots liked to see themselves.[65] The centrality of Presbyterianism to the nationalist notion of Scottish national identity declined in the twentieth century as the importance of the church faded due to secularizing influences.[66] The determinedly pro-unionism of the Kirk and its anti-Labour stance in the interwar era further alienated an affinity with the nationalist movement.[67] While the church did highlight social problems in the 1930s,[68] its strong association with the Conservative Party was seen as a hindrance:

> If nationalism needs the Church the Church also needs nationalism and the Church's need is the greater of the two. But the Church is still blind – or afraid to face the facts. Its illumination will come in due course. It cannot go on for long groping after a policy for Scottish prosperity and welfare without discovering the insuperable obstacle of Westminster government and English domination.[69]

The strong current of anti-Catholic sectarianism further complicated relations with the Kirk with fears that it would divide the nation and exacerbate Catholic and Protestant quarrels.[70] Finally, the emergence of socialists within its ranks did little to soften its hard-line unionism. The reunification in 1929 of the two dominant Presbyterian churches finally healed the rift of the Disruption of 1843 but in so doing formally renounced its connection to the state ending its position as a 'national' church.[71] Although the nationalist movement would continue to use the notion of the covenant as a means of mobilizing popular support, this was largely shorn of its religious connotations in 1948 and 1988. For whatever reason, and perhaps it is worth further investigation, an alliance between political nationalism and the Kirk never really showed much prospect of success, and it is worth pointing out that this went against the traditional nationalist model in Europe in which popular religion was often a crucial mobilizing force.[72]

Education and the promotion of a distinctive Scottish educational tradition was part and parcel of nationalist philosophy and was a further way of highlighting the difference between Scotland and England. The Scottish educational myth of the 'lad o' pairts' in which a boy of humble background (not a girl) could rise in society through education was used to demonstrate that Scottish society was meritocratic and less bound by class than England.[73] It could be utilized by the right as evidence that the individual would rise in society based on ability and talent, but it could also be utilized by the left to show that Scottish society was innately more egalitarian than its southern neighbour.[74] By the 1930s, the independence of the Scottish education system was believed to be under threat because of the tendency to simply adapt English educational reforms to Scottish legal requirements, which was leading to 'a sad decline from Scotland's former proud pre-eminence in education'.[75] For a number of artists and thinkers there was a clearly defined Scottish philosophic and intellectual tradition.[76] The idea of the 'democratic Intellect' was most clearly articulated in the 1960s by George Elder Davie, and the central role allocated to philosophy within the traditional educational curriculum was taken as a truism which was undermined by Anglicization in the nineteenth century.[77] The 'generalist' mode of Scottish thought which worked on the basis of establishing universal principles from which interpretations about the nature of things could be established was replaced by the English one of specialization. The academic debate as to whether this was a process of Anglicization or just the adaptation to the demand of the modern world need not worry us too much here, the point being that in nationalist thought there was a specific Scottish educational and philosophic tradition and it should not be undermined.[78]

The legal system was the most important dimension of the nationalist vision of a distinctive civil society and a constitutional tradition. The law determined the territorial and, therefore, physical reality of Scotland. This strong sense of geographic or territorial identity cut out the need to rely heavily on an ethnic construction which was most commonly associated in Europe in areas where national frontiers and ethnic/linguistic boundaries were not conterminous.[79] Also, it was fundamentally important in ensuring the territorial integrity of Scotland that meant it was one of the few European nations that did not have its borders shifted in the modern period. This is a point that is often overlooked and was one of the key triggers in bringing nationalism in Europe in a political sense to the fore.[80] The legal system was also a reminder of the fact that Scotland was once a nation state and Scots' private law had been guaranteed by the Treaty of Union. The fact that the Scottish legal system was based on Roman law while that of England was based on Common law was an important fact in making it a clearly distinguishable feature and one that meant long-term assimilation was unlikely. It meant all legislation passed in Westminster that applied to Scotland had to conform to Scottish law. It also meant that a fairly powerful group of middle-class Scots had a vested interest in ensuring its preservation, and it is noteworthy how many leaders of the SNP were from a legal background.[81] Also, it has given rise to the notion of a 'Scottish legal nationalism', although the terminology is problematic because many were staunch unionists.[82]

The existence of a clearly defined legal system meant that Scottish nationalisms did not develop as an irredentist nationalism in the twentieth century which was driven by territorial claims. Close to home there was the ethnic division of Ireland with one group determined to unite Ireland and absorb the Northern state on the grounds that Ireland was indivisible, although for some the Protestants were ethnically foreign.[83] For Unionists in Scotland, there was a determination that their fellow country in Ulster would not be abandoned, and this was reinforced by a belief that there was a racial and ethnic component to that argument which emphasized their Saxon, Scottish and English origins as a fundamental difference to the Celtic Irish.[84] Sometimes this was described as Ireland having two distinctive nations within the one island. Whatever advantages notions of ethnicity may have conferred as a mobilizing myth for nationalism, the experience of Ireland highlighted too readily the problems associated with it. The simplistic reality of a national legal system solved a lot of potential problems because it clearly defined Scotland and those within Scotland as being subject to Scottish law.

There was a constant stream of complaints about the administration and passing of law from Westminster. Firstly, the Imperial Parliament in London was overburdened, and this meant that legislation could be held up for years because other matters were deemed more important and Scottish legislation always came second. The Sheriff Courts Act of 1907, for example, was the result of a committee of inquiry which was formed in 1898 and reported in 1904. It had cross-party support and was recognized at the time as an urgent and non-controversial reform, but it took over three years to find the requisite time in parliament to pass the legislation.[85] Both nationalists and devolutionists alike cited other examples of parliamentary congestion to make the case for a Scottish parliament.[86] The second major complaint which was related to the first was that Scottish legislation was often faulty because it was simply adapted versions of the English law and took inadequate consideration of the Scottish legal system. The practice of simply adding clauses to English Bills to cover Scotland was deemed both inappropriate and some argued was the principal determinant of the bad government that impacted on Scottish society:

> The folly of the attempt to meet the difficulties of life and livelihood in Scotland by the application of English methods is reflected in the comparatively backward condition of our country, and in the swelling chorus of complaints at the neglect and vexatious interference of London government.[87]

In particular, it was noted the key areas of education, agriculture, fisheries and health were most affected by legislative neglect. In particular, the habit of adapting English bills meant that 'it would take a skilled lawyer two or three hours to make the necessary adaptions before it could be read as an intelligible whole' but often that meant 'it is presented in a form in which it cannot be readily understood'.[88]

The use of political violence is always problematic in a democracy, and two important factors prevented its emergence as a serious strategy within the evolution of Scottish nationalist political thought. Firstly, Scottish historiography did not produce or rather lend itself to the production of a 'tradition of revolt' in which nationalists could claim that they were only the latest in a long line of patriots who used arms to throw off English oppression. Simply put, there was too big a gap between the Jacobite Rising and the present day, although the 1820 insurrection has been presented as a nationalist revolt.[89] While, theoretically, the tradition of revolt may have been possible, it went against a widely accepted fact that Scotland and England were united not through conquest but by consent. As was explained in Chapter 1, throughout the nineteenth and twentieth centuries, conventional wisdom held that the Union was stable in Scotland precisely because Scotland was not a conquered nation which was in stark contrast to Ireland which, it was claimed, failed to attain the same level of political maturity as the Scots. The legal and law-abiding nature of Scottish society was contrasted with that of Ireland to make the case that if any nation should have home rule, it was the Scots. The Scottish Home Rule Association in 1890 claimed that granting a parliament to Ireland but withholding it from Scotland would be unjust to a loyal, hard-working and intelligent people and 'set a premium on disorder'.[90] Lord Rosebery, although no supporter of home rule, likewise contrasted the behaviour of the Scots and the Irish: 'Justice for Ireland means everything, even to the payment of the natives' debts. Justice for Scotland means nothing but insulting neglect. I leave for Scotland next week with the aim of blowing up a prison or shooting a policeman.'[91] Although it is difficult to assess with any great degree of precision, the debate regarding home rule in the late nineteenth and early twentieth centuries, in which the legally minded behaviour of the Scots was frequently contrasted with the Irish proclivity towards disruption and occasional political violence, may have been a factor in tramlining the Scottish national movement later on into a constitutional and legalist route for political change because that had been firmly established as the norm before the First World War.

The manufacture of a long history of resistance to English conquest had provided the Irish with a narrative in which revolt could be cast as the norm and that Irish patriots by taking up arms were only following the example of their predecessors. That said, it is worth pointing out that Irish nationalist politics were largely constitutional throughout the nineteenth century and that the British government believed that political violence was more likely to come from the Unionist side of the political divide.[92] Also, it is worth speculating whether the 'tradition of revolt' was an intellectual response to the stalemate of the dominance of Westminster parliamentary sovereignty.[93] Would-be nationalist revolutionaries in Scotland were disadvantaged by the peculiarities of the Unionist reading of Scottish history which incorporated the tradition of resistance as a central theme of its own but kept it neatly confined to the pre-Union era. The argument went that resisters such as Wallace and Bruce had kept the nation independent and thus paved the way for Scotland to grow into a mature nation and thus could enter into the Union with honour and dignity.[94] Although a somewhat torturously contorted argument to modern eyes, the idea was that maintaining Scottish independence against English colonial ambition was a necessary prerequisite for creating a genuine Union when it eventually happened in 1707. This allowed the construction of a historiography of Scottish martial prowess and stubborn resistance to English encroachments, but crucially, it was subsumed within a wider unionist framework, and Bruce and Wallace could be presented as paving the way for Union centuries later. This argument was used to explain the contrasting historical experiences of Scotland and Ireland in which it was argued that conquest had made the Irish surly and resentful, while the Scots could enter Union with honour having proven their martial vitality. Irrespective of the merits or otherwise of such arguments, the point remains that it proved difficult to monopolize Scottish history for nationalist purposes as was the case in Ireland.

A point that has to be emphasized in looking at the Irish Easter Rising and the subsequent Anglo-Irish War was that by 1916 there was a nationalist mandate under the current political system in which the electors of Ireland had returned a majority of MPs who were in favour of home rule and the Easter Rising could also be interpreted as the only response possible because Westminster clearly thwarted the popular will of the Irish people.[95] The failure to enact home rule in spite of the fact that this was something which every Irish electorate had voted for since the 1870s showed many nationalists that the parliamentary route was futile and legitimized the right of resistance. Again Scottish nationalists could draw on the parallels that an in-built English superiority in the parliamentary system could thwart the democratic will of any of the constituent nations of the United Kingdom, with the obvious exception of England. Whatever the particular merits of this argument, it did have a logic and although Irish voters had not given an explicit mandate for revolutionary violence, it was possible for the revolutionaries to make the case that their uprising was ultimately the only way to realize what Irish voters wanted, even though they (the electorate) might not realize this themselves.[96] The situation in Scotland was very different. Scottish politics were absorbed by the British party political system, and while there might be variances with England, there was little concrete evidence to show that the will of the Scottish people was being thwarted by Westminster. Although Scotland tended to be more Liberal in the nineteenth century and more Labour in the twentieth, this would be difficult to cite as evidence of a demand for independence. Even when divergence was used as proof for the utility of independence, it did not necessarily follow that there was widespread support for this. Finally, the advent of the National Party and its electoral fortunes was a significant empirical demonstration of the popular support for independence or, more accurately, its absence. Thus we have our second factor in explaining the reluctance to endorse revolutionary violence; it was difficult to justify that there was a mandate from the people or that the will of the people was being thwarted.

That said, revolutionaries seldom require or seek a democratic mandate, and a variety of reasons could be brought forth to justify political violence in the name of the people. Over the course of the twentieth century a variety of reasons have been cited to explain the Scottish population's acquiescence in the Union, ranging from thought control and propaganda to corrupt politicians and their henchmen and women.[97] One of the reasons that pressure group tactics were popular among some advocates, especially of home rule, was that the issue of self-government was obscured by party politics and the ideological divide.[98] With some evidence, it has to be said, if the issue was put to a plebiscite, they argued, it would command a majority, and it was this lack of opportunity for the Scottish electorate to express a view on the issue without the ideological and party political baggage that went with parties that many believed held back the cause.[99] Although there were occasions when frustration at the lack of political progress led some to advocate direct action, it has almost been built in as axiomatic that Scottish independence requires a democratic mandate, irrespective of how just the cause and how beneficial it would be for the Scottish people. Whereas the manufacture of a tradition of revolt in Scottish history was problematic, constitutionalism and the democratic tradition was moulded and used by nationalists to show that the consent of the people was a fundamental requirement of all Scottish political change and that the demand for independence was part of that wider tendency in Scottish political thought in which sovereignty was increasingly described as the prerogative of the people. In the 1980s and 1990s, the process was revised to argue that the existing British Conservative governments did not govern by the consent of the Scottish people because the party did not command a majority of Scottish Westminster seat, and this gave rise to what was described as the 'democratic deficit'.[100] Also, it is worth stressing that the Irish revolution was firmly in the mind of many at the time of the origins of modern Scottish nationalism, and as we have seen in our chapter on history, it was an example that most did not want to follow because the cost was a price that most Scots would not willingly pay. Also, the conclusion of the Anglo-Irish War gave way to the civil war, and it is worth speculating on whether this was a factor in turning many Irish Scots against the notion of Scottish nationalism.[101] A revolutionary road to independence was largely abandoned by the mid-1920s. Firstly, there was a point of principle in which political change could come through non-violent and constitutional means. In looking at the white dominion nations of the empire, Ireland could be cast as the exception rather than the rule, and in 1931 the Statute of Westminster conferred the principle of independence on these nations which was subsequently ratified at the Ottawa Conference in 1932.[102] Secondly, there was a pragmatic issue that the possible threat of violence would deter support for the cause, and the public opprobrium on those who advocated a more militant stance seemed to confirm this as was demonstrated by the widespread denunciation of Clann Alban – a nascent Fascist organization promoted by Hugh MacDiarmid.[103] The impact of the second point was to reinforce the first one in which the peaceful and democratic nature of the movement was repeatedly stressed and highlighted.

A commitment to non-violence was reinforced by the fact that many of the pioneers of the nationalist movement were pacifists, and in the interwar era, pacifism was a growing political force that was becoming increasingly mainstream.[104] In the era after the Great War there was a public revulsion at violence which stemmed from the experience of the trenches, and the turmoil and upheaval caused by revolution was all too apparent in post-1918 Europe. The democratic process was seen to be the only way to legitimately attain political goals and even if this meant availing themselves of the British political system, which was not without its problems. More extremist elements were sceptical about both the efficacy and the ability of conventional party politics under the Westminster system to deliver tangible results that would lead to independence. Indeed, it was argued, this was a key feature of Westminster politics in that once absorbed into the system, Scottish nationalists would be contained and rendered impotent. After all, it was claimed, was this not the experience of both Scottish and Irish home rulers and that had parliamentary means worked, it would have delivered Irish independence. Westminster, it was claimed, was like a spider's web, and any political action could only be successful if it were undertaken independently of it. One of the key paradoxes of the Scottish nationalist movement is that it has sought to use the very same British political system from which it wants to escape and which it has no faith in, as its principal means of attaining independence. More than anything, it was this conundrum of how to engage with the British political system in order to disengage from it that accounts for the painful and long-drawn-out birth of the SNP as a distinct political party.[105]

The sovereignty of the people

Although the movement has values that are democratic, constitutional and non-violent at its ideological core, there is a degree of ambiguity surrounding the legitimacy of the British state. In the normal sense of law and order and what might be described as natural justice, most nationalists would not see much of an issue and stress that they are a law-abiding movement that respects the rights and property of individuals. With regard to the British state, however, there is a degree of conditionality. The case of William Wallace, who was tried for treason in Westminster Hall, was one that nationalists often referred to with his defence that he could not be a traitor to Edward I because he was never his subject: 'I was never liege of Edward, I was never traitor to my King.'[106] The idea that a Scottish national interest supersedes a British or English one is used to counteract the idea of an unconditional loyalty to the British state, irrespective of its legal status. As we shall see, the idea that Scots could owe loyalty exclusively to the Scottish component of the British realm was propounded by Douglas Young in his trial during the Second World War for his refusal to be conscripted.[107] The ability of Westminster to 'entrap' nationalists and home rule movements led some to advocate the withdrawal from London and the setting up of an alternative parliament in Edinburgh, a sort of Sinn Fein policy. It still led to the conundrum that in order to demonstrate a popular mandate, nationalists would have to use the British electoral machinery to stage a withdrawal from it. Furthermore, they would have to win a 'Scottish election' in the sense of winning a majority of Scottish seats. For all practical intents and purposes, whatever the intellectual merits of the proposal, the likelihood of nationalists winning a clear majority of Scottish parliamentary seats on the first-past-the-post system looked like a forlorn ambition. So an abstentions policy still required the creation of the necessary political machinery and apparatus first required to make a political breakthrough before withdrawing.[108]

The ambivalent nature of the nationalist's association with the British political system and the practical difficulties that can ensue from failing to recognize its authority, or rather refusing to recognize its purely English dimensions, can be illustrated by reference to the career of the first SNP MP, Robert McIntyre, who in 1945 after winning a by-election in Motherwell refused to have sponsors from other parties and was denied the right to take his seat. His argument against sponsorship was that this was a purely English parliamentary tradition and not one that he recognized from a Scottish legal or constitutional perspective. Furthermore, as the only SNP member of parliament, the rest of the House of Commons was made up by members from

English-controlled parties, and he had made it explicit in his election manifesto that 'to the English controlled parties I owe no allegiance. My loyalty is to Scotland and her people'.[109] Ultimately, McIntyre backed down and took the oath under protest, but it does illustrate the difficulties in a practical sense of having to operate within a political system with which there is an ambiguous regard to its legality and traditions. The recent example of SNP MPs clapping in the House and being roundly told off by the Speaker is another demonstration of the problems of operating in a political system which is regarded with an ambivalent legitimacy.[110] The paradox of demonstrating that the sovereignty of the Scottish people demands independence by securing an electoral mandate by using the British electoral system is that it de facto pulls the nationalist movement into the British parliamentary system. A cursory glance at history would reveal that the way the British parliament works is very good at neutralizing perceived outsiders. The experience of the Irish Home Rule party in the late nineteenth and early twentieth centuries demonstrates that the system could adapt to forestall any disruption that outsiders may cause, but perhaps more crucially, it shows that an alliance with British political parties to deliver a majority in favour of home rule legislation and reliance on the parliamentary system to deliver objectives has the effect of holding the movement hostage.[111] This was something that Redmond discovered to his cost as his dependence on the parliamentary Liberal Party had become a political liability which would ultimately give rise to Sinn Fein.[112] Even the parliamentary Labour Party was having its doubts about a parliamentary route to Socialism before 1914 as they were also effectively captured by the Liberals.[113] This issue was one that, historically speaking, has only received cursory attention as the need to demonstrate popular support for independence was the overriding concern.

As we shall see when we discuss the relationship with devolution, engagement with the British political process can be a poisoned chalice in that participation – even under protest – can be said to confer legitimacy, and secondly, by making it work, it can philosophically undermine the raison d'etre of the independence project. A primary objective of some devolutionists was to show that independence was not necessary in order to have a greater degree of self-government and would 'kill nationalism stone dead'.[114] The alternative view was that by demonstrating it could work and confer benefits, it was easy to make the argument that if more self-government was better, the process would inevitably lead to independence.[115] One of the principal reasons why nationalists believed that Scottish national interests could never be truly served by the British political system was the fact that Scottish members could always be outvoted by an English numerical superiority. Allied to that assumption is the notion that it is in England's best interests – be that for economic or political reasons – to keep Scotland attached and prevent independence. This idea has been reinforced by the idea that the British state is reluctant to face up to the reality of its post-war decline.[116] So there is the conundrum that nationalists believe that it is in Scotland's best interest to escape from a political system that works to their disadvantage, but the only way to achieve this is to use that same system which by your own logic will not do what is best for you. How to square the circle?

All of which takes us back to the construction of an alternative Scottish constitutional history. As was mentioned in Chapter 1, the use of Scottish history as a legitimation for independence is one of the key planks in the construction of nationalist ideology. From the outset, Scottish nationalists argued that Scotland was a 'sovereign nation'. Lindsay Crawford claimed in 1920:

> Executive legislatures cannot abolish themselves, or sink, or transfer the rights and prerogatives that appertains to them save with the consent of the nation to which they belong and from which they derive their powers and authority. The Scottish parliament had no power to subvert its constitution or sink its prerogative and functions in that of another country without first submitting the Union proposals to the constituencies and receiving the approval of the electorate.[117]

Furthermore, the issue of sovereignty might be regarded as a moot point because Scotland was a nation, and as a result of the recognition that nations have the right to self-determination it follows that Scotland as a nation has the right to exercise its sovereignty and therefore has, so to speak, an inherent sovereignty. Most Unionists would also accept that as a nation, Scotland has sovereignty and the real argument is about whether or not it should be exercised, and if so, what is the mechanism to demonstrate that it should be exercised. So the debate is not whether Scotland is sovereign but rather where and how that sovereignty is expressed. The violations of the Treaty of Union were for some reason enough to regard the existing constitutional relationship between Scotland and England as null and void. The English obligations under the Union

> have been lightly regarded by her [England] and were the Treaty ever a valid document it must have become null and void by England's violations of it. It will be admitted that nothing in such a 'Treaty' may be altered 'save with the consent of the high-contracting parties thereto' which plainly must be secured in the same formal manner in which it was enacted. The setting aside of the supreme authority in Scotland of the Court of Session, the shutting down of the Scottish Mint, Act 5 Geo I of 1718, altering Scotland's obligations in respect to Customs and Excise and the Church Patronage Act are outstanding violations of the 'Treaty'.[118]

As much as anything, a great deal of intellectual endeavour went into demonstrating, as we have seen in Chapter 1, that Scotland was a historic nation but also that in terms of landmass, population, economy and the like, there were lots of other nations that were statistically similar to Scotland. Because nations were inherently sovereign, by demonstrating that Scotland was a nation, both past and present, a large part of the issue of sovereignty was effectively solved.

Furthermore, as a distinct national entity, Scottish constitutional principles could then be used to counteract and undermine both English and British constitutional arguments, particularly that of Westminster's parliamentary sovereignty. The notion of sovereignty of the people as opposed to sovereignty of parliament has become a fundamental constitutional difference between the two nations, and the nationalist argument is that there was nothing explicit in the Union of 1707 that meant that their principles should be abandoned in favour of the English tradition. So using the British electoral system to demonstrate the will of the Scottish people is an area of overlap that can be – from a Scottish constitutional perspective – used quite legitimately. The idea of the sovereignty of the people has been around for a long time though not really articulated in its current form until comparatively recently, and the legal judgement often used to provide its intellectual validity (Cooper) actually states that parliamentary sovereignty is not known in Scottish law but does not specify where sovereignty does lie.[119] The earliest modern manifestation that sovereignty lay with the people would appear to be in the Bannockburn demonstration in 1930 when John MacCormick first broached the idea of a National Covenant. Although the phrase 'sovereignty of the people' is not used, it is clearly implied:

> Another thing has happened during these two years. Not for the first time an Act has been passed – the Local Government Scotland (Act) – which is a contravention of the Treaty of Union entered into in 1707, and we find that there is no court or tribunal which can test the validity of that Act. We find that we are bound to accept whatever law England cares to force upon us in spite of the safeguard of a bargain, and we have therefore decided once and for all without any ambiguity that there is only one authority to which we are appealing, to set up our independent Parliament in Scotland, and that is the authority of the Scottish people. I find it very strange and amusing when I am asked to propose what to do if England will not give us self-government. We are not concerned whether England will give us it or not. England has nothing to do with it. It is for us to make up our minds whether we want it, and if we want it we are going to have it, and in this Covenant we declare our belief and bind ourselves to act on it that the authority of a majority of Scottish citizens is sufficient for setting up of an independent Scottish Parliament.[120]

The use of the idea of the covenant was one that chimed in with notions of Scottish constitutional history. The National Covenant was created in 1638 in response to the policies imposed by Charles I which endeavoured to bring the Church of Scotland more in line with the practices of the Church of England.[121] The original covenant was an agreement between the people and God and thus an appeal to a higher authority than the state, and undoubtedly for MacCormick, the people were a higher authority than the state. Also, by gathering signatures on a petition that constituted a majority of the Scottish electorate, the cumbersome task of contesting elections and all that entailed could be by-passed. Whether that constituted a democratic mandate was, and still is, a bone of contention.

In the nationalist reading of the past, a tradition of the sovereignty of the people was stitched together and traced back to the Declaration of Arbroath and seen in action during the Reformation and the deposition of Mary Stuart, the Covenanting wars of the seventeenth century, the overthrow of James VII in 1689 and the Disruption in the Church of Scotland in 1843. According to Robert McIntyre, the SNP plan for a written constitution was an outgrowth of the Scottish 'liberal human tradition' and that history played an important part in shaping a nation's constitutional development.[122] This narrative of the people rejecting tyranny and asserting their rights of liberty was presented as a form of Scottish constitutionalism that had roots 'deep in our history and its struggle for humanity and freedom from the Declaration of Arbroath onwards. They are … A defence against arbitrary power and provide freedom within the law and use the law as a protector of freedom and justice'.[123] This was a narrative that was easily adaptable and emerged with great force in the controversy surrounding the 'Democratic Deficit' which was used to characterize the Scottish situation during the Thatcherite and Conservative electoral hegemony in the 1980s and 1990s. This was especially the case in relation to the imposition of unpopular policies such as the Poll Tax, which it was claimed had no democratic mandate in Scotland.[124] The use of a popular plebiscite to oppose the privatization of Strathclyde region's water supply in 1994 was indicative of the growing awareness of the power of local mandates that chimed in with wider constitutional debates.[125]

The notion of the sovereignty of the people as a Scottish constitutional bedrock was one that evolved and attained widespread public acceptance in the late 1980 and early 1990s. Lord Cooper put his finger on the conundrum at the heart of the constitutional debate regarding the Union of 1707 in that the Union made for the preservation of Scottish law under a system that propounded the absolute sovereignty of parliament, yet this is not necessarily recognized in Scottish law. This takes us back to a point made by Michael Fry regarding the original Union negotiations in which the Scottish view was that the Union had to be based on principles whereas the English view was that it was an expedient to solve a particular set of problems.[126] This meant that the Union contained the seeds of its own undoing in that once the Scots were absorbed into the English constitutional settlement, the specific stipulations of the Union as a treaty and all its guarantees could be voted down in parliament according to the principle of parliamentary sovereignty. Crudely put, the treaty could be seen as an agreement between two sovereign powers, and therefore because it is an international obligation, it is binding on the Westminster parliament. But once signed, it can be argued, the fulfilment of the treaty's obligations became a domestic issue and was therefore not binding on Westminster. The Scots may have interpreted the Anglo-Scottish agreement as the former, but the English took the latter view, and as they held the majority view, it was the one that would triumph. Hence the belief in nationalist circles that the Union is nothing more than a worthless piece of paper. As we have already seen, the prevailing ideas of constitutionalism for the British parliamentary system were all drawn from English parliamentary conventions. The supremacy of English parliamentary conventions was guaranteed by an overwhelming English majority of MPs rather than constitutional principles. English parliamentary dominance was absolute, and even at its lowest after the 1884 Reform Act, it still accounted for about two-thirds of elected members. So for nationalists, it was fairly easy to make the case that, firstly, there was no British constitutional tradition in any real sense and that the Scots were subject to the English tradition and that, secondly, this vacuum of not having a genuine British constitutionalism opened up the opportunity to construct a distinctive Scottish one to counterbalance and oppose the existing English one.

A number of thinkers associated with the Scottish legal system posited ideas and values over the past one hundred years that helped shape an alternative tradition. As with all aspects of tradition, the veracity of historical analysis is not necessarily what counts but rather the ways it can be shaped and used to form a coherent body of ideas that have a timeless dimension. The system of Roman Law was a crucial difference, and a number of commentators made the point that the English legal system had evolved in a complex and tortuous fashion, whereas its Scottish counterpart retained its core principles at heart and was more of a rational philosophic system.[127] Nationalists trawled through history to back up their claims, and the nineteenth-century Tory and judge Sir Archibald Alison was favourably quoted for his praise of the legislative wisdom of the old Scottish parliament.[128] Historically speaking, the basis of principle made the Scottish legal system simpler, and since the Union of 1707, Scottish law had been warped by a parliamentary system that tagged on Scottish pieces of legislation to English ones that did not do justice to the distinct legal system and consequently bad laws were often the result. Until the creation of the Supreme Court in 2009, the House of Lords was the final court of appeal and had neither sympathy with nor understanding of the Scottish legal system. Nationalist thinkers produced a catalogue of statutes that showed the lack of legal parity under the Union, and this was complemented with a historical list of all the violations of the Union by the British Parliament. Although the system was being warped as a result of attempts at assimilation, the fact remains that it was a different system with a different history, and as such it could be used to construct an alternative constitutional tradition. According to Andrew Dewar Gibb, Regius Professor of Law at Glasgow University and SNP leader between 1936 and 1940:

> It [Scottish law] was a body of law so different from English law that was in 1707 given a supreme court in the House of Lords. That tribunal had for a century and a half no Scottish judge among its members. It was a system so different that from 1707 onwards was handed over for its statutory improvement and development to a legislative body of which the great majority knew nothing and cared nothing about it. When Mr. Muff in the House of Commons expressed thankfulness that he knew nothing of the law in Scotland it was his candour, not his mental attitude that was exceptional. The hardship to litigants caused by this extraordinary arrangement as well as the violence done to the law itself are beyond computation.[129]

Critical in the construction of a Scottish constitutional tradition were the Wars of Independence in which exigency meant that Robert the Bruce had to appeal to the *Communitas* or the community of the realm for support because the traditional parameters of feudalism in itself would not be enough to weld together a sufficient opposition to English imperialism and aggression. Given the disparity of wealth and strength of the two nations, the Scots had to rely on volunteers and developed the system of *Wapenshaw*, which was the mobilization of local communities for self-defence. This meant that Scots from all classes were involved with the defence of the realm and ideas of constitutionalism reflected this all-embracing composition of the nation: 'Every Scot had, so to speak, a spade in one hand and a sword in the other, and an invader was not faced with a section of the people but the whole nation in arms.'[130] It also was posited as the beginning of the Scottish tradition of individualism which was strongly associated with freedom and individual liberty. This individualism, it was argued, was reflected in the Roman legal system. Interestingly, although English historians and philosophers have attached a premium to the influence of individualism and personal liberty in accounting for the development of English ideas of constitutionalism, Scots critics believed just the opposite.[131] The powerful English monarchy was able to use mercenaries and the lack of personal investment in maintaining liberty meant that, according to one Scottish legal thinker, there was a slavish devotion to authority and this was reflected in the complexity of their legal system. The English natural deference to authority was put down to being a conquered people.[132]

For many, the constitutional incoherence of the Union and the fact that it had, in the eyes of many, been subject to repeated violation meant that a shadow of ambivalence was cast over the legality of the British state and whether there should be a strict observance of all aspect of the law. The appeal to some sort of higher Scottish constitutional principle, even though it has always been vaguely defined, has meant that for some nationalists there has been the legitimacy required to break the law. More often than not, such act of disobedience have been related to symbolic acts of defiance that, while having a point of principle, were more about drawing attention to the cause. Also, acts of symbolic law-breaking were usually associated with non-violent protest. Civil disobedience has never been universally endorsed by the nationalist movement because for many there was the danger that far from encouraging more support it might repel moderate opinion. Also, the whole point of a constitutional approach to independence meant that it was not necessary to break the law. The issue involved a lot of complications for the SNP as it could be subject to direct legal consequences if it was seen to be openly advocating violating the law. Although the issue of insurrection has been raised from time to time, the reality is that it had little support both on the grounds of political principle and expediency in the sense that few reckoned it would have any chance of success. As many pointed out, Scotland was neither bound by coercive laws nor subject to military occupation, and there was little evidence that revolutionary violence would garner much popular support.[133]

The tradition of symbolic disobedience, however, has a chequered history and while it may have brought the movement public attention, more often than not, it did not bring any more support. The antics of Wendy Wood's hauling down of the Union flag at Stirling Castle and replacing it with the Lion Rampart certainly caught the imagination of the press. Wood was speaking in Stirling at the annual Bannockburn Day parade and asked the audience whether they would 'allow that flag to fly there on such a day' and called on the audience for volunteers to take it down.[134] She led a group of about one hundred nationalists into the castle which also at that time served as an army barracks, although the soldiers were largely absent due to a sports day. The local guides were brushed aside and the flag taken down to the singing of 'Scots Wha Hae'. The National Party of Scotland (NPS) almost immediately disowned the event as a cheap sensationalist stunt and worried that this would simply confirm the widespread notion that the party was associated mainly with cranks and fanatics. Wood's persona as a bolshie woman who advocated direct action and used her femininity to shame men for their lack of physical action was not the image that the nationalist movement wanted to cultivate. Her habit of dressing like a Jacobite Miss Jean Brodie was a sartorial nationalism that placed her alongside Compton MacKenzie and Hugh MacDiarmid as belonging to the eccentric wing of the movement.[135] Yet, for all the discomfiture of 'respectable' nationalists, Wood was able to gather public attention in a way that legitimate ways could not.¹³⁶

The anti-conscription movement on the eve and during the Second World War was another issue that tore at the movement over the issue of legality. At the SNP annual conference in 1937 it was decided that the party would oppose conscription until the British government acceded to some form of home rule:

> This Conferences declares that the Scottish National Party is strongly opposed to the manpower of Scotland being used to defend an Empire in the government of which she has no voice and all male members of the Scottish National Party of military age hereby pledge themselves to refuse to serve in any section of the Crown Forces until the programme of the Scottish National Party has been fulfilled.¹³⁷

Undoubtedly, it caught the widespread public mood of pacifism, and there was an element of bravado involved. The issue led to a split in the party with moderates worried that this would alienate popular support, and in 1942 John MacCormick led those opposed to anti-conscription out of the party to form the Scottish Convention.¹³⁸ Activists were investigated by the police under the Defence of the Realm Act for running support networks for those refusing conscription, and Arthur Donaldson was briefly imprisoned for his efforts. It was Douglas Young, however, who brought the issue to the fore. The kilt-wearing, six-foot-seven classicist was imprisoned twice for his refusal to register either as a conscientious objector or for war service. Young made a point of saying he was not a pacifist and made his claim against conscription on the basis that the Treaty of Union did not, in his mind, give sanction to the British state to compel Scots to undertake military service outside Scotland. As he argued, 'The Party as a whole supported the war effort and so did he in his own fashion. But Scotland could only be defended by a Scottish Government and a Scottish Army and that is what he stood for.'¹³⁹ The issue did create a lot of publicity and did show a marked radical tendency for the movement. This was made more emphatic because, following the split of 1942, this was the official position of the SNP. In 1944, Young contested the Kirkcaldy by-election and coming second secured a respectable 42 per cent of the vote. Much of his appeal was based around the emotive issue of female conscripted labour in which young unmarried women from Scotland were being sent south to work in factories in England.¹⁴⁰ Also, it should be borne in mind that because of the wartime electoral truce, there was only one official candidate from the Labour Party standing, and it may be the case that Young picked up a host of anti-Labour votes. In any case, at the time, it seemed that the anti-conscription stance did no harm. This seemed to be further endorsed when Robert McIntyre won the Motherwell by-election in 1945.

The failure to maintain the wartime momentum and the distraction of the covenant movement in raising over two million signatures which failed to bring about any discernible outcome led to perhaps the most audacious piece of law-breaking in nationalist lore. In 1944, Compton Mackenzie, in the final volume of his magnum opus, *The Four Winds of Love*, recounted the story of a nationalist plot to 'reclaim' the Stone of Destiny.¹⁴¹ The stone, which was housed in Westminster Abbey, was used by

English monarchs at coronations since it was taken from Scotland by Edward I and was obviously of great symbolic value. In Mackenzie's novel a group of ambitious and committed young nationalists planned to steal the stone and strike a blow against the British establishment, but the press get hold of the plan and the mission is aborted. Yet, on Christmas Eve 1950, four young nationalists did exactly that and broke into Westminster Abbey and successfully removed the Stone.[142] This caused outrage with the Bishop of Canterbury describing it as an atrocity, and the best efforts of the police failed to either retrieve the stone or apprehend its removers.[143] The whole episode was one that was surrounded by romantic myth and the act was fundamentally symbolic. It was a graphic way of bringing to the public's attention a piece of Scottish history that had largely been forgotten, and it also helped to highlight an imperialist dimension to the Anglo-Scottish union that many unionists would find uncomfortable. The stone was eventually returned to the authorities in Arbroath Abbey which had the purposeful effect of drawing attention to and thereby linking its removal to the 1320 Declaration of Independence. Again, this was a further nod towards a distinctive Scottish constitutional tradition.

The attention given to the Declaration of Arbroath in the early 1950s drew attention to the fact that the current monarchy had more of a direct ancestral ink to Robert the Bruce than Edward I, and this historical awareness would somewhat bizarrely raise its head during the coronation of the new monarch Elizabeth in 1953. This was set against a post-war backdrop of economic and social reconstruction and talk of a 'new Elizabethan age' in which a transformative Britain would emerge from the ashes of the Second World War.[144] The Festival of Britain and the new consensus around the Welfare State arguably marked a new and heightened sense of British national identity. The idea that Britishness had to acknowledge and pay due deference to its Scottish component was let down by the hugely symbolic role played by the monarch during the coronation. Much of it was down to cack-handedness and poor public relations, but it struck a raw nerve among the Scottish royalist, middle classes and led to considerable agitation which the nationalist movement was able to capitalize on. The coronation was a major event, the young, glamorous queen was used in many ways to symbolize a rebirth of Britain and it was the first major act of British pageantry to be televised to a mass audience. The use of the numeral 'II', however, hit a discordant note among many historically minded Scots who pointed out that the previous Elizabeth was queen of England only and that the correct numeration should be first of Great Britain. The implication was clear that when it came to numbering the monarchy, the English line took precedence. Although similar gripes emerged over Edward's use of 'VIII' in the early twentieth century, the issue in the early 1950s did take on a more militant note. The use of the numeral was challenged and but this was defeated in the courts because the monarchy can use royal prerogative in relation to titles and is not bound by any tradition. For many Scottish royal purists, the issue was that there was no such stipulation in the Treaty of Union which allowed the English line of the monarchy to take precedence in relation to royal titles and as such it was seen to be a violation of the constitutional rules established by the Union. The reputation of the monarch was not further enhanced when on her first visit north she turned up at St Gilles Cathedral to receive the honours of Scotland in a twinset and handbag.

Sartorially, many considered this an inappropriate way to acknowledge the heritage of the ancient Scottish Crown. and this was yet again evidence that Scotland was not given due deference in the Union. Finally, the monarch referred to herself as the queen of England in the Christmas broadcast of 1953 which was designed to show off the technical prowess of the British Empire as it was transmitted from New Zealand.[145]

The response to the denigration of Scottish honour was quite violent. Tourists shops which carried souvenirs displaying the offending 'II' had their windows put in and, more seriously, new postal boxes which bore the symbol were attacked with explosives (in reality just one).[146] This was a high-profile outrage, and given that the boxes were made of cast iron, it had the potential to turn them into much more serious and deadly bombs considering the effect of shrapnel. The threat and use of terrorism certainly did draw a lot of attention to the issue, and it did have the effect of ensuring that postboxes in Scotland did not have the offending numeral. For a number of commentators since and at the time, the episode was cited as evidence that terrorism did work, although the cumulative effect on public opinion would not have endeared them to the nationalist movement, and, indeed, the campaign pulled many law-abiding constitutionalists into an orbit they would rather not have experienced. The later 1950s also experienced middle-class sensitivities when a recommendation in the Church of Scotland report on ecumenism that said members could elect bishops roused great indignation that a process of Anglicization was at work. What these episodes, either individually or collectively, demonstrate is that the Scottish middle class – at least – had a clear notion of the Union in which the distinctive Scottish element which was enshrined in the Treaty of Union should be respected and honoured.[147] This sense of a distinctive Scottish polity was echoed in Conservative party strategy which used Scottish national distinctiveness as an intellectual bulwark against Labour's supposed socialist centralization. This idea of a separate Scottish constitutional and legal framework was an important backdrop for the development of a nationalist intellectual case to be made in that either the Union was not being honoured or it was not capable of fulfilling its mission of keeping a distinctive Scottish polity alive.[148]

Secret revolutionary organizations which claimed they were capable of using armed resistance as a political tool have emerged from time to time during the 1960s and 1970s. Groups like the 1320 Club and the Scottish Liberation Army have never enjoyed any appeal beyond the fringe and, indeed, depended quite heavily on media attention for publicity which was happily provided because it was believed that this would hinder rather than help the cause of independence. Undoubtedly, there was an element of right-wing authoritarianism that bordered on Fascism in these groups, and some of it was indistinguishable from a militant British nationalism which borrowed very heavily from Scottish military caricatures. In any case, much of it appears to be born of political frustration and had little ideological substance in the sense that movements of national liberation were widespread at the time, but there was no endeavour to portray such movements as anti-colonial or anti-capitalist.[149] The predominantly right-wing complexion of these shadowy organizations in the 1960s ruled out identification with the left, while in the 1970s and 1980s when attempts were made to promote a revolutionary vision, a residue of Irish nationalist influence made it difficult to firmly place them either on the left or on the right. The limited impact that political violence has had on the nationalist movement can be demonstrated by the fact that for many, the would-be revolutionaries were in fact acting as agents provocateurs for the British state.[150]

A legal form of direct action was to engage in public petitions and organize a local plebiscite. The issue of using plebiscites as a way of demonstrating the necessary support either for home rule or independence has always been part and parcel of the discourse in nationalist circles.[151] The one advantage of using a plebiscite was that it would clearly demonstrate whether there was majority support and it was a way to present the issue untrammelled with all the conventional packaging associated with party politics. There were a number of home rule dry runs in parts of Scotland in the 1950s, and the establishment of the Scottish Convention in 1948 which gathered over two million signatures in favour of home rule was seen as a way of by-passing conventional party politics.[152] In spite of an outward appearance of success, the strategy had one fatal flaw in that it was not understood as carrying a mandate in the conventional political sense. This demonstration of support could be ignored by the government of the day because it insisted that should there be support for home rule, it should be demonstrated at the ballot box during general elections. If home rule was as popular as its protagonists claimed, then the electorate would vote for such candidates, and this was the normal way in which the electorate demonstrated their political preferences. The convention was stumped and faded away. In effect, this signalled the end of the pressure group approach to independence or home rule and placed the primary focus on winning elections as this was the first necessary step to demonstrate the will of the Scottish people. In the absence of a Scottish parliament, an electoral mandate could be secured by winning a majority of Scottish Westminster parliamentary seats.

To challenge the idea that the Scots were subjected to the unlimited sovereignty of the Westminster parliament, the nationalist movement has in stages increasingly advanced a notion of sovereignty residing with the Scottish people. This doctrine has become more sophisticated and intellectually evolved as time passed over the course of the twentieth century. The significance that there was a legalistic and constitutional challenge to the fundamental legal facet of the British state has not received the scholarly attention that it deserves, and this has yet to be done, although the rudimentary sketch and outline was produced by the Campaign for a Scottish Assembly in 1988.[153] Although the campaign was in the main supported by parties and institutions that were devolutionist, the argument used to justify the setting up of a devolved parliament was the decidedly nationalist one that the Scottish people were sovereign as was demonstrated throughout their history. It is a point that often goes unnoticed, but by utilizing the idea of the sovereignty of the people to justify devolution, opponents of independence conceded the case that Scottish sovereignty was not limited by the British state, and theoretically it could take as much or as little power as it demanded. The idea of the sovereignty of the people was widely legitimized in the late 1980s and 1990s by the Unionists parties in the argument over devolution. Before examining the arguments put forward by the Labour and Conservative parties at this time, it is worth stressing that both predicated their ideas on the twofold assumption that, firstly, a majority of Scots would not vote for independence and that, secondly, the SNP would not become the dominant political power in Scotland. Because of this, both parties gave free expression to the notion of Scottish sovereignty, safe in the knowledge that it was unlikely to have any meaningful political consequences.

For the Labour Party in Scotland, the creation of a Scottish parliament was seen as an institution which, it was argued, could deflect some of the worse policies coming from the Conservative government and also act as a check on the progress of the SNP because, it was believed – and the polling evidence backed this up – devolution was more popular than independence.[154] The odd thing about Labour's espousal of a Scottish parliament was that it was based, first and foremost, on the fact that Scotland was a nation and not, as would be the case with most systems of devolution, an administrative functionality. The case made by Labour was that as the Scots elected a majority of MPs who were in favour of setting up a Scottish parliament, it was undemocratic of the Conservative government to deny them their wishes. As the Labour MP for Dundee John McAllion put it:

> Scottish sovereignty is not something which Scotland can keep exclusively to itself. We need to pool our sovereignty with other nations where it is in our common interest to do so. However, the decision to pool that sovereignty must be a Scottish decision. We must decide how much of our sovereignty we are prepared to pool and decide with which other countries we wish to place that sovereignty and how much we shall keep to ourselves. The present Union is unacceptable because we are not allowed to make that decision. We are denied the opportunity to decide how much sovereignty we share with the other nations of the United Kingdom. That is why the Union is profoundly undemocratic and why it is ultimately doomed until it learns to transform itself into the decentralised, democratic and reformed Union to which I have referred and which the Labour party intends to implement after the next election. The debate is a matter of the utmost importance to the people who live in Scotland for those reasons and also because of the questions that it asks about the democratic credentials of the Westminster parliamentary system. It is not just a dry, constitutional matter.[155]

The idea of Scotland as a sovereign nation is one that all nationalists would agree with, and just in case there was any doubt about the argument being driven by nationalism, McAllion elaborated: 'The point that I am trying to make is that nationalism can be, and often is, a progressive and liberating force in the modern world. I believe that Scottish nationalism is and can be such a force if it is properly channelled.'[156]

The Conservative retort was that a constitutional restructuring of the British state was a matter for the British government and not something that the Scots could impose on the rest of the United Kingdom. Obviously with an eye on making life as difficult as possible for Scottish Labour home rulers, it was pointed out that 'one party – the Scottish National party – stood for election on one issue alone: the establishment of a self-ruling Scotland with no Westminster connection? Labour and the Liberal Democrats stood for a parliament within the Union'.[157] Being in the Union meant having to accept the will of the majority of British MPs. Conservatives conceded that it would be constitutionally acceptable for the Scots to vote for independence. According to Margaret Thatcher, 'They [the Scots] have an undoubted right to national self-determination; thus far they have exercised that right by joining and remaining in the Union. Should they determine on independence no English party or politician would stand in their way.'[158] The publication of the government white paper, *Scotland in Union: A Partnership for Good*, in 1993 accepted that the current constitutional arrangement was through a partnership of nations, and according to the prime minister, John Major, writing in the forward to the report, 'No nation could be held irrevocably in a Union against its will.'[159] By the time of a majority SNP government in the Scottish parliament in 2011 which was committed to holding a referendum on Scottish independence, the response of the British government was to clearly articulate that the Scots had the right to do this and it had been accepted by previous administrations because 'should a majority of people in any part of the multi-national UK express a clear desire to leave it through a fair and democratic process, the UK Government would not seek to prevent that happening.'[160] None of this should be surprising given that the British state had always been seen as a multinational entity, even though it may not have occupied the central constitutional position that it should have. Even after the vote against independence in the referendum of 2014, the Smith Commission on further devolution established by the prime minister David Cameron conceded the fact that there was nothing in the report that would prevent the people of Scotland from becoming independent in the future if they chose to do so.[161] Finally, a non-binding vote in the House of Commons on 4 July 2018 recognized 'the sovereign right of the Scottish people to determine the form of government best suited to their need'.[162]

Conclusion

The issue of where sovereignty resides had tended to overshadow the much more basic proposition that as a nation Scotland has an inherent sovereignty because all nations have the right of self-determination. The creation of a distinct Scottish constitutional tradition, as much as anything, was about shoring up the idea that Scotland had the full trappings of nationhood. Given the importance of notions of legitimacy, governance and sovereignty in cementing the idea of the nation, it is not surprising that nationalist chose to focus on this to show that Scottish traditions were both distinctive and different from that of England. The issue of the constitutional relationship between Scotland and England was always problematic because the Treaty of Union did not lay down the necessary groundwork for a viable framework in the future, and it is worth noting how a distinctive British constitutionalism failed to develop as opposed to the adaptation of the English constitution to serve British or extra-English interests. The Union did, however, create a paradox for Scottish nationalists because, on the one hand, it legitimized the idea of Scotland as a nation but, on the other, it legitimized the British state from which they wished to escape. This has meant that, unlike most other nationalist movements, Scottish nationalists recognize, albeit reluctantly, that the apparatus and forms of the British state and its political system have to be used in order to achieve their aims. This commitment to using the existing British political apparatus was also reinforced by the widespread aversion to political violence that followed in the wake of the First World War and the Irish Revolution. The development of nationalist constitutional ideas arguably had its biggest impact on the Unionists parties that came to accept the principle of Scottish sovereignty. Devolution rather than independence was the issue on which the divergent wills of the Westminster and the people of Scotland manifested itself. While devolutionists increasingly turned to arguments regarding the sovereignty of the people to legitimize their claims, Conservative opponents accepted that the people were sovereign but that if the Scots wanted to exercise that right it would only apply to the SNP and independence, not devolution. For most of the past century, such ideas were important because they posited an intellectual framework for attaining independence, but the political reality meant there was little opportunity to test this in practice because the nationalist movement until very recently did not have the electoral support to give weight to these arguments. Legally and constitutionally, the ways in which the sovereign will of the Scottish people can be demonstrated in a political sense has been a fundamental building block of the nationalist movement because it was and is the only non-revolutionary and therefore non-violent way in which the sovereignty of Westminster can be challenged.

4

Home rule and unionism

You must know of the great and increasing congestion of business in the Imperial parliament, a congestion which is injurious both to domestic and imperial affairs. Foreign policy especially, suffers through inadequate discussion, for the Imperial Parliament is not a real Empire Parliament. Under present conditions, therefore, Foreign policy cannot be thoroughly probed and tried, as with fire, and to have anything else is fateful to the Empire, and at the present juncture, to the world. This congestion at Westminster has told heavily upon the domestic legislature of the component nations of Britain. But Scotland being the smallest nationality has naturally suffered most.
    – D. MacKinnon, interim general secretary, the Scottish Home Rule Association, to Rt. Hon. Andrew Bonar Law, prime minister, 26 October 1922

In this chapter we will discuss the wider intellectual world with which the Scottish national movement engaged. This is important because it provides the broader perspective that is necessary to see political movements in the round. In the same way that a discussion of socialism that fails to mention capitalism has a missing element, so too with the debate surrounding Scottish independence that does not engage with home rule and Unionism. The quote above shows the importance of context because the world that brought forth the Scottish national movement was still the world of the British Empire and, to a large extent, it was responsible for framing the debate regarding self-government; moreover, the experience of the dominion nations was an important point of reference for both home rulers and unionists. More than will be realized today, it shaped the contours of much of the discussion. This chapter explores the issues surrounding the differences between those who were home rulers and those who believed in independence and relates how they were often grouped together historically on the basis of wanting some form of constitutional change. It also examines the relationship of nationalism to home rule in the sense that whereas devolution is not dependent on nationality for its functionality, the former was always predicated on the fact that the Scots needed a parliament because they were a nation. Furthermore, when the issue of democracy is factored in, the discussion becomes more problematic in that for many the parliament was the forum where the decision to stay within a devolved settlement or move on to independence would be taken, but the

Figure 4 The National Party of Scotland at the Glasgow University election for rector (1928) when Compton Mackenzie was narrowly defeated by the prime minster Stanley Baldwin (Source: *Scots Independent*).

Left to right: The Duke of Montrose (who was not a member), Compton Mackenzie, R. B. Cunningham Graham, Hugh MacDiarmid, James Valentine and John MacCormick. The last two were members of the Glasgow University Scottish Nationalist Association.

substantive point was that such a decision was the right of the Scottish people to take and such a forum was necessary for this purpose. The idea that self-government was a process that would lead to independence appeared to be borne out by the experience of the 'white dominion' nations in the empire, and for many nationalists of a pragmatic mind, devolution was an important first step because it would begin the process of building up a state apparatus which would make the final stop towards independence less of a leap into the unknown. As we shall see, it was precisely for those reasons that Unionists opposed home rule, but in any case, Conservatives were always sceptical as to the value of constitutional change. The extent to which unionism was a coherent philosophy will be explored because there were oscillations between support for unionism and assimilation. Finally, the ways in which unionism was a way of masking a competitor British nationalism will be explored because to some extent the issue in Scotland has boiled down to a choice of a 'big-nation' or a 'small-nation' nationalism.

The unbalanced Union

The relationship between those who have advocated for Scottish independence and those that have sometimes been seen as allies, namely home rulers, and those that have been seen as their principal opponents – Unionists – created a Scottish political ecosystem that was different from the wider British political environment in which it existed. A sort of political tidal pool, so to speak. It is by examining this wider habitat that we can reconstruct the connections and interactions that made up the intellectual world in which Scottish nationalism existed. In particular, it is important to focus on the engagement with home rulers or devolutionists because they have been fellow travellers in the quite literal sense that they are on the same road but have a destination that is, figuratively speaking, one stop before the nationalist's disembarkation point of independence. It is also important to point out straight away that the issue of devolution in British political history is predominately related to the question of nationalism or national identity in the sense that the units of devolution or home rule have focused on the historic nations of Ireland, Scotland and Wales.[1] Although arguments relating to greater efficiency and administrative restructuring have frequently been advanced in favour of devolution, the fact remains that no one has seriously started from scratch and posited a scheme of dispensing administrative or political power on any other criteria except that of historic nationality.[2] Furthermore, because of the recommendations of the 1954 Balfour Commission on Scottish Affairs, many aspects of British government were administratively directed to the Scottish Office which meant that the expansion of centralized British state power in the post-war era paradoxically reinforced the distinctive dimension of governmental administration in Scotland and marked it out from the rest of the United Kingdom. Wherever it was practically possible, the report concluded, government activity should be administered from Edinburgh via the Scottish Office.[3] The growth of British state power in the post-war era was reflected in the expansion of the Scottish Office. Although there is a considerable time lag, in Scotland, administrative devolution predates its political equivalent. Usually it is the other way round.

There is an intellectual conundrum at the heart of the policy of devolution in the United Kingdom. It is often seen as giving special powers and dispensations to the smaller nations because they have complained of being dwarfed by England, but this does not fundamentally address the issue of the unbalanced nature of the Union because England still dominates politically, socially, culturally and economically as a result of its overwhelming size compared to Wales, Scotland and Northern Ireland.[4] The current constitutional arrangement still leaves the big obstacle of England, in that for an effective form of federalism or equitable devolution to exist in the United Kingdom, the largest nation in the Union would have to be artificially broken down into smaller units that have little or no historical resonance in order to create some form of equitable harmony of size and function between the various components that would make up the new system of government. This has proven to be unpopular.[5] For devolution to work as an effective form of governmental administration in the United Kingdom, as was recognized by the minority recommendation in the Kilbrandon

Report on the Constitution published in 1973, genuine balance and regional equality could only be achieved by administratively splitting the English nation asunder.[6] There is a real suspicion that devolution has emerged in the British state, to use an inelegant but descriptive phrase, as a bastardized form of federalism.

The focus on the smaller historic nations as the base units for devolution has ensured that there is a very considerable intellectual overlap between Scottish home rulers and nationalists because both camps agree that Scotland is a nation, its people have sovereignty and it should have a government best suited to meet its needs. As we shall see, the issue of national sentiment as the key driver of constitutional reform has meant that there have been frequent endeavours to disguise this fact by playing up the utility of administrative benefits and hence why what started out as home rule in the period after the First World War was increasingly transformed into devolution in the post-war era because the latter sounded less of a sop to national distinctiveness and nationalism. Having said all that, it is undoubtedly the case that for some, the distinctive needs of Scottish society can be satisfied by devolution without having to go as far as independence. And this remains a resolute view among many. But also, as we shall see, some devolutionists have argued that the journey is more important than the destination, and they have had an open mind as to where the stopping point should be. This is a point we shall return to later on in this chapter.

Many nationalists of a pragmatic mind made the argument that if the goal of independence is to be reached, then setting off for a devolved Scottish parliament makes for a sensible first leg of the journey. The Labour home ruler J. M. MacDiarmid made the point that the creation of an independent nationalist movement that would compete against the Labour Party in elections would alienate sympathetic elements in the political mainstream, which would make the creation of a home rule parliament less likely, which in turn would make independence less likely:

> If the National Party persists in a policy of injuring and opposing all who aim at Scottish management of Scottish affairs unless they abandon all other causes than home rule, then I can safely predict that the youngest present members of the NPS will be mouldering in their graves and home rule still in the future.[7]

There was always this dilemma facing those who argued that the creation of a home rule parliament was a necessary first step for independence. On the one hand, it was only by demonstrating popular support at the ballot box for a distinct national party that would push the mainstream parties into legislating, but on the other, this policy could also potentially increase hostility. Before the advent of devolution in the 1990s, the nationalist movement can be divided into two camps. On the one hand, there were the fundamentalists who advocated outright independence of the kind associated with the nation state and that anything less was unacceptable. On the other, there were the gradualists who advocated a 'stepping stone' policy of greater devolution as a first step on the road to independence.[8] The division was amplified along the lines of strategy with fundamentalists believing that an independent political party was a necessary means of delivering greater autonomy, while gradualists tended to believe that common ground could be found with home rulers and devolutionists within the mainstream British parties. This hard and fast division was rarely apparent in reality with most having a foot in either camp. Furthermore, the dichotomy is not as great as it might first appear. Most fundamentalists have accepted that some powers are better than none, and only the ultra-purist would insists that there should be outright independence or nothing.[9] Furthermore, there have been many gradualists whose commitment to greater powers of self-government have no fixed end point and will go as far as pragmatism prevails or the will of the Scottish electorate demands. This was especially the case if home rulers accepted that the Scottish people were sovereign because it could then be argued that the Scottish parliament represented the will of the people and as such it did not matter

> whether a man believes that Scotland should be an independent Republic with complete separation from England or believes that the future Scots government should only make the minimum of changes to the existing Union with England, or even that Scotland should have foreign affairs, army, navy air force, to be managed by the Westminster Parliament, so long as he accepts the principle above.[10]

For many, the journey was more important than the destination, and there is a tendency among some to see devolution as a process with an undetermined end. It is perhaps best described as a sort of constitutional magical mystery tour in which the end point could turn out to be independence, but it is not necessarily framed as its ultimate objective, although, tantalizingly, it could be. The metaphor of devolution as a journey was the one used by Donald Dewar, the first first minister of Scotland and a leading architect of the devolution settlement. According to the second first minister, Henry McLeish:

> Donald Dewar had a speech where he's making the point that this is a journey, we don't know what the destination is. He also made the point that he can't believe that the UK government has such a soft underbelly that there won't ever be any more changes to the constitution of the UK. This was a person who was thinking achievement and thinking to the future. And that came through on that day ... Some people were apprehensive about destination unknown. We had no idea at that point but we had reached that critical day where everything changed.[11]

The important point was that with democracy as the driver, the constitutional destination could not be predetermined.

Since the creation of the Scottish parliament, it would appear that devolution is a process, rather than an event, and there has been the accumulation of more powers showing that the constitutional boundaries were not fixed. The 'power grab' post-Brexit shows that the process is not all one-way either. An election study conducted in the wake of the opening of the Scottish parliament in 1999 found that most Scots regarded devolution not as the 'settled will of the people' as was frequently claimed but rather as beginning a process of constitutional change.[12] Although most of the respondents may not have been aware of it, this corresponded with the view of home rule or 'self-government' as it was widely understood in the past. The idea of devolution as a process has been reinforced, paradoxically, by the Conservative Party and home rule opponents because it was claimed that political devolution was merely the first step on the road to independence. Scottish Tories claimed that there was little or no difference in the objectives of home rulers and those that wanted political separation because the former would lead to the latter and this was why the party campaigned against the creation of a Scottish parliament in the referendums in 1979 and 1997. As the legislation was going through Westminster to set up the Scottish parliament, there was still an unrepentant chorus that devolution would let the nationalist genie out of the bottle. According to the Conservative member of parliament (MP) Michael Ancram:

> If the Government's claims that they want the United Kingdom to be maintained and Scotland's place in it to be strengthened are genuine, fairness in this Parliament is paramount. They should welcome our efforts to find an answer that works, but instead they are making an enormous political miscalculation, which is becoming a habit for them. Only six months ago, they campaigned hand in hand with nationalists for a yes vote in the referendum and, as my hon. Friends remember, told their supporters that they had the measure of the Scottish National party. In haunting words, the Secretary of State for Defence, the right hon. Member for Hamilton, South (Mr. Robertson), said that devolution would kill nationalism stone dead. Stone dead? Nationalism is trampling all over them. Opinion polls consistently show what Conservative Members warned about throughout the devolution referendum. We said that the creation of a focus for nationalism would not weaken nationalism, but strengthen it. We were mocked for our pains. Opinion polls now show nationalists running Labour neck and neck for seats in a Scottish Parliament. The Government are running scared – they could not have got it more wrong if they had tried. They apparently believed that the credibility that they had bestowed on the SNP would fade away once the referendum was over.[13]

Unionist opposition to devolution was based on a belief that once the process was begun, it would end up with independence and those who argued otherwise were being naive. This attitude was firmly established in the later nineteenth century as it formed the main plank of opposition to Irish home rule with the claim that it was a cover for Irish republicans that wanted to break up the British Empire.[14] While ambiguity may have been cultivated on both sides of the political divide between home rulers and nationalists because each saw it as a way of maximizing support, there was less ambivalence among Unionists opponents who argued that devolution was a ruse to make independence seem more acceptable. Before the advent of political devolution in the 1990s, it was common practice to bracket everyone who is in favour of greater powers of devolution or self-government as belonging to a small 'n' nationalist camp, and, historically speaking, this is how the movement for greater autonomy has tended to be seen.[15]

The reality of course is that, strictly defined, independence and devolution are two radically different political policies, which have opposing objectives and desired outcomes; one is to dissolve the United Kingdom and create a new Scottish state and the other is to strengthen and make more effective the existing government apparatus. This division has become much more apparent with the creation of the Scottish parliament as devolutionists have achieved their objective and argue that the constitutional journey has gone far enough. Today the big divide in Scottish politics is largely based around support or opposition to independence rather than the axis of left and right, which was the case for much of the twentieth century. To some extent, this new division has grafted itself onto the old divisions by claims that an independent Scotland would be more likely to have left-leaning social democratic governments in contradistinction to England where there is a tendency for right-wing governments. The different objectives associated between independence and devolution were not so obvious before the days of the Scottish parliament because there was a tendency to conflate nationalists and home rulers when dealing with a unitary British political system.[16] The fact that both wanted a Scottish parliament, albeit for different purposes, was held to be more important. This fundamental point of principle of the purpose of the parliament tended to be lost sight of and the *Claim of Right* produced by the Scottish National Convention in 1989 tended to gloss over these issues by placing the emphasis on the issue of democracy in the sense that the Conservative government which had little electoral support in Scotland refused to countenance any constitutional change:

> We, gathered as the Scottish Constitutional Convention, do hereby acknowledge the sovereign right of the Scottish people to determine the form of Government best suited to their needs, and do hereby declare and pledge that in all our actions and deliberations their interests shall be paramount.
> We further declare and pledge that our actions and deliberations shall be directed to the following ends:
> To agree a scheme for an Assembly or Parliament for Scotland;
> To mobilise Scottish opinion and ensure the approval of the Scottish people for that scheme; and
> To assert the right of the Scottish people to secure implementation of that scheme.[17]

To illustrate how much has changed in terms of the current political debate one only has to look at the changing terminology of Scottish politics. The term 'Unionist' was, more or less, exclusively used to describe those who opposed home rule in the 1980s and 1990s, while those in favour of a devolved Scottish parliament tended to be described as 'nationalist'.[18] Although never hidden from view, creating a Scottish parliament according to devolutionists would lead to a strengthening of the British state by reconstituting its government by bringing it closer to the people. According to William Cowan, the sponsor of the first Scottish home rule bill to make it to the statute book in 1913:

> Our cause is unanswerably strong both from a legislative and administrative point of view. A Scottish Office in London can never be other than a geographical absurdity. It is admittedly the centre of an efficient bureaucracy. No one disputes

that. It governs Scotland more or less autocratically – largely by methods of administrative decree. I do not blame the members of that bureaucracy. They are courteous and considerate, especially to Scottish Members. But they can do very little to mitigate evils for which they are not responsible. Scottish legislation – what there is of it – is initiated mainly by the permanent heads of the various Departments. If these Departments are situated in Edinburgh they are out of touch with the Scottish Members here. If they are situated in London they are out of touch with the Scottish people.[19]

Although devolutionists would make pragmatic and administrative justifications to bolster their claims, the appeal to nationalist sentiment in support of the creation of a Scottish parliament always tended to predominate. Cowan claimed that

history justifies the demand. The Scottish people never voluntarily renounced their ancient Parliament. It was filched from them … since 1707 protests have been heard against a transaction which took too little into account both the sentiments and interests of a proud and ancient people who had maintained their independence for centuries against tremendous odds.[20]

Almost sixty years later, the Kilbrandon Report came to the same conclusion.[21] The appeal to history and Scottish sentiment in support of devolution was undoubtedly a major factor in spooking Unionists because, for them, if nationhood was the basis for a Scottish parliament, then the argument would be to follow it through to its logical conclusion of statehood. This suspicion was reinforced because for those seeking independence, the prime objective of creating a devolved Scottish parliament would be that it would make it easier to leave the British state by setting up the embryonic apparatus required for statehood. According to Neil MacCormick, a leading nationalist constitutional theorist, once a Scottish parliament had acquired a real measure of economic and financial power, the subsequent steps to full independence would be reasonably simple.[22] This view was able to command a degree of cross-party consensus and was shared by the most trenchant opponent of devolution, the Labour MP for Linlithgow Tam Dalyell:

The position now is, as it has always been – devolution in anything resembling the form in which it is proposed is a staging post, a halfway house, or a springboard to something else. Liberal Democrat Members think that it will lead to federalism – I see them nodding, so I am not distorting their position. Scottish National party Members think, as I do, that this is a paving Bill – I see them also nodding – towards the dissolution of the United Kingdom. [HON. MEMBERS: 'Independence.'] It is coming to that. That, rightly or wrongly, is what I think.[23]

As should be obvious, the political objectives of independence and devolution are miles apart and irreconcilable, yet the two have often gone hand in hand over the course of the twentieth century, and it is only since the independence referendum of 2014 that the width of the gulf has become apparent between the two philosophies.

Home rule or devolution?

In essence, the conflation between independence and devolution is understandable because, at heart, the debate is about the appropriate political state for Scottish nationhood. A key argument in support of home rule has been the idea that devolution is enough to both reassert Scottish nationality and promote a national interest. In other words, statehood is not necessarily a requisite state of being for a nation and devolution can cater to most of those issues and needs that an independent state normally fulfils. A key element in this argument is that it is possible to have the best of both worlds – a form of self-government while remaining under the apparatus of the British state with the advantages that this conferred, especially in regard to international affairs which was an area of great volatility for much of the twentieth century.[24] In more recent times, this argument has focused on the idea of a fiscal transfer or, in other words, that Scotland is subsidized by England and devolution allows Scots to have a level of public expenditure that independence could not afford. Needless to say, nationalists disagree with this prognosis. A neglected aspect of this argument is that the Union makes England poorer and intellectually shows that Scottish Unionists do tend to take English support for granted.[25] Others have a focus on strengthening the effectiveness of British government by making it more pluralistic and responsive to local needs which has helped to accommodate the diverse nature of the British state. In the words of Tony Blair, 'We can celebrate and recognise the differences in our nations within the UK because the unity of the UK should be based not on conformity, but diversity.'[26] As will be discussed below, a salient factor, and for many its most important aspect, has been its potential to stop independence by providing a halfway house to statehood. This was especially the case when it looked as if the Scottish National Party (SNP) might emerge as a major electoral force, as was the case in the 1970s, or in the 1980s and 1990s when Conservative governments were able to impose unpopular policies on Scotland in spite of having little electoral support north of the border and led to fears that independence would emerge as the best way to avoid the so-called democratic deficit.[27] These pragmatic reasons and ones of electoral calculation, arguably, have outweighed the potential benefits and possible dangers to the British state. Thus devolutionists can be separated into two camps: those whose primary focus see it as a benefit for the United Kingdom by stopping the SNP and the campaign for independence, but that could include creating greater democratic accountability and a more pluralist system of government. Then there were those whose interest is purely centred on Scotland and the benefits it would bring, largely in circumventing unpopular policies associated with right-wing London governments.[28] Needless to say, there are many who would see themselves as having a foot in both camps as neither were mutually exclusive.

Conservative opposition to Scottish devolution, although there have been various flirtations in the post-war era,[29] is fundamentally based around a predisposition to be suspicious of constitutional change. This has been a feature of British Conservatism since its inception as a party and remains a central pillar of its political philosophy that can be traced all the way back to Edmund Burke's denunciation of the French Revolution.[30] The stalwart defence of tradition and the existing social and political order tend to be overlooked in discussions of Scottish Conservatism, which in recent time has focused more on its unionism, but it has not always highlighted enough that defence of the Union is part of a wider dispensation to protect and entrench the existing constitutional status quo. For example, the best illustration of an aversion to constitutional reform can be seen in the history of the issue of reform of the House of Lords which shows consistent and entrenched Tory opposition.[31] A clear exposition of scepticism regarding devolution was expressed by Margaret Thatcher's incoming Scottish secretary of state, George Younger, when repealing the Scotland Act of 1978 after it failed to secure the necessary mandate of over 40 per cent of the electorate voting in favour:

> We have debated this subject for almost 10 years. What, I wonder, have we learnt from it. First, we should have learnt that constitutional change cannot easily or lightly be used as a gimmick for gaining votes in the short term. Politicians and the media have vied with each other over the last 10 years to express enthusiasm for one or other version of this cause. It is clear now that the people were much more hard-headed and sceptical about what was happening than anyone gave them credit for, and the referendum proved that they were much harder-headed than many of those who sought to advise them. Secondly, we have surely learned that devolution by itself produces no panaceas for the problems that we politicians are elected to try to solve. The main effect of the devolution cause over the past seven or eight years has been not to solve any of our problems but to divert our attention from them. Indeed, it has delayed solutions to many matters which are of far greater importance to the average person living in the average constituency in Scotland. Thirdly, we have surely learnt that the electorate in Scotland has a higher opinion of our existing constitution than many of the politicians who are operating that constitution. With that in mind, I believe that we can now see the way ahead fairly clearly on this issue.[32]

Conservatives are against any tinkering with the Union precisely because they are conservatives. As Iain Hutchison pointed out, the Scottish Tories did not modernize to the same extent as their southern counterparts in post-war era and still retained an aristocratic and tweedy persona well into the 1960s.[33] In other words, Conservatism, rather than unionism, explains the largest part of traditional Tory hostility to devolution. As will be discussed later in this chapter, there is a danger of retrospectively enhancing the idea of unionism in the past in order to accommodate the contemporary paradigm of seeing Scottish politics exclusively through the constitutional prism. Or to put it more crudely, we are in danger of throwing out the Scottish Tory baby with the Scottish Unionist bath water.

For parties on the left and in the centre, the ideological position is much more complex. Devolution can and is presented as a mechanism for a more equitable dispersal of political power among the population and a way of positing greater democratic accountability and checking the growth of centralized state authority. It brings government closer to the people and has all the hallmarks normally associated with liberalism and progressivism. In the Liberal Party, this aspect of decentralization of power is evidenced by the long-standing commitment to federalism.[34] In the Labour Party, there has been a commitment to devolution through supporting the power of local government against the encroachments of central government, and this formed one of the major set-piece battles against Thatcherite reforms in the 1980s, especially the attack on Labour run councils in London and Liverpool.[35] Because many nationalists have supported the creation of a devolved Scottish parliament as a stepping stone strategy to independence and because devolution begins the process of building up a state infrastructure, there has been an understandable scepticism as to using this as a preventative measure for independence, irrespective of any potential benefits in terms of bringing the decision making closer to the people. In more recent times, this debate has been most clearly articulated in the Labour Party where sceptics in the 1970s warned that devolution would act as the superhighway to independence, and once established, a train of constitutional momentum would become unstoppable.[36] This argument that constitutional 'appeasement' would simply whet the appetite of nationalism has a long pedigree and was the main argument used against proponents of home rule. As was spotted by Conservative critics in the 1980s, the espousal of devolution, rather than home rule, was a way of trying to distance the policy from its association with nationalism and national identity. Malcolm Rifkind, the secretary of state for Scotland, chided his Labour opposition:

> There have been calls for home rule, demands for Parliaments and requests for a Prime Minister of the territories concerned. Perhaps we have given insufficient consideration during the past 10 years to why the Labour party has steered clear of such terminology. There have been no references to home rule, only adherence to a much more clinical and sterile term – devolution – which is hardly likely to set alight any great passion or interest in such a mundane approach to the problems of government. There have been no calls for a Scottish Parliament, merely for an assembly, which, by definition, has reduced relevance and significance. Most important, the executive head of the assembly to which the Labour party refers, is to be called not a Prime Minister, Premier or Chief Minister, but First Secretary – a magnificent title, normally more relevant to a senior official in a trade union or a senior official in the central committee of the Soviet Communist party … The Labour party's reluctance to use the terminology that one usually associates with a genuine campaign for home rule is of great significance. The reason is quite simple. Opposition Members know perfectly well that the terminology which refers to home rule, to Parliaments and to Prime Ministers is the language of nationalism. They are conscious of the fact that they are opening a Pandora's box which they believe, by their addiction to a sterile indifferent terminology, they will somehow be able to conceal. There is a basic and fundamental inconsistency between the Labour party's claim to speak for the Scottish people, and claiming that they deserve a legislature of their own, and its refusal to use the terms usually associated with such a political philosophy.[37]

While there was a wariness about the 'national' dimension in promoting devolution and the creation of a Scottish assembly or parliament because of the danger of stoking up political nationalism, at the same time, there was a recognition that Scottish sentiment was increasingly politicized and that it had to be accommodated.

With the emergence of the SNP as a political force in the 1970s, such points of principle relating to democratic accountability and decision making were put aside and devolution was largely endorsed first and foremost as a way of halting the nationalist juggernaut. Shorn of ideology or principle, a pragmatic reason for supporting devolution in the Labour Party was that it would offer a safer constitutional option to the electorate that would help undermine the electoral progress of the SNP, and it would also acknowledge the importance of Scottish national sentiment. There was a catch-22 with the engagement with devolution in that by explicitly acknowledging the legitimacy of Scottish national sentiment as a political force by saying that the Scots should have the right to a government best suited to their needs, it offered no logical reason why the same argument could not be made for independence, the very policy it was supposed to stop. Having said that from a purely theoretical perspective, devolution does have the potential to form the most significant bulwark to independence as it can be presented as a compromise that combines the best of both constitutional worlds: greater self-government without the attendant disruption and dangers of separation. Indeed, the key argument made by devolutionists in the 1980s and 1990s was that a failure to offer some form of devolution would only encourage support for independence and that the biggest danger to the Union came from those who sought to preserve it without reforming it. From the historian's perspective, it is too early to judge whether devolution will kill nationalism stone dead or whether it is the superhighway to independence, but it certainly looks like a policy that was 'damned if you do, damned if you don't'.

Indeed, historically speaking, a central argument frequently used by supporters of devolution was that it would make the British state more effective as its political process was overburdened at Westminster. This was especially the case in the late nineteenth and early twentieth centuries, and this Brito-centric approach was conditioned by the need to calm fears that it would stoke the embers of separation in Ireland by arguing that the principles relating to self-government should be applied across the United Kingdom. In this way, it could be argued that the Irish were not being given special treatment. Rather it was a wider reform of the role of the state and its administration, and this debate took place at a time when the functions and activities of government were increasing.[38] The idea that devolution would help to modernize the British state tied in with wider notion of 'national efficiency' in the Edwardian era.[39] Dealing with a wide spectrum of issues that ranged from the trivial to the vital, from the regional to the national and from the private hobby horses of individual MPs to issues of international magnitude meant that parliament was a busy place with sittings that would last well into the night. It was not a model of effective government, especially as the demands on its time were growing rapidly and the range of its responsibilities were increasing. It was argued that insufficient time was spent on important matters of state because of what was described as 'parliamentary congestion'.[40] Devolution would disperse decision making on minor issues out into the regions, and this would allow the government in London more time to focus on the big issues of the day and make for more effective government. In the late nineteenth and early twentieth centuries, parliamentary congestion was cited by devolutionists as the main reason to disperse political power as it would benefit both central government and the geographical fringes which were not accorded enough political priority. Numerous examples were cited to show how ineffective the system was and one example was the Dundee Docks Extension Scheme which was tabled as a private member's bill and regarded as of vital local importance; it was delayed time and time again because insufficient time was allowed for parliament to vote it through. There was a substantial litany of cases of parliamentary congestion and legislative neglect and delay. According to Scottish home rule activists in the period after the First World War:

> In the ten years 1900 to 1910 selected as a representative decade in pre-war times, the number of non-financial Government Bills passed by the Commons was 328. These occupied 483 days of parliamentary time, but no fewer than 207 of these days were devoted to the ten principal bills, including the Education Bill of 1902, the Licensing Bill of 1908, and the Old Age Pensions Bill of 1908, The other Government measures were passed in 276 days. Some were doubtless little more than formal, and most probably aroused little opposition; but when all allowances are made, these Bills received an absurdly inadequate amount of consideration. Most of them slipped through in the small hours of the morning or during the slackness of the weekend. These facts show that the House of Commons cannot give adequate consideration of the legislation necessary for all the nations of the United Kingdom, separately and conjointly.[41]

The consequence of congestion was that legislation was often delayed or dropped. Large sums of money were spent by the government without a vote or proper scrutiny, all because there was insufficient time. The lottery of the private member's bill meant that local important issues were often decided more by luck than design. So although there was always a suspicion that devolution was a mechanism that might advance the cause of Scottish nationalism, there was also a compelling argument that it could help modernize the archaic British parliamentary process. Devolution or home rule has this in-built schizophrenic quality in which opponents and proponents can argue that it can either progress or retard independence and strengthen or undo the unity of the British state. Because of its Janus-like quality, it has had supporters and detractors in all the political parties, but because it could theoretically lead to drastically different outcomes, it was not a policy that fitted with a large swathe of middle-ground political opinion, and, indeed, at a time of 'consensus' politics, it was absent from the run-of-the-mill political discourse.[42] It may be significant that devolution emerged as an issue in British politics just as the post-war consensus was breaking down in the 1970s.[43]

The schizophrenic dimension of devolution was further reinforced by suspicions from the nationalist side. It was an ingrained assumption among many nationalists that devolution was primarily a political ploy designed to thwart not just independence but any form of self-government. Because devolution was a reorganization of the British state, it was argued, it would require the blessing and approval of the British government. It was an article of faith among many nationalists that Westminster would not countenance any constitutional change that would weaken its power, and for some such as Roland Muirhead, it even meant that should the SNP win all the parliamentary seats, change would still not be forthcoming.[44] As we have seen, Scottish home rule could be tied into a wider scheme of devolution that would be dependent on its implementation on a wider acceptance of regional government throughout England, and this was unlikely to happen. It was a frequent jest of Conservatives that both English Liberals and Labour MPs were not particularly enthused about the scheme because as one Scottish Tory pointed out:

> I was asking why it is Radical Members for England are not bringing forward a measure of this kind. Everybody knows that they do not bring in a measure to establish a Parliament of this kind because they know that in that Parliament their party would be impotent. As a matter of fact, England is Conservative or Unionist, and at the present moment the English Unionist Members are in a very considerable majority in this House.[45]

After all, this was used to stymie Irish home rule. Winston Churchill announced his unlikely conversion to home rule all round, as federalism was described, in Dundee with emphasis on different parts of the United Kingdom having their own parliaments. The problem in Ireland would be solved by either having a separate parliament for Ulster or, as was sometimes suggested, bringing Northern Ireland under the jurisdiction of Edinburgh.[46] The premise underlying this scheme of home rule all round was that it had to be implemented in all parts simultaneously which meant that it was unlikely ever to happen given that there was little appetite for English regional government. This meant that Liberal sceptics of Irish home rule could sign up to the plan and claim that they supported the project, safe in the knowledge that it was unlikely to be delivered. The same argument could also be made about the Labour Party when it was in power. Furthermore, the fate of the Irish home rule party graphically illustrated the impotence of Irish home rulers working within the British parliamentary system because they were dependent on English members to ensure a majority, which never transpired.

The promise of home rule was seen by a fairly consistent sceptical wing of the Scottish nationalist movement as a means of diffusing the nationalist impulse by getting Scots to commit to a scheme which had no prospect of being delivered. Certainly, there was considerable evidence that could be cited to prove that Westminster would not deliver, as Scottish home rule bills failed to be enacted in 1914, 1920, 1924 and 1927. The Labour government of 1945–51 failed to enact a bill in spite of the fact it was on the Scottish Labour manifesto. Furthermore, in spite of the endeavours of the Scottish National Convention to mobilize public support in the form of a petition of about two million, attitudes had hardened against both devolution and home rulers who were bandied together with the SNP. According to Arthur Woodburn, the Scottish secretary of state, it was a charlatan movement that was disruptive and destructive, and he hinted that it was a quasi-terrorist organization:

> The point I am making is that the people I am describing were at that Convention; everyone I have been describing is a leader of a particular section of that Convention, and when the Press refer to these heterogeneous elements I am

merely pointing out to innocent people the danger of being wrapped up in a movement which may take them along roads over which they have no desire to travel. In the present world situation, it is essential that this country should speak in the councils of the nations with one voice, and that Parliament should give no encouragement to the suggestion that there is any intention on the part of Scotland to do other than stand together with England and Wales in one of the greatest democratic partnerships the world has ever seen.[47]

A Tory flirtation in 1967, the so-called Declaration of Perth came to nought, as did Labour's attempts in the period 1974–79.[48] Although devolution was finally enacted in 1997, it is worth remembering that for the century preceding it, the majority of Scottish MPs for the majority of the time were in favour of it.[49] So it was easy to see why a number of nationalists believed it was a stalling device.

As devolution was a modification or readjustment in terms of the relationship with central government, it was therefore dependent on parliamentary approval and the consent of the major British political parties. For many nationalists, devolution had no prospect of success because it could not overcome the in-built English majorities in the established political parties. A central aspect of both the Scottish and Irish nationalist perspective held that because home rule would ultimately lead to independence, this would not be in the interests of England to support it because it would denude them of the resources of both respective nations. Although Scottish nationalists had an ambivalent relationship with the idea that Scotland was a colony, this basic premise shows that, intellectually at least, there was a form of acceptance that the relationship was colonial, otherwise there could be no reason for arguing that the English political elite would see devolution and independence as being against their interests. It was this complete lack of faith in the established British parties' commitment to devolution that led a significant number of home rulers to join the independent national party, primarily as a means to demonstrate to the other parties that home rule or some form of self-government was electorally popular. So for a number of early members of the National Party, the organization was seen primarily as a catalyst and the creation of a Scottish parliament would still largely be delivered by the British parties.[50] Others took the opposite view and the extent of nationalist distrust of Westminster can be illustrated by quoting from the SNP's post-war constitutional policy:

> On the election to the British Parliament of a majority of Scottish National members from Scotland, a Scottish Constituent Assembly shall be summoned either a) in virtue of an Act of Parliament passed by the agreement of the English members or b) failing such an agreement, by the Scottish National members acting in terms of the authority conferred upon them by the Scottish electorate.[51]

The belief that the British parties would take home rule seriously only if they faced an electoral challenge that would cost them votes acted as an ideological glue that helped to unite those who were in favour of independence, those who were home rulers, those who have no faith in the British political parties and those who believed that the British parties would deliver if they had an incentive.[52]

Self-government

The conflation between those who wanted devolution and those who wanted independence can also be explained by historical context. The modern nationalist movement emerged in the interwar period, and it is worth remembering that for many who had lived through the era of the Irish Question in British politics, the label 'nationalists' was frequently applied to and used by Irish home rulers.[53] One of the major reasons why, historically, there was such an overlap between devolutionists and nationalists is that probably up until the 1950s the difference between them was not that clear cut. When Scottish home rule emerged as an issue in the wake of the Irish Question in the 1880s, it was invariably set within the context of the British Empire. And it is worth keeping in mind that although the Irish Free State came into existence in 1922, there was still an 'imperial' dimension in that Eire was a member of the Commonwealth and the king was still head of state and the British or English national anthem still had an official status.[54] The conflict with Ireland was something that interwar Scottish nationalists wanted to play down for obvious reasons and quoted with approval the statement by Senator Sir John Keane, a director of the Bank of Ireland who claimed that there 'has emerged a new and different loyalty – a loyalty not to Westminster or to British Rule, but to the larger conception of King and Commonwealth'.[55] In the interwar era, devolution or federalism was the dominant mode of government in the white settler colonies, and there was an expectation that if this was good enough for the dominions, then it ought to be applied in a domestic context in the British islands. Consequently, many of the main arguments that were made to justify the creation of a Scottish parliament were framed as a way of strengthening and reinforcing the empire.[56] As we have already mentioned, it would make government more efficient by separating the domestic from the imperial and allow the parliament in London more time to deal with international issues. The Duke of Montrose quoted with approval the words of Britain's foremost pre-war imperial advocate Joseph Chamberlain: 'Get rid of everything in Parliament which is not absolutely essential to the security and integrity of the Empire. It is only in this way that we can relieve our over-burdened Parliament of work which prevents it from giving due attention to Imperial affairs.'[57] Montrose, as a moderate devolutionist, placed most emphasis on devolution or self-government as something which would strengthen the unity of the United Kingdom because 'out of plurality will come a greater unity than ever before, and the freedom for self-expression will be in keeping with the spirit which has proved so successful and binding throughout the whole British Empire'.[58]

Others, however, saw the same process as leading in an entirely different direction because self-government was seen as a process in which local parliaments evolved to take on more powers and responsibilities as was demonstrated by the experience of the dominions.[59] So although the terms 'self-government' and 'home rule' were fairly nebulous concepts, they did fit into an established intellectual context that gave them more meaning than might be apparent from our own contemporary perspective. In the aftermath of the First World War, for example, home rulers believed that devolution would have meant that Scotland would have been represented at the Versailles Peace summit in 1919.⁶⁰ This was because the dominion nations of the empire were represented and the assumption was that home rule was a similar process as to what had happened in the 'white' colonies which would eventually culminate in independence. Although the term 'independence' was hardly ever used, 'self-government' was the more common way of expressing a process for the greater accumulation of constitutional and political power. In terms of what self-government meant in the dominion context, we would understand that today as being a form of statehood, although there were bonds of sentiment and a constitutional role for the monarchy.⁶¹ It is worth pointing out because it has largely been forgotten that the origins of the mindset and mental world of Scottish independence was very much conditioned by the experience of the British Empire, and a lot of the concepts and terminology carried on into the post-imperial age. In the 1950s or even 1960s, the overwhelming example of independent states that could act as an inspiration or template for the Scottish national movement would be places like New Zealand or Canada.⁶² After the fall of the Berlin Wall, the intellectual focus has become more Eurocentric and places like Estonia and Slovenia are now more likely to be cited as examples of successful independent states.

The term 'self-government' could be understood as devolution or independence, although for many in the period before the Second World War they were one and the same. The history of the 'white dominions' showed that there was a gradual assumption of greater powers that ended with full control of foreign policy in the Statute of Westminster in 1931 which was ratified in the Ottawa Agreement of 1932.⁶³ Although ostensibly independent countries, the 'white dominions' clearly identified themselves as belonging to the 'British group of nations', and although not coming to much, there were constant efforts to create formal economic trading relationships with the empire in the 1930s in response to the Great Depression.⁶⁴ This British world view was evident in the policy of the SNP when it was created in 1934 which stated that its primary objective was 'independence within the British Group of Nations'.⁶⁵ In early home rule tracts, the example of the dominions was one that was frequently cited to show that self-government did not lead to the disintegration of the British world, and, indeed, many presented this as an inevitable trend that would eventually reach the mother nations:

> So far as its white population is concerned, the British Empire is a Home Rule Empire. The great White Dominions enjoy self-government in such large measure to make them rather sister than daughter nations and yet they are all loyal members of the Empire. They are even separately represented on the Assembly of the League of Nations and determine their own foreign policy.⁶⁶

Certainly in the period after the First World War, the idea of self-government or home rule could be construed as something which would eventually lead to statehood and complete independence as we would understand it. Hence the Conservative opposition to Irish home rule, but also in the 1930s, there were die-hard opponents of the Government of India Bill in 1935 because it created a federal system of government with some degree of autonomy.⁶⁷ When the National Party of Scotland was in the process of being created, there was considerable debate as to the terminology to be used, and the option of 'independence within the British group of nations' was chosen not just because it could encompass traditional home rulers but also because it fitted with an established schemata that many could relate to. Having said that, it was also made very clear in the discussions that sovereignty should reside with the Scottish parliament in relation to international affairs. As Robert Muirhead argued in 1934:

> The central principle of the policy of the National Party of Scotland is that the future Scottish Parliament should have the final decision on all Scottish questions, including Scotland's action in regard to questions affecting other countries – in fact the Scots National Parliament must be sovereign and independent. This does not imply separation from England or the reverse.[68]

Given the generally accepted idea that the Scots had the right to self-determination because they were a recognized nation, Muirhead's argument was that constitutional issues should be decided by the people through the Scottish parliament. In many respects, this was a way to sidestep the issue of devolution or independence by arguing that only the future parliament could decide.

By setting the argument for home rule within the context of the empire and using the example of the 'white dominions', it was possible to present the issue in a familiar and non-threatening context and, indeed, argue that it was both a progressive and natural development that was a common feature in the 'British' world. As was frequently asked, why should the Scots not have the same rights and privileges as the daughter nations, especially given their role in bringing them to maturity and nationhood?

> Scotland has never been a mere province of England. She has made her independent contribution to the Commonwealth of Free Nations which are called the British Empire. That Empire has been built with the blood and brains of Scotsman no less than Englishmen.[69]

While there was obviously an expedient reason for home rulers and nationalists to keep the issue of devolution or independence ambivalent in order to maximize support from both camps, when looked at in its historical context, the dichotomy is not necessarily so obvious as there was a considerable overlap in terms of meaning. The setting of the issue of home rule within the framework of the British Empire, which was unavoidable because of when the movement emerged in the interwar era, has meant that much of the intellectual baggage was carried forward into more modern times without it necessarily being apparent to most observers. For many in the period up to the 1960s, it would not be unreasonable to assume that home rule would begin a process that would inevitably lead to independence as the term 'self-government' largely implied that it was the beginning of a political evolution that had led to statehood in the British dominions. And it is worth pointing out that Scottish society in the post-war era witnessed extensive emigration to the 'white Commonwealth' and kept these 'new' nations in the public eye.[70] All of which brings us to a partial revision to the conventional understanding of the historic division in the national movement between fundamentalists and moderates. The tendency to see this as a split based on ideology surrounding devolution or independence overlooks the extent to which it was a division over strategy. For many, a devolved parliament was a necessary precursor to independence in the sense that it was pointless trying to walk before learning to crawl. In short the division between those in favour of home rule and independence may not appear as great as it is sometimes presented in the sense that a devolved Scottish parliament could act as a stepping stone to independence, but if not, that would be something that would be decided by the Scottish people expressed through their parliament, the point being that it would be their sovereign right to choose. A more nuanced examination of the interplay between ideology and strategy helps to explain some of the seemingly contradictory positions that were held at times by members of the movement ranging from hardliners such as Douglas Young, moderates such as John MacCormick and committed activists such as Isobel Lindsay.[71]

The issue of the relationship between home rule or devolution and independence has a chequered history in British politics and the question of whether or not the former was simply a staging post to the latter had been a recurrent theme, although as we have seen, when understood in the context of the early and mid-twentieth century this is not as incongruous as it seems. Parnell's statement that 'no man has the right to fix the boundary to the march of a nation. No man has the right to say his country thus far shalt thou go and no further' was, and has been, subject to a variety of interpretative examinations with many concluding that his view was that Ireland would not stop with devolution but go all the way towards independence.[72] More often than not, this has been the principal argument against forms of devolution, not that there is a problem with devolution itself but that when it is combined with notions of nationhood it will lead to independence. Not surprisingly, many nationalists have supported devolution precisely because it was seen as the first step on the road to independence. For practical purposes, however, this has created an intellectual conundrum. For nationalists who endorse the 'stepping stone' approach to independence and advocate as many powers as possible under a devolution settlement, they face the key Unionists argument against further devolution which is that it will be used precisely for the purpose of taking a step nearer independence. Against this, there is no intellectually honest response. Furthermore, nationalist gradualists also have to make an alliance with committed devolutionists whose principal argument has been that some form of self-government is the best way to stymie the march to independence, and, indeed, they have often argued that the failure to enact some form of devolution would be the best support for the cause of independence. This was the argument that emerged in the 1980s when the Conservative Party's uncompromising attitude to home rule, it was claimed, would end up producing the exact opposite effect and increase the popular demand for independence. Historically, what has emerged is a rather awkward alliance of convenience between nationalists and devolutionists who while both wanting the same thing, often want it for different purposes. Furthermore, in the post-empire era, the differences between devolution and independence have become sharper and the intellectual overlap has been much reduced. Another mundane point, but one worth emphasizing, in the period after the Second World War social expectation of the state and hence the role of government has greatly expanded in a way that would not have been envisioned by the early devolutionists and home rulers. The increasing functions of government and the state have been a complicating factor in this debate, and a central argument against home rule and independence that emerged from the 1930s in response to the economic consequences of the Great Depression was that economies of scale are greater the larger and more centralized the state is. The advent of Keynesian economics in the period after the Second World War consolidated this orthodoxy.[73]

The tactical alliance between those who want independence and those who want devolution has meant that nationalists have not focused much attention on the philosophical underpinnings of devolution and have tended to couch support for it within a broader framework of greater democracy and accountability. As was mentioned earlier in Chapter 3, by committing and actively engaging with the devolution process, the nationalist movement has conferred a degree of legitimacy on the British state, and while the devolutionary process in the imperial context led to independence where geographical distance played a large part, it is not necessarily the case that the stepping stone route is guaranteed, especially when the intellectual orthodoxy was that devolution would hold back the tide of nationalism, more so when the policy became associated with creating an anti-independence buffer. With the advent of the Scottish parliament, devolutionists are now more clearly seen as veering towards unionism than, as was previously assumed, nationalism. Furthermore, it would appear that the devolutionary line in the sand is much more rigid than nationalists had previously assumed.[74]

Unionism

Just as devolution has proved to be an intellectual hurdle for the nationalist movement to overcome, so has unionism. Most nationalist movements elsewhere have not had to face a unionist challenge; they may have experienced an assimilationist movement or foreign force, but the problem the nationalist movement in Scotland has to deal with is that the main source of its opposition comes from within Scotland, not without, and the key ideology that gives legitimacy to the British state has a seductive narrative that permits the existence of nationhood without statehood.[75] William Mitchell Ramsay, the Regius Professor of Humanity (Latin) at Aberdeen University, in the Romanes Lectures of 1913 at Oxford gave a clear and articulate account of the Anglo-Scottish Union and its relationship with nationalism and national identity. Ramsay set out what in essence could be described as the conventional thinking that underlay Scottish unionism as a political philosophy. Although there was a tendency to see historical development in a deterministic way that was typical of the Whig school of history at the time in which the greater absorbed the smaller, Ramsay was lecturing on Dante's notion of the wise and just monarch that would bring order and stability and how this laid the foundations for an empire which would guarantee peace. He used the Scottish case to illustrate the ways in which mature nationalism or nationality could be accommodated to a higher ideal. It is worth quoting at length:

> For my own part, I should refuse to regard as evil a power [nationalism] which has been steadily growing through modern history. It is a great power, which may

be turned (like every vast power) to evil or to good purposes; but to condemn it as evil is to declare that the tide of European development has been for a long time setting steadily towards evil. To pronounce such a condemnation no one is obliged, who remembers that the peace which is really good is a positive power, the force of order, and not a mere negative condition. It is the orderly balance of active and powerful forces ... I propose to take an example from history, one with which I have some small opportunity of becoming familiar, because it has entered into and made my character from infancy. I mean the union of the two warring parts of Scotland with each other, and the union of England and Scotland in one country: two processes which may be taken together, and which are, perhaps, not always rightly understood ... There were no insuperable difficulties to be overcome in this union, as events have shown; and yet there were considerable difficulties. There were very diverse elements to be fused in one nation, the Gaelic, the Briton, the Saxon, and the Norse, which presented at least two very diverse types – types which remain as diverse to the present day ... Circumstances in the thirteenth century were bringing about the union of England and Lowland Scotland gradually and naturally. The process was slow, but inevitable. It was merely accidental that Lowland Scotland was severed from England: there is on the whole probably less natural racial diversity between Lowland Scotland and North England than there is between North and South England, and certainly far less diversity than exists between the Gaelic Highlands and the mixed Lowland population of Scotland. The mutual hatred and antipathy between Highlands and Lowlands was exceedingly strong, and persisted to a comparatively recent time ... In the thirteenth century it seemed likely that Lowland Scotland would go with England, and that Oxford would continue in increasing degree to be the University of the Scots.

This was not to be, however, because Edward I of England set his sights upon conquering Scotland and that helped to reinforce Scottish national identity.

> But a great king, one of the greatest in many respects that ever sat on the English throne, saw clearly the process which was going on, and took steps to accelerate it by diplomacy, by dynastic arrangements, and finally by war. The result was that the union was postponed for centuries. Real national union cannot be won by war and compulsion; the few apparent exceptions are only apparent, and serve to define more clearly the real nature of the process ... Yet the First Edward was, in a sense and to a certain degree, right. I do not mean that he would have defined his position and his motives in the same way as we might – but, in the wider view of history, what he was attempting was to weld the diverse peoples into a strong united nation. The attempt was premature. The tough intractable nature of the northern races was not ready for the process of union. They could not accept the same ideals and the same sentiments that ruled in the south. Those who successfully opposed the English king were struggling to preserve a nationality, which the 'Hammer of the Scots' would have probably annihilated, rather than developed; and the nation would have been united only at the sacrifice of one stubborn and therefore useful element. The separatists and 'patriots' who resisted him and overcame his son

were narrower in their aims, while he had the Imperial outlook. Yet, after all, a true instinct recognizes in their policy the creation of the Scottish nationality, and reverences them as having contributed to the making of a greater Britain ... In 1603 the process was nominally completed; but the unity that resulted was more dynastic than real: there was no common feeling or patriotism. The process was made possible by religious causes: the forces of Protestantism were strong enough to compel a union of the two kingdoms, and the English hatred felt for the Catholic countries carried wide support even among the English Catholics. But religion has never had such a hold on men of Western Europe as to make men into a nation and to dominate their hearts and overbear the other causes that work on them. The two peoples remained in heart and ideals almost as diverse as before. Nor did the closer union through the amalgamation of the Parliaments in 1707 produce a real unity. It was a political device; but it did not remould the hearts of men.

For Ramsay, history and institutional structures are only part of the story and the real Union is one of the mind and the ideas that sustain it.

I venture to think that the unity of England and Scotland is the work of Walter Scott ... who touched the heart of both countries, and made each appreciate the excellences of the other. The real union is a matter of idea, of thought, of common mental inheritance and occupation, of mutual appreciation and respect ... The point at which I am aiming is to answer the question, whether national idiosyncrasy and national pride are necessarily hostile to the union of two or more distinct races. Speaking for my own side, I should be surprised to learn that as a race the Scots are less proud of their nationality and its heroes, or less attached to their historical memories, than they ever were at any period in the past. I believe they are only more intensely Scottish, as a rule, than they formerly were ... The truth is this. The more intense is the spirit of nationalism in its highest and best form, the more powerful is the appreciation of the wider Imperial patriotism. In the fostering of that Imperial patriotism the worst possible course would be to discourage and try to extirpate the national idiosyncrasies, and to aim at a dead level of universal similarity to one general type. The truest Scotsman, the most characteristic and typical Englishman, is the best and most patriotic citizen of the Empire. Each may find it difficult to appreciate the other. If I may venture to quote my own experience, the most remarkable nature, the one which I have found it hardest to gauge or to comprehend, the one which oftenest impresses me with its unsuspected and unfathomed depths, is not that of any foreign, nor even Oriental nation, but the Englishman. And they say that the Englishman can never learn to appreciate the music of the Scottish bagpipes, except in a few cases where he has heard it in the last and most critical moment of a long and hard-fought battle. The story is familiar to all of the old Scot who, after forty-five years of a business life in London, confided sadly yet appreciatively to a young compatriot that it took a long time to learn how clever those stupid English are. He learned his lesson, however, and his respect grew ... If we argue from the particular case which has been quoted to the general law, nationalism is good when it can be combined with a sense of a higher unity; and the first condition of such combination is that the two or more diverse nationalities can share certain sufficing aims and ideals, and can respect and admire each other, remaining conscious of their diverse individuality, regarding the idiosyncrasies of the other with perhaps a humorous but not an unkindly eye, no one nationality seeking to compel the others into an unwilling similarity with itself. Such compulsion may sometimes succeed in annihilating the weaker nationality; but it can never produce a unity in which each member profits by the strength of the other, and finds its complement in the other.[76]

In a clear and concise way, Ramsay set out the case that the Union did not diminish Scottish nationality and clearly articulated the idea that it was a partnership that brought out the best in both the Scots and the English. There was no coercion, no endeavour to eradicate Scotland or absorb its nationality and, furthermore, belief in the Scottish nation as a nation actually increased and promoted patriotism. In many ways, this can be seen as an encapsulated form of the essence of Scottish unionism before the First World War.

In recent times, historians have become more aware of the force of unionism in relation to the development of Scottish national identity and for some a form of 'unionist nationalism' has been used to explain why nationalism, in the conventional sense, was held at bay. Put simply, unionist nationalism encourages a duel identity in which Scots can be both Scottish and British, and furthermore, these national identities reinforce one another. In most cases of nationalism in another European countries there is a jealous exclusivity. Take, for example, the case of Germany and Russia in relation to being Polish. The notion of a German Pole or a Russian Pole would seem like a contradiction as the essence of being Polish was to escape from the clutches of both German and Russian domination. Similarly, the 'West Briton' of Ireland showed that the symbiosis of British and Irish was not one easily achievable and in the protestant enclaves in the north, the British identity was based on denying any relationship with being Irish.[77] The fact that for most of the period since the Union the Scots have been comfortable with both a British and a Scottish identity has meant that Scottish nationalists have had a difficult ideological obstacle in that there was no foreigner holding back independence, nor an alien occupation binding them in the British state and no obvious 'other' to blame for their political plight. Although a number of scholars have noted the peculiarities of the Scottish case, it is worth emphasizing that it does not fit easily with the standard model of European independence movements of the nineteenth and twentieth centuries.[78]

Having said all this, there are a number of issues that need to be addressed before progressing with the discussion. The first and most obvious one is terminology. As Alastair Raffe noted, there is a looseness about the terms used when discussing both nationalism and unionism, and while etymological exactitude can stifle debate, the fact remains that unionism and nationalism are opposing political creeds so a 'unionist nationalist' is a contradiction in terms.[79] A nationalism that does not seek statehood is not a nationalism as most people would understand it. There may be similar characteristics to nationalism such as pride in Scotland, Scottish history, Scottish people and Scottish achievements, and it may even display a degree of chauvinism in thinking that Scots are the best people in the world. Yet, if we apply the same characteristics to, say, people from Yorkshire, we would not describe that as nationalism because Yorkshire is not a nation. The correct term would be 'localism', and the fact that Scotland is a nation somehow allows the same characteristics to be portrayed as nationalism, even though the most cardinal aspect of nationalism – the acquisition of statehood – is missing. This must surely make us pause for thought to question whether such a description is appropriate. In one respect, if we change the descriptive term from 'unionist nationalism' to 'unionist localism', we can legitimately ask if this alters the paradigm and if it holds up in terms of historical analysis. If it does, then semantically it would make more sense to use this terminology. Also, it chimes in with a key element in Conservative political thought in Britain which stresses the importance of locality.[80] That said, we can see why unionism is a powerful force in Scotland because it has the ability to offer an alternative narrative of nationhood to the traditional one told by nationalists in which the destination ends with independence and statehood. Furthermore, if Unionists believe that their political philosophy is one based on a historic union between two nations, it is difficult to gainsay this. Caustically, we might describe it as nationality without responsibility.

One thing that we must be aware of is the danger of imposing on the past our own contemporary ideologies. The attraction of stretching ideas and beliefs into the past is that the longer they have existed, the greater the legitimacy that can be conferred upon them. There has been a tendency of late to stretch the idea of the Anglo-Scottish Union, and hence, unionism, back to John Mair, the Scottish philosopher and his publication of *History of Greater Britain* in 1521.[81] Contemporary political ideas such as unionism and nationalism simply have no resonance in the intellectual word of the sixteenth century, and it would be a bit like claiming that Dante and his idea of 'universal monarchy' was the originator of the European Union.[82] Ideas can only really be understood in the context of their own time and to associate them with events in the future is clearly anachronistic. In part, the 'Pocockian turn' in early modern history which has drawn attention to the multinational dimension in the Stuart era has arguably, if unintentionally, led to a sort of tramlining in which the British state becomes a sort of historical inevitability, and thus anything associated with this has its historical significance magnified, often at the expense of a broader European perspective. After all, James VI was the wisest fool in Christendom, not just Britain.[83] While the Anglo-Scottish Union has been around for three hundred odd years, the reality is that it has not been served by a consistent political philosophy and the extent to which this could be presented as a coherent ideology, as we shall see, is questionable. It ought to be borne in mind that modern-day unionism is not much older than nationalism and that, as we have seen, its entrance into Scottish politics in the 1880s was based on the Irish and not the Scottish Union. The term 'unionism' is very much missing from Scottish political discourse before this date. The absence of unionism in Scottish political history can be explained by the fact that it is very much a philosophy based on defending the union with England and, as for most of the period since 1707, there has been no threat to the Union and hence no need for unionism to defend it. There is a danger that contemporary concerns have pushed for a post-hoc intellectual construction of a political philosophy in a period where it served no function or need. This point can be illustrated by bearing in mind that many Scots in the nineteenth century were quite happy to use the term 'England' for the name of the state. David Livingstone and Robert Louis Stevenson, for example, described themselves as Englishmen when speaking in an international context.[84] Political leaders from Palmerston to Salisbury regularly described the state as England, even when in Scotland, and this roused no considerable ire.[85] Gladstone in his 'Midlothian Speeches', in spite of his Scottish parents, talked about 'England's role in the world' and even the Scottish aristocrat Lord Rosebery could give a speech to students in Glasgow University and state 'that when I speak of England, I do not mean just these two Islands'.[86] It was not just politicians who described the state as England; most of the Scottish press did the same.[87] So for a big chunk of the nineteenth century it is quite clear that politicians and much of the population in Scotland have no understanding of what we would describe as modern unionism. While at the same time as such statements were being made, it is also possible to find clear articulations of Scottish national identity. One problem with the past is that it is under no obligation to make sense to the present, and clearly Scots in the nineteenth century carried ideas that were mixed together in a way that while seeming contradictory to us today did not trouble people at the time. If unionism emerged as a Scottish political philosophy, it does not make its presence felt arguably until the twentieth century, and probably its main driver, intellectually, was Scottish nationalism. All of which poses the question whether Scottish unionism can exist without Scottish nationalism and vice versa? Does one only make sense and have purpose if it exists with the other because on their own they have no meaning? If this is the case, then both are the products of the early twentieth century.

Another issue to address is that unionism was a clearly formulated political philosophy that set out that Scotland was a nation in its own right and had joined with England to create the British state. Unionism was not *unitarism* and did not advocate for a homogenized British state and accepted that there were differences between Scotland and England and that these should be respected.[88] In essence unionism argued that there was no need for separate political representation to give expression to Scottish nationhood. The original formulation of unionism emerged in relation to Gladstone's conversion to Irish home rule in 1886. It was argued that the Irish as a nation did not need home rule to express their politics and that the existing constitutional relationship should be maintained without change.[89] Edward Carson, the doyen of Irish unionism, was born in Dublin and represented a Dublin constituency.[90] With partition, unionism was increasingly confined to the North and based around ideas of ethnicity in the sense that Ulster Protestants were British and not Irish. Ulster unionism is primarily an ideology that aims to keep Northern Ireland British and unlike its Scottish counterpart does not acknowledge a distinctive Irish dimension.[91] Whereas Scottish unionism stresses that there is no conflict of interest in terms of having both a Scottish and a British identity and, indeed, that they are mutually reinforcing, the same cannot be said for Northern Ireland Unionism and Irish identity, although in recent years there have been endeavours to heighten the sense of a distinctive Ulster identity.[92] That there are very different understandings of unionism suggests, paradoxically, as a British conception, it has no philosophic coherence. 'Unionism' is primarily a Scottish and Ulster construct, and this begs the further question: where is English unionism? While there are, and have always been, English Unionists, there has not been an accompanying ideological or philosophical movement to give intellectual weight to England as a member of a multinational union. The reasons for this are not hard to find. For many, England and Britain were one in the same, and, equally, the sheer numerical dominance and weight of England within the Union meant that it did not require the philosophic props that the minority Irish and Scots needed. In an almost paradoxical way, the British state is held together by the coherence provided by the fact that its largest member accounts for over 80 per cent of its population and that the Scots, Welsh and Northern Irish, no matter the political issues, will always exist in a fundamentally unbalanced Union. The existence of separate Scottish, Ulster and increasingly Welsh unionisms that are different and, apart from a commitment to maintain the British state, do not share much of a similar philosophical underpinning simply adds to the amorphous nature of unionism.[93]

Assimilation?

Furthermore, there has been ambivalent dimension within Scottish unionism that oscillates between unionism in the sense of a union between England and Scotland and an assimilationist vision where both countries are effectively the same. To some extent this has given Scottish unionism a schizophrenic feature, and there were clearly a number of Scottish Unionists who were, to all intents and purposes, Unitarians. For some, Scottish history came to an end in 1707, as expressed by Lord Rosebery at the inauguration of the Scottish History Society in 1886.[94] The Unionist MP for Wigtonshire and Scottish history buff Sir Herbert Maxwell, in his *Robert the Bruce and Scottish Independence*, which went through various editions in the late nineteenth and early twentieth centuries, did not recite the chapter and verse of how Wallace and Bruce preserved Scottish independence which would enable the Scots to freely enter into Union in 1707 but instead took the altogether more pessimistic view that it led to centuries and conflict with England. If King Robert had simply been defeated, none of this misfortune would have happened.[95] Following the Speakers Conference of 1919 on Scottish home rule in the House of Commons, James Kidd, the Unionist MP for Springburn, claimed that Scotland was past the stage of nationality and argued that it had been 'absorbed' into the larger political unit. His statement is worth quoting to show how far removed it was from a notion of the union as based on a partnership:

> Home Rule at this stage of our progress sets out deliberately to cultivate the idea of nationality. Devolution, on the other hand, starts on the presupposition that the nation has been absorbed in the larger political unit. That is challenged by the claims of a spurious nationality. [HON. MEMBERS: 'How spurious?'] Spurious in the sense that you are trying to resuscitate that which has grown into something larger … Home Rule and Nationalist feeling has been warmed up for the last few years by the somewhat indiscriminate talk about the rights of little nations. I hope I shall have the assent of the House to the statement that the rights of little nations, and the exercise of those rights, must always be dependent upon

two considerations. The exercise must be consistent with the legitimate interests of the larger political unit, and, secondly, and this is much the more serious consideration, the exercise of those rights must always be subject to the higher law, which, in order to secure the better life of all mankind, compels co-operation. I hope I am fair in putting these limits to the rights of little nations … Scotland, perhaps, is the very best example the world can afford of the continuous growth of political development … Nationhood is merely a stage in the progress of a people. Some have not reached it, some have passed it. Ireland, on her own confession, has reached a stage between the two. To talk of the rights of small nations when you speak of the Balkans, and then to use the same phrase-in relation to Scotland, is to go very near to offering an insult to the people of Scotland. Scotland has passed the stage of nationhood. Her nationhood has been absorbed-in a wider area.[96]

A question for future historians to address is the extent to which the First World War and the creation of the Irish Free State not only hardened Scottish unionism against any constitutional change but also, and perhaps inadvertently, created an inbuilt suspicion of Scottish sentiment and ideas of Scottish nationality. According to Noel Skelton, who first used the term 'property owning democracy',[97] Scottish national sentiment was a beast best left undisturbed:

It is my firm conviction that if you were to set Scotland on the path of separation, however tentative and hesitating were the steps taken to begin with, you would be rousing ancient fires, you would be touching feelings, you would be putting in motion centrifugal forces which, once set in motion, you could not control; and I believe that, take it long or take it short, if you give up the Union between England and Scotland, you are taking a course of action which leads you to complete separation. In any case, it is not a convenient place for Scotland to stop at, because Scotland is not a Dominion … if you were to rouse these ancient national feelings in Scotland, you would stir forces the strength of which you do not realise. Further I say, and I say with all the force that I can command, there is no halting place in logic, in history or in the genius of a people, once you leave Union, to complete separation. It is well that those who are flirting with these ideas should clearly see that such, at all events, is the probability … It is unnecessary for me to refer to the case of Ireland, which is a special case, but take the case of Norway and Sweden. They were two countries living apparently in complete harmony, but ancient feelings of separate nationality burst out and, for reasons which are very hard for a foreigner to understand, they felt separation was the only course. It was easy enough, and I do not suppose anyone would maintain that Sweden or Norway or the world suffered particularly from Norway becoming a separate Kingdom. But nobody can contemplate with patience the idea of such an event happening within our own shores. The effect upon Scotland, as a Scotsman I hesitate to contemplate, but I say the effect on England would be very serious too, and the effect on the Empire would be extremely serious as well. The House has to recollect that Scotland has played a considerable part in the development of this great Imperial structure and not only that, but I think no Member, not a

> Scotsman, will disagree or think I am blowing the national trumpet when I say that the Scottish people do add a definite flavour and strength to the Imperial centre, namely, the United Kingdom. If you deprived England of the assistance of Scotland in its work and task as the centre of the Empire you would weaken England. I know one's own experience with the peoples of the Dominions has been that they keep a specially warm corner in their hearts for Scotsmen, and I do believe it would be dangerous to the Empire to take any step which would run the risk of breaking up the United Kingdom.[98]

Skelton's central contention was that the experience of the dominions, if applied to the mother nations, would lead to both the disintegration of the British state and therefore the empire because it would lead to a polarization in which Scottish nationality was no longer the unproblematic prop to British identity, but one, like its Irish counterpart, that had the potential to unravel the entire British enterprise. As we shall see, this marked an increasingly schizophrenic phase in the intellectual development of unionism, and one way out of the difficulty of reconciling any potential conflicts was to move from the idea of Union as a partnership to one where Scottish identity was firmly a subset of British identity. This was not a dual national identity but increasingly a singular identity associated with the idea of British nationality in which Scottish identity was only a part. The extensive Conservative involvement in the 'Scotland is British campaign' during the Devolution Referendum in 1979 showed little signs of a nuanced understanding of the meaning of unionism: 'Our purpose is to develop a campaign among Scots emphasizing our common nationhood with the rest of the people of Britain and seeking support in persuading Parliament and Government that the Devolution Bill endangers that common British nationhood and should be withdrawn.'[99] As will be discussed below, the issue of unionism is made more complex by the idea of competing British and Scottish national identities.

The Conservative Party in the immediate period before the First World War was not in a happy place. It had lost three general elections in a row, and it was expected that the Liberal government's abolition of plural voting, in which business owners were given an additional vote for their work's place of residence, would cost the party between thirty and forty seats.[100] The one policy which seemed to offer the Conservative Party hope was the issue of Irish home rule because Ulster resistance could mean that it would have to be imposed on Protestants in Ireland at the point of British bayonets, which, it was believed, the British electorate would not stand for.[101] Needless to say, North of the Border, the party which amalgamated with the Liberal Unionists (Liberals who opposed Irish home rule in 1886 following Gladstone's change in policy) in 1912 to form the Scottish Unionist Party, was equally opposed to the creation of a parliament in Edinburgh. As has been pointed out previously and is obvious from the preceding discussion, unionism was largely about Ireland; however, the Scottish party chairman Sir George Younger issued a memorandum on Scottish home rule in which he pointed out the danger that in the next general election, which was scheduled for 1915, should the Liberals win most Scottish seats, they would claim that they had an electoral mandate.[102] In the two general elections in 1910, the Liberal party won fifty-eight and fifty-seven seats, respectively, out of seventy-two (including the two university seats) and the Liberal hegemony looked unlikely to shift. The memorandum is interesting for the insight that it gives into Scottish unionism as a political philosophy: 'Take up a positive and, if need be, aggressive policy and point to the importance which Scottish national patriotism has played and still must play in the wider patriotism of the British Empire.'[103] What this statement clearly demonstrates is that Scottish national sentiment was a subset of a more important and larger British national sentiment. Clearly it is not regarded as of equal weight. Indeed, according to Younger's argument, it is hard to see what the difference is compared to a strong regional identity. The obvious distinction was that Scotland was once a nation in a way in which English regions were not, but in terms of its function and its place within the wider structure of British identity, it serves the same purpose. Scottish patriotism only has meaning as a prop to British patriotism and has no independent existence. The idea of Scotland as a region was reinforced by the assertion of Sir Henry Craik who claimed that different parts of Scotland had more in common with other parts of England than they had with other parts of Scotland:

> There are hundreds of men who have branches of their business in both towns, and who spend half the week in Manchester and the other half in Glasgow. That is not the case as between Glasgow and Edinburgh. Is there any connection between Aberdeen and the ports on the west coast of Scotland? Will anyone deny that Aberdeen and Newcastle are as closely connected as they possibly could be? Speak to any of the people in Aberdeen, and you will find that any pilot or captain on the trading vessels going from one place to the other is familiar to people in both towns. Is there any close connection between Inverness and Edinburgh?[104]

At the same time, Craik would cite his own and others' sense of Scottish nationality, patriotism and love of country:

> There is nothing I love more than my country. Every tradition of hers, every habit, every foot of her soil is dear. I have steeped myself in her history, and I have even, I am sorry to confess, been tempted to destroy good paper in trying to write something about her history. I am full of that love, and I yield to no man in that.[105]

But it was a vision carefully tailored to only engage with the past, the individual activities of Scots, and had a particular focus on Scots who did not reside in Scotland but had made their mark elsewhere in the world. In short, it was a very British version of Scottish identity.

Big-nation nationalism

One important point to consider regarding unionism that has not received sufficient attention from historians is that it offered Scots the option to buy into aspects of English identity through the medium of the British state. This meant that Scots could abandon the notion of being a small nation and acquire all the trappings and pretentions of belonging to a larger nation and great power. As we have seen, small nations did not have good press in British political discourse during the nineteenth and twentieth centuries.[106] A frequent refrain was one of disdain for the small and, hence, internationally insignificant nations. Sir Henry Craik, Tory MP and historian, asked, 'Do hon. Members think that their country's great name and fame, or that their patriotism, is to be pitted upon the establishment of a little Parliament of 140 people in Edinburgh? Do hon. Members think that their patriotism is to be formed and supported only upon that?'[107] It was frequently claimed that the fact that Scots occupied high positions within the empire, within the British political and legal establishment, and that many Scots had been prime ministers showed not only that the Union worked for individual Scots but it gave them access to positions or power in a state that had global significance, and without the Union, the Scots would be relegated to international insignificance.[108] Furthermore, all the problems identified by home rulers and Scottish nationalists, whatever their legitimacy and merit, were more than adequately compensated by the benefits of belonging to a great power. According to Bob Boothby, 'Prior to 1707, the Scots were a miserable pack of savages ... It was the Union that turned the Scots into an Imperial race.'[109] The option to engage in the full panoply of Great Power status was obviously an aspect that many Scottish unionists relished, but it is not necessarily the case that they did so as members of a small nation in a union with a larger nation, that in reality they saw Britain as a nation and not a composite state made up of different nations. John Buchan, Walter Elliot, James Maxton, Tom Johnston and most Scottish politicians in speeches at Westminster regularly referred to Britain as the nation.[110] In other words, what unionism does is set up a competitor nationalism to Scottish nationalism in which the choice is between big-nation nationalism or small-nation nationalism. This is a factor that has not received much attention from historians or political scientists because, in reality, many of the key tropes expressed by Unionists in terms of British Great Power status, history, institutions and traditions can be understood in terms of national identity and even nationalism.[111]

An intellectual puzzle that has not been addressed, but was pointed out by Scottish nationalists as we shall see below, is: Can nationalism as conventionally understood admit of two distinct loyalties? Does unionism require that Scottish identity be subservient to the wider British identity, and if this is the case, how can this be a partnership? Furthermore, as we have seen and what continued well into the twentieth century and still exists today, this meant regularly turning a blind eye to a conflation in terms of the nation between England and Britain which arguably reached its peak during the Second World War – 'who do you think you are kidding Mr Hitler if you think old England is done' – in spite of constant complaints from the Scottish press.[112] One way of squaring the circle, in an almost literal sense, is to use the idea of 'concentric circles' in which social identities can overlap with one another and thus Scottish identity can co-exist with British identity, but this sidesteps whether this is a 'national' identity, or more precisely two national identities, because the idea is essentially the same as the relationship between regional and national identities. The idea of concentric circles works because the interface of the local, regional, national, territorial or geographic ensures that it always progresses from smaller to bigger, for example, Yorkshire/English/British/European and, therefore, Scottish/British has the same relationship as local and national. To illustrate the problem of using concentric circles in relation to nationality, imagine using the same formula in relation to other aspects of social identity such as class or religion. A working-class/middle-class identity or a Protestant/Catholic identity becomes problematic in way that a working-class Protestant identity or a middle-class Catholic identity does not. In short, the Scottish and British identity can only work because they do not both belong to the same social category.[113]

How nationalists engaged with the idea of unionism and how it fitted within their wider intellectual universe was an important part of their world view. The extent to which unionism was regarded as a legitimate ideology in the sense that it made sense and was a coherent way of expressing a political point of view was something that nationalists would have to engage with. In the interwar era, the extent to which there was a public perception of unionism as a political philosophy which the vast majority of Scots agreed with is problematic. The term was used in a fairly uncritical way and usually as a Scottish descriptor of the Conservative Party without much emphasis placed on the Anglo-Scottish Union. Furthermore, in a bipolar British political system in which political loyalty was largely determined by class, the issue had little significance among the key issues of the day. In the 1930s, the issue of the Union came to the public's attention largely as a consequence of the damage inflicted on the Scottish economy as a result of the Great Depression and a sense that the Scots were suffering disproportionately and that government policy was more favourable to the southeast.[114] For the two main Unionist parties, the economic argument formed the mainstay against any arguments for both home rule and independence. The Conservatives used a form of subsidy argument which argued that the Scots were the net beneficiaries of a fiscal transfer and argued that either a home rule or an independent parliament would have less funds and the consequent economic disruption caused by the economic downturn in the 1930s would be considerably greater. At times, there was a very negative defence of the Union which even irritated conventional Conservative supporters. The statement by the former chancellor Sir Robert Horne was hardly evidence of a confident Unionist:

> The Welsh are showing the kind of wisdom that is generally attributed to the Scot, because, knowing that the amount of their unemployment is so much greater than that elsewhere, probably they realise that they would find great difficulty in providing unemployment benefit by themselves, and they are wiser to rely on the richer country than to seek any separation. Let us see how this argument runs. 'Unemployment is rife in Scotland. Therefore, there should be a Scottish Parliament.' It is perfectly obvious that there is some missing premise in that syllogism. How does it require to be stated? 'Unemployment is rife in Scotland; Parliaments are the cure for unemployment; therefore, there should be a Parliament in Scotland.' You have only to state the proposition in that way to see how false the whole assumption is. Are Parliaments the cure for unemployment? What has this Parliament been doing ever since the War and how much has it achieved to cure unemployment.[115]

For the Labour Party home rule was obviated by the rise in centralized planning then in evidence in the Soviet Union in which social and economic problems would be tackled by state intervention, and to make the best of rational and scientific principles these were best done at the largest scale which meant that home rule would no longer be needed as a means to alleviate social and economic hardship. Without a social and economic purpose, the key rationale behind support for home rule was lost. Furthermore, intellectually, as we have seen in Chapter 2, the small nation was seen as an anachronism and a bar to greater efficiency in left-wing circles and nationalism was associated with the bourgeoisie and deflected from the real interests of the working class. As the Labour MP George Buchanan put it in the House of Commons

> As regards the demand for Scottish Home Rule, Parliament would do well not to dismiss it with the cheap sneers which so often greet demands for reforms of that kind. There is a genuineness behind this demand. It is, as I have said, in the main a middle-class movement. I and the few who sit here with me, welcome it in so far as it represents the progress of human liberation, a progress which has gone on in Ireland and is going on in India, which has captured our Colonies and is now moving into Scotland. We welcome that movement but we hold that the movement is only good in so far as- it applies itself to the great poverty problems in our midst. We say that far greater than Home Rule for Scotland, or for England, or for Ireland are the great fundamental economic problems, the problems of a community which is producing untold wealth and untold poverty. Whether you have Parliaments in London and Edinburgh and Dublin or not does not matter if the problems of economic want and economic misery are not solved. No Parliament and no Government, local or national, will last or will have a meaning for the people, which does not wipe out needless poverty in the country which it governs.[116]

A point not sufficiently recognized by historians is that the emergence of the British state added a new and vital element in the intellectual construction of unionism in interwar Scotland. Although it would take the impact of the Second World War to bring to fruition the reality of the power of state intervention as a mechanism for socio-economic regeneration, it was already becoming apparent in the 1930s that the link between socio-economic improvement and the state was the way of the future. For many of a leftward persuasion, the choice was between using the existing apparatus or building a new one. That said, throughout the 1930s, a foot was kept in the self-government camp, and even in the 1945 Labour Manifesto Scottish home rule remained as a sort of totem to the radical past.[117] Furthermore, as the term 'Unionists' was associated with the Conservative Party, Labour in Scotland never made an explicit endorsement of the term, and throughout the post-war era, the party always had a significant element of parliamentary MPs who were favourable to the creation of a Scottish parliament.[118] Even when not in favour of devolution, many were still sensitive to Scottish sensibilities as exemplified by Labour MP Arthur Woodburn:

> We have no objection to our English friends remaining English and being proud of their heritage and destiny. They can sing, 'There must always be an England', but they must not object to our singing, 'There must always be a Scotland'. This cold

war which has gone on for a couple of hundred years between English people and ourselves is due to the lack of appreciation of these national feelings, and I am of the opinion that this indifference to national feelings, that unfortunately exists in England, was largely the cause of our losing America, might have lost us India, and certainly helped us to lose Ireland. Carried to an exaggerated extent, it could result, in spite of our economic loss, in the loss of Scotland.[119]

Furthermore, working-class solidarity was an effective way to create an alternative pan-British community of interests without the need to refer to the Union.[120]

England or Britain?

At its most simple, nationalists could refuse to engage with the arguments of unionism and deny its legitimacy. Often Unionists were simply dismissed as 'Anglo-Scots' who were collaborators with England against their own country's interests. The use of the term Anglo-Scot was quite deliberate and implied that those who upheld the Union were doing so at the behest of England. In contradistinction to Ireland where the term 'West Briton' was frequently used to describe those against Irish independence, the term 'North Briton' was rarely used.[121] The notion of a treachery against one's own nation was one that appealed to popular ideas of Scottish history in which the governing classes had consistently worked against the interest of the people and where their own interests were tied up with the British or English state. This tied in with a traditional radical vision in which the aristocracy were cast as the villains of the piece.[122] From the collaborators of Edward I of England down to the landowners who expelled their kinsmen from the land during the Highland Clearances, there was a clear narrative of aristocratic perfidy that only needed a tweak to show that their actions of self-interest were driven by the needs of the English or British ruling class. In the modern era, this argument further chimed in with a view that linked aristocratic privilege with imperialism and sought to portray the Conservative Party as one in which the interests of its higher echelons were of paramount importance and those who helped were lackeys and lickspittles. Those Scots who served their masters' interests were cast as unthinking and blinded to the harm they were doing to the national interests. A servile class had emerged in Scotland that was willing to perpetuate the interests of the ruling class. On occasion this type of argument could also spill over into Anglophobia in which the English in Scotland were portrayed as a sort of fifth column and 'a danger which undoubtedly threatens them of being absorbed by the swarming thousands of the south'.[123] Such arguments, however, were intellectually vacuous and did little to explain the current political situation in which the majority clearly endorsed parties which supported the union. It is probably the case that some of these outbursts were driven by frustration at the lack of political progress. While greater circumspection was used in relation to the Labour Party, there was an explanation that socialists were being duped and that common sense would eventually lead to the realization that independence was a more socially just outcome than the Union.[124] As the movement sought to both increase support and gain greater credibility, it was recognized that Anglophobia and the more intemperate rhetoric was an electoral liability. The purges of the 1930s and 1980s by the leadership tended to conflate Anglophobia and fundamentalism as one and the same thing.[125]

A more nuanced argument sought to cast the role of the 'Establishment' as the villains of the piece, and in essence the nature of the debate focused on the fact that those who had most to lose from Scottish independence or home rule were those who were benefiting most in society and hence those most anxious to preserve the status quo. Although not as blunt as the argument that the nobility and elite of Scotland had always betrayed the nation in order to further their own interests, it did point out that the most significant opposition to self-government usually came from those in elite or established positions. The growing nationalist agitation in the early 1930s led to the creation of the Movement to Oppose Agitation for a Scottish National Parliament.[126] Some four hundred eminent people who were drawn from the world of business and the arts and headed by four dukes signed an anti–home rule declaration which was described by nationalists as 'the same type as those who were on the infamous Ragmans Roll of six hundred years ago [those who signed fealty to Edward I's claim of overlordship of Scotland] – men who were ready to sell and betray their country to England'.[127] The reason cited by nationalists for opposition to self-government was that such individuals put 'personal interests and political inertia before the urgent claims of Scotland for a chance to live and prosper' and that they desired that Scotland 'should remain a northern appendage of England, neglected and exploited for English ends'.[128] For nationalists the fact that many of the business community were against self-government was not based on an economic rationale, but rather it was because they were the ones who were profiting most from the status quo.

The Unionist case against Scottish self-government rested on a basic proposition that the affairs and economies of Scotland and England were so integrated that there was nothing practical to be achieved by disaggregating them. Indeed, it was contrary to the interests of both. The main thrust of the Unionists argument from the 1930s was fundamentally economic and 'in the material matters of industry, trade and commerce … for the solution of the new problems that follow on modern developments … any legislative separation would dry up rather than fructify the channels of material and spiritual development'.[129] Unionists pointed out that there was no desire or objective to remove the national status of Scotland, and some even argued that home rule would be a diminution in status as this was something that only applied to daughter or dominion nations, whereas Scotland was a mother nation of the empire. The Unionists also argued that just as Scotland was not represented in the Commonwealth or the League of Nations, neither was England, and both nations were represented by Britain. Finally, Unionists made the point that having an English majority within parliament was a small price to pay for all the advantages of Great Power status that being a member of the Union entailed.[130]

From the outset, the main argument against unionism and the British state was the majoritarian one that as the English were in the majority, their interests would always outweigh that of the Scots. A key component of this argument is the assumption that the Union was passed to satisfy English national interests and that the British state was simply a way to further the interests of the English nation. This argument was outlined in 1920 by Rhuraidh Erskine of Mar:

> It is imagined by many Scotsmen that the English Parliament is a British parliament; the English Army a British Army; the English throne a British throne, and so on; but for the life of me I cannot see why this should be so. It would appear indeed that the only thing which our pro-Britons allow to be definitely and unequivocally English is the English language; but it is a pity that they are not so clear-sighted with respect to the other institutions I have named. The Teutonic character of the English parliament is not affected by the fact that a small minority consisting of Scots and Welsh Celts sit in it. The home of that parliament is Westminster, from which it never budges. It is ruled by a distinctly English majority; therefore with what face can a Scotsman or a Welshman contend that it is British? The same line of argument applies to the other typically English institutions that I have named; which in origins, genius and intent are all essentially English.[131]

For Scottish nationalists, far from being abolished in 1707, the English nation continued under its new guise of Britain, and the regularity with which the terms England and Britain were conflated was cited as evidence of the essential continuity in the minds of most English commentators. The idea that Britishness was in essential conflict with Scottishness was based on the fact of an English numerical superiority which was so large as to prevent a meaningful British entity. Also, at this point, it is worth pointing out that the nationalists did not register or engage significantly with the idea of Unionism until late in the 1930s and much preferred to engage with the construct of British. In part this was due to the idea of Unionism being associated with the politics of Ireland. The idea of Unionism as a competitor philosophy was not much in evidence, and more often than not during the interwar era the term was used in lieu of Conservative, and although ostensibly unionist, it was hardly ever used for the Labour Party. An appeal to Scottish Conservatives made the following argument:

> Conservatives in Scotland have got into the way of calling themselves Unionists, partly because of their entanglement with English politics and partly because of a feeling that the word Conservative suggest a reactionary, one who clings to institutions and principles whose day is over, merely because they have a venerable past.[132]

Although never really articulated in a black-and-white manner, a key argument against unionism was that it served as a cover for British or English nationalism and that many of the criticisms of Scottish nationalism that were used by Unionists could be levelled back at them with greater accuracy. As we have seen in Chapter 2, the idea of small-nation nationalism was used to disassociate Scottish nationalism from the more virulent and aggressive form of nationalism that was associated with larger nations and imperialism. The opposition of some elements of the Conservative Party to the Self-Government of India Act of 1935 was used to demonstrate the imperialist vision of British nationalism, especially as many of the key opponents of Scottish home rule were equally virulent in their opposition to greater autonomy for India: 'The British are trying on India the trick which almost worked in Ireland. Pakistan is Ulster.'[133] At the end of the day, the major difficulty that unionism posed for the national movement was that the majority of their fellow countrymen and women endorsed it and that was an awkward fact to explain away. There was nothing to be gained in denigrating the political choices of their fellow Scots, so nationalist rhetoric has evolved to remove England and unionism from much of its debate. The focus of nationalist fire has been on 'London' or 'Westminster' government which removes ordinary English and Scots people from the target and pushes the blame for Scotland's ills on the British elite.

Conclusion

As a result of being a minority movement for most of its history, the nationalist movement could not afford to alienate potential supporters, and this meant that it had to have a modus vivendi with the home rule and devolutionist movement. In part, this was made easier because there was a considerable overlap for much of the century in terms of meaning and membership with a number believing that a devolved parliament would be a necessary first step to independence and that it would mark the beginning of a process that would lead to self-government, which in the context of the British imperial experience meant independent statehood. The 'stepping stone' policy, and, in more recent times, 'independence by stealth' in which more powers are accrued to the parliament in Edinburgh, has always commanded a lot of support in the movement. Even devolutionists who did not believe in independence still used the argument of Scottish nationality to justify the creation of a Scottish parliament. Arguments regarding administrative efficiency and the like failed to divert attention away from the fact that the project was a nationalist one, albeit with a small 'n'. At the end of the day, devolution was not the Gorgon that killed independence stone dead but rather Aladdin who let the genie out the bottle. Evidence of this is to be found in the fact that the fundamental political divide in Scotland today is between independence and unionism. The latter's close connection to Conservatism makes perfect philosophic sense in that there has traditionally been a suspicion of radical change, especially in regard to the constitution. There is no doubt that unionism has been a salient factor in revitalizing Conservatism in Scotland in recent years, but the extent to which unionism has the same intellectual coherence as nationalism in Scotland is very much up for question. Firstly, as we have seen unionism means different things in Scotland and Northern Ireland and has no real equivalent in England. Crudely put the Ulster Unionists see themselves as British not Irish, the Scottish Unionists see themselves as Scottish and British and in England, English and British are the same thing. Finally, there is the issue that what the real divide is not the political philosophies of unionism and nationalism but rather a competition between two competing nationalisms: Scottish and British. Unionism, theoretically at least, regards Britain as a multinational state, but much of the language and ideas that shore it up regard it, first and foremost, not as a state but as a nation.

5

Ideology: Left, right and the state

Just as the nineteenth century had been dominated by the emergence of nations and the demand of nation states, so the twentieth century was dominated by the clash between nationalism and ideologies, between independence for each separate state and new universalisms. Wars and revolutions blurred the battle-lines. These were shifted by growth crises of scientific and technological progress and by the social consequences of economic expansion; by the expansion of the state, by tense waves of democratisation and anti-liberal movements; by imperialism and colonial policy, and also by decolonization and neo-colonialization.
– Bracher, *The Age of Ideologies: A History of Political Thought in the Twentieth Century*, 147

As one of Germany's most eminent historians and political scientist eloquently points out, the twentieth century was the age of ideologies, and this had a profound impact on both the development of the state and its relationship with nationalism. In this chapter we will discuss the difficulties associated with a national movement that sought to portray itself as a moderate and neutral force in navigating the ideological divide in the twentieth century. How does a party that aims to transcend class pitch its electoral message, and how does it reconcile its left- and right-wing elements within the one movement? Should the national party acquire policies like other political parties, or should it focus on the single issue of independence? Also, the creation of an independent Scottish state begs the question of what that state would do to make a material difference to the Scottish people. Whether nationalists liked it or not all these questions meant having to engage with the ideological spectrum and the issues surrounding class interests. One strategy to get round questions of ideology was to focus on what was described as Westminster mismanagement in which independence on its own would make a material difference irrespective of any ideological dimension. Another way was to strive for ideological neutrality and aim for the centre. As we shall see, the Scottish National Party (SNP) tended to gravitate towards the middle ground, even though the rank-and-file membership has tended more to the left. Finally, because British political parties over the course of the twentieth century tended to fight for the centre ground, it was a crowded area which pushed out the SNP. Furthermore, in the post-1945 period up until the mid-1970s there was a consensus that the state

Figure 5 Cartoon from the *Scots Independent* (1935) illustrating the point that government policies work to the advantage of England against Scotland (Source: *Scots Independent*).

should take the lead in guaranteeing the socio-economic well-being of citizens which meant an extension of state power. For the national movement this created a dilemma because it would mean an extension of the power of the *British* state in Scotland which was the very state they wanted to leave, but state intervention was the norm in the small Western European nations that were held up as a model for Scotland to follow. In an endeavour to distinguish themselves in a crowded market, there was a premium on coming up with policies that would give the party a distinctive identity and mark them out from the British parties.

Navigating the ideological divide

The most important factor in the world of politics in the period after the First World War was the ideological divide between the left and the right. In essence, this division was based around the conception that class was the most important indicator of political behaviour because this determined, theoretically at least, support for political parties that would best further the interests for the working class and the middle class, respectively.[1] With the exception of the United States, most democracies evolved a political system in which forces of the political left (representing the working class and trade union movement) challenged forces of the political right (representing the middle class and the interests of property).² Central to these arguments was the role of the state, with the left favouring greater government regulation and intervention to ameliorate social and economic conditions for the people (usually those on the lowest income), while on the right, there was a scepticism and suspicion of the state because it could circumvent and curtail the rights of the individual (usually those with the most income).³ Although this is a very crude and unsophisticated reading of the main political development in the twentieth century in Europe, most politics has tended to be explained in terms of the left–right dichotomy and the oppositional forces of capital and labour. Naturally, the world of politics was much more complex and nuanced, and the shifts into areas between the left and the right gave rise to the greatest explanatory force in modern political history. Whatever its drawbacks and inadequacies, the ideological axis from left to right is still the arena in which most political debate takes place. To all intents and purposes, any serious political movement or party must engage with this model as it has been the main intellectual framework for both the understanding and the engagement with the world of politics. And while the language of class and the left–right dichotomy may have gone out of fashion in recent years, from a historical perspective, it has dominated the language of politics (and perhaps still does so), it has shaped the political landscape and has been the main interpretive lens through which the political world is understood.⁴ This has been the intellectual arena in which the national movement has had to develop over the course of the twentieth century.

The key objective of the Scottish national movement has been and is the reacquisition of statehood. So the relationship of the population to the state and the role of state intervention and action is obviously one area that has to be of importance to nationalists because their main argument is that a Scottish state is a necessary thing to improve the well-being of Scots. Whereas in the nineteenth century, nationalist movements in the main were led by the middle class and the intelligentsia, expectations on the state at that time were not that significant. Foreign policy, war and peace and general aspects regarding tariff and trade were the usual limits of state power, and government was largely absent in the lives of most of the population.⁵ In the period after the First World War, the role of government and the state has increased massively. The emergence of the Soviet Union in which state action and planning transformed a peasant backwater economy into an industrial superpower had a profound impact on thinkers from the left in terms of expectations as to what state intervention could achieve as far as economic and social engineering was concerned.⁶ After the experience of the interwar depression and the role of the state during the Second World War, government intervention became the norm in the Capitalist West in the post-war era.⁷ This was especially the case when it had to be demonstrated that 'tweaking' of the economy by demand management mechanisms could deliver higher standards of living for the population in the Capitalist West than the Communist East.⁸ And within the West, attitudes to the extent of state involvement in society and politics were largely determined by the ideological spectrum with those on the left more in favour and those on the right tending to be more suspicious, although more often than not, this was more about emphasis than ideology in the age of consensus.⁹ So attitudes to the state and its role in society and economy inevitably involved engaging with the ideological axis, and this was something that nationalist politicians in Scotland would struggle to avoid. Furthermore, as we shall see, the role of the state was complicated by the fact that nationalist attitudes to state intervention meant potentially supporting the growth of the British state in Scotland if that meant delivering government-driven social and economic policies. This created an intellectual conundrum in that taking a position on the ideological axis could end up involving support for increasing the British state presence in Scotland, which is the very opposite of the policy of independence.

The centrality of social class in relation to the ideological spectrum raises an important issue when discussing nationalism because as a political philosophy it usually stresses the unity of the nation, whereas class focuses on the fundamental divide in society based on material prosperity.[10] Traditionally nationalism has shied away from class because of the emphasis on the nation as the fundamental political unit, and in nationalist narratives the usual dichotomy is one that represents natives against foreigners, be that as invaders, colonists, enemies or whatever.[11] The idea that the nation has an essential unity is one that is immediately compromised when discussing social class because it shows that it is divided.[12] Furthermore, because most nations are divided into working-class and middle-class elements, the idea of the uniqueness of any nation is arguably undermined, and identifying with a social class across national boundaries potentially creates an alternative loyalty based on class that supersedes loyalty to the nation. Traditionally, for those on the left, the primacy of class surmounts that of nation, and, indeed, nationalism is often presented as a bogus ideology that has the prime function of diverting the working class from their true material interests and legitimizing the economic, social and political dominance of the bourgeoisie. In the words of Marx, 'The workers of the world have no nation', although the meaning of this can be interpreted as they have no ownership or investment in the nation.[13] As a comparative latecomer in European terms, Scottish nationalism arrived after the heyday of middle-class bourgeois nationalism of the nineteenth century into the class-dominated ideological world of the twentieth. While a number of artists such as Hugh MacDiarmid and Hamish Henderson adapted their nationalism to the ideological demands of Marxism and a number of Marxists, such as Tom Nairn, adapted their Marxism to nationalism, it has been difficult for the movement as a whole to shake off its nineteenth-century intellectual inheritance.[14] Or perhaps it is more accurate to say that it has been more difficult to adapt what was largely a nineteenth-century philosophy to twentieth-century political realities. The problem can be best illustrated by looking at the role of class in the development of Irish historiography over the course of the twentieth century where the role of nationalism was the dominant mode of historical explanation until the late 1960s. The Great Famine, for example, as Cormic O'Grada points out, was to modern Ireland what the Revolution was to France, but it did not occupy the central historical place that it ought to in the nation's history.[15] Social class was the single biggest determinant as to whether someone would live or die during the Great Hunger, but this salient fact was largely obscured by the dominance of nationalist narratives that tended to portray the victims as a largely undifferentiated mass described as the 'Irish People'.[16] Acknowledging class and class interests makes it much more difficult to construct narratives that project national unity.[17]

Although class was probably the dominant issue in British politics in the era before the First World War, by 1924 this was manifested much more explicitly by the dominance of the Conservative and Labour Parties that made a direct appeal to their specific class constituency.[18] The Liberals, which had tried to focus on class conciliation rather than class conflict, were squeezed out because they had supported a minority Labour government in November 1923. The short-lived Labour government of 1924 showed the brutal reality of class-based politics. Class warriors in the Conservative Party denounced the Liberals for letting the socialists into government, while Labour denounced the Liberals for bringing down a reformist and moderate government that was trying to do its best for ordinary working-class people. In 1923 there was almost a three-way split in terms of support for the political parties in Scotland, but after 1924 class polarization turned it into a two-way split between Labour and the Conservatives.[19] Having said this, it is important to remember that while this model of using class as a determinant of political behaviour works in the main, there is enough variation in the system to make it much more complex. If this was the case, then there would be uninterrupted socialist governments across Europe throughout the twentieth century given that the working class constitutes the majority of the electorate in all countries.[20] A large number of voters have never voted on the basis of class interests, and many often identify with a different class to the one that the strict socio-economic parameters would consign them to. By and large, however, the dichotomy of Conservative and Labour has been the dominant theme in British politics which was reinforced by the first-past-the-post electoral system which worked against the interest of smaller parties.[21] Although this has started to break down partially in the late twentieth century with the rise of a three-party system in the United Kingdom and a four-party system in Scotland, it is worth remembering that many still regard the duopoly of political power as the normal state of affairs. Class is still the main determinant of political behaviour, although it has recently come under threat with the rise of 'identity' politics in which issues such as gender, sexuality, environmentalism and the like have emerged to challenge the primacy of class as the principal determinant of political behaviour.[22] Scottish nationalism has frequently been cited as part of this new phenomenon of 'identity' politics, but the reality of course is that as a political organization, the SNP has been in existence since before the Second World War and the constitutional question has arguably been a key part of Scottish politics since the 1970s, and in terms of longevity, it will soon overtake the Irish Question.[23] While nationalism is normally associated as an ideology of the right, this usually but not exclusively is associated with established state politics. Certainly for most of the nineteenth and early twentieth centuries, nationalist movements that sought independence from larger states tended to be associated with the middle class and would probably fit in the right-wing ideological axis.[24] This is especially the case in Central and Eastern Europe in the interwar period when the Soviet Union was regarded as the greatest imperialist threat to independence. In the post-war era, nationalist independence movements shifted in the main to the ideological axis of the left as it was largely driven by anti-imperialist movements in the Third World that sought to liberate themselves from European empires.[25]

In its most pure and abstract form, the issue of Scottish independence is not a left- or right-wing issue, although that is the perspective that many adopt when assessing its virtues or faults. The simple reason for this is that most people who are politically engaged tend to have a position that is located on the ideological perspective. Left-wingers will assess the merits of Scottish statehood and independence from that position, as will right-wingers. That is the reality of politics, and there are probably few people who will approach the issue from a purely neutral ideological perspective. Having said all that, independence is about a form of government and a mechanism for the implementation of policy which could be either left or right, but for many protagonists there is a tendency to predict the future ideological complexion of an independent Scotland and the type of policies that would be implemented. As was discussed in Chapter 2, there has always been a long tradition of expedient arguments for independence because it would lead to the creation of a particular form of society that has a particular ideological dimension. More often than not, this was left wing. Before the creation of the National Party of Scotland (NPS) in 1928, Iain Gillies argued that the issue of independence and an ideological position were inseparable:

> To my mind, Scotland's need is a National Party, advocating full-self-government; anti-jingo and anti-militarist; strongly radical in general outlook, prepared to face the issue of housing and land reform on Socialist lines. These two problems at least ... I feel that ... some such progressive platform, our position would be clearer and greater support forthcoming. Convince the Scottish progressive that Westminster action is futile, prove by our radical policy that we are not reactionary and I believe we shall get our necessary support.[26]

For Gillies and others, Scottish independence was a mechanism that would make the delivery of certain ideological objectives in the field of social and economic policy more likely than the current constitutional arrangement in which policy was shaped by the ideological complexion of parliamentarians at Westminster. This expedient form of nationalism in which it served a higher purpose was the one advocated by Clydeside revolutionary John Maclean, and for many on the left this pragmatic nationalism was given further intellectual weight by the republication of the writings of the Scottish/Irish socialist and revolutionary James Connelly.[27] Not everyone shared this view that a committed ideological position would add weight to the cause, and there was a suspicion that by tying the party to a specific programme it was just as likely to lose as much support as it would gain. Throughout the history of the nationalist movement there have been periodic bouts of dispute regarding the issue of moderation versus radicalism, which can be best summed up as a competition between those who favour a centrist position and those who leaned more to the left. The traditional right have not had a strong influence on the SNP except for a brief period of time in the 1930s.[28] Normally, each side claimed that their particular vision of Scottish independence was likely to garner more support than the current policies on offer. Given that the failure to attract electoral support was a hallmark of the party's progress until the mid-1960s there was plenty of scope to blame one side or the other, and this was used as a justification to change policy. In most cases the division was between a cautious leadership and a more radical and impatient rank and file, and not without some degree of justification, those at the top could blame certain elements of giving the party a bad name. The Scottish National Congress (SNC), for example, was a constant thorn in the side of the party leadership with its often outlandish demands and unrealistic proposals such as setting up an unelected chamber as a political counterweight to Westminster.[29] Also, there were always a number of individuals whose nationalism was a consequence of their commitment to left-wing principles and who found the conservatism of the national movement and its 'broad church' strategy either too stifling and left or were expelled. One such figure was Oliver Brown who was a prolific writer and ardent critic of capitalism and imperialism. For Brown Scottish independence was the best way to defeat both, and his trenchant style and no-holds-barred approach made many in the leadership feel uncomfortable. He would eventually set up his own organization, the Scottish Socialist Party. Brown himself acknowledged that he was a bit of a political loner: 'I had found the perfect political party that aligned with all my principles and there was unity and harmony until the second member joined.'[30]

At the time of the origins of the national movement, for some nationalists, the issue could be reduced to a basic point of principle, namely that it is right for Scots to govern themselves and debates around policy or what an independent Scotland can do was a matter to be left to the post-independence Scottish electorate: 'On all the so-called great political issues brought forward by the present political parties the National party said that all those issues were of no importance whatever to Scotland until Scotland had the power to decide them for herself.'[31] Time and again, critics would argue that any flirtation with an ideological position was doomed to failure and a handicap on progress. C. M. Grieve (Hugh MacDiarmid) with typical acerbity condemned the dullness associated with policy detail which he loathed with all his artistic temperament:

> Scotland's worst disease is its appalling love for and dependence on the calculable. I am protesting against the idea that a scheme for developing the poultry industry, or re-afforesting part of Sutherlandshire, or re-establishing a Parliament in Edinburgh, or in short any scheme to do anything at all, political, economic, commercial or industrial – except to rouse a distinctive and dynamic spirit in Scotland again, and without any cut-and-dried schemes let that spirit find its own forms, no matter how unpredictable and how unrelated to anything in our past history they may be – has anything whatever to do with Scottish nationalism.[32]

There was a danger with such a strategy, however. Independence can be described as a policy objective in the sense that it is a change in the nature and structure of government and that, in and of itself, as we have already mentioned, can be construed as ideologically neutral. That said, its association with nationalism, however, is an altogether different proposition. This was especially the case in the interwar era when the growth of nationalism and Fascism was firmly on the public's radar, and while nationalism was instrumental in attaining independence, the idea that it was a political philosophy that had a validity on its own terms was one that many were suspicious of. For a number of pragmatists in the movement, independence would make sense and become attractive to the majority of the Scottish electorate only when it could be explained 'to the man in the street in bread and butter terms'.[33] It was a fairly constant refrain among critics of the nationalist movement that it was driven by romantics and cranks and that it was hopelessly impractical.[34] The idea that being in a state of independence on its own or, as some put it, a 'national awakening' would usher in a new and vibrant Scotland reinforced this perception. Quite often these eulogies to the nation chimed in with the rhetoric that was being heard in Germany and Italy:

> The rebirth of a nation is an event of world importance ... To begin with we should have the dignity and prestige of our country re-established, and moreover, the self-respect and the influence of our nationals the world over would be enhanced. The Scottish race would become heirs to the inspiring heritage which is the birth right of the children of free and vigorous nation. To regain for our native land the independence without which our nationality must wither and for our race that freedom which exalteth its soul, the presentation of our cause must be worthy of its true greatness and transcending importance. Who can deny that as a consequence of long years of political subjection our national story has been stained and soiled? Who therefore will assert that we should be content with anything less than the freedom that will enable us to develop our national resources to their very utmost, and as a nation highly resolve to live up to the finest ideals of which our race is capable? This is the freedom on which the ordered progress of mankind depend, and we as a nation have to learn the great and serious truth , that Scotland's greatest glory can never be attained, nor can the struggling masses of our people be given the opportunities to which they are entitled by blindly following blind leaders in the arid wastes of imperialism or the parched and barren deserts of socialism ... This is the freedom we demand for Scotland; for the preservation of our race it is imperative that we take full control of those things which belong to us.[35]

One of the reasons why many gravitated to the world of practical politics in the interwar era is that any semblance of mystical nationalism and appeals to national consciousness – and there were the odd rumblings of this among party activists – was a fear of being tarred with the Fascist brush. One of the reasons that nationalism was promoted by many in interwar Europe was the idea that it could appeal above class interests and that the needs of the nation were more important than any sectional or class grouping. Indeed, MacDiarmid did call for a form of Scottish Fascism claiming that 'we in Scotland have been for too long grotesquely over-democratised'.[36] Given that class was the single biggest dividing factor within societies, and that this division seemed to harden and become more polarized in the wake of the impact of both the First World War and the Great Depression, the idea that nationalism could bring harmony was one espoused by right-wing organizations to heal the divisions of democracy.[37]

Because the movement believed that 'practical' politics were essential to establishing the credibility of the case for independence, the majority felt that the overly rhetorical and emotional appeals to a 'national awaking' would undermine the seriousness of the proposition. The party turned its face against extremism, and it is no surprise that one of the first resolutions put before the newly formed SNP in 1934 was against Fascism:

> The Scottish National Party is opposed to fascism and dictatorships in any shape or form being fully persuaded that it is repugnant to the ancient Scottish ideal of liberty and the Party repudiates the suggestion implicit in Fascist policy, that Parliamentary Government on democratic lines has proved a failure and maintains that until Scotland has resumed self-government, parliamentary government in Scotland on modern lines has not been tried.[38]

Given that nationalism was on the rise in Europe between the wars, this was a clear statement that the party saw itself as different from the right-wing movements that emerged in protest at the failure of Liberal Democracy to address the social and economic consequences of the Great Depression. In any case, most of these movements manifested themselves in established states.[39] Any whiff of mystical nationalism would make people think the Scottish movement was a variant on a wider European theme. Also, the language of a 'national awakening' was dismissed as meaningless and void of reason. While many could see the populist attraction of an appeal to the 'big picture' precisely because it did not need details and practical solutions, this approach was condemned as fraudulent, dishonest and dangerous: 'If the policies of Hitler and Mussolini and Japan are Nationalism: then Nationalism is indeed a world danger of the first magnitude.'[40] People would naturally want to know what kind of policies an independent Scotland would pursue, particularly in what ways they would be different from what was on offer at the moment. Furthermore, as the party was seeking an electoral mandate for independence the obvious question that arose is that until they constituted a majority of Scottish members, what position would SNP members of parliament (MPs) take on a range of issues in the Westminster Parliament. If they took none, then it might be asked what the point in electing them was. For example, Sir Alexander MacEwen argued for an ambitious programme of government intervention in Scotland to build up infrastructure such as roads, houses and hydroelectric power, as well as encouraging the development of newer industries such as aviation and motor cars.[41] Whether or not many of the criticisms were justified, the idealist streak within Scottish nationalism has led many of its critics to claim that the movement lacked any practical sense of realism. This association with romanticism was compounded by the fact that many of the party's high-profile supporters such as Hugh MacDiarmid and Compton Mackenzie had used language and concepts similar to far-right nationalism and Fascism. This criticism obviously took its toll as the party leadership evolved into an almost caricature of Presbyterian dourness, seriousness and moral rectitude.

Although a number of nationalists believed that the issue of Scottish self-government was enough on its own to attract voters to a political party set up specifically for that issue, it soon became apparent that the NPS was not a voter magnet. If the party saved its deposit, it was considered a good result and throughout the 1930s and beyond a key question was how to increase support among the electorate.[42] The heart of the problem was that the NPS and, subsequently, the SNP were organizations dedicated to one specific policy: Scottish independence or self-government. Apart from those who believed in this specific policy, the party had no natural constituency or ready-made cadre of voters. The process that had largely shaped the politics of Scottish and British society into one based on class in the early twentieth century did not leave a natural space for those who advocated for independence or self-government. Home rule was just one of the many issues that populated the political environment in the Edwardian era, but like land reform, temperance, church disestablishment and other issues that were either swept away or repackaged into a rhetoric of class interest, it did not fit naturally into the new realities of the post-1918 era.[43] A single issue is a difficult sell in the world of practical politics. Like love and peace, or kindness to animals, many will endorse it, but in a world dominated by political parties that serve up a whole range of policy options, it is unlikely to acquire the necessary sense of priority to overwhelm those more mundane packages of issues that political parties bundle together into a form of ideology. With the realization that one core policy was not enough to attract sufficient voters, the national movement had to give a deeper meaning to the concept of Scottish independence by illustrating in a practical way what difference it would make to the lives of ordinary voters. As soon as one enters into the world of practical politics, that means engaging with conventional ideology and the left and right axes of politics. Also, as would have seemed to have been the case, if the espousal of Scottish independence on its own did not motivate the electorate, then the different and unique policies that could be applied in an independent state become the most important way to attract voters. And again, this means engaging with the left–right axis. All of which raises the issue of electoral calculation. If it becomes necessary to win a mandate from the electorate, then this will require a pitch to the voter that will have to secure as much support as possible, and this will involve an appeal to the ideological shading which is most reflective of Scottish society. Unlike other parties which may promote interests based on an ideological conviction or identification, the national movement has to circumvent all policies to the central objective of winning independence by securing an electoral mandate. Although all political parties have to balance a pragmatic sense of whether their policies will be popular with an ideological conviction, for the national party, this is especially acute. Furthermore, unlike the Conservative and Labour Parties, it does not have the safety net of a reservoir of support based on class interests. And if this was not all problematic enough, there is the issue that the British parties operate on a left–right axis, and in a crowded political marketplace, how do nationalists posit something that can both engage with the left–right axis but also stand out as different from the traditional Labour and Tory offerings? Even if nationalists opt for an ideological neutrality by going for the middle, they would still face competition from Liberals. Such complexities and issues have helped to mould a distinctive nationalist approach to the ideological dimension of practical politics and have been an important factor in the promotion of what would come to be seen as a distinctive brand of policies and ideological positioning.

One of the main objections to forming a separate national party which would contest elections on a ticket for independence and, at the same time, promote specific policies was that in doing so it would alienate potential supporters of Scottish self-government. As we have already mentioned, the world of practical politics often involves picking a side and therefore leads to divisions. For example, a programme of land reform, which was always quite close to the movement's heart, might win over rural workers in the

Highlands and Islands but, at the same time, could potentially alienate farmers and estate owners who did not want the state to interfere in the rights of property. In the 1930s, the radical argument was:

> At the present time we have at least two million acres of good land suitable for small holdings, not to mention millions of acres classed as 'sporting estates' ... the problem we have to face is how to get the able-bodied unemployed to leave the town areas and take up land where it is available and waiting for the willing cultivator.[44]

This would have dismayed most of the farming community and the SNP post-war policy of land reform proposed a national survey first 'to determine whether it is in the national interest to develop land for agriculture, afforestation, industry, housing or recreation, and to indicate the areas most suitable for improvement and reclamation'.[45] Vagueness and ambiguity were often used as ways to avoid alienating voters. The natural riposte to the problem of not pleasing all the people all of the time was that so long as the policy was endorsed by the majority and not the minority, there was little to worry about. Such a view, however, could lead to accusations of populism and an unprincipled form of politics which was in stark opposition to the claim that Scottish independence was akin to a moral crusade. With a fairly hostile press, such accusations would damage what limited credibility existed. This was especially the case in the 1930s when the movement seemed to be breaking into the traditional ranks of the middle-class professional class. According to the Tory MP and novelist John Buchan:

> There is the crank, with whom we need not concern ourselves. If he were not a, Scottish Nationalist, he would be a Communist or a Fascist or some other extravagance. Then there is a considerable section of young people who are Nationalists on romantic, historical or literary grounds. That is a respectable type. You may say that that is only a phase with them, and that it will pass. Yes, but it is also found among young people who are hard-headed, ambitious and practical; who are shaping out for themselves careers in medicine, law and business. Very few of that class would agree for a moment to any of the schemes of Home Rule at present put forward, but they all feel the dissatisfaction. They all believe that much is wrong with Scotland, and that it is the business of Scotsmen to put it right.[46]

As with all political parties, there was a desire to be taken seriously and perhaps an extra sensitivity when it came to criticism from the establishment.

The electorate was complex, and there were capable and functioning political competitors in existence which made attempts to 'game' elections very difficult. As we have seen, there were a number of purist minds who were apt to claim that it was pointless in promoting specific policies or projecting detailed visions of the future because this was only something that could be done by the post-independence electorate. In short, it was the decision of a future post-independent Scottish electorate, and there was no point in trying to circumvent this process. As a matter of democratic principle, no decisions could or should be made about Scotland's future until independence was achieved. Such views did not lend weight to the development of credible policies, nor did it encourage conviction in the policies that were adopted by the party. As we shall see, the principle of Scottish independence required unity and as much support as possible, and practical politics and ideology created divisions and alienation. As the editor of the *Scots Independent* put it in 1934:

> The bread and butter propaganda has been very successful up to a point, and it must be continued, and even expanded, but far more will be needed in a time of industrial recovery, even if it is only spasmodic and partial, as it will probably be. We must remember that nations cannot live by bread alone, and give heed to the spiritual essentials of national life ... To put it another way, we must make a kind of religion of nationalism, and infuse into our propaganda the spiritual passion that is so conspicuous in the Communist movement.[47]

A left-wing case for Scottish independence would put off those of a right-wing persuasion and vice versa. Even for some of a committed ideological position, the promotion of Scottish self-government should be one of studied neutrality. Furthermore, detailed discussion was likely to distract from the main issue. One consequence of this was that many in the movement did not take seriously the raft of policies proposed at national conferences, and on a number of occasions, such as the issue of conscription just before and during the Second World War when the party officially opposed it, discipline would fall apart.[48] Also, it is worth pointing out that in the days before the creation of an independence party, many self-government activists naively assumed that the principle of the issue was such that its benefits were self-evident and required little or no explanation as to its potential practical benefits. This tendency to expect people to see that independence was a virtue that required no elaboration at worst further exacerbated hostility to the promotion of practical policies and at best meant that they failed to take them seriously.

Until the SNP explicitly committed itself to a left-of-centre ideological position in the mid-1980s, there were three factors that largely determined nationalist policy in regard to the ideological spectrum.[49] Firstly, there was what might be described as the politics of grievance that did not depend on any ideological perspective because it focused attention on the ways in which Scotland was treated unfairly or unjustly within the Union. For example, it might be claimed that Scotland was comparatively overtaxed or received less than its proportionate share of public expenditure. In essence this argument buttressed the idea that independence on its own would improve matters by removing the bias and iniquities that were said to exist in the Union. Secondly, there was the idea that policy could be constructed from an ideologically neutral perspective that would eschew class and class interest altogether and avoid the need to support or alienate one side or the other in the main divide that governed Scottish political loyalties. This was an altogether trickier proposition which had to avoid the pitfalls of a vacuous appeal to national interests but have the necessary economic credibility to give it a chance of garnering electoral support. An example of this type of cross-class appeal might be the argument that more goods are bought which are produced domestically, rather than ones which are imported. Both the workers and bosses could potentially benefit from such a policy. Thirdly and finally, especially in the crowded British ideological market, there was an endeavour to come up with distinctive policies that were quite different from any British counterparts. This distinguishability was important because it could be used to demonstrate the argument that Scotland needed specific policies of its own and not Scottish variants of British solutions. Furthermore, if such policies could be tied into notions of a Scottish tradition, so much the better. As we shall see, a disproportionate amount of nationalist policy focus was directed towards housing, education, fishing and agriculture precisely because it was possible to promote a distinctive national slant on these activities.[50] Although Peter Lynch is correct to observe that there are broad periods in which policy reflected a distinctive strand, the reality is that the interplay of these three factors cumulatively over time helped to embed a nationalist political tradition and its own distinctive take on the ideological spectrum.[51]

Grievance

From a philosophical perspective the idea that there was no point in taking policy decisions before the independent Scottish electorate could have a say made perfect sense, but even before the creation of the national parties in the late 1920s and early 1930s, the world of practical politics was rendering the idea of ideological neutrality redundant. To advance the idea that the principle of Scottish self-government was one that commanded the support of the Scottish people would still require its political implementation and that would mean it would require legislation, which in turn meant, in all likelihood, the involvement of political parties at Westminster. As we have discussed in Chapter 4, the conflation of home rule, self-government and independence tended to blur lines of clear definition with many if not seeing them as one and the same thing, then certainly believing them to be politically related and belonging to the same philosophical family. The non-party Scottish Home Rule Association which was re-established following the end of the Great War in 1918 professed a studied political neutrality but urged members and supporters to vote for candidates and parties that were committed to self-government. In reality, this meant the Labour Party, as the Tory Party was opposed to home rule and the Liberal Party, which was in favour, was in decline after 1924 and had little chance of its prospective candidates being elected. The fact that the Conservative Party was historically against and the Labour and Liberal parties were in favour of home rule meant that there was already an ideological divide with the idea of self-government being associated with the left and not the right. Even though the Liberal Party was of the centre, its keenest advocates of home rule before the First World War tended to belong to the left of the party, and there is a case to be made that the idea of self-government was part and package of what might be called the 'radical tradition' which passed to the Labour Party after 1918.[52] Interestingly, the intensity of opposition to home rule in the Conservative Party, historically at any rate, seems to align with the ideological spectrum with right-wingers such as Sir James Lithgow in the interwar era and Michael Forsyth in the post-war era being implacably opposed with moderates such as Walter Elliot and Malcolm Rifkind being less agitated.[53] Although it was this resultant dependency on established political parties and its failure to deliver in the 1920s that led some to argue for a political party set up for the sole purpose of promoting Scottish self-government, the fact remains that by that time Scottish self-government was already clearly identified as having a provenance of the left. Furthermore, attempts in the late 1930s, late 1940s, mid-1970s and late 1980s to mobilize public opinion and support but rely on the mechanism of established parties at Westminster to deliver still tended to show a clear bias more towards the Labour Party rather than the Conservatives.[54]

When the NPS was formed in 1928, there was considerable debate whether the party should be a single-ticket organization with a studied ideological neutrality or whether, in order to build up its credibility and support, it should acquire policies that would augment and further its electoral appeal. Part of the difficulty faced by the new party was that the issue of self-government had never been put to an electoral test on its own, and while many were convinced that the single issue was enough to command widespread electoral support, others believed that public support for the principle would not necessarily translate into votes. From the outset of the creation of a national party, there was an in-built intellectual tension between what could be described as indicative policies which would show how an independent Scotland would work and a wariness of being drawn into the world of practical and ideological politics because of its inherently divisive nature. The guiding principle for Roland Muirhead was one of democracy, and he believed that the world of practical politics was a distraction:

> The Scottish people must drop their minor difference and combine to obtain self-government. After a Scottish parliament was obtained then the Scottish people and their representatives can divide into as many division as they care and fight out their differences in their own chamber.[55]

As was discussed in the previous chapter, the elasticity between home rulers and those who advocated for independence was demonstrated by the point that Muirhead made that once some form of parliament was established, it would be up to the Scots to decide and that before then, debate was almost meaningless. What effectively turned the tide towards a more practical engagement with politics is the Scottish Home Rule Association had more or less become an adjunct of the Labour Party in the 1920s and, according to its critics, it would never succeed because 'they were more or less attached to or worked through one of the present political parties and the failure of the attempts to obtain home rule, due to the English element in these parties'.[56] In the case the Scottish Home Rule Association or other non-party groups such as the Scottish National Conventions of the 1940s and 1980s, many of the leading figures belonged to established British political parties and the argument was made that the cause of home rule would always be undermined by the primacy of party loyalty.[57] This issue between principle and practicality would be a constant source of intellectual tension throughout the history of the nationalist movement and tended to be heightened when the electoral progress of the party seemed limited. If the party did poorly it was blamed on either policies that were putting people off or the party needed more and better policies. This debate rumbled through the 1930s and for those on the left:

Those who engineered the fusion of the National Party of Scotland and the Scottish Party surely could not have recognised that if the party was to grow, it must look to do so from Labour voters, since Unionists and Liberals (what is left of them) are afraid of home rule as they see clearly that if Scotland gets self-government she will have a radical and labour government, and they hate the idea of socialism in power.[58]

Several years later, the SNP chairman Andrew Dewar Gibb, who had stood as a Conservative candidate in the 1920s, resigned because 'any pretence that the party is not overwhelmingly socialist must now be abandoned … It has become intolerable for me to be constantly confronted with articles in the *Scots Independent* which I find myself in total disagreement'.[59] Furthermore, just as lack of electoral progress opened up the left–right divide, it also reignited the debate as to whether the national movement should contest elections or act as a pressure group:

To my mind active nationalism must proceed by sections, some fighting die hard elections, others forming self-government groups within the Liberal, Labour and Tory parties. What part is the SNP to take in the future? It cannot take complete charge of the movement so long as it manifests its present constitution.[60]

The failure to make an electoral impact was a central aspect on pushing John MacCormick towards the idea of a Scottish National Convention in the late 1930s which would eventually culminate in the Scottish Covenant Association in the late 1940s when two million signatures were gathered in favour of home rule.[61] Furthermore, the supposed advantage of the cross-party, single-issue, pressure group approach is that it could obviate the need for any ideological engagement. Labour was sympathetic in the late 1930s, when the SNP ceased to pose any electoral threat and in November 1936, SNP activists campaigned to help elect the Labour candidate, Robert Gibson, in the Greenock by-election which had been caused by the death of the National Liberal secretary of state for Scotland Sir Godfrey Collins.[62] MacCormick made a tactical error of standing as an 'Independent Nationalist' in the Paisley by-election in 1948 against Labour and did so with the tacit support of the Liberal and Conservative Parties. Although Labour was reassessing its stand on Scottish home rule, this electoral threat hardened attitudes against the Covenant Association.[63] It is also worth pointing out that poor elections results for the SNP in the general election of 1979 led to internecine warfare between the left and right and after lacklustre performances in the elections of 1983 and 1987, the Liberal and Labour Parties felt confident about exploring cross-party engagement in support of devolution.[64] In a movement that is a broad church, the ideological trip wire is one that is especially sensitive and ready to amplify divisions over strategy or policy.

In the early years of the nationalist movement, the key figure in promoting the link between practical politics and independence was Tom Gibson who argued that unless the Scottish electorate could be shown the benefits of independence in bread and butter terms it would always remain an abstract concept in the minds of most voters. As such, it could command a lot of lip-service support, but it would never mobilize many to cast their vote for it. Gibson was also wary of taking too much of an ideological position lest it scare off potential recruits who would object to either a right- or left-wing perspective. Having said that, Gibson was inclined to a traditional Liberal position on matters concerning the economy and was wary of state interference. As is often the case, those on the centre tend to describe themselves as ideologically neutral when in fact occupying the centre ground is every bit as ideological as those on the left or the right, respectively.[65] Furthermore, Gibson wanted to rid the movement of its association with romantics and demonstrate that there was a strong practical dimension to independence, and he was helped in this endeavour by his background in business management. This was probably a factor in his scepticism as to left-wing politics, and he was also married to Elma Campbell who was active in the Conservative Party at Glasgow University before becoming a founder member of the National Party which all indicated an inclination towards the centre-right. For Gibson, an engagement with economics meant the recitation of facts and figures and extensive use of statistical abstracts to demonstrate intellectual credibility. He was instrumental in limiting the influence of colourful and eccentric literary types such as Compton Mackenzie and Hugh MacDiarmid and played a leading part in steering the movement away from those that sought to emulate the Irish road to independence.[66] For Gibson, the movement had to demonstrate a firm grasp of the hard facts of economics and all its practical implications and be able to show a sceptical electorate that had come to see politics in terms of class interests how an independent Scotland could deliver a higher standard of living for all Scots. Gibson sought to dislocate the issue of economics from the dichotomy of working-class versus middle-class interests and substitute it with a model based on Scottish-versus-English interests. This was quite a balancing act and the way that Gibson was able to reconcile any conflicting ideological dimensions of a left versus right approach was to draw up an economic critique of Westminster government that showed the comparative disadvantages to Scotland as a whole that tended not to focus on sectional interests:

> It has become apparent to all of us that, in the industrial and commercial world, Scotland is not occupying the position in which she formerly stood and by reason of her pioneer work, and the world-famed skill of her tradesmen, the position in which we have every right to expect her to stand today. London's paralysing grip on our industries and money, heavy taxation, English political influence abroad, the callous indifference of the Westminster parliament to our requirements, and the want of national feeling and action due to the divisions among our people consequent upon the present English party political system, are undoubtedly the main contributory factors that have led to our present serious position. It is obvious that the first thing to do is to get rid of these retarding influences. Equally obvious, the most effective way of doing this is by setting up again our own parliament and thus creating a national outlook leading to national action.[67]

This argument was reinforced by claiming that in terms of the allocation of government spending, Scotland did not get a proportionate share based on the size of its population or that in the application of subsidies and tariffs in relation to specific industries which there was a disadvantage to the Scottish economy compared to the south: 'So long as the seat of Government remains in England, it is difficult to understand why people cannot accept as an indisputable fact that England must benefit directly and indirectly from any Scottish money spent on Government services in that country.' Furthermore, Gibson deconstructed the official figures and claimed that in the period from 1921 to 1931 'the increase in English general expenditure is 43.57% more than the increase for Scotland'.[68] Official facts and figures were mined to demonstrate that there was statistical evidence to show that Westminster government worked against a Scottish national interest. In 1921, it was pointed out that the Scots paid almost £120 million in taxes but only £33 million was spent in Scotland with the rest deemed for Imperial purposes. The fact that no separate records were issued thereafter was taken as evidence that Scotland was ill-served by the distribution of taxation.[69] This approach suggested the ways in which the Scottish economy was underdeveloped and would arguably be stronger with independence.

Gibson argued that even the raw statistical information on its own, if it was presented in the right way, would lead to positive conclusions in favour of independence. For example, the 1920s witnessed a decline in the amount of trade coming into Scottish ports compared to that in England, and especially London which increased by 40 per cent, and Gibson argued that this was a key factor in leading to industrial closure.[70] Issues such as taxation, government spending, industrial closures and the like could be used to show that there was a bias against Scotland with a non-ideological implication that independence on its own, regardless of which party was in power, would produce a better set of statistics. Roland Muirhead made the claim that 'Scotland pays to the London treasury the whole of its taxes from year to year, and only gets less than a third as grants for Scottish purposes ... England was like a Vampire, sucking the life blood of Scotland'.[71] According to Gibson, Scots were paying for the upkeep of London which he reckoned was a major factor in depressing Scottish wages.[72] The same implications could be drawn from figures on housing, living standards, wages and other indicators of social well-being. Infant mortality figures showed that in 1925 deaths decreased by fifty-five per thousand in England while the decline in Scotland was only nineteen per thousand. The figures for new housing per head of population showed that the figure in England was double that of Scotland.[73] The debate could be further widened by drawing on international comparisons with other small nations. The official figures, for example, showed that the Scots were much more heavily taxed than other small European nations.[74] A key objective of Gibson was to move the debate away from the abstract principle into the world of practical politics. This critique of Westminster government would become a standard template for nationalist arguments that would draw attention to the ways in which independence would push up economic well-being by rectifying the bias and faults of the current system of doing business and had the added advantage that it could keep away from the ideological divisions of left and right. Gibson used the conclusion of the World Economic Conference of 1933 to make the point that Scotland should put its own interest ahead of that of England:

> No country can be expected to make a sacrifice of itself for the sake of others. It is doubtful if indeed whether the world as a whole would not lose rather than gain

by any such sacrifice, since every country has its own contribution to the general prosperity, which can only be a viable contribution if it is prosperous itself. Its own progress must be its first concern.[75]

Arguably one major drawback of this approach is that it tended to be negative in its approach and placed all the blame on Westminster.

The idea that Westminster acted as a drain on Scottish resources continued into the post-war era. According to Catherine Snodgrass, a lecturer in geography at the University of Edinburgh, there was a constant drift south of excess taxation and talent, and this was reinforced by higher government expenditure:

> In these days of large government spending there is the obvious revenue loss. In free countries, even if taxes are high, the proceeds are spent within the country, apart from embassies etc, which is reciprocated, and on contributions to such bodies as the United Nations, but in our case much that is taken out in taxes is spent in England ... The Government continually stalls at giving the figures of the net amount taken out, but among the lowest of the estimates suggested recently is £40 to £80 millions per year ... how much employment and how many amenities and improvements are we losing in this way? This process going on for decades has created a descending spiral in Scotland by enabling higher pay and more posts to be provided in England, including those in the Higher Civil Service and in many publicly financed research institutions, with the resultant drain by emigration both in the 1920s and in recent years ... Moreover the drain is to a large extent composed of highly skilled and educated people and the reverse side is that Scotland has too few opportunities for such people and smaller proportions of them living and working in it compared with free countries of like size and development. Consequently there is an inadequate number of highly educated people with the same traditional background as the majority of the people compared to what there would be in a real living democracy.[76]

In the nineteenth century conventional wisdom held that Scotland put in more financially than it took out and official figures seemed to back this up until the government stopped producing them in 1921.[77] In the absence of reliable official figures, from then up until now, it is held as an article of faith by both nationalists and unionists that Scotland is either heavily subsidised by or a substantial over-contributor to the British exchequer. In the 1930s, Unionists turned to this negative defence which reached its apogee or nadir, depending on perspective, in the late 1980s with the 'subsidy junkies' taunt that featured during Scottish questions at Westminster.[78] In the 1980s, the debate revolved around the fact that the Scots received a higher proportion of *identifiable* expenditure, but the major problem with using this as a reliable index of net transfers of spending and income is that it related to only 60 per cent of government expenditure with the remaining 40 per cent described as *unidentified*, and, as was pointed out at the time, most *unidentified* expenditure took place in the south-east in the form of research and development, mortgage relief, tax subsidies and the like.[79] The latest series of statistics, GERS (Government Expenditure and Revenue in Scotland) is largely based on estimates and, as has been pointed out by Richard Murphy, cannot be used as a basis for assessing the prospects for an independent Scottish economy.[80] Strangely, in the land that invented political economy, the debate regarding the financial interaction between Scotland and England and the economics of Scottish independence has found it difficult to break the shackles of narrow accountancy.[81]

The middle ground

As the raison d'etre of the national party was to secure independence by means of an electoral mandate, this meant winning the votes of a majority or a sizable chunk of the Scottish electorate. In effect, a new electoral constituency would have to be forged out of the existing ones that were predominantly based on class. Furthermore, simply by dint of being nationalists, there was an intellectual commitment to an ideal that the interests of the nation had to surmount those based on class, so the very tall order facing the national party in electoral terms was to convince a significant number of working-class and middle-class Scots that their best interests were served by independence and they should prioritize the nation before that of class. This would be especially difficult given that class was the stark political reality in British society until the 1960s.[82] As we mentioned in the previous chapter, this appeal was complicated because it also meant putting the interests of the Scottish nation above that of the British nation, and although rarely acknowledged, Scottish nationalism was additionally having to compete electorally against a form of British nationalism. An interesting question for some future PhD student is the extent to which 'class' acted as a cover for British nationalism in Scotland in terms of political allegiance. Although most individuals in the national movement would have identified with being on the left, it never promoted itself as a champion of the working class even though this might have theoretically secured an electoral mandate, given that this group must have constituted between two-thirds and three-quarters of the electorate.[83] Obviously there was a squeamishness about making a direct appeal to one class or the other as this would obviate the idea of a 'national' interest and also, there was probably a realization that this corner of the market was already captured by its political competitors.

Throughout the history of the SNP there has been a tendency to eschew class-based politics and instead try and create a sort of Scottish consensus that was somehow able to bridge the gap between the social classes. The idea that it was possible to create a Scottish political and ideological consensus was certainly helped by what had been the political experience before the First World War. After 1918, Scottish nationalists looked back to the unchallenged electoral dominance enjoyed by Liberals in Scotland after 1832 and the fact that this was in marked contrast to the experience in England to make the case that there was a distinctive Scottish political tradition. John Bright was quoted with approval when he claimed in 1843 that if the Scots 'were separate from England, they might have a government wholly popular and intelligent to a degree which I believe does not exist in any other country in the world'.[84] This led many to advocate the idea of 'radicalism' as an inherently Scottish political stance in the hope that it would have the same appeal that it had in the era before the First World War. This might have made sense had the Liberal hegemony continued after the war, but it was split apart by the impact of class polarization. For some, this radical tradition had passed to the Labour Party with many conflating the idea of a radical tradition with one that was inherently left-wing.[85] Therefore, it was argued that the party would have to adopt a left-of-centre ideological stance in order to maximize electoral support, but rather than state this openly it tended to promote itself as 'radical' to avoid the association with either class politics or the left–right spectrum and often took shelter in old pre-war Liberal ideas such as land reform. According to John MacCormick:

> My own outlook in politics is radical, and I know that I cannot help letting that radicalism show through my nationalist speeches. Is it not possible that we should boldly proclaim as our policy for a Self-Governing Scotland and indicate that even before we get Self-Government, out members in Parliament will be irrespective of Party divisions unfailing in the progressive side ... I believe that radicalism is the only real political bent of the Scottish people and that in expressing it we would be expressing our national character ... I mean by radical that they favour neither Capitalism as we know it now, nor Socialism as expressed by the Labour Party.[86]

For a number in the movement, however, there was a danger that the party would frighten off more moderate right-wingers and thus tended to push a more non-ideological perspective or at least claim that as a movement it was not biased in favour of one class against the other. As ever with the foray into the world of practical politics, the failure to win widespread electoral support was frequently attributed to having the wrong type of policies. Either the party was too left-wing or too right-wing or too political, and this was the reason for electoral failure: 'When a right-wing organisation is fused with a left-wing organisation the whole body suffers a set-back.'[87] Most of the disputes tended to revolve around the left and right axis which was always grist to the mill of the non-ideological proponents. For some, such as the novelist Neil M. Gunn, the problem was having a mixture of left and right policies: 'Any patchwork programme – partly socialist – party Tory etc. is not the slightest use ... either the party adopts one of the existing economic faiths such as socialism or liberalism and goes all out on it on a national basis or ... it acts through all the other parties.'[88] The issue of ideology would always remain problematic because until the party started to win elections, there could be no real litmus test as to the impact of nationalist policies on the electorate.

A major problem that emerged with the party's engagement with ideology is that Scottish political behaviour in the interwar era did not conform to what many expected. No consensus emerged and politics remained divided in the 1920s. Up until 1924, there was almost a three-way split between Labour, Liberal and the Conservative Parties, and thereafter politics was dominated by a Labour Conservative divide until 1931 when a government of National Unity won a landslide in the general election. In 1935, a Labour recovery could not defeat the vagaries of the first-past-the-post system and the National Government (in reality by this time a Tory front) continued to dominate Scottish politics until the end of the Second World War.[89] All of this made it difficult to determine a Scottish political consensus, and while there was a in-built bias towards the left in the national movement, the fact remained that although the working class was a majority of the electorate, this was not reflected in class interest-based voting. If there was a consensus in Scottish politics, the interwar era offered no clue as to where it lay. Much of the political culture of the home rule movement had a distinctly pre-war Liberal heritage and the new class-based realities of the interwar period was for many a strange and unfamiliar territory, even for those who formerly belonged to the Labour Party. Roland Muirhead, Walter Murray and J. L. Kinloch were three important figures in the early nationalist movement who started out in the Liberal Party.[90] For some, like many in interwar Europe, a 'national' policy – however that was defined – would act as an antidote to the class divisions which had sundered society. And while many in the national movement were not of the same political persuasion as the far-right nationalists on the continent, there was still an element that naively believed that the promotion of the Scottish national interest would, in and of itself, surmount class differences:

> The Scottish National Party makes no appeal to class interests, to sectional or sectarian prejudices, or to out-worn political creeds. It takes its stand on the urgent necessity for all men and women of good will in Scotland to unite in the work of national redemption ... The Party has one aim – the reconstruction of Scottish national life. It has only one article of faith – the right and obligation of the Scottish Nation to Self-government ... The Scottish National Party will reconstruct the industrial and economic life of Scotland. Its policy will be designed to promote:
>
> 1. Development of National resources – minerals, water power, forestry, and rural industries.
> 2. Adaptation of Scottish industrial equipment to modern conditions.
> 3. Readjustments of the balance between town and country
> 4. Development of Scottish agriculture and fishing on economic lines, both in regards production and marketing.
> 5. Development of direct Scottish overseas trade, and a careful scrutiny of the effects of tariffs, and trade agreements on Scottish industry.
> 6. Growth of Scottish tourist traffic.
> 7. Reorganisation of finance.
>
> Scotland can be saved by one thing and one thing only; a mighty upsurge of the national will, a firm grasp of the truth that Scotland's future must be planned and fashioned within Scotland's borders, a resolve to build for Scotland a new prosperity, with a realisation that this can only be done through a Scottish legislature and a Scottish Government ... the crusade for a Scotland that will be better, richer and happier – a Scotland that will take her place among the nations.[91]

This type of statement was fairly common and demonstrated a number of the key handicaps in trying to formulate policy that eschewed the left and right axes. Firstly, it tended towards blandness and fairly general statements of intent that were short on detail and lacking in specifics but with plenty of rhetorical flourish. Secondly, as was discussed in Chapter 2, it tended to reflect the common nationalist ideal that the soul of the nation resided in the rural environment, and hence there was more focus on landholdings, farming, fishing and the agricultural community. This also tended to chime in with an idea that rural society was more in favour of traditional Liberal values which reinforced the party's centrist ideological position. In part, this was driven by pragmatism in that there was a weak Labour challenge in northern rural and Highland constituencies, and it was believed that a traditional Liberal programme might pay dividends in carefully choses seats.[92] It also probably reflected the influence of the Irish Free State's policy on rural regeneration which though much admired in Scotland at the time had a major retarding impact on Irish economic development.[93] Finally, it was clearly recognized that such appeals chimed in with much of what was circulating on the European mainland and that it was necessary to disassociate itself from militant nationalism and Fascism. It was claimed that

> freedom is in danger. Individual liberty is everywhere being assailed by Fascism, Communism or bureaucracy. The Scottish National Party does not ask its members to flaunt black shirts, green shirts or red shirts. It appeals to the love of liberty and the traditions of democracy, which are the most cherished characteristics of the Scottish race. The Scottish National Party offers a rallying ground for all who believe in true national unity, and not in party or class warfare.[94]

One consequence of blaming Westminster government for the 'underdevelopment' of the Scottish economy was a promotion of greater self-sufficiency or autarky in the sense that many sectors could grow due to the expansion of domestic demand at the expense of imports. This was not particularly new, nor was it fundamentally different from most of the ideas regarding political economy in the period from the Great Depression until the 1980s. The economic downturn of the 1930s encouraged protectionism throughout the world, and the idea that domestic industry and commerce could expand by reducing imports was fairly commonplace.[95] In Britain there was what Martin Daunton describes as 'insular capitalism' in that there was a largely free domestic market, but the state would use its regulatory powers to control the engagement with the global economy in order to ensure a balance of payments in that exports and imports were of the equivalent value, that the value of Sterling remained constant and that economic growth was neither too fast nor stagnant.[96] Excessive government manipulation of economic growth led to the notorious 'stop go' economy of the 1950s and early 1960s when politicians endeavoured to engineer boom conditions to coincide with elections and then immediately had to apply the brakes as the balance of payments deficit increased.[97] The Keynesian Revolution during the Second World War in which the state would use interventionists powers to regulate the economy to ensure maximum output for the war effort could be applied to peacetime conditions to stimulate and control economic growth to ensure that there was no repeat of the depression in the 1930s by creating demand to ensure employment levels remained high.[98] This had the effect of largely depoliticizing government intervention as a consensus emerged among Labour and the Conservatives that this was now an established facet of policy. One of the major problems facing nationalist policy advocates in the period after 1945 was that the British state was much more proactive than it had been in the interwar era.

The post-war period still focused on grievance and autarky as the key elements in what was described as Scottish reconstruction. Apart from the issues regarding economic efficacy, the policies offer an interesting insight into what were seen by nationalists as the socio-economic priorities for an independent Scotland. Furthermore, the nationalists were able to add another dimension to their prognosis of the future and that was the idea that Britain was destined to decline in terms of its global position in a world that was increasingly dominated by the superpowers of the Soviet Union and the United States. Writing during the war, Arthur Donaldson did not reckon there was a positive outlook for the British state in the post-war world:

> It is not impossible, in fact if the war should last as long as seems likely, that most nations will similarly repudiate their national and private debts and this their competitive positions in world markets will not have materially changed. The plain facts are that the U.K. possibly faces one of the greatest upturns the world has ever seen and that neither a continuation of capitalism or the introduction of socialism is likely to prevent the reduction in our lifetimes of the British Isles from their present position as the seat of a World Great Power to either the subordinate factor in a new Europe or an appendage to an Empire centred overseas, probably in the USA.[99]

Many nationalists believed that the best course of action for the new political realities of the post-1945 period was to try and steer a path through the ideological middle, and this reinforced the centrist position which has been the mainstay of the SNP's stance since its inception. In many respects it simply reflected the prevailing ideological climate in post-war Britain in which the Welfare State and the mixed economy were packaged as utilizing the best of socialism and capitalism while avoiding the worst excesses of both the Soviet and American systems.[100] As Robert McIntyre put it:

> Is it to be the happy hunting ground for big business and unscrupulous monopolies? Is it to be a bureaucratic state in which we are labelled and controlled from the crèche to the crematorium in the name of all but for the good of none? ... Practical measures must be undertaken to help to secure the independence, wellbeing and happiness of the people of Scotland.[101]

The guiding principle behind the nationalist adoption of the political middle was not that it would attract the most voters but rather that it would alienate the least. Also, there was a constant lip service to the mythical Scottish consensus in that it had a form of ideological neutrality wherein it did not set out to appeal to one particular class or section of society: 'The National Party kept clear of ideologies, representing as they did, the opposing economic forces.'[102] Again there was an ingrained belief that independence or self-government would be to the advantage of both capital and labour because it would 'free our national economy from the control of foreign and domestic manipulators and to introduce as the only economic law which we can recognise the needs and resources in the material and labour of our own country'.[103] One particular problem of this reading of political behaviour was that it did not take into account class loyalties and the impact the first-past-the-post electoral system had on political geography. The pivotal role the centre ground played in securing electoral majorities was because the class spectrum gave both main parties their core support. This meant that the centre ground was the only realistic area in which new voters were going to be found. It would be very unlikely that a stockbroker would vote Labour and equally unlikely that a miner would support the Conservatives. This idea of the rigidity of the class spectrum determining political behaviour meant a focus by both main parties on the middle ground: the natural political territory between the two as it was this area that had to be captured in order to ensure electoral success.[104] One major problem facing the SNP is that it has no natural class constituency and while the centre ground was important in determining the outcome of British political contests, it is not necessarily the case that on its own it is the most popular political position. Its pivotal role in politics is to augment either the left or right into creating a majority position.

Apart from the problem of potential voter alienation, a key difficulty with adopting an ideological position based on class was the issue of trying to promote something distinctive and different from the existing British political parties. After all, if you are a working-class Scot, why vote for independence if your class interests are better served by a British Labour government, and would an independent Scotland offer something better for a middle-class Scot than a Conservative government in Westminster? From the left-wing perspective, this was especially problematic, especially in the post-war era. One of the key experiences of the Second World War was that the state had considerable powers that it could use to effect social and economic change. This was especially the case in Scotland in which there was considerable economic dislocation with the attendant social problems of long-term unemployment, poor housing, poverty and the like which followed in its wake. The use of demand management economics associated with Keynesianism meant that there was now the prospect of the state bringing about solutions to the problems that had haunted interwar Scottish society. The British government could now fund public housing, schools, hospitals, roads and other social amenities, and it could use its considerable powers to boost economic activity by increasing public expenditure or cutting taxes. The state was now also a major employer as about 20 per cent of the British economy was nationalized and what were key industries in Scotland such as coal and steel were now owned by the state. There is no doubt that the social contract in which the citizen could rely on the state from the cradle to the grave to secure his or her best socio-economic interests was popular in Scotland.[105] The slowness of Labour to deliver on its post-war promises were instrumental in securing a victory for the Conservatives in the 1951 general election, and in 1955 the party won just over 50 per cent of the total vote in Scotland, the only time this happened in the post-war period. The 'white heat of technology' of Labour's Harold Wilson Labour Party in which greater state intervention was promised to deliver more prosperity helped to ensure that Labour would be seen as being more committed to using the levers of government power and planning in Scotland, and this witnessed the party start to open up a convincing lead over the Conservatives. Undoubtedly, it was Labour's ability to present itself as more committed to the Welfare

State and the planned economy that explains its better performance in Scotland compared to the Conservatives. As key industries declined and new industries failed to appear by the 1970s, there were greater expectations among the Scottish public that more state intervention was needed. Shipbuilding and car manufacturing were two areas of industrial activity that received increasing amounts of state aid in the late 1960s and early 1970s. The increasing use of government economic intervention demonstrated the growing public expectation that the state was responsible for socio-economic well-being.[106]

The state

British state intervention posed a number of particular problems for Scottish nationalists. Firstly, there was the appeal of the British state that was obviously working in electoral terms and for all practical intents and purposes, it would not be easy to offer counterfactual options based on the creation of a separate Scottish state in a way that would readily strike a chord with the voter. The important point about state intervention is the action regardless of which state is doing it. The only possible alternative would be to offer more or less of what is already happening. In one respect it would be like switching a supplier from one that was tried and tested to one that was not. With minimal or little state intervention in the interwar era, critiques of Westminster government tended to focus on the uneven nature of policy and could offer a plethora of possible developments that could be undertaken by a Scottish parliament. The issue of land use being a good case in point where land that was undeveloped could be brought under cultivation and used to create small holdings which would help to end rural depopulation. One major difficulty in the post-war era was that given the wide range of state intervention, it was difficulty to show how Scottish state intervention would be different or better. For the electorate it may not matter whether it is a Scottish or British state that is building council houses; the key thing is that municipal housing demand is met. Also, it was not clear how a Scottish state could undertake such activities and do them differently or better given the post-war predilection to trust and use 'experts' in determining social and economic policies. Tower blocks, for example, emerged as housing orthodoxy because this was the best way to create cheap housing as quickly as possible by using the minimum building materials, and this type of construction was not confined to the United Kingdom. This was advocated as a solution by experts and picked up by politicians of all political hues because it was 'scientifically' shown to be the best option. The old method of building discrete houses with gardens and the like was too costly and would take too long to satisfy the aspirations of the voters. In purely intellectual terms, it was hard for nationalists to come up with counter-proposals, and in effect they were only able to criticize major government policy on points of detail or offer minor suggestions. The first SNP MP, Robert McIntyre, for example, in the debate on health in Scotland at the end of the war used his own personal experience as an expert in public health to raise technical issues on tuberculosis and government policy preventing doctors from transferring from their current posts into areas where they were arguably more needed.[107] The other thing that nationalists could do in regard to state intervention was to point out and criticize when targets and objectives were not made. Archie Lamont, for example, set out the ways in which the government failed to deliver on its promises in the Clyde Valley Plan to bring new industries to Scotland and scale back on the reliance on the old traditional industries associated with coal, steel, heavy engineering and shipbuilding. As Lamont pointed out, the Scottish economy was more dependent on the old industries in the late 1950s than at any time during the interwar period.[108] Given the enormity of state intervention in the period from 1945 to 1976, nationalist were often forced to focus on the fringes of policy as that was the only area in which there was space and no competition from the British state. Usually this involved policy in the traditional areas of agriculture, fishing, education and housing as these were the areas covered by the Scottish Office.

The second way in which British state intervention caused problems for nationalists is that it increased the power of the state that they wanted to leave, which could make escape more difficult. The reform of the Scottish Office which took place in the late 1930s following the Gilmour Inquiry increasingly concentrated powers in the hands of the Scottish secretary of state that bypassed normal parliamentary scrutiny. This led some in the Labour Party to re-engage with the issue of forming a Scottish parliament as a way of creating a democratic check on the secretary of state who was compared to a colonial governor general. This development was significant because it marked the beginning of using devolution as a specific policy to check and balance the power of central government, rather than see home rule as a sort of open-ended policy.[109] Also, there was an element of pragmatism in this move as the Labour Party had been frozen out of increasing corporate developments which involved business but not trade unions in terms of consultation. It was the momentum from this development that carried on through the war which conditioned a half-hearted manifesto pledge in 1945 to create a Scottish parliament. This impetus was blunted by the fact that Labour held the position of secretary of state in Churchill's coalition and Tom Johnston, who was a formidable political figure by all accounts, opened up the corporate form of government to include Labour and the trade unions. Johnston was a creative thinker who used administrative devolution as an alternative to political devolution by creating the Committee of the Ex-Secretaries of State for Scotland as a means to push plans for post-war reconstruction.[110] He also used the Scottish Grand Committee of the House of Commons to much better effect and brought it to sit in Scotland for symbolic effect.[111] Furthermore, the exigencies of the war itself pushed the issue of Scottish home rule down the political agenda. Wartime emergency planning and intervention, for example, more or less created the infrastructure for the National Health Service in Scotland. The post-war era entailed a significant growth in the powers of the government in Scotland, and this was backed up by a massive expansion in the number of civil servants in the Scottish Office which increased from 2,300 in 1937 to 10,000 by the time of Margaret Thatcher in 1979.[112] Johnston was able to breathe new life into the Union by taking a number of actions that demonstrated the ways in which future British governments could have an impact on improving the socio-economic well-being of the populations. The promotion of ideas on post-war reconstruction and, in particular, Sir Patrick Abercrombie's *Clyde Valley Plan* demonstrated the potential of the transformative powers of the state.[113] The commonly held political assumption was that this trend in government intervention would not stop once the war was over.

During the period of the first Labour governments from 1945 to 1951, nationalist thunder was stolen as the Conservatives advanced a particular critique of the nationalization of key industries. It was argued that for Scotland this was a policy that effectively 'de-nationalized' the Scottish economy as more control would move southward as London exerted greater direct power through the nationalized sectors and industries. About a fifth of the economy which was previously managed in Scotland was now transferred south. No doubt there was a cynical element to Tory campaigning in which Scottish sentiment could be mobilized against the Labour government. Winston Churchill, when touring Scotland, claimed at Ibrox Stadium in front of 22,000 supporters that if he was Scottish he should be a nationalist to prevent the takeover of Scottish industry and reassert Scottish control.[114] This theme was echoed in a Unionist pamphlet *Scottish Control: Scottish Affairs* published the following year, and the Scottish Conservatives made great play of the issue in the elections of 1950 and 1951. The extent to which Scottish unease about greater centralized state control fed into the campaign for home rule manifested by the Scottish National Covenant in which more than two million signatures pledged their support is a point of discussion. But certainly in the late 1940s and early 1950s there was quite an increased manifestation of what might be called 'nationalist sentiment', albeit with a small 'n'. The issue facing the nationalist movement was that although there was public sympathy and support for self-government, however that may be defined, it had difficulty manifesting itself in electoral terms and, furthermore, a direct association with any campaign against state policies would lead to a close identification with the Tories which would hamper the party in terms of its image and its idea of ideological neutrality. As we have seen, John MacCormick who was the leader of the Covenant campaign, dented the idea of political neutrality by standing as a 'Independent' in the Paisley by-election of 1948 with a close relationship with the Liberal Party and the tacit support of the Tories who stood down to give him a clear run against Labour. Although MacCormick polled reasonably well, his loss seemed to dent the claim that home rule was as important as its protagonists claimed. This action did not endear the home rule movement to the Labour leadership and the Covenant and its two million signatures which was established in 1949 was dismissed by the claim that if the issue was so important then people could elect candidates on that ticket to Westminster to press the claim.[115] Conservative sympathy against excessive centralization dissipated once they were in power after 1951 and was reinforced by the work of the Catto Committee's Report on the Financial Relations between Scotland and England.[116] By late 1951, the economic argument against home rule or devolution was emerging as another element in the post-war consensus. According to the Earl of Home, at that time the minister of state for Scottish affairs:

> Sentiment is a virtue, and without sentiment no country has a soul. But in such matters which affect work and wages, housing and the whole range of the social services and social benefits, agricultural prices and food subsidies, the structure of organised labour, and taxation, sentiment must be tempered and tested by the

facts. I do not believe that any thoughtful Scotsman would contest it, and I do not believe that anyone who put his signature to the Covenant would thank any Minister of any Government who acted precipitately on sentiment and endangered lowering the standard of living of our people in Scotland.[117]

In the post-war era, the British state was extensively promoted as being the critical factor in maintaining the social and economic well-being of Scottish voters.

The third problem faced by nationalists in the debate regarding the role of state intervention was that there was little opportunity to offer distinctive policies of their own. Indeed, there was little substantive difference between the political offerings of the Conservatives and Labour Parties, more often than not the debate was about the ability to deliver than policy, and coming up with something different would have gone against the established intellectual orthodoxy of the day. A good example of this is council house building where Labour and the Conservatives tried to outbid each other in terms of targets set and achieved.[118] Nationalist policy put a bit more emphasis on crofting and rural areas, but the statement that 'only by planning on a national scale can conditions which for so long have been a disgrace to the civilised nations be remedied' could have been taken from either a Labour or Conservative manifesto of the 1960s.[119] Given that state intervention was the norm in the Western democracies in the period after the Second World War, it was less easy for nationalists to isolate the example of small nations from the larger ones when economic growth was broadly comparable across continental Western Europe.[120] Nationalists could and did model what could be achieved by way of state intervention by an independent nation, but there was little in the way of a substantive difference from what was already being offered by the two main parties.[121] The awkwardness of the issue of British state intervention may help explain its gravitation towards the centre and the tendency to blunt an overt left-wing perspective. Take the following example by Billy Wolfe writing in 1973:

> While I accept the facts of the so called 'class war' and the need for the working class in various places and in various times to close ranks and pursue class warfare, in order to combat exploitation and achieve a fairer distribution of wealth, I believe that in a participating democracy, social justice can be achieved with a minimum of the old class warfare, through legislation which ensures more participation and a much fairer distribution of wealth and which outlaws what we in the SNP call 'undue concentration of wealth' in a few hands. In fact by treating everybody as workers and by putting the interests of the people as a whole before the interests of any one section, and especially by spending far more of the nation's wealth on educating our people in social responsibilities and in the value and pleasure of cultural pursuits, we can gradually eradicate these class barriers.[122]

When the party made its electoral breakthrough in 1974, it described its policies in its October Manifesto of that year as being 'social democratic'. Arguably this ideological dimension was blurred by its neutrality in the House of Commons where it opted to vote on issues case by case based on merit. Furthermore, it was argued that it would neither favour the Labour nor the Conservatives, and its voting patterns accordingly showed that it was not especially biased to one side or the other. All this took place when the Labour government of the day had the narrowest of majorities which it lost in 1976 and had to rely on Liberal support.[123] Ideological fault lines opened up following the poor result in the general election of 1979 when the SNP share of the vote collapsed from just over 30 per cent to 17 per cent and its number of MPs declined from eleven to two. The fact that the SNP had voted against the Labour government leading to its downfall and the subsequent victory of Margaret Thatcher entered into Labour Party folklore. The studied neutrality of the nationalist movement in a British context together with the ambivalence on state intervention and the fact that the party seemed to do best in Tory voting areas in Scotland was used by the Labour Party to brand the movement as 'Tartan Tories'. In reality, the reason why the SNP did well in previous Tory voting areas was because they acted as an effective focal point for the anti-Tory vote. The resulting schisms and splits in the National Party following the poor election result in 1979 were described by the then party chairman, Gordon Wilson, as a 'plague of Jacobites and Jacobins' as right- and left-wing factions emerged.[124]

The crises facing the British state in the 1970s helped to promote a left-wing critique of the British state and its relationship to Scottish nationalism. Most famously associated with Tom Nairn and his *The Break Up of Britain* (1979) which argued that the British state was a survival of an early phase of capitalism that kept some aspects of feudalism alive and was basically a historical accident that had survived into the present. Others postulated that what was happening in Britain was a crisis of capitalism and that the Scottish situation was a form of colonialism which would eventually be overturned.[125] This more avowedly leftist approach was not one that was favoured by the party leadership and the early 1980s was replete with New Leftist anti-capitalist critiques of the Scottish situation that sought to tie the issue of Scottish independence more firmly to the mast of a left-wing perspective.[126] This view held that the key to the political future lay with the working class and that any attempt to gain independence without addressing this central issue was doomed to failure. The 1980s would witness the rise of a new generation of thinkers who became associated with the journal *Radical Scotland* that tied the issue of home rule and independence more firmly to the left.[127] The fact that the stalwart opposition to home rule came from the Conservative Party further reinforced the identification of a left-wing bias in favour of Scottish self-government. In the period from 1983 to 1997 anti-Conservatism was the dominant force in Scottish electoral politics, and this had the effect of convincing many in the nationalist movement that if there was a Scottish political consensus that they should seek to represent, it was not to be found on the right.[128] The broad coalition of forces that gathered together to promote home rule in the name of civic society further confirmed this anti-Conservative bent. One further issue that helped establish the idea of a left-leaning consensus was that political behaviour between Scotland and England had begun to diverge and constituencies in Scotland that had a socio-economic make-up that would have made them safe Conservative seats in England returned either Labour or Liberal candidates.[129] Even though tactical voting in Scotland took a toll on the number of Conservative MPs, the fact that the share of the vote collapsed to just under a quarter in the late 1980s and early 1990s showed that there was a significant difference between Scotland

and England. As the Scottish socio-economic profile was increasingly becoming the same as that south of the border, a separate political culture was used to explain the electoral divergence. For nationalists and others, this was taken as proof positive that the Scots were more left-wing inclined, more in favour of the mixed economy and supportive of the welfare state. In order to win an electoral mandate, the party would have to reflect the view of the Scottish electorate, and the fact that the English electorate was more right-wing was used as a further bolster for the argument in favour of independence.[130] And while the SNP became more clearly identified with the left in the 1980s, as James Mitchell pointed out, the reality, if not the perception, was that the party had always had a leftish hue.[131]

Difference

While the ideological spectrum was unavoidable, as were the consequent disputes and disruptions that followed in its wake, one of the features that marks the intellectual development of the national movement because it held the potential for greater unity was the need to try and be different from their British competitors. One of the key drivers of this tendency was the idea that there was a national political perspective and policies had to be adapted to this. Obviously the greater difference such policies had compared to those on offer from the British political parties, the more it could be argued that this was a consequence of the different political culture in Scotland. The idea that there was a distinctive way of doing politics North of the Border was an article of faith, but quite what this was remained for the most part elusive. Often this would set them down different political routes and arguably it is this willingness to dally with unorthodox ideas that has helped the modern SNP accommodate itself to a left-of-centre position that increasingly tried to present policies as being emblematic of a wider Scottish political culture.[132] This need to plough a different furrow manifested itself in the 1930s when a number of activists advocated for the adoption of the economics of the Douglas Social Credit movement. Clifford Douglas wrote *Social Credit* in 1924, and it set out to apply the principles of engineering in designing an economic system that would ensure that consumption would be the driver of production and rectify scarcity of goods – which was the principal means to make profits – by increasing purchasing power. These ideas gained considerable currency in the dominions and were mooted as a cure to the problems of the Great Depression. In Scotland, Hugh MacDiarmid utilized the ideas of Social Credit to formulate what he called 'Neo Gaelic Economics', although in reality most of what was proposed was gibberish:

> The difference between Russian Bolshevism and neo-Gaelic Communism will lie in the attitude to the arts. Can a Gaelic state in the light of tradition be envisaged in which the keystone of the arch would be the creation, recognition, and use of genius – in which, as a consequence, the synthesis of all the elements would be, not towards the most backward, but towards the most advanced, in which the utmost freedom would be the conscious and co-operative aim of all, and in which the mere means of life would be relegated to as subordinate a place as possible in

relation to the ends? Such a state of society would be in profound harmony with the essentials of the Gaelic genius.[133]

MacDiarmid, who had as little time for economics as understanding of the subject, above all craved a distinctive policy that would stand out as something different from what was on offer from the main political parties, and this was a factor that led him into his support for both Fascism and Communism. Chris Harvie has perhaps too kindly described MacDiarmid as having an 'ideological inconsistency' when it is probably more accurate to say that he had no real ideological commitment other than what would, as he saw it, further his artistic ambitions and promote Scottish independence.[134] That said, Douglas Social Credit did win quite a significant number of followers within the national movement precisely because it did help make the nationalist message more distinctive.[135]

This desire to promote a particularly Scottish vision of policy that differentiates the programme of the SNP from its British competitors found expression in the ideas of Robert McIntyre who laid out the aims of the party in 1946, and this was the position that served throughout most of the post-war era until the 1980s. In terms of socio-economic matters there was a strong emphasis on the rights of the individual and a frequent point made by McIntyre in his many speeches was that the individual was being squeezed by both the forces of impersonal capitalism and big government. The individual had a right to private property and the right to choose private healthcare and education if they wanted. A focus on state bureaucracy and its impersonal qualities was a way of attacking the Labour government's programme of nationalization in an indirect fashion. The historian Harry Hanham posited that such ideas were similar to some of the social democrat-type movements that existed in the 'white dominions', again demonstrating the enduring influence of the imperial legacy.[136] Just as other nationalists had argued that small-nation nationalism was a form of preserving ideas of individuality, so McIntyre and others in the leadership in the post-war era saw a distinctive furrow in trying to steer a path between the big combinations that threatened the role of the individual, namely big government, big trade unions and big business. Also, it avoided the left–right dichotomy. These forces, it goes without saying tended to be more pronounced in big states and the state intervention of the small state was not as impersonal, so the argument went. Also, to counteract the reach of the state, there was an emphasis on local government as a way to bring a democratic input back to the local community at a time when powerful forces were reshaping society. McIntyre wanted to steer a middle path, as he saw it, between the excesses of socialism on the one hand and the excesses of capitalism on the other. The party programme of 1946 did make the case that there should be state intervention and planning and did talk about the need for a fair distribution in society. A key component was to diversify the economy and develop the Highlands and rural areas:

> Planning must be forward looking and creative, and in Scotland it should be directed towards a better distribution of work and people between the industrial belt and the rest of the country. It should aim at ensuring the fullest use of natural resources consistent with the welfare of the community and family life.[137]

In keeping with the rights of the individual and local democracy, the party was also pledged to ensure that the growth of state and business monopolies was kept firmly in check:

> The economic safeguard of democracy lies in the diffusion of economic power. The concentration of economic power in either state or private monopolies is inimical both to the freedom of the individual and to the proper functioning of democratic government. In order to ensure democratic control of the economic structure of the state it is essential therefore either to eliminate or to subject to strict supervision all private monopolies and restrict state monopolies to the minimum. It is in the national interest to increase the technical efficiency of small and medium size production units in every way as, for example, by encouraging cooperation for research and marketing. Where, however, technical efficiency requires very large productive units and thus monopoly or virtual monopoly such monopolies must be state owned.[138]

In a way, this was trying to engage with some of the key development in the post-war British economy. Firstly, by linking democracy with property and seeing the proliferation of small business as an important indicator of well-being it was trying to posit an alternative to the idea that the state should command the pillars of the economy as was promoted by the advocates of nationalization. While the notion of the mixed economy was one that was accepted as an orthodoxy in post-war Britain, by asserting the importance of small business, the SNP was pushing for what it saw as an important sector, especially as a residual fear was that much of the control of business on Scotland was drifting south. This would also chime in well with the interest of the countryside and rural communities in which the party hoped to do well, believing that previous Liberal strongholds had helped slow down the ingrained class interest of both the Labour and Conservative Parties.[139]

The SNP argued that 'the standard of living of the people depends on the distribution as well as the amount of the national income and national wealth, it is desirable that economic activity should be distributed throughout all parts of the country and that there should be no great inequalities in individual wealth and income'.[140] What was not clear was the role of the state in redistribution of wealth and the use of state intervention. There is a sense, although it was never really articulated to any great extent, that the nationalist vision of an independent Scotland was based on a predominantly semi-rural economy comprising of many small and medium-sized businesses and, as far as possible, the main capacity of the economy should be internally generated. Much of this was the logical outcome of arguing that the economy had been mismanaged by Westminster, therefore a better controlled economy would be able to expand and this could be done relatively painlessly by substituting exports for home-grown production.[141] A focus on agriculture and fisheries suggested a predilection for autarky, and it aimed for the 'fullest development of the home production of food' as this was a fundamental national policy 'in order to provide a sure basis for the physical health of the people and to achieve a wise balance economically between town and country'.[142] In part, a major factor in the nationalist predilection for the rural and small business economy was down to the fact that it would take the economic profile closer to that of other small European nations.[143] Also, the relative importance attached to the farming and fishing sector was one of the reasons why there was a strong sense of Euro-scepticism in the party until the 1980s.

While there was clearly an element that wanted to create a set of distinctive policies that made the party stand out from both Labour and the Tories, there is also a throwback to the dominant Scottish political culture of the period before the First World War. By attempting to steer a middle course between the left and the right and by endeavouring to extol both the rights of the individual and the positive dimension of state intervention, there was a harking back to the 'New Liberalism' of the early twentieth century.[144] The New Liberalism (which is not to be confused with Neo Liberalism) stated that the rights of the individual were paramount and the state should not interfere with those rights, which the individual should be able to exploit to the best of their abilities. This was the classic Liberal doctrine, but what made it new was that it also recognized that without a minimum standard of economic and social well-being and education, such individual freedoms were worthless. Therefore, it was the duty of the state to provide a social infrastructure that would provide the opportunities for individuals to exploit to the best of their abilities their freedoms.[145] Although it is always difficult to chart the movement of ideas with precision, there is a historical consensus that the ideas of the New Liberalism were very strong in Scotland before the First World War and that these passed into the post-war Labour Party, where they then subsequently made their way into the early SNP. A key conduit for this process was the Young Scots Society which included Tom Gibson, Roland Muirhead and J. L. Kinloch.[146] Robert McIntyre had been a member of the Labour Party in his student days and was the foremost champion of the rights of the individual and advocated the creation of a Scottish Bill of Rights that would enshrine in law a 'defence against arbitrary power and provide freedom within the law and use the law as a protector of freedom and justice'.[147] He had an instinctive suspicion of left- and right-wing ideology and believed his position in the middle was 'neutral' in the sense that it was, as many liberals think, non-ideological:

> The Scottish National Party was often accused in the past by those thirled to orthodox socialist conceptions of being reactionary and chauvinistic, and by those of the right of being another type of socialist party. Instinctively the National Party kept clear of the tentacles of either of those parties or their ideologies, representing as they did, the opposing economic forces within industry and the economy fighting for its control ... We beware of ideologies ... in the beginning they may have a fine ideal. The ideologies produce a scheme, a system, a faith, with or without works which they believe will bring their ideal about. In due course they get stuck with the system of thought rather with the original ideal and you have an ideology for its own sake. Its original purpose goes, the human reasons and moral considerations which initiated the process become lost and forgotten ... the ideology becomes the god and everything that serves it becomes justified.[148]

Because the movement stressed the primacy of independence above that of ideology, McIntyre argued that pragmatism should be its guiding principle especially in relation to working out what were the obligations of the state and what were the responsibilities of the individual.[149] The extent to which this represented a continuity with the New Liberalism of the early twentieth century is a point for debate, but it was created as a result of the need to try and manufacture a philosophy that was different from that of its British opponents and at the same time anchor itself in a Scottish intellectual tradition.

Conclusion

From the outset, the Scottish national movement has had more members who were of a left-wing political disposition than those who were of the right, although there were and are a number of the latter. The relationship with the ideological spectrum was made complex by the fact that a central aspect of strategy was that independence should always come first, even though there have always been a significant number of 'instrumental' nationalists who saw an independent Scotland as the most effective means to realize a particular ideological vision, usually associated with the left. Furthermore, both as a means of maximizing support, but also of manufacturing moral legitimacy, the movement has had to eschew any notion that it would exclude any elements within society and that it would seek to represent all. This meant that it adopted the common nationalist trope of pitching its appeal beyond class and the inability or reluctance to talk about class limited the range of its ideological engagement to the centre. It was further constrained by a determination not to be associated with populist nationalism, which toned down its language and appeal to the 'people'. The need to demonstrate credibility on socio-economic policy, but without appealing to one section of society or the other, pushed forward a narrative of grievance and a particular focus on maximizing domestic production and consumption. In the marketplace of political ideas, the need to have an identifiable selling point pushed the party towards a focus on agriculture and rural society, in part because it was neglected by Labour, which tended to focus on its urban electorate and the Conservative focus that catered more for the specifics of the English countryside. Arguably the desire to steer a middle way between the Labour Party and the Conservative Party in the post-war era when the middle ground was already heavily contested meant that a premium was placed on policies that could help give the SNP a more distinctive profile. Because ideology came second to independence it meant that the national movement was easy to characterize as an organization of the left or right by its political opponents. Also it meant that ideological divisions within the movement were never far from the surface and could break through during times of crisis. Perhaps, most significantly, it pushed pragmatism as a counterpoise to questions of ideology.

Conclusion

Scotland is the only country which has ever voluntarily given an alien culture precedence in its schools, and eschewed its own. Scottish literature and Scottish history should form the staple of the literature and history lessons in our schools. There is no earthly reason why English literature should be taught to any greater extent than German, French or Italian. The re-Scottisisation of Scottish education is a programme that no sane Scot can oppose. Any attempt to do so is to put himself in a position no citizen of any other country – above all no Englishman – would contemplate for a moment.
– C. M. Grieve, 'Towards a Scottish Renaissance: Desirable Lines of Advance',
Scots Independent, May 1929, 89

In the quote above, Hugh MacDiarmid was one of many critics who argued that the Scots did not act and behave like a normal nation and that this had an impact in terms of the development of culture and identity. Tom Nairn called it the 'Tartan Monster' and described Scottish culture as 'deformed' and famously or infamously argued that Scotland would not be free until the last minister was strangled by the last edition of the *Sunday Post*.[1] As a nation, Scotland has been extensively psychoanalysed by cultural critics, and for non-nationalists like Edwin Muir, the trauma is located with John Knox and the Reformation.[2] But for most the trouble began with the Union of 1707, and at the time of the emergence of the national movement there was a widespread assumption that the terminus of the process begun in 1707 would be the extinction of Scottish identity:

> More powerful nations than the Scots have lived and died; and their dead languages have been preserved only in the mortuary of the schools. Even the language of the Scots is dying before the corpus of the nation has succumbed, because the ubiquitous and more commercially convenient vehicle of their political conquerors has been substituted and accepted. Thus with the children denied access to the fount of their cultural heritage, the time is rapidly approaching when shall arise an Anglicized generation which, without the aid of a glossary, cannot read Burns, not to mention Dunbar and the other genuine makers of Scottish poetry and literature. The process of Anglicization would then be complete with the spectacle of a dead

nation, dumb to its own mother tongue, but speaking its adopted language with a perfect accent that only a born imitator could acquire.[3]

In retrospect, such fears were unfounded and overly pessimistic, but the important fact to emphasize because it is often forgotten is that much of the creation of the national movement and its subsequent development have been driven by a quite legitimate fear of national decline, if not national extinction. For those in doubt as to whether there has been a decline, had the population distribution of the British mainland remained consistent in its national profile from 1707, the current population of Scotland would be twice what it is today. If it had kept pace in the twentieth century with other small Western European nations, it would now stand at about eight million, rather than its current figure of about five-and-a-half million. The debate about Scottish independence is one that is rooted in perceptions of decline, but it rarely comes to the surface. Unionists argue against independence *because* of decline – Scotland is too poor and small – while nationalists argue in favour of independence to *reverse* the process of decline. The idea of Scottish decline forms a central plank of both philosophies and also an uneasy consensus if ever there was one.

If we date the origins of the campaign for Scottish independence to the Scots National League (SNL) which was founded in 1920, then the national movement has had a century to evolve and develop a mature understanding of nationalism and one that is more suited to the contemporary world than many of its compatriots across time and space. The distance from political success is not necessarily a bad thing for the evolution of ideas, and while it has only been in the past decade and a half that the Scottish National Party (SNP) has emerged as the major force in Scottish politics, it has done so with a century's worth of development under its belt. While it may be argued that it has been the peculiar circumstances of the early twenty-first century that has propelled the issue of Scottish independence to the top of the political agenda, the fact that there has been a long and sustained political debate in relation to national identity and nationalism in Scotland has perhaps ensured that some of the more visceral and extreme notions that have emerged elsewhere in Europe have not appeared in Scotland. The emergence of a popular national movement that is social democratic, cosmopolitan and welcoming and supportive of refugees and immigrants is not the norm, and it has been described as a post-nation nationalism.[4] In England, the tendency for a knee-jerk reaction to categorize discussion about ideas of nationalism and the nation as the intellectual property of the far right, coupled with a reticence on the part of those on the left to engage with the question for fear of legitimizing it, arguably has led to a widespread public and political immaturity in which cartoonish notions of British exceptionalism paved the way for Brexit.[5] The history of English nationalism and English national identity remains remarkably understudied in academia.[6] For any nation, this is not a healthy state of affairs.

While one should always be wary of the dangers of citing exceptionalism in history, the Scottish historical experience is difficult to pigeonhole. It does not conform to the model where a nation is colonized and absorbed into a bigger territorial entity only to re-emerge either through revolution, conflict or imperial disintegration at a later date. Nor does it chime in with many of what Norman Davies describes as

Europe's 'Vanished Kingdoms' where the process of absorption and assimilation was completed.[7] The history of Scotland shows that it had achieved a fairly advanced stage of statehood in the medieval and early modern periods and that the Union of 1707 failed in its objective to make an incorporating or complete Union in which Scotland was absorbed into the English state. Unlike the French state which engaged in a process of Frenchification and centralization in the nineteenth century, the British state was remarkably decentralized and British society was strongly provincial. Not that you would know from reading the history books which have an overwhelmingly London-centric perspective.[8] Scotland retained enough of a historical residue to prevent its complete assimilation, and, paradoxically, in the twentieth century when the British state massively increased its presence in Scotland, it did so in an administratively devolved way which reinforced the territorial dimension of Scottish politics. One way of looking at the historical development of Scotland is to see the Union as creating a constitutional twilight zone in which nationhood was strong enough to withstand the absence of statehood, but as time passed, statehood has come to be seen as a necessary condition of nationhood, and devolution, which is a form of semi-statehood, has simply reinforced that trend. If Scotland does become independent, historians in the future will no doubt see the growth of government in the twentieth century, be that administrative or political devolution, as simply the tendons of the state reconnecting after being severed in 1707.

Throughout this book, we have largely described those who have advocated for the independence of Scotland as the *national* movement and not the *nationalist* movement. As we have seen there has always been a delicate and nuanced relationship with the idea of nationalism in the sense that beyond independence, it serves no purpose. Theoretically, the movement on completion of its goal ceases to have a raison d'etre and contains the seed of its own destruction. In the meantime, expedient or instrumental nationalism, civic or liberal nationalism and small-nation nationalism have been used as a way to distinguish the movement from the more virulent forms of the political philosophy. But there is another important dimension to the movement which is to reinforce the idea that there is a distinctive *national* aspect to Scottish politics, and this has been a secondary function of the SNP, albeit one that makes the case that Scotland is a nation and has a national interest which is best served by being an independent state. In a political area which has been dominated by British political parties, although often adopting a Scottish guise, arguably it has been the SNP which has consistently kept the issue of there being a distinctive Scottish political dimension at the fore. As a political party, the SNP ought to be measured by its electoral success which until comparatively recently was nothing to write home about. But this only tells one part of the story; a key aspect of its function and existence was to maintain the idea that Scotland still survived as a political entity and prevented the wholesale assimilation into the British system. The articulation of a Scottish national interest, which the movement has constantly promoted, is an important one in that it has helped to normalize the debate and take the sting out of the nationalist tail. The broad acceptance that there is a Scottish national interest by all political parties in which, for example, educational attainment can be judged by international comparisons has meant that it is possible to talk about Scottish politics in the same way that we would describe Angela Merkel as pursuing a German national interest, but that does not make her a nationalist. The normalization of the national in Scottish political debate has been an important factor in both making it mainstream but also preventing it being hijacked by extremists.

As historians know only too well, nothing lasts forever. The political future of the British Islands remains uncertain, but one way of explaining that uncertainty is to postulate that what we are witnessing is not so much the growth of Scottish, Welsh and, at different stages, Irish nationalism in the late twentieth and early twenty-first centuries but rather the disintegration and collapse of British nationalism and British national identity back into its original constituents. Of course, the elephant in the room is English nationalism and the way that in the past decade or so it has been the principal driver of British state disintegration by encouraging the growth of independence movements in Scotland and Wales and a reunification movement in Ireland.[9] It is interesting to note that the last bastions of Britishness are increasingly to be found in Scottish, Ulster and Welsh unionism. For English nationalists, the Celtic peripheries have never mattered anyway, and the genuine lack of concern for the future of the 'precious union' must cause alarm for those that stress the primacy of their British identity in Scotland. In one sense, the debate regarding independence can be seen as a competition between two nationalisms: British and Scottish, big nation and small nation, Great Power or small power and now isolationist/Global Britain or European Unionist. British unionism has obscured that dichotomy, but the growth of English nationalism has blown away the fig leaf of unionism as a historic British partnership. Perhaps the most significant question to address is why unionism has not been able to accommodate the recent rise of English nationalism and national identity. That, however, is for another book and another historian.

Notes

Introduction

1. https://www.spectator.co.uk/article/scottish-independence-has-become-a-zombie-policy (although the convention is to give the date when online sources are accessed, I have dispensed with this as it consumes a lot of space for no good reason).
2. Currently the percentage of under-thirty-five in favour of independence stands at somewhere in the high sixties, but it is worth remembering the young were also more in favour in the 1970s. William L. Miller, *The End of British Politics? Scots and English Political Behaviour in the Seventies* (Oxford, 1981), 112. Currently, it is more than twice as high as in 1974.
3. On the recent political history of Scotland, see T. M. Devine, *Independence or Union? Scotland's Past and Scotland's Present* (London, 2017); Iain Macwhirter, *Tsunami: Scotland's Democratic Revolution* (Glasgow, 2015); and Rob Johns and James Mitchell, *Takeover: Explaining the Extraordinary Rise of the SNP* (London, 2016).
4. Margaret Thatcher, *The Downing Street Years* (London, 1993), 624.
5. For a good overview of the subject in its historical context, see James Mitchell, *The Scottish Question* (Oxford, 2014).
6. This is a different take from Ben Jackson's recent book, *The Case for Independence: A History of Nationalist Political Thought in Modern Scotland* (Cambridge, 2020), which focuses on the period after 1960 and examines the idea of independence in left-wing intellectual circles whereas this study is a broader examination of the wider movement with a focus on the political activists.
7. J. R. Seeley, *The Expansion of England: Two Courses of Lectures* (London, 1883), 131; and J. R. Green, *A Short History of England* (London, 1876), 689, for example.
8. See, for example, Neal Acherson, 'Scotland, Brexit and the Persistence of Empire', in Stuart Ward and Astrid Rasch (eds), *Embers of Empire in Brexit Britain* (London, 2019), 71–9. For a discussion which points out that it is fundamentally changes in Englishness that is driving the constitutional question, see Ailsa Henderson and Richard Wyn Jones, *Englishness: The Political Force That Is Transforming Britain* (Oxford, 2021).
9. Sir Reginald Coupland, *Welsh and Scottish Nationalism: A Study* (London, 1954), xvii.
10. Ibid., 414.
11. See Stuart Ward and Astrid Rash (eds), *Embers of Empire in Brexit Britain* (London, 2019); and Bernard Porter, *Britain before Brexit: Historical Essay on Britain and Europe* (London, 2021), 183–247.
12. Scott Hames, *The Literary Politics of Scottish Devolution: Voice, Class and Nation* (Edinburgh, 2019); Jackson, *The Case for Scottish Independence*; Malcolm Petrie, 'Anti-Socialism, Liberalism and Individualism: Rethinking the Realignment of Scottish Politics, 1945–1970', *Transactions of the Royal Historical Society*, vol. 28 (2018), 197–217; and Naomi Lloyd-Jones, 'Liberalism, Scottish Nationalism and

the Home Rule Crisis, c. 1886–1893', *English Historical Review*, vol. 129, 538 (2014), 862–87.
13. The key early studies were H. J. Hanham, *Scottish Nationalism* (London, 1969); Jack Brand, *The National Movement in Scotland* (London, 1978); Keith Webb, *The Growth of Nationalism in Scotland* (London, 1978); and Michael Keating and David Bleiman, *Labour and Scottish Nationalism* (London, 1978).
14. For a good overview of the issues, see Murray G. H. Pittock, *Scottish Nationality* (Basingstoke, 2001).
15. On the history of the SNP, see Richard J. Finlay, *Independent and Free: Scottish Politics and the Origins of the Scottish National Party, 1918–1945* (Edinburgh, 1994); Paula Somerville, *Through the Maelstrom: A History of the Scottish National Party, 1945–1967* (Stirling, 2013); Peter Lynch, *SNP: A History of the Scottish National Party* (Cardiff, 2013); Gerry Hassan (ed.), *The Modern SNP: From Protest to Power* (Edinburgh, 2009); James Mitchell and Gerry Hassan (eds), *Scottish National Party Leaders* (London, 2016); Ewen Cameron is currently completing a PhD on the party in the 1970s at Strathclyde University.
16. The following review articles are useful. James Kellas was a pioneer of Scottish political science and his 'Political Science and Scottish Politics', *British Journal of Political Science*, vol. 10, 3 (1980), 365–79, is still worth looking at. Two useful starting points are James Mitchell, 'The Study of Scottish Politics Post-Devolution: New Evidence, New Analysis and New Methods?', *West European Politics*, vol. 24, 4 (2001), 216–33; and Neil McGarvey, 'New Scottish Politics, New Texts Required', *British Journal of Politics and International Relations*, vol. 3, 3 (2001), 427–44.
17. James Mitchell, *Conservatives and the Union: A Study of Conservative Party Attitudes to Scotland* (Edinburgh, 1990).
18. James Mitchell, *Strategies for Self-Government: The Campaign for a Scottish Parliament* (Edinburgh, 2001).
19. James Mitchell, 'Factions, Tendencies and Consensus in the SNP in the 1980s', *Scottish Government Yearbook, 1990*, 49–61.
20. James Mitchell, Lynne Bennie and Rob Johns, *The Scottish National Party: Transition to Power* (Oxford, 2011).
21. Mitchell, *Scottish Question*.
22. For a discussion of the issues, see Richard J. Finlay, 'Does History Matter? Political Scientists, Welsh and Scottish Devolution', *20th Century British History*, vol. 12, 2 (2001), 243–50.
23. Iain McLean, 'The Rise and Fall of the Scottish National Party', *Political Studies*, vol. 18, 3 (1970), 357–72.
24. For an intelligent discussion on the importance of definitional precision, see Alastair Raffe, '1707, 2007, and the Unionist Turn in Scottish History', *Historical Journal*, vol. 53, 4 (2010), 1071–83.
25. For a discussion on Scottish Unionism, see Colin Kidd, *Union and Unionisms: Political Though in Scotland, 1500–2000* (Cambridge, 2008).
26. The term was invented by Graeme Morton, *Unionist Nationalism: Governing Urban Scotland, 1830–1860* (East Linton, 1999), who acknowledges the contradictory nature of this term.
27. See Murray Stuart Leith and Daniel P. J. Soule, *Political Discourse and National Identity in Scotland* (Edinburgh, 2012), 13.
28. In doing this I have followed Michael Freeden, *Ideology: A Very Short Introduction* (Oxford, 2003).

29. For a discussion of the complexities involved, see Gary Alan Fine and Kent Sandstrom, 'Ideology in Action: A Pragmatic Approach to a Contested Concept', *Sociological Theory*, vol. 11, 1 (1993), 21–38.
30. H. T. Dickinson, *Liberty and Property: Political Ideology in 18th Century Britain* (London, 1979), 6.
31. Colin Coote, *A Companion of Honour: The Story of Walter Elliot in Westminster and Scotland* (London, 1965), 48.
32. In particular, see Alan Bold, *MacDiarmid: A Critical Biography* (London, 1988); Marjory McCulloch, *The Novels of Neil M. Gunn: A Critical Study* (Edinburgh, 1987); and Cory Gibson, *The Voice of the People: Hamish Henderson and Scottish Cultural Politics* (Edinburgh, 2017).
33. The classic study of pressure groups in the nineteenth century is D. A. Hamer, *The Politics of Electoral Pressure: A Study in Victorian Reform Agitation* (London, 1977).
34. Finlay, *Independent and Free*, 251–3.
35. See Derek Heater, *National Self-Determination: Woodrow Wilson and His Legacy* (London, 2014), 21–78.
36. See Hugh Seton-Watson, *Nations and States* (London, 1977), 143–93.
37. R. C. Snelling, 'Peace Making 1919: Australia, New Zealand and the British Empire Delegation at Versailles', *Journal of Imperial and Commonwealth History*, vol. 4, 1 (1975), 15–28; and Margaret McMillan, 'Canada and the Peace Settlement', in David Mackenzie (ed.), *Canada and the First World War* (London, 2005), 379–408.
38. Ronan Fanning, *Fatal Path: British Government and the Irish Revolution, 1910–1922* (London, 2013).
39. Susan Pederson, *The Guardians: The League of Nations and the Crisis of Empire* (Oxford, 2015), 44–77.
40. See K. C. Wheare, *The Statute of Westminster and Dominion Status* (London, 1949).
41. David McCrone, *The Sociology of Nationalism: Tomorrow's Ancestors* (London, 1998), 63.
42. For a short history of Scotland written by a nationalist activists, see James Halliday, *Scotland: A Concise History* (Edinburgh, 1996); and J. M. Reid, *Scotland: Past and Present* (Oxford, 1959). Halliday was a trained academic historian and the average reader would not be aware of any overt bias, while Reid was a nationalist polemicist. For a one-volume history of Scotland, see M. Lynch, *Scotland: A New History* (various ed.); and Allan I. Macinnes, *A History of Scotland* (Basingstoke, 2015). The medieval and early modern period could do with being served with a comparable volume like T. M. Devine, *The Scottish Nation: A Modern History* (London, 2012). On the emergence of the Scottish Kingdom, see Dauvit Broun, *Scottish Independence and the Idea of Britain: From the Picts to Alexander III* (Edinburgh, 2013).
43. Hagen Schulze, *States, Nations and Nationalism: From the Middle Ages to the Present* (London, 1998), 137–97.
44. Anthony D. Smith, *Nationalism* (Cambridge, 2010), 95–129. For a wider discussion of the nation and history, see Stefan Berger, Mark Donovan and Kevin Passmore (eds), *Writing National Histories: Western Europe since 1800* (London, 1998); Stefan Berger with Chris Conrad, *The Past as History: National Identity and Historical Consciousness in Modern Europe* (Basingstoke, 2014); and Stefan Berger and Chris Lorenz (eds), *Nationalizing the Past: Historians as Nation Builders in Europe* (Basingstoke, 2010).
45. For example, the Scots National League, the Scottish National Movement, the National Party of Scotland, the Scottish National Convention and the Scottish National Congress.

46. There is a vast literature on the subject but a good starting point is Umut Ozkirimli, *Theories of Nationalism: A Critical Introduction* (London, 2000); and Steven Grosby, *Nationalism: A Very Short Introduction* (Oxford, 2005).
47. Barton Swaim, 'Scotland's Post-National Nationalism', *The Washington Post*, 29 August 2016. https://www.washingtonpost.com/opinions/global-opinions/scotlands-post-national-nationalism/2016/08/27/ce607152-6afb-11e6-ba32-5a4bf5aad4fa_story.html.
48. BBC Broadcast, 27 September 1938: https://www.bbc.co.uk/archive/chamberlain-addresses-the-nation-on-his-negotiations-for-peace/zjrjgwx.
49. See W. K. Hancock's polemic, *Argument of Empire: A Penguin Special* (London, 1943).
50. Perhaps the best-known advocate of Soviet expansion was the historian E. H. Carr. See Jonathan Haslam, *The Vices of Integrity: E. H. Carr, 1892–1982* (London, 1999), 93.
51. Ian Kershaw, *To Hell and Back: Europe 1914–1949* (London, 2016), 16–18.
52. Alvin Jackson, *Home Rule: An Irish History* (Oxford, 2004), 156.
53. For a recent collection of the impact of the Declaration on Scottish history and culture, see Klaus Peter Muller (ed.), *Scotland and Arbroath, 1320–2020: 700 Years of Fighting for Freedom, Sovereignty and Independence* (Leck, 2020).
54. On the revolutionary dynamic of the covenant, see Terry Brotherstone (ed.), *Covenant, Charter and Party: Traditions of Revolt and Protest in Modern Scotland* (Aberdeen, 1989); and on Ulster, see A. T. Q. Stewart, *The Ulster Crisis: Resistance to Home Rule, 1912–14* (London, 1969).
55. For the European context, see Tibor Frank and Frank Hadler (eds), *Disputed Territories and Shared Pasts: Overlapping National Histories in Modern Europe* (Basingstoke, 2015).
56. The Treaty of Union covers about twelve pages depending on the size of print. Compare this with the eighty pages of text in the Treaty of Rome.
57. The phrase was popularized by David McCrone, *Understanding Scotland: The Sociology of a Stateless Nation* (London, 1992), but the 'Stateless' was dropped in the post-devolution editions.
58. This was the thrust of Alfred Zimmern, *The Third British Empire: Being a Course of Lectures at Columbia University* (Oxford, 1926).
59. Speech made in Cork, 21 January 1885.
60. In 1912 the Scottish Liberal Unionists and the Scottish Conservative Party merged to form the Scottish Unionist Party, although the Union in question was the Irish one. It acted as an independent party until 1965, when it was absorbed into the wider British Conservative party and its name was changed to the Scottish Conservative and Unionist Party. By the late 1970s it was completely controlled by Conservative Central Office. For a nuanced discussion of the Conservative Party in Scotland and the relationship with Unionism, see David Seawright, *An Important Matter of Principle: The Decline of the Conservative and Unionist Party* (London, 2018 edn), 127–57.
61. Gwyn A. Williams, *When Was Wales? The History, People and Culture of an Ancient Country* (London, 1985), which demonstrates the difficulties of applying simplistic and retrospective categories on the past.
62. House of Commons Debates, 7 July 1857, vol. 146, col. 1049.
63. *Daily Record*, 29 November 1932. It is worth noting that Stanley Baldwin, the leader of the Conservative party at the time, published his collected speeches with the title, *On England and Other Addresses* (London, 1926), which was reprinted in 1938.

64. Colin Kidd has adapted Michael Billig's notion of banal nationalism to make the case that the reason Unionism does not have a greater presence in the nineteenth and twentieth centuries is that it was taken for granted and understated. The Union was part of the 'wallpaper of Scottish political life'. Kidd, *Union and Unionisms*, 23-4. While the presence of the Union may have been understated and a relatively unacknowledged political reality, it is quite another thing to imply that a fairly complex political philosophy is evidenced by this. Furthermore, Billig's notion also implied an extensive engagement with the nation, albeit not necessarily noticed, especially in relation to popular culture. What would probably make more sense is to say that 'banal' British nationalism in Scotland was an important prop of the Union, but is that the same thing as unionism? Michael Billig, *Banal Nationalism* (London, 1995), especially chapter 5, 'Flagging the Homeland Daily'.
65. M. Cragoe, '"We Like Local Patriotism": The Conservative Party and the Discourse of Decentralisation, 1947–51', *English Historical Review*, vol. 122, 498 (2007), 965–85.
66. Keating and Bleiman, *Labour and Scottish Nationalism*.
67. This became a key feature of the post-war era and was first set out in Robert McIntyre, *Some Principles for Scottish Reconstruction* (Glasgow, 1944).
68. The only available study of Douglas is by Bob Hesketh, *Major Douglas and Alberta Social Credit* (Toronto, 1997). The fact that Douglas was influenced by the Protocols of the Elders of Zion may help explain his current obscurity.
69. The classic account is by Michael Freeden, *The New Liberalism: An Ideology of Social Reform* (Oxford, 1986).

1 The historic nation

1. On the Scottish border in the medieval period, see John Sadler, *Border Fury: England and Scotland at War, 1296–1568* (2005). It is worth noting that the 'territorial' dimension of modern British politics has been picked up more by political scientists than historians. See James Mitchell, *Devolution in the United Kingdom* (Manchester, 2012).
2. See Aviel Roshwald, *Ethnic Nationalism and the Fall of Empires: Central Europe, Russia and the Middle East, 1914–23* (London, 2000); Volker Prott, *The Politics of Self-Determination: Remaking Territories and National Identities in Europe, 1917–1923* (Oxford, 1916); and Larry Wolff, *Woodrow Wilson and the Reimagining of Eastern Europe* (Stanford, 2020).
3. On the longer term consequences of the Paris Settlement, see Alan Sharp, *The Consequence of the Peace: The Versailles Settlement, Its Aftermath and Its Legacy, 1919–2015* (London, 2015).
4. See Robert Lynch, *The Partition of Ireland, 1918–25* (Cambridge, 2019); and Diarmid Ferriter, *The Border: The Legacy of a Century of Anglo-Irish Politics* (London, 2019).
5. Richard J. Finlay, 'Thatcherism, Unionism and Nationalism: A Comparative Study of Scotland and Wales', in Ben Jackson and Robert Saunders (eds), *Making Thatcher's Britain* (Cambridge, 2012), 165–80.
6. This was a notion advocated by Rory Stewart in the BBC series 'Border Country: The Story of Britain's Lost Middleland' (2014) and developed in his *The Marches: A Borderland between England and Scotland* (London, 2017).

7. On the formation of the early kingdom, see Dauvit Broun, *Scottish Independence and the Idea of Britain: From the Picts to Alexander III* (Edinburgh, 2007).
8. Robert Bartlett, *The Making of Europe: Conquest, Colonization and Cultural Change, 950–1350* (London, 1993), 40–2.
9. Norman MacDougall, *An Antidote to the English: The Auld Alliance, 1295–1560* (East Linton, 2001).
10. On the evolution of the ideas that vindicated the idea that the Scots were a distinctive people with their own history, see William Ferguson, *The Identity of the Scottish Nation: An Historic Quest* (Edinburgh, 1998).
11. See 'Introduction' in Stefan Berger and Eric Storm (eds), *Writing the History of Nationalism* (London, 2019), 1–19. For a fairly comprehensive collection of volumes of essays on European nations, nationalism and national identities, see the title series 'Writing the Nation: National Historiographies and the Making of Nation States in 19th and 20th Century Europe', in Stefan Berger, Christoph Conrad and Guy P. Marchal (eds), funded by the European Science Foundation and published by Palgrave.
12. On Irish historiography, see D. George Boyce and Alan O'Day (eds), *The Making of Modern Irish History: Revisionism and the Revisionist Controversy* (London, 1996).
13. For example, see Jorg Hackmann, 'German East or Polish West? Historiographical Discourses on the German Polish Overlap between Confrontation and Reconciliation, 1772–2000', in Tibor Frank and Frank Hadler (eds), *Disputed Territories and Shared Pasts: Overlapping National Histories in Modern Europe* (Basingstoke, 2015), 92–125.
14. R. W. Seton-Watson, *The Rise of Nationality in the Balkans* (London, 1917).
15. For example, this was the view of Hector MacPherson, *Scotland's Debt to Protestantism* (Edinburgh, 1912), 25–35. MacPherson was a Liberal who was very active in the home rule movement until his death in 1924.
16. The origins of this idea come from Max Webber, *The Protestant Ethic and the Spirit of Capitalism* (London, 1905); and R. H. Tawney, *Religion and the Rise of Capitalism* (London, 1926), but the impact of the Reformation on 'deforming' Scottish culture is mainly associated with someone who was not a nationalist; see Edwin Muir, *John Knox: Portrait of a Calvinist* (London, 1929) and *Scott and Scotland* (London, 1936). But for many left-wing nationalists, the processes of capitalism and Anglicization have gone hand in hand. See Tom Nairn, *The Break-Up of Britain: Crisis and Neo-nationalism* (London, 1981 edn), 120–3.
17. For example, Archie Lamont writing in the *Scots Independent*, June 1937, 3, criticizing the attempt to stoke sectarianism for political gain.
18. For a discussion of Scottish historiography, see Marinell Ash, *The Strange Death of Scottish History* (Edinburgh, 1980); Colin Kidd, *Subverting Scotland's Past: Scottish Whig Historians and the Creation of an Anglo-British Identity, 1689–1830* (Cambridge, 1993); Richard J. Finlay, 'Controlling the Past: Scottish Historiography and Scottish Identity in the 19th and 20th Centuries', *Scottish Affairs*, vol. 9, 1 (1994), 127–9; James Coleman, *Remembering the Past in Nineteenth-Century Scotland: Commemoration, Nationality, Memory* (Edinburgh, 2014); and Graeme Neil Forsythe, 'The Presbyterian Interpretation of Scottish History', PhD, Stirling University (2003).
19. The classic exposition of this was Thomas Charles Thomson, *Scotland's Work and Worth*, 2 vols (Edinburgh, 1909).
20. On the changing nature of the historiography of the Scottish Reformation, see Michael Lynch, 'In Search of the Scottish Reformation', in Edward J. Cowan

and Richard J. Finlay (eds), *Scottish History: The Power of the Past* (Edinburgh, 2002), 73-95.
21. For some like Lord Rosebery the Scots had surpassed the need for statehood and their Scottish patriotism was a 'subordinate' one to their wider British imperial patriotism. See 'The Patriotism of a Scot', Speech, 4 November 1882, reproduced in *Miscellanies*, vol. II (ed.), John Buchan (London, 1921), 111-27.
22. For a typically celebratory account of the Scots in America, see Duncan A. Bruce, *The Mark of the Scots* (London, 1996).
23. This idea was propounded by Thomas Carlyle, *Essays*, vol. iv (London, 1839), 137; *Fortnightly Review*, vol. 22 (1874); and *Contemporary Review*, vol. 61 (1892), 437-4.
24. *Past and Present*, vol. I (1843 edn), chapter ii. A good example of this view can be seen in the opening of the Wallace Monument in Stirling when it was claimed that 'the rose of England never bloomed so fair as when entwined with the thistle of Scotland', quoted in James Coleman, 'Unionist Nationalism in Stone: The National Wallace Monument and the Hazards of Commemoration in Victorian Scotland', in Edward J. Cowan (edn), *The Wallace Book* (Edinburgh, 2007). The idea of 'Unionist Nationalism' in which unionism is based on a form of nationalism is propounded by Graeme Morton, *Unionist Nationalism: Governing Urban Scotland 1830-60* (East Linton, 1999).
25. Rosalind Mitchison, *A History of Scotland* (London, 1970), 311. This and other similar judgements are based on comparisons with England which was at this time pioneering the development of national debt, which meant greater state record keeping for the purposes of tax and revenue collection. Scotland had no national debt and hence did not have the state apparatus associated with this, as was the case for most of Europe at this time, which would provide a more appropriate comparison.
26. For an interesting study that points out that the growing national debt of England and subsequently Britain was a way of ensuring that the elite had a vested financial interest in the survival of the state, see Bruce G. Carruthers, *City of Capital: Politics and Markets in the English Financial Revolution* (Princeton, 1999). Charles I was notorious for not paying royal debts, the Tulip Mania in the Netherlands in 1637 led to a crash, England had a crisis with revaluation in 1696 and the Scotsman Robert Law bankrupted France in 1720, the same year the South Sea Bubble burst and effectively bankrupted the newly formed British state.
27. Athol L. Murray, 'Administration and Law', in T. I. Rae (ed.), *The Union of 1707: Its Impact on Scotland* (London 1974), 1.
28. R. H. Campbell, *Scotland since 1707: The Rise of an Industrial Society* (London, 1965), 56-7.
29. Allan I. Macinnes, *Union and Empire: The Making of the United Kingdom in 1707* (Cambridge, 2007), 285.
30. John Oldmixon, *The History of England during the Reigns of William and Mary, Anne and George I* (London, 1735), 396.
31. T. M. Devine, 'The Union of 1707 and Scottish Development', *Scottish Economic and Social History*, vol. 5, 1 (1985), 23-40.
32. See David Dickson, *New Foundations: Ireland, 1660-1800* (Newbridge, 2000 edn), 109-43.
33. Lord Rosebery, 'The Union of England and Scotland', in John Buchan (ed.), *Miscellanies: Literary and Historical*, vol. II (London, 1923), 71-104.
34. For the myriad characterizations of Wallace, see Edward J. Cowan (ed.), *The Wallace Book* (Edinburgh, 2007).

35. See Tom Garvin, *Nationalist Revolutionaries in Ireland, 1858–1928* (Oxford, 1987), chapter 5; D. George Boyce, *Nationalism in Ireland* (Baltimore, 1982), 295–303; Paul Bew, *Ideology and the Irish Question: Ulster Unionism and Irish Nationalism, 1912–1916* (Oxford, 1994), 71–91; and Michael Laffin, *The Resurrection of Ireland: The Sinn Fein Party 1916–23* (Cambridge, 1999).
36. See Colin Kidd, *British Identities before Nationalism: Ethnicity and Nationhood in the Atlantic World, 1600–1800* (Cambridge, 1999); and 'The Ideological Uses of the Picts, 1707–c.1990', in Cowan and Finlay (eds), *Scottish History: The Power of the Past*, 169–91.
37. See John Kendle, *Ireland and the Federal Solution: The Debate over the United Kingdom Constitution, 1870–1920* (Montreal, 1989).
38. *Scots Independent*, September 1934, 170.
39. 'Self-Government in Practice: A Report of a Delegation Appointed by the Scottish National Party to Visit Northern Ireland, the Irish Free State and the Isle of Man to Study Certain Aspects of Self-Government' (Glasgow, 1935), 1–2; and John M. MacCormick, *The Flag in the Wind* (1955), 67.
40. Mar frequently wrote on this in his journal *Guth na Bliadhna* (1903–8); see, for example, December 1904, 8. See also the important biography by Gerard Cairns, *No Language, No Nation: The Life and Times of the Honourable Ruaraidh Erskine of Mar* (Perth, 2021).
41. Although not specifically named, it would appear that the work of Eoin MacNeill, a founder of the Gaelic League and distinguished Irish historian, was influential in the 'Celtic' accounts of Scottish history. See F. X. Martin and F. J. Byme (eds), *The Scholar Revolutionary: Eoin MacNeill, 1867–1945 and the Making of the New Ireland* (Shannon, 1973).
42. Seumus Mac Garaidh, 'Scotland: A Nation Once Again', *Liberty*, July 1920, 67.
43. *Pictish Review*, December 1927, 14.
44. NLS, Acc. 6058, box 1, Erskine of Marr to Tom Gibson, 11 May 1926.
45. NLS, Acc. 5916, Lewis Spence, notes April 1926.
46. Liam Mac Gill Iosa, 'English Atrocities', *Liberty*, March 1920, 25.
47. Liam Mac Gill Iosa, 'England Unchangeable: The Same Today as 1707', *Liberty*, May 1920, 43.
48. William Gillies, 'Westminster and Its Scottish Associations III – When Cromwell Conquered Scotland', *Scots Independent*, September 1929, 141.
49. Lindsay Crawford, 'Scotland a Sovereign Nation', *Liberty*, April 1920, 38.
50. Editorial, 'Scotland's Position', *Scots Independent*, January 1927, 5.
51. H. C. MacNeacail, 'The Road to Freedom', *Liberty*, August 1920, 77.
52. Ian Michael Smart, 'The Political Ideas of the Scottish Covenanters, 1638–88', *History of Political Thought*, vol. 1, 2 (1980), 167–93.
53. See A. T. Q. Stewart, *The Narrow Ground: The Roots of Conflict in Ulster* (2nd edn, 1989), 168.
54. Liam Mac Gill Iosa, 'English Atrocities', *Liberty*, March 1920, 26.
55. Art O'Brien, 'Ireland's National Struggle: A Lesson in Politics', *Scots Independent*, June 1928, 122.
56. MacNeacail, 'The Road to Freedom', 78.
57. Liam Mac Gill Iosa, 'England Unchangeable: The Same Today as in 1707', *Liberty*, May 1920, 43. The quote is from William E. H. Lecky, *A History of England in the Eighteenth Century*, vol. 4 (1906 edn), 338.
58. For a modern survey of seventeenth-century Irish history, see Raymond Gillespie, *Seventeenth Century Ireland* (Dublin, 2006).

59. A. M. MacGregor-Arbuckle, 'What Is a Scot', *Scots Independent*, May 1927, 8.
60. H. C. MacNeacail, 'The Celtic Decline in Scotland', *Scots Independent*, March 1931, 71–2. On Andrew Lang, see Catriona M. M. MacDonald, 'Andrew Lang and Scottish Historiography: Taking on Tradition', *Scottish Historical Review*, vol. 94, 239 (2015), 207–36.
61. Ian Gillies, 'Was Scott's Influence Malign for Scotland? The Saxon v. Gael Myth', *Scots Independent*, June 1929, 107.
62. Angus Clark, 'An End to Humbug: Kilti-cism Is Not Enough', *Scots Independent*, June 1928, 114.
63. Lindsay Crawford, 'Scotland: A Sovereign Nation', *Liberty*, April 1920, 37.
64. Patrick M. Geoghegan, *Liberator: The Life and Death of Daniel O'Connell* (Dublin, 2012).
65. Richard J. Finlay, 'The Wallace Cult in the Nineteenth and Twentieth Centuries', in Cowan, *The Wallace Book*, 176–93, 235–6; and Graeme Morton, *William Wallace: Man and Myth* (Stroud, 2001), 94–135.
66. Liam Mac Gill Iosa, 'Bannockburn and Its Lessons', *Liberty*, June 1920, 59.
67. H. C. MacNeacail, 'Bannockburn and Robert Bruce', *Scots Independent*, June 1927, 1.
68. Reprinted with an introduction by Brian D. Osborne (Glasgow, 1999).
69. See Finlay, 'Controlling the Past'.
70. On this, see R. Anderson, *Education and Opportunity in Victorian Scotland* (Edinburgh, 1989).
71. H. C. MacNeacail, 'Kingdom and Republic', *Liberty*, January 1921, 6.
72. On John Maclean, see David Howell, *A Lost Left: Three Studies in Socialism and Nationalism* (Manchester, 1986); Brian Ripley and John McHugh, *John Maclean* (Manchester, 1989); and Henry Bell, *John Maclean: Hero of Red Clydeside* (London, 2018).
73. Liam Mac Gill Iosa, 'John Maclean and the Crown', *Liberty*, June 1921, 83.
74. Iain D. Patterson, 'The Activities of the Irish Physical Force Organisations in Scotland, 1919–21', *Scottish Historical Review*, vol. 72, 193 (April 1993), 39–59.
75. William Gallacher's account is in *Revolt on the Clyde: An Autobiography* (London, 1936), 248–70; see Ripley and McHugh, *John Maclean*, for a more nuanced discussion, 124–45; Douglas Jones, *The Communist Party of Great Britain and the National Question in Wales, 1920–1991* (Cardiff, 2017), regularly discusses Scotland; and Ragnheidur Kristjansdottir, 'Communism and the National Question in Iceland and Scotland, c.1930 to c.1940', *Historical Journal*, vol. 45, 3 (September 2002), 601–19.
76. Scots National League, *Some Arguments for Scottish Independence* (Edinburgh, 1923), 16–17.
77. Liam Mac Gill Iosa, 'Subordinate Patriotism', *Liberty*, July 1920, 73.
78. NLS, Acc. 3721, box 81, 'Record of the Scottish National Convention, 28 May, 1927'.
79. For example, R. L. Cassie, 'Scotland before Race', *Scots Independent*, May 1831, 192.
80. See Gordon Donaldson, *Scotland: The Shaping of a Nation* (1980), who writes on page 15. 'The future of Scotland lay in the main with two races who arrived in the sixth century.' The Conservative MP and former chancellor of the exchequer Sir Robert Horne made the claim that the Highlanders 'belong to a different race ... as the real original inhabitants of the country could be entitled to claim home rule for themselves'. House of Common Debates, 24 November 1932, vol. 272, col. 244.
81. These ideas are given expression in the Eighth Duke of Argyll, *Scotland as It Was and Is* (1887). For a rejection of ethnology in explaining Scottish history, see George Dott, 'Scotland before Race', *Scots Independent*, September 1931, 174.

82. Art O'Brien, 'Ireland's National Struggle: A Lesson in Politics', *Scots Independent*, June 1928, 123.
83. On the Union, see Christopher A. Whatley, *The Scots and the Union: Then and Now* (Edinburgh, 2014); Allan I. Macinnes, *Union and Empire: The Making of the United Kingdom in 1707* (Cambridge, 2007); and T. M. Devine, *Independence or Union: Scotland's Past and Scotland's Present* (London, 2016).
84. On regnal union, see Jenny Wormald's classic 'James VI and I: Two Kings or One?', *History*, vol. 68, 223 (1983), 187–209; and on the civil wars, see Allan I. Macinnes, *The British Revolution 1629–1660* (2004).
85. Lindsay Crawford, 'Scotland a Sovereign Nation', *Liberty*, April 1920, 37.
86. For a modern discussion of Jacobitism, see Daniel Szechi, *The Jacobites: Britain and Europe, 1688–1788* (2nd edn, Manchester, 2019); and Murray G. H. Pittock, *Jacobitism* (Basingstoke, 1998).
87. On the Irish Jacobites, see Eamonn O' Ciardha, *Ireland and the Jacobite Cause 1685–1766: A Fatal Attachment* (Dublin, 2000).
88. The Jacobites rarely feature in nationalist historical discussion because Celtic Republicans did not like the idea of monarchy, and moderate nationalists largely endorsed the idea that Presbyterianism had risen up against Stuart despotism in the later seventeenth century; hence the tendency to use the idea of the covenant as a constitutional mechanism to represent the will of the people. That said, Compton Mackenzie was more sympathetic to Jacobitism; see his *Catholicism and Scotland* (1936), 130–45. On the continuing claims of Jacobitism in the modern era, see Murray G. H. Pittock, *The Invention of Scotland: The Stuart Myth and Scottish Identity, 1639 to the Present* (London, 1991).
89. *Home Rule for Scotland: The Case in 90 Points* (Glasgow, 1922), 40–1.
90. Contrast Lindsay Crawford, 'Scotland a Sovereign Nation II', *Liberty*, May 1920, 41, 'Since England obtained the Treaty of Union she has never relaxed her efforts to reduce Scotland to the position of an English province', with the statement in *Home Rule: The Case in 90 Points*, 33, that the Union 'removed serious fiscal and political hindrances to the commercial and social progress of both nations'.
91. NLS, Acc. 6058, box 1, Tom Gibson, 'Memorandum on the Scottish Home Rule Association', June 1924.
92. *Standard*, May 1922, 77.
93. See Richard J. Finlay, *Independent and Free: Scottish Politics and the Origins of the Scottish National Party, 1918–1945* (1994), 1–29.
94. The conventional accounts of the Union that were in use in the early twentieth century were James MacKinnon, *The Union of England and Scotland: An International Study* (London, 1886); The Glasgow Herald (ed.), *The Union of 1707: A Survey of the Events and the Texts of the Articles of Union* (Glasgow, 1907); and A. V. Dicey and Robert Rait, *Thoughts on the Union between England and Scotland* (London, 1920).
95. A point made by Duncan H. Macneill in *The Scottish Realm: An Approach to the Political and Constitutional History of Scotland* (Glasgow, 1947), 37, in which he argues that repeated conquest had made the English more servile than the Scots.
96. Frequent reference was made to the role of conquest in Westminster in the debate on the state of Ireland in 1844. For example, see *House of Commons Debates*, vol. 72, col. 684, Lord John Russell, 13 February 1844.
97. Alexander Shaw, *House of Commons Debates*, vol. 154, col. 1618, 26 May 1922.
98. *Scotia: The Journal of the St. Andrew Society*, vol. II (1908), 143.

99. See Richard J. Finlay, 'National Identity in Crisis: Politicians, Intellectuals and the "End of Scotland", 1920-1939', *History*, vol. 79, 256 (June 1994), 242-59.
100. H. C. MacNeacail, 'The Eclipse of Scotland', *Scots Independent*, November 1926, 9.
101. A. A. W. Ramsay, 'The End of an Auld Sang', *Scots Independent*, December 1932, 28.
102. Duncan H. McNeill, 'This Scotland: Unconquered – But Subordinated', *Scots Independent*, July 1934, 136.
103. 'Clan Scotland', *Scots Independent*, November 1933, 12.
104. See *Home Rule: The Case in 90 Points*, 38.
105. See C. de B. Murray, *How Scotland Is Governed* (Edinburgh, 1938), 66-84.
106. John M. MacCormick, 'The Scrap of Paper: Should We Accept the Local Government Act', *Scots Independent*, March 1930, 54.
107. James Alston, 'Aspects of Self-Government', *Scots Independent*, January 1932, 39, 42.
108. Ibid.
109. Angus Clark, 'The Decay of Scotland', *Scots Independent*, November 1927, 1.
110. H. C. MacNeacail, 'The Reform of Education: How Our History Is Mangled in the Schools', *Liberty*, 9 October 1920, 119.
111. Editorial 'Should We Repeal the Union?', *Scots Independent*, August 1932, 147.
112. Finlay, 'National Identity in Crisis', 250.
113. 'Scotland's Golden Age', quoted from Dr H. W. Thompson, *A Scottish Man of Feeling*, (London, 1931) in *Scots Independent*, September 1931, 165.
114. William Bell, *Rip Van Scotland* (Oxford, 1930), 29.
115. This was a frequent Unionist retort, House of Commons Debates, vol. 272, col. 339, 24 November, 1932.
116. See Finlay 'National Identity in Crisis', 244-9.
117. For the traditional positive view, see John Hill Burton, *The Scot Abroad* (London, 1864); for the negativity of the interwar era, see John Torrence, *Scotland's Dilemma: Nation or Province* (Edinburgh, 1939), 15; and for a modern discussion, see T. M. Devine, *To the Ends of the Earth: Scotland's Global Diaspora, 1750-2010* (London, 2012).
118. See G. M. Thomson, *Scotland: That Distressed Area* (Edinburgh, 1935), 21-9; and Andrew Dewar Gibb, *Scotland in Eclipse* (London, 1930), 49-55.
119. See J. M. MacDiarmid, *The Deer Forests and How They Are Bleeding Scotland Dry* (Glasgow, 1926); Finlay, *Independent and Free*, 62-3.
120. On Europe, see R. Boyce, *The Great Inter-War Crisis and the Collapses of Globalisation* (London, 2009).
121. See R. H. S. Robertson, 'The Output of Scientists in Scotland', *Eugenics Review*, vol. 52-3 (1960), 71-82.
122. Richard J. Finlay, 'Nationalism, Race, Religion and the Irish Question in Inter-War Scotland', *Innes Review*, 42 (1991), 46-76.
123. The classic model of this narrative is Thomson, *Scotland: That Distressed Area*, but it is echoed in J. A. Bowie, *The Future of Scotland* (Edinburgh, 1939); James A. A. Porteous, *Scotland and the South: Economic and Financial Relations* (Glasgow, 1947); and Donald MacKay, *Scotland 1980: The Economics of Self-Government* (London, 1977).
124. The classic nationalist account of the Scottish role in the empire is Andrew Dewar Gibb, *Scottish Empire* (London, 1937).
125. Henry George, *Scotland and Scotsmen* (Glasgow, Scottish League for the Taxation of Land Values, no date but based on a speech delivered at Glasgow City Hall, 18 February, 1884), 13.

126. Bell, *Rip Van Scotland*, 28.
127. For the impact of the empire, see Richard J. Finlay, 'For or Against? Scottish Nationalists and the British Empire', *Scottish Historical Review*, vol. 71, 1, 2 (1994), 184–206.
128. 'History in Our Schools', *Scots Independent*, January 1928, 45–6. See also Bruce Lenman, 'The Teaching of Scottish History in the Scottish Universities', *Scottish Historical Review*, vol. 52, 154 (October 1973), 165–90; and Gordon Brown, *My Scotland, Our Britain: A Future Worth Sharing* (London, 2015), 63–5, which endorses the lack of teaching of Scottish history in the post-war era.
129. Richard J. Finlay, 'The Declaration of Arbroath and Scottish Nationalist Constitutional Thought in the 20th Century', in Klaus Peter Muller (ed.), *Scotland and Arbroath 1320–2020: 700 Years of Fighting for Freedom, Sovereignty, and Independence* (Leck, 2020) (Scottish Studies International series no. x), 307–25.
130. For example, see his *Lord Rosebery's Address on Sir William Wallace at the Sixth Centenary Celebration of the Battle of Stirling* (Stirling, 1898).
131. Scottish Home Rule Association, *A Protest against the Mis-use of the Terms 'England' and 'English' for 'Britain' and 'British', Its empire, Its People and Its Institutions* (Edinburgh, c. 1890).
132. *Glasgow Herald*, 15 May 1903.
133. Many English historians at the time simply assumed that this was the case. See J. R. Seeley, *The Expansion of England: Two Course of Lecture* (London, 1883), 131; and J. R. Green, *A Short History of England* (London, 1876), 689.
134. Richard J. Finlay, 'Scotland and Monarchy in the Twentieth Century', in William L. Miller (ed.), *Anglo-Scottish Relations from 1900 to Devolution and Beyond* (Oxford, 2005), 28–32.
135. G. Gregory Smith, *Scottish Literature: Character and Influence* (London, 1919); MacDiarmid's essay was originally published in the *Modern Scot* and is republished in Duncan Glen (ed.), *Selected Essays of High MacDiarmid* (London, 1970), 56–75; see also Nairn, *Break-Up of Britain*, 138.
136. Michael Hechter, *Internal Colonialism: The Celtic Fringe in British National Development* (London, 1973).
137. See the debate of the place of Scottish history in the school curriculum in the 1990s. Sydney Wood and Fran Payne, 'The Scottish School Curriculum and Issues of National Identity', *Curriculum Journal*, vol. 10, 1 (1999), 107–21.
138. On Scottish historiographical development in the 1970s and 1980s, see T. M. Devine, 'Whither Scottish History?', *Scottish Historical Review*, vol. 72, 195 (1994), 1–3.
139. On the influence of left-wing ideas on the development of nationalist thought from the 1960s onwards, see Ben Jackson, *The Case for Scottish Independence: Nationalist Political Though in Scotland, c.1960–2014* (Cambridge, 2020), 123–73.
140. Owen Dudley Edwards, *A Claim of Right for Scotland* (Edinburgh, 1989).

2 Nationalism

1. The *Edinburgh Evening News*, for example, ran a series of cartoons depicting the nationalist movement as a Scottish version of the Nazi Party in the mid-1930s. Gavin Bowd, *Fascist Scotland: Caledonia and the Far Right* (Edinburgh, 2013), while containing a number of useful insights, makes the elementary mistake of using the

reports of undercover policemen and giving them far too much credibility, especially in relation to Arthur Donaldson who was under surveillance by the authorities for his anti-conscription activities during the war. Hearsay from undercover policemen is not reliable evidence, and it ignores the extent to which throughout history spies have always exaggerated the importance of their information. The 1320 Club which emerged in the 1960s was frequently described as a quasi-fascist group, and similar accusations have been made against Siol nan Gaidheal (Seed of the Gael) in the period from the late 1970s.
2. Robert D. McIntyre, *Some Principles for Scottish Reconstruction* (Glasgow, 1944).
3. This was a prominent view among many who vacillated between the need for an independent political party that contested elections on its own manifesto and, on the other hand, using pressure group tactics on existing political parties. See R. J. Finlay, 'Pressure Group or Political Party: The Nationalist Impact on Scottish Politics, 1928–45', *Twentieth Century British History*, vol. 3, 3 (1992), 274–97.
4. NLS, Acc. 3721, box 6, Roland Muirhead to M. A. MacCrouther, 8 October 1928.
5. This was one of the fundamental issues that dominated the debate about the creation of an independent national party in Scotland. See Richard J. Finlay, *Independent and Free: Scottish Politics and the Origins of the Scottish National Party, 1918–1945* (Edinburgh, 1994), 71–126.
6. Walter Murray (ed.), *Scottish Home Rule: The Case in 90 Points* (Glasgow, 1922), 20.
7. The leader of the SNP, Nicola Sturgeon, discussed some of the problematic issues surrounding the notion of 'nation' and 'nationalism' in the 2017 Edinburgh International Book Festival with the Turkish writer Elif Shafak. See https://www.edbookfest.co.uk/news/scotland-s-first-minister-admits-nationalism-a-difficult-word-at-book-festival.
8. John Hutchison, 'Nationalism and War: A Review of the Literature', *Studies on National Movements*, vol. 4 (2019), http://eprints.lse.ac.uk/101028/1/nationalismandwar.pdf.
9. There is an extensive literature on nationalism. John Breuilly (ed.), *The Oxford Handbook of the History of Nationalism* (Oxford, 2016); and Liah Greenfeld, *Nationalism: A Short History* (London, 2019) are good starting points from the perspective of the historian. For the theoretical discussion, see Anthony D. Smith, *Nationalism* (Cambridge, 2010).
10. For an early discussion that links nationalism with emotionalism, see Max Sylvius Handman, 'The Sentiment of Nationalism', *Political Science Quarterly*, vol. 36, 1 (March 1921), 104–21.
11. Ghita Ionescu and Ernst Gellner (eds), *Populism: Its Meaning and National Characteristic* (London, 1969) and more recently Jan Werner Muller, *What Is Populism* (2017); and Roger Eatwell and Matthew Goodwin, *National Populism and the Revolt against Liberal Democracy* (London, 2018).
12. The term was coined by Fritz Stern, *The Politics of Cultural Despair: A Study of the Rise of Germanic Ideology* (London, 1974 edn), and this work examined the intellectual roots of Nazism.
13. Although political scientists and social theorists are aware of the variety of forms of nationalism, they still tend to see them as different manifestations of the same phenomenon. A classic study is Hans Kohn, *The Idea of Nationalism: A Study in Its Origins and Background* (London, 1944). For a more recent discussion on the complexities of varieties of nationalisms, see Hedva Ben-Israel, 'Nationalism in Historical Perspective', *Journal of International Affairs*, vol. 45, 2 (1992), 367–97; and

Geert Van Cleemput, 'Clarifying Nationalism, Chauvinism, and Ethnic Imperialism', *International Journal on World Peace*, vol. 12 (March 1995), 59–97.
14. For example, Mussolini argued that nationalism came as a result of the state and not vice versa, and as we shall see, a common defence used by independence movements in Europe was that small nations were not capable of mounting aggressive wars against their neighbours. The break-up of Yugoslavia, however, demonstrated that small nations were not immune from the worst excesses of nationalism. See Susan L. Woodward, *Balkan Tragedy: Chaos and Dissolution After the Cold War* (London, 1995).
15. Anthony D. Smith, *The Ethnic Origins of Nations* (Oxford, 1999 edn), 47–50; and Joep Leerssen, 'Nation and Ethnicity', in Stefan Berger and Chris Lorenz (eds), *The Contested Nation: Ethnicity, Class, Religion and Gender in National Histories* (Basingstoke, 2011), 75–104.
16. On irredentist nationalism, see Oliver Zimmer, *Nationalism in Europe, 1890–1940* (Basingstoke, 2003), 50–80.
17. See, for example, Alvin Jackson, 'Unionist History', *Irish Review*, vol. 7 (1989), 58–66; Patrick J. Roche, 'Northern Ireland and Irish Nationalism: A Unionist Perspective', *Irish Review*, vol. 15 (1994), 70–8; Sabrine Wichert, 'The Role of Nationalism in the Northern Ireland Conflict', *History of European Ideas*, vol. 16, 1–3 (1993), 109–14; and Diarmaid Ferriter, *The Border: The Legacy of a Century of Anglo Irish Politics* (London, 2019).
18. Richard English, 'Defining the Nation: Recent Historiography and Irish Nationalism', *European Review of History*, vol. 2, 2 (1995), 193–200.
19. See Ian Adamson, *The Cruthin: A History of the Ulster Land and Its People* (Belfast, 1974), which claims that the original inhabitants of Ireland were Picts, who, he argues, were a different people from the Irish Celts and the plantations of the seventeenth century were the Picts returning to their homeland.
20. 'Nicola Sturgeon Admits to Difficulties of SNP Name', *Financial Times*, 18 August 2018.
21. For a collection of essays on the connection between liberalism and nationalism in the nineteenth century, see Ivan Zoltan Denes (ed.), *Liberty and the Search for Identity: Liberal Nationalism and the Legacy of Empire* (Budapest, 2006).
22. Kossuth was given the freedom of the city of Glasgow, 18 November 1858. John McAdam took part in the Risorgimento and was in regular contact with leading European nationalists; see Janet Fyfe, *Autobiography of John McAdam* (Scottish History Society Texts, 1980).
23. For a discussion on civic nationalism, see Richard J. Finlay, 'Thatcherism, Civil Society and the Road to Home Rule: Scotland 1980–97', in A. Murdoch (ed.), *The Scottish Nation, Identity and History: Essays in Honour of William Ferguson* (Edinburgh, 2007), 136–55.
24. Liam De Paor, *On the Easter Proclamation and Other Declarations* (Dublin, 1997).
25. See David McCrone, *Understanding Scotland: The Sociology of a Stateless Nation* (London, 1992), 104–27.
26. On the relationship between the two phenomena, see Jonathan S. Hearn, 'Scottish Nationalism and the Civil Society Concept: Should Auld Acquaintance Be Forgot', *Political and Legal Anthropology Review*, vol. 20, 1 (1997), 32–9.
27. Finlay, 'Thatcherism, Civil Society and the Road to Home Rule'.
28. T. M. Devine, *To the Ends of the Earth: Scotland's Global Diaspora, 1750–2010* (London, 2012), 147–93, 270–89.

29. Daniel John Evans, 'Welshness in "British Wales": Negotiating National Identity at the Margins', *Nations and Nationalism*, vol. 25, 1 (2019), 167-90.
30. Cynthia J. Neville, *Violence, Custom and Law: The Anglo Scottish Border Lands in the Later Middle Ages* (Edinburgh, 1998); Andy King and David Simpkin (eds), *England and Scotland at War, c.1296-c.1513* (Leiden, 2012); and Jenna M. Schulz, *National Identity in the Anglo Scottish Borderlands, 1552-1652* (Woodbridge, 2019).
31. Peter Hume Brown, *History of Scotland to the Present Time*, vol. I (Cambridge, 1899), 8; for a modern perspective, see Dauvit Broun, 'The Birth of Scottish History', *Scottish Historical Review*, vol. 76, 201 (1997), 4-22.
32. On ethnicity in the early modern period, see Colin Kidd, *British Identities before Nationalism: Ethnicity and Nationhood in the Atlantic World* (Cambridge, 1999); and 'Teutonist Ethnology and Scottish Nationalist Inhibition, 1780-1880', *Scottish Historical Review*, vol. 74, 197 (1995), 45-68.
33. On the relationship between race and ethnicity, see Stephen Spencer, *Race and Ethnicity: Culture, Identity and Representation* (London, 2014).
34. See Murray Pittock, *The Invention of Scotland: The Stuart Myth and Scottish Identity from 1689 to the Present* (London, 1991), 85, for a discussion of the impact of Walter Scott's vision of Scottish history; for the full-blown vision of Scotland as an invented tradition, see Hugh Trevor-Roper, *The Invention of Scotland: Myth and History* (London, 2014). For an example of the dismissal of the idea of a coherent Scottish national identity, see the debate in the House of Commons on the Scotland and Wales Bill on 16 February 1977, vol. 926, cols 553-631, where a number of Conservative MPs denied the existence of Scotland as a nation.
35. House of Commons Debates, 24 November 1932, vol. 272, cols 252-3.
36. For example, 'The Mixture of Races Has Produced an Admirable Variety of Qualities', *Celtic Monthly: A Magazine for Highlanders*, vol. 22 (1914), 148.
37. Nannie K. Wells, 'An English View of the Celt', *Scots Independent*, November 1930, 4.
38. Andrew Lang argued that the opposing armies of Robert the Bruce and Edward II were of the same race, for example; but E. M. Barron, *The Scottish War of Independence* (London, 1914) argued for the significance of Highland resistance. While Barron's view of the Wars of Independence were supported by nationalists, he himself was a vigorous opponent of home rule.
39. See in particular Michael Hechter, *Internal Colonialism: The Celtic Fringe in British National Development* (London, 1975).
40. See John M. MacKenzie and T. M. Devine (eds), *Scotland and the British Empire* (Oxford, 2011).
41. Tony Brewer, *Marxist Theories of Imperialism: A Critical Survey* (London, 1990).
42. This theme comes out in John Prebble, *Mutiny: Highland Regiments in Revolt, 1743-1804* (London, 1977).
43. Derek Hastings, *Nationalism in Modern Europe* (London, 2017), 157-99; Ian Kershaw, *To Hell and Back: Europe, 1914-49* (London, 2016); and Oliver Zimmer, *Nationalism in Europe, 1890-1940* (Basingstoke, 2003).
44. Among the first prominent studies on nationalism emerging during the First World War were the works by the Scot Robert Seton Watson, *The Rise of Nationality in the Balkans* (London, 1917); and *Europe in the Melting Pot* (London, 1919).
45. Derek Heater, *National Self-Determination: Woodrow Wilson and His Legacy* (London, 2014).
46. Zara Steiner, *The Lights That Failed: European International History, 1919-33* (Oxford, 2005).

47. League of Nations Union, Education Committee, *History Teaching in Relation to World Citizenship* (London, 1938), 14.
48. John MacArthur, 'Scotland a Nation', *Liberty*, December 1919, 1.
49. Murray, *Scottish Home Rule*, 5.
50. 'Petition National de l'Ecosse pour obtenir sa Represantation au Congress de la Paix', *Scottish Review*, Spring 1919, 377.
51. Eduard Benes 'The Position of the Small Nation in Post War Europe', *American Journal of Sociology*, vol. 49, 5 (March 1944), 390–6.
52. Murray, *Scottish Home Rule*, 18.
53. R. Erskine of Marr, 'Scotland and the "New" World', *Liberty*, July 1920, 65.
54. On this issue in relation to the history of political thought, see Richard Whatmore, *What Is Intellectual History* (Cambridge, 2016), 4–12.
55. *Scots Independent*, April 1931, 93.
56. Murray, *Scottish Home Rule*, 44.
57. *Scots Independent*, January 1931, 34.
58. Roland Muirhead, 'The Forthcoming General Election', *Scots Independent*, November 1928, 7.
59. *Scots Independent*, April, 1933, 80.
60. *Scotsman*, 25 November, 1932.
61. For the growing movement towards a 'national' strategy, see R. H. Campbell, 'The Committee of Ex-secretaries of State for Scotland and Industrial Policy', *Scottish Industrial History*, 2 (1979), 1–10.
62. 'The Local Government Bill', *Scots Independent*, February 1929, 40.
63. Led by the SNP provost of Stirling, Robert McIntyre, *British Pathe News*, 16 March 1968.
64. Finlay, 'Political Party or Pressure Group?'
65. H. J. Hanham, *Scottish Nationalism* (London, 1969), 77.
66. Open Letter by the Council of the Royal Incorporation of Architects in Scotland, April 1930.
67. Charles Milne, Unionist MP for West Fife, argued that insufficient time was devoted for the purpose of Scottish legislation, House of Commons Debates, vol. 272, col. 301, 22 November 1932.
68. Murray, *Scottish Home Rule*, 5–6.
69. David B. Knight, 'Identity and Territory: Geographical Perspectives on Nationalism and Regionalism', *Annals of the Association of American Geographers*, vol. 74, 2 (1982), 514–31.
70. Angus Clark, 'The Basis of Nationalism: Lessons of Past Failures', *Scots Independent*, April 1930, 68.
71. *What Scottish Nationalism Stands For* (leaflet for the Kilmarnock by-election printed December 1933).
72. Speech given at Scotland's Day Rally, 21 June 1930, quoted in *Scots Independent*, July 1930, 2.
73. For a discussion of the complexities of definitions, see John Breuilly, *Nationalism and the State* (Manchester, 1993), 1–16.
74. For example, Roland Muirhead, who was the largest financial donor to the nationalist movement until the 1950s, believed that the national party only needed to establish that self-government was electorally popular and the Labour Party in Scotland would join the cause, which he would once again support. See his correspondence with J. M. MacDiarmid (Labour's Scottish land spokesperson), NLS, Acc. 3721, box 5, April 1932.

75. B. Haddock, 'State and Nation in Mazzini's Political Thought', *History of Political Thought*, vol. 20, 2 (1999), 313–36.
76. NLS, Dep. 207, box 15, Neil Gunn to Tom Gibson, 3 April 1933.
77. See Finlay, 'Pressure Group or Political Party', 280–90.
78. Tom Gibson argued that socio-economic policies could be advanced as 'preparatory to the effecting of comprehensive schemes of national development by an independent Scottish parliament'. NLS, Acc. 6058, Box 1, Gibson to Erskine of Marr, 21 March 1927.
79. Andrew Dewar Gibb, *Scotland Resurgent* (Stirling, 1950), 4.
80. Ibid.
81. Robert F. Muirhead, 'Nationalism and War', *Scots Independent*, May 1932, 107.
82. William Bell, 'Nationalism as a Biological Process', *Scots Independent*, December 1929, 17–18.
83. W. G. S. Adams, 'The Basis of Constructive Internationalism', *The Annals of the American Academy of Political and Social Science* (1915), 217–29; and report of his public lecture at McGill University, Montreal, 'Aspects of Progress in the Twentieth Century', *Scots Independent*, July 1931, 141.
84. *Einstein on Cosmic Religion and Other Opinions and Aphorisms* (New York, 1931), 68, quoted in *Scots Independent*, February 1931, 60.
85. There seems to be a prima facie case for the influence of Mazzini on Scottish nationalist philosophy, but it is hard to pin down any specifics although he is mentioned frequently en passant, which tends to suggest an assumption that his ideas are well known. Denis Mack Smith, *Mazzini* (Yale, 1996) always differentiates between his Scottish and English friends and circles and Christopher Harvie (*The Lights of Liberalism: University Liberals and the Challenge of Democracy, 1860–1886* (1976)) notes his influence on the Scots at Oxford.
86. Archie Lamont, *Small Nations* (Glasgow, 1944), 9.
87. Compton Mackenzie, *The North Wind of Love*, vol. II (London, 1949), 14–62.
88. C. M. Grieve, 'Scottish Nationalism versus Socialism', *Scots Independent*, February 1929, 42.
89. Christine Orr, 'Why I Believe in Scottish Nationalism', *Scots Independent*, September 1931, 168.
90. *Scots Independent*, October 1931, 188.
91. See J. F. Kendle, *Ireland and the Federal Solution: The Debate over the United Kingdom Constitution, 1870–1921* (Montreal, 1989).
92. 'Federal Europe', *Scots Independent*, March 1940, 1.
93. NLS, Acc. 5927, box 3.
94. Jim Sillars, *Scotland: The Case for Optimism* (Edinburgh, 1986), 181–90.
95. Michael Russell (ed.), *Stop the World: The Autobiography of Winnie Ewing* (Edinburgh, 2004), 84–5.
96. Georgios Varouxakis, 'Great versus Small Nation: Size and National Greatness in Victorian Political Thought', in Duncan Bell (ed.), *Victorian Visions of Global Order: Empire and International Relations in 19th Century Political Thought* (Cambridge, 2007), 136–59.
97. W. K. Hancock, *Argument of Empire* (London, 1943), 78.
98. H. A. L. Fisher, *The Value of Small States: Studies in History and Politics* (Oxford, 1914).
99. For example, see J. R. Seeley, *The Expansion of England: Two Courses of Lectures* (London, 1883), 132; and J. R. Green, *A Short History of England* (London, 1876), 689.

100. Alan Cassels, *Ideology and International Relations in the Modern World* (London, 1996), 100–1.
101. Watkin Davis, 'Education for Internationalism', *Hibbert Journal*, January 1922, 343–52.
102. The issue of nationalism was a regular feature in the annual Geneva Institute of International Affairs public lectures, published as *The Problems of Peace*. See, in particular, *Ninth Series: Pacifism Is Not Enough* (London, 1935), 14–103; and *Thirteenth Series: War Is Not Inevitable* (London, 1938), 56–102.
103. Hancock, *Argument of Empire*, 13–16.
104. This was especially the case by the late 1930s. See 'Mass Unemployment in the Capitalist Countries and the Task of the Trade Unions', *The Communist International*, vol. 14 (1937), 621–31.
105. In particular, see the published work of the American Marxist Annie Louise Strong, *The New Soviet Constitution: A Study in Socialist Democracy* (London, 1937); *Lithuania's New Way* (London, 1941) and *Inside Liberated Poland* (London, 1945). For a Scottish Labour apologist, see the Govan MP Neil Maclean, *The Moscow Trial (January 1937) and Two Speeches by Joseph Stalin* (London, 1937).
106. On British wartime attitudes to the Soviet Union, see Martin Kitchen, *British Policy towards the Soviet Union during the Second World War* (Basingstoke, 2014); and on the *Times* editorial justifying the Soviet occupation of the Baltic States, see Jonathan Haslam, *The Vices of Integrity: E. H. Carr, 1892–1982* (London, 1999), 93.
107. G. D. H. Cole, *Europe, Russia and the Future* (London, 1942), 6.
108. Frank Lorimer, *The Population of the Soviet Union* (London, 1946), 54.
109. George Orwell, *Notes on Nationalism* (London, 1945), 19. Also, see the Anglo-centrism of A. J. P. Taylor in his *English History, 1914–45* (London, 1965), v, with his curt dismissal of the 'Scotch'.
110. Arthur Turner, *Scottish Home Rule* (Oxford, 1952), 73.
111. Archie Lamont, *Small Nations* (Glasgow, 1944), 64.
112. See, for example, Edwyn Bevan, *Hellenism and Christianity* (London, 1921). Also it is worth pointing out the impact that Greek nationalism following the First World War had on the Scottish movement; see Compton Mackenzie, *Greek Memories* (London, 1932). MacDiarmid also served in Greece during the war.
113. Compton Mackenzie, *Marathon and Salamis* (London, 1934).
114. Lamont, *Small Nations*, 14.
115. Hugh MacDiarmid, *Albyn: Or Scotland and the Future* (London, 1927), 15–19. For a common English establishment view that the early modern Scottish state failed to develop sufficiently to support a viable 'national consciousness', see Royal Institute of International Affairs, *Nationalism: A Report* (Oxford, 1939), 22.
116. *Scots Independent*, December 1929, 15.
117. 'The Significance of Nationalism: A Challenge to Insincerity in Politics', *Scots Independent*, March 1929, 59. The idea that nationalists kept the vision alive in spite of overwhelming public scepticism is articulated in Mackenzie, *North Wind of Love*, 128–9.
118. A big factor in explaining this phenomenon was that the interwar era witnessed the growth of statistical compendiums and the information was much more readily available, often through the auspices of the League of Nations. John Stevenson points out that this was reflected within British society as a whole; see *British Society, 1914–45* (London, 1984), 320.

119. For a recent biography, see Henry Bell, *John Maclean: Hero of Red Clydeside* (London, 1918).
120. John Maclean, *Accuser of Capitalism* (1986; reprint of speeches from the dock), 35.
121. E. H. Carr, *The Conditions of Peace* (London, 1942), 64.
122. A view argued by Sir William Beveridge, 'A World Safe for Small Nations', *Observer*, 2 May 1943.
123. This was especially pronounced in the 1930s. For a taste of the statistical use of underperformance, see G. M. Thomson, *Scotland: That Distressed Area* (Edinburgh, 1935).
124. Most recently this was the idea of the 'Arc of Prosperity'; see Alex Salmond in the *Scotsman*, 12 August 2006.
125. Thomson, *Distressed Area*, 21–65, 79–92.
126. J. Lee, *Modern Ireland* (Cambridge, 1989), 321–9.
127. Giovanni Fredrico, 'Natura Non Fecit Salrus: The 1930s as Discontinuity in the History of European Agriculture', in Paul Brassley, Yves Segers and Leen Van Molle (eds), *War, Agriculture and Food: Rural Europe from the 1930s to the 1950s* (London, 2012), 15–33.
128. Atsuko Ichijo, *Scottish Nationalism and the Idea of Europe, Concepts of Europe and the Nation* (London, 2004), 20; Michelle Facos, *Nationalism and the Nordic Imagination: Swedish Art of the 1890s* (London, 1998); Joshua Hagen, *Preservation, Tourism and Nationalism: The Jewel of the German Past* (Aldershot, 2006), 1–19; and Kenneth R. Olwig, 'Landscape, Monuments and National Identity', in Guntram H. Herband and David H. Kaplan (eds), *Nations and Nationalism: A Global Historic Overview* (Oxford, 2008), 59–72.
129. See Ewen A. Cameron, *Land for the People? The British Government and the Scottish Highland, 1880–1925* (East Linton, 2001); Leah Leneman, *Fit for Heroes: Land Settlement in Scotland after World War I* (Aberdeen, 1989); and John Burnett, *The Making of the Modern Scottish Highlands, 1939–1965: Withstanding the Colossus of Advancing Materialism* (Dublin, 2010).
130. J. MacDiarmid, *The Deer Forests and How They Are Bleeding Scotland White* (Edinburgh, 1926).
131. Thomas Burns, *The Real Rulers of Scotland* (Glasgow, 1944), 37.
132. See Lesley Riddoch, *Huts: A Place Beyond – How to End Our Exile from Nature* (Edinburgh, 2020).
133. *Scots Independent*, June 1930, 98.
134. T. M. Devine, *Clanship to Crofters' War: The Social Transformation of the Scottish Highlands* (Manchester, 2013), 209–28.
135. Finlay, 'End of Scotland', 251.
136. 'Creative Nationalism: Being Extracts from the Address Delivered by Mr Compton Mackenzie on the Occasion of His Installation as Lord Rector of Glasgow University', *Scots Independent*, March 1932, 72.
137. *Scots Independent*, September 1930, 149.
138. *Scots Independent*, November 1930, 3.
139. Marjory Palmer McCulloch, *Scottish Modernism and Its Contexts, 1918–59: Literature, National Identity and Cultural Exchanges* (Edinburgh, 2009), 113–31.
140. Kenneth Buthlay (ed.), *Hugh MacDairmid: A Drunk Man Looks at the Thistle* (Edinburgh, 1987).
141. Compton Mackenzie, *The Four Winds of Love* (London, 1937–45), eventually published in eight volumes with two volumes each for *The East Wind of Love* (1937);

The South Wind of Love (1938); *The West Wind of Love* (1940–2) and *The North Wind of Love* (1944–5).
142. Elliot Green, https://blogs.lse.ac.uk/politicsandpolicy/scottish-nationalism-sta nds-apart-from-other-secessionist-movements-for-being-civic-in-origin-rat her-than-ethnic/.

3 Constitutionalism

1. Sir David Lindsay Keir, *A Constitutional History of Modern Britain* (London, 1961), 290.
2. The idea of the armed struggle is one most often associated with ideas of resistance to colonialism and was most widely applied in the process of decolonization in the European empire, but anti-imperialism was also used by a number of European minority nationalist movements. For a recent overview on the relationship between empire and resistance, see Nuno Domingos, Miguel Bandeira Jeronimo and Ricardo Roque (eds), *Resistance and Colonialism: Insurgent Peoples in World History* (London, 2019); and for specific example of the 'armed struggle' in Europe, see Richard English, *Armed Struggle: The History of the IRA* (Oxford, 2003); and John L. Sullivan, *ETA and Basque Nationalism: The Fight for Euskadi, 1890–1980* (London, 2016).
3. Dean Kostantaras, *Nationalism and Revolution in Europe, 1763–1848* (Amsterdam, 2020).
4. Iain MacLeay and Andrew Murray Scott, *Britain's Secret War: Tartan Terrorism and the Anglo-American State* (Edinburgh, 1990).
5. The offending item was blown up in Edinburgh, 1952; see *Scots Independent*, March 1953, 2.
6. See K. Theodore Hoppen, *Ireland since 1800: Conflict and Conformity* (London, 2nd edn, 1999), 1–56.
7. James Mackinnon, *The Union of Scotland and England: An International Study* (London, 1896), 524.
8. Ibid., 514.
9. Published by the *Glasgow Herald* as *The Union of 1707: A Survey of Events and the Text of Articles of Union* (Glasgow, 1907).
10. William Ferguson, *The Identity of the Scottish Nation: An Historic Quest* (Edinburgh, 1998), 22–3.
11. Sharon Korman, *The Right of Conquest: The Acquisition of Territory by Force in International Law and Practice* (Oxford, 1996).
12. Robert McIntyre, SNP leader from 1947 to 1956, was a passionate advocate of the right of self-determination for nations that were absorbed within the Soviet Union and argued consistently and constantly for their liberation. His manuscript collection in the National Library of Scotland has an extensive collection of English-language journals and pamphlets in support of minority nations within the Soviet Union; NLS acc. 12917. On Baltic resistance to the annexation, see John Hiden, Vahur Made and David J. Smith (eds), *The Baltic Question during the Cold War* (London, 2008); on Francoist Spain, see Daniel Conversi, *The Basques, Catalans and Spain: Alternative Routes to Nationalist Mobilisation* (London, 2000), 98–104, 109–41; and on the nationalists perspective that Northern Ireland was 'occupied territory', see Graham

Spencer, *From Armed Struggle to Political Struggle: Republican Tradition and Transformation in Northern Ireland* (London, 2015), 20–48.
13. On the Conquest of Ireland, see Steven G. Ellis, *Ireland in the Age of the Tudors 1447–1603: English Expansion and the End of Gaelic Rule* (London, 2014); and Padraig Lenihan, *Consolidating Conquest: Ireland 1603–1727* (London, 2008).
14. M. D. R. Foot, *Resistance: An Analysis of the History of European Resistance to Nazism, 1940–45* (London, 1976), 76–8; P. Lagrou, *The Legacy of Nazi Occupation: Patriotic Memory and National Recovery in Western Europe, 1945–65* (Cambridge, 2000), 38–79, 197–292; Philip Cooke and Ben H. Shepard (eds), *Hitler's Europe Ablaze: Occupation, Resistance and Rebellion during World War Two* (London, 2013). It is also worth pointing out that in the Easter Proclamation of the Irish Republic it is stated: 'In every generation the Irish people have asserted their right to national freedom and sovereignty; six times during the past three hundred years they have asserted it in arms.'
15. H. J. Paton, *The Claim of Scotland* (London, 1968), 32.
16. See Alvin Jackson, *Home Rule: An Irish History* (Oxford, 2004), 8–142; Michael Laffan, *The Resurrection of Ireland: The Sinn Fein Party, 1916–23* (Cambridge, 1999), 122–69; and for an overview of the issue, see Ronan Fanning, *Fatal Path: British Government and Irish Revolution, 1910–22* (London, 2013).
17. G. C. Bolton, *The Passing of the Irish Act of Union: A Study in Parliamentary Politics* (Oxford, 1966); and James Kelly, Patrick Geoghegan and Michael Brown (eds), *The Irish Act of Union: A Study in High Politics, Bicentennial Essays* (Dublin, 2001).
18. James Kelly, *Prelude to the Union: Anglo Irish Politics in the 1780s* (Cork, 1992).
19. *Scots Independent*, January 1929, 26.
20. A. V. Dicey, *England's Case against Home Rule* (London, 1887).
21. *MacCormick v. Lord Advocate* (1953) SC 396 – Court of Session on Appeal.
22. It is important to note that Lord Cooper was also a historian and was one of the first in the twentieth century to appreciate the constitutional significance of the Declaration of Arbroath; see his *Supra Crepidum: Presidential Addresses delivered to the Scottish Historical Society* (1951).
23. See, for example, T. D. Wanliss, *Bars to British Unity or a Plea for National Sentiment* (Edinburgh, 1895); and William Mitchell, *Home Rule for Scotland and Imperial Federation* (Edinburgh, 1892).
24. For the importance of the constitutional position of the Church of England in the eighteenth century, see J. C. D. Clark, *English Society, 1660–1832* (2nd edn, Cambridge, 2000), 256–318.
25. On religion in Scotland at the Union, see Jeffrey Stephen, *Scottish Presbyterians and the Act of Union 1707* (Edinburgh, 2007), 1–40.
26. J. C. D. Clark, *The Language of Liberty, 1660–1832: Political Discourse and Social Dynamics in the Anglo-American World* (Cambridge, 2008), 62–75, 153–67.
27. See Andrew L. Drummond and James Bulloch, *The Scottish Church, 1688–1843* (Edinburgh, 1973), 19–22.
28. *A Selection from the Earl of Marchmont's Papers*, vol. III (1831), Viscount Stair to Lord Godolphin, 22 February 1707, 447.
29. Geoffrey Holmes, 'The Hamilton Affair of 1711–12: A Crisis in Anglo-Scottish Relations', in Geoffrey Holmes (ed.), *Politics, Religion and Society in England, 1679–1742* (London, 1986), 83–108.
30. Geoffrey Holmes and Clyve Jones, 'Trade, the Scots and the Parliamentary Crisis of 1713', *Parliamentary History*, vol. 1, 1 (1982), 47–77.

31. Debates in the House of Lords quoted by John Oldmixon, *The History of England during the Reigns of King William and Queen Mary, Queen Anne, George I* (London, 1735), 384–5.
32. On the political divide in England, see W. A. Speck, *Whig and Tory: The Struggle in the Constituencies, 1701–1715* (London, 1970); and Julian Hoppet, 'Party Politics and War Weariness in the Reign of Queen Anne', in Trevor J. Dadson and J. H. Elliot (eds), *Britain, Spain and the Treaty of Utrecht, 1713–2013* (London, 2014), 9–18.
33. Annette M. Smith, *Jacobite Estates of the Forty-Five* (Edinburgh, 1982), 2–31.
34. Ryan Mallon, 'A Church for Scotland? The Free Church and Scottish Nationalism after the Disruption', *Scottish Church History*, vol. 49, 1 (2020), 1–24; and David W. Bebbington, 'Religion and National Feeling in Nineteenth-Century Wales and Scotland', *Studies in Church History*, vol. 18, *Religion and National Identity* (1982), 489–503.
35. National Association for the Vindication of Scottish Rights, *Statement of Grievances* (Edinburgh, 1853).
36. Scottish Home Rule Association, *The Evils of Centralisation and Its Cure* (Edinburgh, 1898).
37. John MacCormick, 'The Scrap of Paper: Should We Accept the Local Government Act', *Scots Independent*, March 1930, 54.
38. John M. MacCormick's role as a constitutional thinker has been overshadowed by that of his son, Neil MacCormick, who was Regius Professor of Public Law at Edinburgh University. See John's semi-autobiographical account, *Flag in the Wind: The Story of the National Movement in Scotland* (1955). Neil had a prolific output with perhaps *Questioning Sovereignty: Law, State and Nation in the European Commonwealth* (Oxford, 1999) being his best-known work. For an appreciation of Neil's significance as a legal scholar, see Neil Walker (ed.), *MacCormick's Scotland* (Edinburgh, 2012).
39. MacCormick, 'The Scrap of Paper'.
40. MacCormick always tended to a moderate position; see Richard J. Finlay, *Independent and Free: Scottish Politics and the Origins of the SNP, 1918–1945* (Edinburgh, 1994).
41. James Alston, 'Aspects of Self-Government', *Scots Independent*, January 1932, 42.
42. Quoted in MacCormick, 'Scrap of Paper'.
43. The subtitle of the Mackinnon's book, 'An International Study', gives the game away.
44. *Journal of the House of Lords*, vol. 17, 11 December 1704, 595, 13 December 1704, 602.
45. To my knowledge, this is not a point picked up by historians on either the Scottish or Irish Unions.
46. Usually attributed to William Ferguson, *Scotland's Relations with England: A Survey to 1707* (Edinburgh, 1994), but he does not actually use this phrase.
47. For a contemporary English critique of the Union that was not at all flattering, see *Valpone or Some Remarks on Some Proceedings in Scotland Pertaining to the Union and the Protestant Succession* (1707).
48. William L. Sachse, *Lord Somers: A Political Portrait* (Manchester, 1975), 259.
49. 6. Ann. C. 6. For the post-Union administration of Scotland, see P. W. J. Riley, *English Ministers and Scotland, 1707–1727* (London, 1964).
50. Harold Williams, *The Correspondence of Jonathan Swift*, vol. II (Oxford, 1963), 115.
51. Sachse, *Lord Somers*, 308–9.
52. For a recent discussion on the Anglo-centric development of the constitution in Britain before the advent of entry into the European Union, see Vernon Bogdanor, *The New British Constitution* (London, 2009), xi–xiii.

53. To date only P. W. J. Riley has looked at the Union from an English historical perspective; see *The Union of England and Scotland: A Study of Anglo Scottish Politics of the Eighteenth Century* (Manchester, 1978).
54. A. V. Dicey and R. S. Rait, *Thoughts on the Union between England and Scotland* (London, 1920).
55. Robert S. Rait, *The Scottish Parliaments* (London, 1924), 295, 484.
56. Dicey and Rait, *Thoughts on the Union*, 171.
57. For an overview of the historiography on the Scottish dimension of the Union, see C. A. Whatley, *Bought and Sold for English Gold? Explaining the Union of 1707* (Edinburgh, 2001).
58. Lady Francis Balfour, *Lord Balfour of Burleigh* (London, 1924), 97.
59. 'The Coronation and Scotland', *The Scottish Antiquary or Northern Notes and Queries*, vol. 16, 61 (1901), 11–19.
60. William Ferguson, 'Imperial Crowns: A Neglected Facet to the Background of the Treaty of Union, 1707', *Scottish Historical Review*, vol. 53, 155 (1974), 22–44.
61. Richard J. Finlay, 'Scottish Monarchy in the Twentieth Century', in William L. Miller (ed.), *Anglo-Scottish Relations: From 1900 to Devolution* (Oxford, 2004), 62–75.
62. Sir William Edward Whyte, *The Local Government (Scotland) Act: A Popular Exposition of Its Provisions* (London, 1932), 2–11.
63. Tom Gallagher, 'The Press and Protestant Popular Culture: A Case Study of the Scottish Daily Express', in Graham Walker and Tom Gallagher (eds), *Sermons and Battle Hymns: Protestant Popular Culture in Modern Scotland* (Edinburgh, 1990), 193–212.
64. Hector MacPherson, 'What Scotland Owes the Covenanters', *Scots Independent*, October 1930, 165.
65. A very good example of this is James Barr, *The Scottish Covenanters* (London, 1946); and see Edward J. Cowan, 'The Covenanting Tradition in Scottish History', in Edward J. Cowan and Richard J. Finlay (eds), *Scottish History: The Power of Past* (Edinburgh, 2002), 121–47.
66. Callum G. Brown, *The Death of Christian Britain* (2009), 170–93, dates the rapid decline from the 1960s.
67. S. J. Brown, 'A Victory for God: The Scottish Presbyterian Churches and the General Strike of 1926', *Journal of Ecclesiastical History*, vol. 42 (1991), 596–617.
68. In particular, on the pioneering work of George MacLeod, see Ron Ferguson, *George MacLeod: Founder of the Iona Community* (Glasgow, 1990).
69. *Scots Independent*, June 1932, 115.
70. *Scots Independent*, April 1934, 81.
71. A. C. Cheyne, *Studies in Scottish Church History* (Edinburgh, 1999), 287.
72. The link between Catholicism and nationalism in Poland, Ireland and Slovakia is pretty well established. Again religion was a factor in the break-up of the Austro-Hungarian Empire. See James C. Kennedy, 'Religion, Nation and Representation of the Past', in Stefan Berger and Chris Lorenz (eds), *The Contested Nation: Ethnicity, Class, Religion and Gender in National Histories* (Basingstoke, 2011), 104–35; Bernard Wasserstein, *Barbarism and Civilisation: A History of Europe in Our Own Time* (Oxford, 2007), 34–7; Stuart Philip W. Barker, *Religious Nationalism in Modern Europe* (1914); and Stuart Mews (ed.), *Religion and National Identity: Studies in Church History* (Oxford, 1982).
73. The classic study of education in Scotland is R. D. Anderson, *Education and Opportunity in Victorian Scotland* (Edinburgh, 1989); and for a recent overview, see

R. D. Anderson, Mark Freeman and Lindsay Paterson (eds), *The Edinburgh History of Education in Scotland* (Edinburgh, 2015).
74. Lindsay Paterson, 'Liberation or Control: What Are the Scottish Education Traditions of the Twentieth Century?' in T. M. Devine and R. J. Finlay (eds), *Scotland in the Twentieth Century* (Edinburgh, 1996), 230–49.
75. *Scots Independent*, April 1931, 92.
76. In the nineteenth and for much of the twentieth century, this tended to be associated with Protestantism. For an example of this, see Hector MacPherson, *The Intellectual Development of Scotland* (London, 1911). On poetry, see the Saltire pamphlet by Iain Paul, *The Scottish Tradition in Poetry* (Edinburgh, 1948); on philosophy, see Henry Laurie, *Scottish Philosophy in Its National Development* (Edinburgh, 1902).
77. George Elder Davie, *The Democratic Intellect: Scotland and Her Universities in the Nineteenth Century* (Edinburgh, 1964) and *The Crisis of the Democratic Intellect: The Problem of Generalisation and Specialisation in Twentieth Century Scotland* (Edinburgh, 1989).
78. This argument is most clearly articulated in Andre Lockhart Walker, *The Revival of the Democratic Intellect* (Edinburgh, 1998).
79. Aviel Roshwald, *Ethnic Nationalism and the Fall of Empires: Central Europe, Russia and the Middle East, 1914-23* (London, 2000), 34–70, 156–98.
80. See Tibor Frank and Frank Hadler (eds), *Disputed Territories and Shared Pasts: Overlapping National Histories in Modern Europe* (Basingstoke, 2010).
81. The relationship between politics and law in Scotland is a relatively unexplored area in history. Also, a historical, as opposed to a legal, study of the development of law after the Union is very much needed. In the meantime, see Megan Dewart, *The Scottish Legal System* (London, 2019); and the Stair Society, *An Introduction to Scottish Legal History* (Edinburgh, 1958).
82. For example, see Hector L. MacQueen, 'Legal Nationalism: Lord Cooper, Legal History and Comparative Law', *Edinburgh Law Review*, vol. 9, 3 (2005), 395–406.
83. On Ireland, see Robert Lynch, *The Partition of Ireland, 1918-25* (Cambridge, 2019), 1–11.
84. This is a neglected aspect in the discussion of Unionism, but the idea of 'race' as a divide in Ireland was something frequently alluded to by Unionist politicians. For example, Austin Chamberlain tartly remarked that the florid language in a communique to the Ulster Unionist needed toning down as 'we were not now writing to Celts, but Anglo-Saxons'; quoted in Fanning, *Fatal Path*, 295. It is also worth pointing out the role of the leader of the Conservative Party, the Canadian born Ulster Scot Andrew Bonar Law; see Lynch, *Partition of Ireland*, 64.
85. Thomas Alexander Fyfe, *The Sheriff Courts Act, 1907 as Amended by the Sheriff Courts Act 1913* (Glasgow, 1913), 1–10.
86. Walter Murray, *Scottish Home Rule: The Case in Sixty Points* (Glasgow, 1912), 3–15.
87. *Scots Independent*, April 1930, 63.
88. A. A. MacEwen, *Thistle and the Rose: Scotland's Problem Today* (Edinburgh, 1932), 67.
89. Peter Berresford Ellis and Seumas Mac a' Ghobhainn, *The Scottish Insurrection of 1820* (London, 1970).
90. *Protest of the Scottish Home Rule Association against the Denial or Delay of Scottish Home Rule* (Edinburgh, 1890).
91. Quoted in Robert Rhodes James, *Rosebery* (1963), 130.
92. This is the argument made by Fanning in *Fatal Path*.

93. The standard work is Charles Townsend, *Political Violence in Ireland: Government and Resistance since 1848* (Oxford, 1985).
94. See Colin Kidd and James Coleman, 'Mythical Scotland', in T. M. Devine and Jenny Wormald (eds), *The Oxford Handbook of Modern Scottish History* (Oxford, 2012), 72–7.
95. Charles Townsend, *Easter 1916: The Irish Rebellion* (London, 2015); and Diarmaid Ferriter, *A Nation and Not a Rabble: The Irish Revolution, 1913–23* (London, 2015), 99–162.
96. Tom Garvin, *The Evolution of Irish Nationalist Politics* (Dublin, 2005), 116, 119.
97. See *Scottish Review*, Winter 1919, 406; William Bell, *Rip Van Scotland* (London, 1930), 10–45; and J. Torrence, *Scotland's Dilemma: Nation or Province* (Edinburgh, 1937).
98. Finlay, 'Pressure Group or Political Party'.
99. This argument was advanced by John MacCormick and formed the basis for his idea of the Scottish Convention; see Finlay, *Independent and Free*, 211–25.
100. See Paolo Dardanelli, 'Democratic Deficit or the Europeanisation of Secession? Explaining the Devolution Referendums in Scotland', *Political Studies*, vol. 53, 2 (2005), 320–42; and James Mitchell, 'Summoning the Harpies: Legitimacy and the Anglo-Scottish Relationship', *Scottish Affairs*, vol. 68 (2009), 36–44.
101. It is worth speculating whether disillusionment with nationalism because of the Irish Civil War was a factor in turning a number of Scottish-Irish politicians against the idea of Scottish home rule. John Wheatley dropped the idea in the late 1920s; see David Howell, *A Lost Left: Three Studies in Nationalism and Socialism* (Manchester, 1986), 229–65. Patrick Dollan almost went out of his way to emphasize his Britishness during the Second World War; see Daniel Carrigan, 'Patrick Dollan and the Labour Movement in Glasgow', Glasgow University MPhil. (2014), 107–49.
102. K. C. Wheare, *The Statute of Westminster and Dominion Status* (Oxford, 1949).
103. *Scots Independent*, May 1929, 90 and June 1929, 103. See David Goldie, 'Hugh MacDiarmid: The Impossible Persona', in Scott Lyall and Marjory Palmer McCulloch (eds), *The Edinburgh Companion to Hugh MacDiarmid* (Edinburgh, 2011), 125–36, for the awkward nature of his politics and the reaction of party chairman, Roland Muirhead: 'I do not agree with Grieve and his idea of Fascism', NLS, Acc. 3721, box 5, letter to Arthur Donaldson, 16 June 1930.
104. Muirhead, Donaldson and Robert McIntyre, for example, were all pacifists. Pacifism was also significant in the anti-conscription campaign which emerged among the ranks of the SNP in the late 1930s and lasted throughout the war; see Finlay, *Independent and Free*, 206–10, 227–9. On pacifism as a political movement in the interwar era, see Martin Ceadel, *Pacifisms in Britain, 1914–45: The Defining of a Faith* (Oxford, 1980).
105. The issue of contesting elections as a distinct political party that led to the formation of the SNP had a long-drawn-out and chequered history; see Finlay, *Independent and Free*.
106. Quoted from the play by SydneyGoodsir Smith, *The Wallace* (Edinburgh, 1960), 156.
107. D. C. C. Young, *The Free Minded Scot: The Trial of Douglas C. C. Young in the High Court of Edinburgh* (Glasgow, 1942).
108. There was a sort of chicken-and-egg quality to the Sinn Fein policy or 'Carnwath policy' as some nationalists named it after George Lockwood of Carnwath, a Scottish Jacobite who advocated a unilateral withdrawal from Westminster because, as much as anything, it was the fact that Sinn Fein won such an overwhelming majority of Irish seats in 1918 that gave legitimacy to their

withdrawal from Westminster. Without winning a majority of Scottish seats, a withdrawal would make little or no sense and would be devoid of its important political symbolism. On the Carnwath Policy, see H. C. MacNeacail, *Lberty*, October 1920, 77.
109. NLS, Acc. 10090, McIntyre Collection, file 25, Manifesto, Motherwell 1945.
110. https://www.telegraph.co.uk/news/politics/SNP/11633831/Show-some-respect-John-Bercow-tells-SNP-in-slap-down-over-applause.html.
111. See Alan O'Day, *Irish Home Rule, 1867–1921* (Manchester, 1998), 240–66; and Alvin Jackson, *Home Rule: An Irish History* (Oxford, 2005), 106–75.
112. On Redmond's legacy, see Dermot Meleady, *John Redmond: The National Leader* (London, 2018), 1–10.
113. Ross McKibbin, *The Evolution of the Labour Party, 1910–24* (Oxford, 1974), xvi.
114. George Roberston, Labour shadow secretary of state for Scotland, 1997.
115. This incremental approach of using devolution as a stepping stone to independence has always had its adherents within that national movement; see Antonia Dodds and David Seawright, 'The Politics of Identity: Scottish Nationalism', in Michael O'Neill (ed.), *Devolution and British Politics* (London, 2013), 92–3. This was the view of Tam Dalyell, *The Question of Scotland: Devolution and After* (Edinburgh, 2016), which is a rehash of his earlier work, *Devolution: The End of Britain* (London, 1977).
116. Tom Nairn, *The Break-Up of Britain* (London, 1979).
117. Lindsay Crawford, 'Scotland, a Sovereign Nation', *Liberty*, April 1920, 37.
118. Lindsay Crawford, 'Scotland, a Sovereign Nation II', *Liberty*, May 1920, 41.
119. Murray Pittock, 'Scottish Sovereignty and the Union of 1707: Then and Now', *National Identities*, vol. 14, 1 (2012), 11–21.
120. Special supplement, *Scots Independent*, July 1930, 5.
121. For the importance of a 'national' dimension in this episode, see Allan I. Macinnes, *Charles I and the Making of the Covenanting Movement, 1625–41* (Edinburgh, 2003).
122. Robert McIntyre, 'How the SNP See Politics', *Glasgow Herald*, 25 July 1968.
123. Robert McIntyre, Speech to SNP Conference, 1977, NLS, Acc. 10090, File 126.
124. Ray Michie MP (Liberal Democrat Argyll and Bute), House of Commons Debates, 16 December 1991, vol. 201, col. 38.
125. *Glasgow Herald*, 9 March 1994.
126. Michael Fry, *The Union: England, Scotland and the Treaty of 1707* (Edinburgh, 2006), 218–19.
127. D. H. McNeill, *The Historical Scottish Constitution* (Edinburgh, 1971), 40–4.
128. The Scottish Secretariat, *Scotland's Scrap of Paper: The Treaty of Union of 1707* (Glasgow, 1930), 4.
129. Andrew Dewar Gibb, *Scotland Resurgent* (Stirling, 1950), 142.
130. McNeill, *Historical Scottish Constitution*, 18–19.
131. Alan Macfarlane, *The Origins of English Individualism: Family, Property and Social Transition* (London, 1979).
132. McNeill, *Historical Scottish Constitution*, 50.
133. See the SNP leadership correspondence on the 1320 Club in the mid-1960s, NLS, McIntyre Papers, Acc. 10090, file 120.
134. *Glasgow Herald*, 27 June 1932.
135. Wood's association with militancy was also reinforced by her claim that she negotiated a truce on behalf of the Scottish nation with the IRA during the Second World War. *Scots Independent*, April 1939, 8–9.

136. See Wendy Wood's autobiography, *The Autobiography of a Patriot: Wendy Wood, Yours Sincerely for Scotland* (London, 1970).
137. *Scots Independent*, July 1937, 4.
138. Finlay, *Independent and Free*, 228–32.
139. *Scots Independent*, 'Report of the Annual Conference', July 1942.
140. NLS, Muirhead Papers, Acc. 3721, box 4, file 59, Kirkcaldy by election.
141. Compton Mackenzie, *The North Wind of Love, book one* (London, 1944), 144, 236–57.
142. See Ian R. Hamilton, *The Taking of the Stone of Destiny: The Exiting True Story of How the Stone of Scone Was Returned to Scotland* (London, 1992).
143. H. J. Paton, *The Claim of Scotland* (London,1968), 59.
144. Peter Hennessy, *Never Again: Britain, 1945–51* (London, 2006).
145. Richard J. Finlay, 'Scottish Monarchy in the Twentieth Century', in William L. Miller (ed.), *Anglo Scottish Relations from 1900 to Devolution* (Oxford, 2004), 62–75.
146. *Scots Independent*, March 1953, 2.
147. Tom Gallagher, 'The Press and Protestant Popular Culture: A Case Study of the Scottish Daily Express', in Graham Walker and Tom Gallagher (eds), *Sermons and Battle Hymns: Protestant Popular Culture in Modern Scotland* (Edinburgh, 1990), 193–212.
148. *Scottish Control of Scottish Affairs: Unionist Policy* (Glasgow, 1949), for example, claimed that Labour's policy of nationalization had the effect of 'de-nationalizing' Scotland by increasing the amount of London control over the Scottish economy.
149. See, for example, the piece in the *Sunday Telegraph* (Supplement), 175, 9 February 1968: 'Who are the Scottish Nationalists' (15).
150. It has become part of nationalist folklore that MI5 regularly endeavours to infiltrate the movement. See the novel by James Robertson, *And the Land Lay Still* (London, 2010), which features the character Jimmy Bond as the MI5 would-be infiltrator.
151. M. C. Dyer, 'A Nationalist in the Churchillian Sense: John MacCormick, the Paisley By-Election of 18th February, Home Rule, and the Crisis in Scottish Liberalism', *Parliamentary History*, vol. 2, 3 (2003), 285–307; and James Mitchell, *The Scottish Question* (Oxford, 2014), 87–113.
152. James Mitchell, *Strategies for Self-Government: The Campaign for a Scottish Parliament* (Edinburgh, 2001), 150–60.
153. See Owen Dudley Edwards (ed.), *A Claim of Right for Scotland* (Edinburgh, 1989).
154. This was a consistent finding from opinion polls which were collated and published annually in the *Scottish Government Year Book* (Edinburgh 1976–92).
155. House of Commons Debates, vol. 237, col. 36, 7 February 1994.
156. Ibid., col. 30.
157. House of Commons Debates, vol. 237, col. 61, Phil Gallie, Conservative MP Ayr, 7 February 1994.
158. Margaret Thatcher, *The Downing Street Years* (London, 1993), 624.
159. Cmd. 2225, March 1993, 5.
160. Cmd. 8554, *Scotland Analysis: Devolution and the Implications for Scottish Independence* (2013), 32.
161. *Report of the Smith Commission for Further Devolution of Powers to the Scottish Parliament* (2014), 12.
162. House of Commons Debates, vol. 664, 4 July 2018.

4 Home rule and unionism

1. For the issue of devolution in British political history, see Vernon Bogdanor, *Devolution in the United Kingdom* (Oxford, 1999), 1–19; and James Mitchell, *Devolution in the United Kingdom* (Manchester, 1990), 1–16.
2. This was used in the late nineteenth and early twentieth centuries as a way to bolster the existing arguments of basing devolution around nationality, and in the case of Ireland, it was seen as a way of not surrendering in public to nationalist demands. For a contemporary examination of the limited powers put forward for Ireland, see Walter James Shepard, 'The Government of Ireland (Home Rule) Bill', *American Political Science Review*, vol. 6, 4 (1912), 564–73.
3. Cmd. 9212, *Royal Commission on Scottish Affairs, 1952–1954* (1954); and James Mitchell, *Governing Scotland: The Invention of Administrative Devolution* (Basingstoke, 2003), for the period before the Second World War; and Ian G. C. Hutchison, 'Government', in T. M. Devine and R. J. Finlay (eds), *Scotland in the 20th Century* (Edinburgh, 1996), 46–63, for the post-war era.
4. This point is made perceptively by Norman Davies in his *Vanished Kingdoms: The History of Half-Forgotten Europe* (London, 2012), 679–85.
5. For the argument that English federalism was used as a means to stall Irish home rule, see Patricia Jalland, 'United Kingdom Devolution 1910–14: Political Panacea or Tactical Diversion?', *English Historical Review*, vol. 114, 373 (1979), 757–85.
6. Cmd. 5460, *Royal Commission on the Constitution 1969–1973*, vol. II, *Memorandum of Dissent by Lord Crowther-Hunt and Professor A. T. Peacock* (1973).
7. NLS, Muirhead Mss, Acc. 3721, box 5, 6 April 1932, J. M. MacDiarmid to Roland Muirhead.
8. H. J. Hanham, *Scottish Nationalism* (London, 1969), 169, first coined the terms 'fundamentalist' and 'gradualist'.
9. As evidenced by the SNP's decision to campaign for a Scottish assembly and a Scottish parliament in the referendums in 1979 and 1997, respectively.
10. Minutes of the Scottish National Council of the National Party of Scotland, 3 February 1934, 66.
11. Quoted in Gemma Fraser, 'The Birth of a Parliament', *Holyrood*, 21 January 2019.
12. David Denver, James Mitchell, Charles Pattie and Hugh Bochel, *Scotland Decides: The Devolution Issue and the Referendum of 1997* (London, 2000), 213–15.
13. Michael Ancram, House of Commons Debates, 6 May 1998, vol. 311, col. 735.
14. Jeremy Smith, *The Tories and Ireland: Conservative Party Politics and Ireland and the Home Rule Crisis, 1910–14* (Dundalk, 2000); Richard Shannon, *The Age of Salisbury, 1881–1902: Unionism and Empire* (London, 1996), 149 passim; and John Ramsden, *The Age of Balfour and Baldwin, 1902–1940* (London, 1978), 78–126.
15. See Murray Stewart Leith and Daniel P. J. Soule, *Political Discourse and National Identity in Scotland* (Edinburgh, 2012), 13; and Lindsay Paterson, *The Autonomy of Modern Scotland* (Edinburgh, 1994), 18.
16. Most historical accounts of Scottish nationalism tend to see the emergence of the modern SNP as an outgrowth of the campaign for Scottish home rule in the late nineteenth and early twentieth centuries and include the demand for devolution and independence as being part and parcel of the same phenomenon of the campaign for constitutional change that is driven by the politicization of Scottish national identity or sentiment. For a good overview, see James Mitchell, *Strategies*

for Self-Government: The Campaign for a Scottish Parliament (Edinburgh, 2001). According to the Kilbrandon Report: 'Modern Scottish nationalism might be said to have started in 1853, with the setting up, with a considerable measure of support from the Scottish local authorities, of the National Association for the Vindication of Scottish Rights. Since then the fortunes of the nationalist movement have fluctuated, and it has been subject to a number of splits and re-groupings. But the basic idea of the resumption of self-government by Scotland has continued to receive some kind of support throughout, and in more recent years the movement, while still commanding only minority support, has become a well-established feature of Scottish life, *Royal Commission on the Constitution*, vol. I, section 339.

17. See Owen Dudley Edwards, *Claim of Right for Scotland* (Edinburgh, 1989), for a wider discussion of the issues.
18. Liberal Democrats and Labour supporters, for example, shied away from the idea of being labelled 'Unionists', in the main because this was a term historically used to describe Conservatives and had connotations with Ulster. Obviously seeking to make political capital, Tories tended to label all proponents of constitutional change as nationalists; Bill Walker, Conservative MP for Tayside North, referred to Labour Nationalists and Liberal Democrat Nationalists, for example, House of Commons Debates, 7 February 1994, vol. 237, col. 43. A number of attempts were made to create a cross-party constitutional reform/home rule/devolutionist movement such as Common cause and United Front, but a collective term for devolutionists never caught on, nor was it able to compete with the short-hand terms of nationalist and Unionist.
19. William Cowan, Liberal MP (East Aberdeenshire), House of Commons Debates, 30 May 1913, vol. 53, col. 476.
20. Ibid., col. 475.
21. *Royal Commission Report on the Constitution*, vol. I, section 333.
22. Neil MacCormick, 'Independence and Constitutional Change', in Neil MacCormick (ed.), *The Scottish Debate: Essays on Scottish Nationalism* (Oxford, 1970), 68.
23. House of Commons Debates, 6 May 1998, vol. 311, col. 744.
24. Scottish National Assembly, *A Blueprint for Scotland* (Glasgow, 1948).
25. A recent work making this argument is John Lloyd, *Should Auld Acquaintance Be Forgot: The Great Mistake of Scottish Independence* (Cambridge, 2020). According to 'official' figures Scotland costs England £250 million a week, so not that far behind the EU.
26. Quoted in Jo E. Murkens, Peter Jones and Michael Keating, *Scottish Independence: Legal and Constitutional Issues* (Edinburgh, 2002), 12.
27. See Michael Keating, 'Reforging the Union: Devolution and Constitutional Change in the United Kingdom', *Publius*, vol. 28, 1 (1998), 217-34.
28. See Denver et al., *Scotland Decides*, 27-48.
29. See Gordon Pentland, 'Edward Heath, the Declaration of Perth and the Scottish Conservative and Unionist Party, 1966-70', *20th Century British History*, vol. 26, 2 (2015), 249-73.
30. Emily Jones, *Edmund Burke and the Invention of Modern Conservatism, 1830-1914: An Intellectual History* (Oxford, 2019).
31. See Cmd. 7027, *The House of Lords Reform* (2007), 8-19.
32. House of Commons Debates, 20 June 1979, vol. 968, col. 1338.
33. Iain G. C. Hutchison, *Scottish Politics in the Twentieth Century* (Basingstoke, 2000), 113.

34. J. E. Kendle, 'The Round Table Movement and "Home Rule All Round"', *Historical Journal*, vol. 11, 2 (1968), 332–53.
35. For Labour's commitment to strong local government, see Sue Goss, *Local Labour and Local Government, A Study of Changing Interests, Politics, and Policy in Southwark, 1919 to 1982* (Edinburgh, 1988), 135–58; John Carvel, *Citizen Ken: A Biography of Ken Livingstone* (London, 1984); and Derek Hatton, *Left Inside* (London, 1988).
36. The classic account of this is Tam Dalyell, *Devolution: The End of Britain* (London, 1977).
37. House of Commons Debates, 27 January 1988, vol. 126, col. 332.
38. John Kendle, *Federal Britain: A History* (London, 1997), 58–79.
39. The classic account is G. R. Searle, *The Quest for National Efficiency: A Study in British Politics and Political Thought, 1899–1914* (London, 1971).
40. Adam Evans, 'A Lingering Diminuendo? The Conference on Devolution, 1919–20', *Parliamentary History*, vol. 35 (2016), 3, 315–35.
41. *Scottish Home Rule: The Case in 90 Points* (Glasgow, 1922), 10.
42. The classic account of the emergence of post-war consensus politics is Paul Addison, *The Road to 1945: British Politics and the Second World War* (London, revised edn, 1993). On the post-war era, see David Dutton, *British Politics since 1945: The Rise, Fall and Rebirth of Consensus* (London, 1997).
43. Martin Holmes, *The Labour Government, 1974–79: Political Aims and Economic Reality* (London, 1987); and for a contemporary take which did relate the growth of Scottish nationalism to the declining economic fortunes of the British state, see Tom Nairn, *The Break-Up of Britain: Crisis and Neo-nationalism* (London, 1977).
44. *What Is the Scottish National Congress?* (Glasgow, 1950), 3.
45. Sir George Younger, Conservative MP for Ayr, House of Commons Debates, 30 May 1913, vol. 53, col. 503.
46. Jalland, 'United Kingdom Devolution 1910–14: Political Panacea or Tactical Diversion'.
47. House of Commons Debates, 16 November 1949, vol. 469, col. 2098.
48. For Labour's relationship with home rule, see Michael Keating and David Bleiman, *Labour and Scottish Nationalism* (London, 1979), 175–89.
49. Based on personal manifesto commitments, pledges given to home rule movements and parliamentary votes, it can be said with considerable confidence that between 1906 and 1922 there was a clear majority, in the period 1923–31 the Scottish Home Rule Association claimed a majority, in 1945 there would be a nominal majority and from 1974 to 1997 there was a clear majority.
50. Richard J. Finlay, *Independent and Free: Scottish Politics and the Origins of the Scottish National Party, 1918–1945* (Edinburgh, 1994), 1–29.
51. *Policy of the Scottish National Party* (Stirling, n.d.), 2.
52. For much of its history, the national movement has oscillated between the strategy of being a distinct political party and a looser cross-party grouping. See Richard J. Finlay, 'Pressure Group or Political Party: The Nationalist Impact on Scottish Politics, 1928–1945', *20th Century British History*, vol. 3, 3 (1993), 274–93.
53. See D. G. Boyce, *Englishmen and Irish Troubles: British Public Opinion and the Making of Irish Policy, 1918–22* (London, 1972), 25–43.
54. Diarrmid Ferriter, *The Transformation of Ireland* (Woodstock, 2007), 353–5.
55. Scottish National Party, *Self-Government in Practice* (Glasgow, n.d. [1936]), 23.
56. For example, *Scottish Home Rule: An Imperial Necessity* (Edinburgh, 1911).
57. The Duke of Montrose, *Self-Government for Scotland* (Glasgow, 1933), 4.

58. Ibid., 11.
59. Carnegie Endowment for International Peace, *Autonomy and Federation within the Empire of Self-Governing Dominions* (London, 1921); and Robert MacGregor Dawson, *The Development of Dominion Status, 1900–1936* (London, 1965), 54–135.
60. Walter Murray (ed.), *Home Rule for Scotland: The Case in 90 Points* (Glasgow, 1922), 4–5.
61. For the influence of Empire, see Richard J. Finlay, 'For or Against: Scottish Nationalists and the British Empire, 1919–39', *Scottish Historical Review*, vol. 71, 191/2 (1992), 184–206. For the widespread use of the term 'self-government' in relation to political freedom in the Asian and African colonies, see Stephen Howe, *Anti-Colonialism in British Politics: The Left and the End of Empire, 1918–64* (Oxford, 1998).
62. Catherine P. Snodgrass, *Scotland in the Modern World: A Plea for Freedom, Self-Government and Full Participation* (Stirling, 1959), 4, although examples of long-established small nations in Western Europe, such as Denmark, were also cited.
63. Robert Pentland Mahaffy, *The Statute of Westminster* (London, 1932).
64. John Darwin describes the wider imperial sentiment among the white dominions as 'Britannic Nationalism'; see his *The Empire Project* (London, 2011), 144–80.
65. *Scots Independent*, February 1933, 53.
66. Murray, *Home Rule for Scotland*, 2.
67. Carl Bridge, *Holding India to the Empire: The British Conservative Party and the 1935 Constitution* (London, 1986), 60–2.
68. NLS, Acc. 12917, McIntyre collection, 106, minutes of the national executive of the National Party of Scotland, 66.
69. MacEwen, *Thistle and the Rose*, 128.
70. T. M. Devine, *To the Ends of the Earth: Scotland's Global Diaspora, 1750–2010* (London, 2012), 270–89.
71. Douglas Young took the lead in the anti-conscription campaign during the Second World War and was identified by many moderates as a fundamentalists, but he was relaxed about SNP members joining other political parties and supported MacCormick's National Convention. See Paula Somerville, *Through the Maelstrom: A History of the Scottish National Party, 1945–67* (Stirling, 2013), 28–9. MacCormick's pragmatism tends to mask his ideological position; see M. C. Dyer, 'A Nationalist in the Churchillian Sense: John MacCormick, the Paisley By-Election of 18th February, Home Rule, and the Crisis in Scottish Liberalism', *Parliamentary History*, vol. 2, 3 (2003). Isobel Lindsay abandoned party politics in the early 1980s to become a founding member of the cross-party campaign for a Scottish assembly; see Tom Freeman, 'Isobel Lindsay's Radical Road to Devolution', *Holyrood*, March 2019.
72. Speech at Cork, 21 January 1885. See F. S. L. Lyons, 'The Political Ideas of Parnell', *The Historical Journal*, vol. 16, 4 (1973), 749–75. For a historiographical overview, see Frank Rynne, 'No Man Has the Right to Fix the Boundary to the March of a Nation: Fixing the Boundaries of Irish Nationalism, 1882–85', *Revue Française de Civilisation Britannique*, vol. 14, 2 (2019), https://doi.org/10.4000/rfcb.3714.
73. For a study of the post-war economy, see Richard Saville, *The Economic Development of Modern Scotland* (Edinburgh, 1985).
74. See Neil McGarvey, 'Has Scottish Devolution Been a Success', https://strathprints.strath.ac.uk/35737/.
75. See Colin Kidd, *Unions and Unionism: Political Thought in Scotland 1500–2000* (Cambridge, 2008); Alvin Jackson, *The Two Unions: Ireland, Scotland and the Survival of the United Kingdom, 1707–2007* (Oxford, 2011); Graeme Morton, *Unionist*

Nationalism: Governing Urban Scotland, 1830–1860 (East Linton, 1999); and Paul Ward, *Unionism in the United Kingdom, 1918–1974* (Basingstoke, 2005).
76. W. M. Ramsay, *The Imperial Peace: An Ideal in European History* (Oxford, 1913), 15–21.
77. See Thomas Paul Burgess (ed.), *The Contested Identities of Ulster Protestants* (London, 2015); William Kelly and John R. Young (eds), *Ulster and Scotland: History, Language and Identity, 1600–2000* (Dundalk, 2004); and Iam Adamson, *The Identity of Ulster: The Land, Language and People* (Belfast, 1991).
78. Tom Nairn, *The Break-Up of Britain: Crisis and Neo-Nationalism* (London, 2nd edn, 1981) was a pioneering study of the peculiarity of Scottish history and its complex relationship to nationalism.
79. Alasdair Raffe, '1707, 2007 and the Unionist Turn in Scottish History', *The Historical Journal*, vol. 53, 4 (2010), 1071–83.
80. The association with the Tory Party and the 'Squireocracy' in which local landowners are the dominant political force is one that dates back to the late seventeenth century. The importance of the local Conservative Party organization can be seen in John Ramsden, *The Age of Balfour and Baldwin* (London, 1978), 45–65, 218–44; and Hutchison, *Scottish Politics*, 73, points out that the Scottish West Central organization had 150,000 members in 1953.
81. Colin Kidd, 'Unionism a Very Scottish Idea', 16 May 2013, IPPR, https://www.ippr.org/juncture/unionism-a-very-scottish-idea.
82. For a discussion of Mair's work within its proper historical context, see Roger A. Mason, 'Kingship, Nobility and Anglo-Scottish Union: John Mair's *History of Greater Britain* (1521)', *Innes Review*, vol. 41, 2 (1990), 182–222.
83. J. G. A. Pocock's seminal article 'British History: A Plea for a New Subject', *Journal of Modern History*, vol. 47, 4 (1975), 601–21, began the process of a revision of early modern Scottish, English and Irish history. For a good précis of the historical debate, see Allan I. Macinnes, *The British Revolution, 1629–60* (Basingstoke, 2004).
84. David Livingstone dedicated his *Voyages on the Zambesi* to Lord Palmerston, prime minister of England, while Stevenson described himself as English in his *South Seas Letters* but did articulate the difference between the English and Scots; see Sidney Dark, *Robert Louis Stevenson* (London, 1931), 7–10.
85. Disraeli referred to the state as England in a speech at Edinburgh after being given the Freedom of the City; see George Earle Buckle, *The Life of Benjamin Disraeli: Earl of Beaconsfield*, vol. 3 (London, 1914), 2921; Palmerstone did the same in Perth and Glasgow, *The Examiner*, 1 October 1853, 633; and Salisbury when asked by the Scottish secretary if he would say Britain rather than England curtly replied that he would not; Lady Francis Balfour, *Lord Balfour of Burleigh* (London, 1924), 93.
86. W. E. Gladstone, *Midlothian Speeches, 1879* (various editions); and Lord Crew, *Lord Rosebery*, vol. 1 (London, 1931), 139.
87. For other examples, see Richard J. Finlay, 'National Identity, Union and Empire', in John M. MacKenzie and T. M. Devine (eds), *Scotland and the British Empire* (Oxford, 2011), 287–8.
88. The classic study of this is James Mitchell, *Conservatives and the Union: A Study of Conservative Party Attitudes to Scotland* (Edinburgh, 1990).
89. See James Winder Good, *Irish Unionism: Modern Ireland in the Making* (London, 1920), which sets out the argument of unionism in relation to the Anglo-Irish landowning class and the economic power of the protestant elite. This was unionism before its 'Ulsterfication'.

90. A. T. Q. Stewart, *Edward Carson* (Dublin, 1981).
91. Patrick Buckland, *The Factory of Grievance: Devolved Government in Northern Ireland, 1921–39* (Dublin, 1979); and Graham Walker, *A History of the Ulster Unionist Party: Protest, Pragmatism and Pessimism* (Manchester, 2004), 87–139.
92. Paul Gardner, *Ethnic Dignity and the Ulster-Scots Movement in Northern Ireland: Supremacy in Peril* (London, 2020).
93. Richard Wyn Jones, 'Ever Looser Union: The Future of the UK', *British Academy Review*, vol. 22 (2013), 8–11.
94. Lord Rosebery, 'Address to the Scottish History Society', 1886.
95. Sir Herbert Maxwell's *Bruce and the Struggle for Scottish Independence* (London, 1898), 272–4.
96. House of Commons Debate, 16 April 1920, vol. 127, col. 2045.
97. David Torrance, *Noel Skelton and the Property Owning Democracy* (London, 2010).
98. House of Commons Debates, 24 November 1932, vol. 272, col. 358.
99. Quoted in Graham Walker, 'The Scotland Is British Campaign 1976–78', *Scottish Affairs*, vol. 61 (2007), 82.
100. On the Edwardian Conservative Party, see Frans Coetzee, *For Country or Party: Nationalism and the Dilemmas of Popular Conservatism in Edwardian England* (Oxford, 1997), 126–58.
101. M. L. Connelly, 'The Army, the Press and the "Curragh Incident", March 1914', *Historical Research*, vol. 84, 225 (2011), 535–57.
102. Sir George Younger, 'Memorandum on Scottish Home Rule', 15 May 1914, Bonar Law Papers, British Library.
103. Ibid.
104. House of Commons Debates, 16 April 1920, vol. 127, col. 2024.
105. Ibid., col. 2021.
106. Georgios Varouxakis, 'Great versus Small Nation: Size and National Greatness in Victorian Political Thought', in Duncan Bell (ed.), *Victorian Visions of Global Order: Empire and International Relations in 19th Century Political Thought* (Cambridge, 2007), 136–59.
107. House of Commons Debates, 16 April 1920, vol. 127, col. 2021.
108. See the debate in the House of Commons, 24 November 1932.
109. *The Nation*, 9 March 1929.
110. This is based on a fairly random search of parliamentary speeches on https://www.theyworkforyou.com/ wherein Scottish politicians used the term 'nation' in the post-war era.
111. See Richard Weight, *Patriots: National Identity in Britain, 1940–2000* (London, 2002), 10–56.
112. Sonya O. Rose, *Which People's War: National Identity and Citizenship in Wartime Britain, 1939–1945* (Oxford, 2003), 197–239.
113. The idea of concentric circles was used by T. C. Smout, 'Perspectives on Scottish Identity', *Scottish Affairs*, vol. 6 (1994), 101–13; and for the theory, see Anthony D. Smith, 'A Europe of Nations: Or a Nation of Europe?', *Journal of Peace Research*, vol. 30, 2 (1993), 129–35.
114. See Richard J. Finlay, 'National Identity in Crisis: Politicians, Intellectuals and "The End of Scotland?", 1920–1939', *History*, vol. 79, 256 (1994), 242–59.
115. House of Commons Debates, 24 November 1932, vol. 272, col. 341.
116. Ibid., col. 292.
117. See Thomas Burns, *Plan for Scotland* (Glasgow, 1937), preface by Clement Attlee, 4.

118. Keating and Bleiman, *Labour and Scottish Nationalism*; and Ian Donnachie, Christopher Harvie and Ian S. Wood (eds), *Forward! Labour Politics in Scotland, 1888–1988* (Edinburgh, 2001).
119. House of Commons Debates, 1 February 1955, vol. 536, col. 915.
120. A very good example of the way an appeal to British working-class solidarity could be used to make the case for the Union can be seen in James Maxton's speech on Scottish local government where he argued against agricultural relief as it would benefit Scottish landowners and makes the case that improved food consumption by the British working class would be the best policy:

    > As I read the situation for agriculture, the problem is to see that the population of Great Britain have the necessary money in their pockets that will enable them to purchase British agricultural products as against the cheaper products that are imported, by patriotic British citizens, from China, Holland and other parts of the world. Margarine has got to be bought by the working classes in place of butter. Preserved eggs have to be got in place of new, fresh laid eggs that the home farmer can so easily produce. It seems to me that the intelligent way to stimulate British agriculture is to make it possible for the people of Great Britain, by enhanced purchasing power, to purchase wholesome commodities produced by the farmers of their own land rather than to have to depend upon second-rate, unfresh, adulterated products from other countries. (House of Commons Debates, 20 February 1929, vol. 225, col. 1224)

121. The term 'West Briton' was used regularly by Irish nationalists to refer to Unionists. For a literary example, see James Joyce's short story, *The Dead* (1914), when Gabriel is denounced as a West Briton because he wrote for the *Daily Express*.
122. The best example of this type of history is Tom Johnston, *Our Scots Noble Families* (London, 1909).
123. Lewis Spence, 'The English Peril in Scotland', *Standard*, March 1922, 41.
124. Malcolm MacColl, 'The Faint Cry of the Forward', *Scots Independent*, October 1927, 1.
125. See Finlay, *Independent and Free*, 116–18; and Gordon Wilson *SNP: The Turbulent Years, 1960–1990* (Stirling, 2009), on the expulsion of Siol nan Gaidheal (204–5).
126. *Scots Independent*, January 1931, 42.
127. *Scots Independent*, December 1932, 17.
128. Ibid.
129. Scottish Conservative and Unionist Party, *Scottish Nationalism* (Glasgow, 1932).
130. Ibid.
131. Erskine of Mar, 'The British Superstition', *Liberty*, 2 October 1920, 103.
132. *Scots Independent*, July 1931, 151.
133. See Oliver Brown's acerbic, *Stepmother Britain* (Glasgow, 1945), 36–7.

5 Ideology: Left, right and the state

1. There is a vast literature on this subject, but for what might be described as a traditional left-wing perspective, see Ralph Miliband, *The State in a Capitalist Society* (London, 1969); and from a right-wing perspective, see Keith Middlemass, *Politics in an Industrial Society: The Experience of the British System since 1911* (London, 1979).

2. Stefan Berger and David Broughton (eds), *The Force of Labour: The Western Labour Movements and the Working Class in the Twentieth Century* (London, 1995).
3. See Ben Jackson, *Equality and the British Left: A Study in Progressive Political Thought, 1900-64* (Manchester, 2011); and Lawrence James, *The Middle Class: A History* (London, 2018), 309-407.
4. For an series of essays on the relationship between social class and ideology in England and the British state, see Ross McKibbin, *The Ideologies of Class: Social Relations in Britain, 1880-1950* (Oxford, 1994).
5. John Breully, *Nationalism and the State* (Manchester, 1993), 30-46.
6. Ludmila Stern, *Western Intellectuals and the Soviet Union, 1920-1940: From Red Square to the Left Bank* (London, 2006), 86-132; and Giles Udy, *Labour and the Gulag: Russia and the Seduction of the British Left* (London, 2017).
7. Peter Baldwin, *The Politics of Social Solidarity: Class Bases of the European Welfare State, 1875-1975* (Cambridge, 2008), 1-55; and Peter Clarke, *The Keynesian Revolution in the Making, 1924-36* (Oxford, 1988).
8. Barry Eichengreen, *The European Economy since 1945: Coordinated Capitalism and Beyond* (Princeton, 2008), 86-129.
9. See Roger Middleton, 'Economic Policy and Management', in Roderick Floud, Jane Humphries and Paul Johnson (eds), *The Cambridge Economic History of Modern Britain, Volume II 1870 to the Present* (Cambridge, 2014), 476-506.
10. See Harvey J. Kaye and Victor Kiernan, *History, Classes and Nation States* (Cambridge, 1988), 138-66.
11. Hagen Schulze, *States, Nations and Nationalism* (London, 1996), 159-74.
12. Ernest Gellner, *Nations and Nationalism* (London, 2nd edn, 2006), 118-31.
13. Shlomo Avineri, 'Marxism and Nationalism', *Journal of Contemporary History*, vol. 26, 3/4 (1991), 637-57. For a Scottish discussion on the issues, see James D. Young, 'Nationalism, Marxism and Scottish History', *Journal of Contemporary History*, vol. 20 (1985), 337-55.
14. Tom Nairn's seminal *The Break-Up of Britain* (London, 1977); and Eric J. Hobsbawm's 'Reflections on "The Break-Up of Britain"', *New Left Review*, vol. 105 (1977), 3-23. For a discussion on the emergence of left-wing neo-nationalism in Scotland, see Ben Jackson, *The Case for Scottish Independence: A History of Nationalist Political Thought in Modern Scotland* (Cambridge, 2020); as to whether Nairn is a nationalist or a Marxist from a Marxist perspective, see Neil Davidson, 'In Perspective: Tom Nairn', *International Socialism*, March 1999, https://www.marxists.org/history/etol/newspape/isj2/1999/isj2-082/davidson.htm.
15. Cormic O Grada, *Ireland: A New Economic History* (Oxford, 1995), 173-6.
16. On the academic reticence on the Famine, see Liam Kennedy, *Colonialism, Religion and Nationalism in Ireland* (Belfast, 1996), 182-23; and James S. Donnelly Jr, *The Great Irish Potato Famine* (Stroud, 2010), 209-45.
17. Interestingly there is a historiographical consensus that class conflict became more pronounced and class divisions more entrenched during the Second World War in Britain, which goes against popular understanding of the event. See Kenneth M. Morgan, *Britain since 1945: The People's Peace* (Oxford, 2001), 3-29; Angus Calder, *The Myth of the Blitz* (London, 1992); Malcolm Smith, *Britain 1940: History, Myth and Popular Memory* (London, 2000), 111-30; and Lucy Noakes and Juliette Pattinson (eds), *British Cultural Memory and the Second World War* (London, 2013).
18. John Belcham, *Class, Party and the Political System in Britain, 1867-1914* (London, 1990).

19. M. Cowling, *The Impact of Labour, 1920-24* (London, 1971), 341–413; Ross McKibbin, *The Evolution of the Labour Party, 1910-1924* (Oxford, 1984), 112–23; Trevor Wilson, *The Downfall of the Liberal Party, 1914-1935* (London, 1966), 285–324; G. R. Searle, *The Liberal Party: Triumph and Disintegration, 1886-1929* (Basingstoke, 1992), 141–60; and John Ramsden, *The Age of Balfour and Baldwin, 1902-1940* (London, 1978), 154–243.
20. The classic account of working-class conservatives is Robert T. Mackenzie and Allan Silver, *Angels in Marble: Working Class Conservatives in Urban England* (London, 1968); but see also Martin Pugh, *The Tories and the People, 1885-1935* (London, 1985).
21. Martin Pugh, *The Evolution of the British Electoral System, 1867-1987* (London, 1988), 16–20.
22. Francis Fukuyama, *Identity: Contemporary Identity Politics and the Struggle for Recognition* (London, 2018).
23. James Mitchell, *The Scottish Question* (Oxford, 2014), 87–156; and M. C. Mast, *Shaping Ireland's Independence: Nationalist, Unionist and British Solutions to the Irish Question, 1909-1925* (London, 2019).
24. Benedict Anderson, *Imagined Communities: Reflections on the Origins and Spread of Nationalism* (London, rev. edn, 2016), 113–40.
25. Frank Furedi, *Colonial Wars and the Politics of Third World Nationalism* (London, 1994), 143–233. It is also worth pointing out that in Western Europe in the Cold War era a number of nationalist movements adopted a Marxist revolutionary perspective; see Michael McKinley, '"Dangerous Liaisons?": The Provisional Irish Republican Army, Marxism and the Communists Governments of Europe', *History of European Ideas*, vol. 15, 1–3 (1992), 443–9; and Robert P. Clarke, *The Basque Insurgents: ETA 1952-1980* (Maddison, 2005).
26. NLS, Tom Gibson Papers, Acc. 6058, box 1, Iain Gillies to Tom Gibson, 3 February 1926.
27. Connolly's writings were reprinted by the Irish Transport and General Workers Union in the 1930s and pamphlets appear in the following archive collections of nationalist leaders in the National Library of Scotland, Muirhead, McIntyre, Donaldson and Gibson. He was regularly cited in the *Scots Independent* and other nationalist publications. On Connolly, see Shaun Harkin, *James Connolly: A Reader* (Chicago, 1918).
28. For the history of the SNP, see Richard J. Finlay, *Independent and Free: Scottish Politics and the Formation of the Scottish National Party, 1918-1945* (Edinburgh, 1994); Paula Somerville, *Through the Maelstrom: A History of the Scottish National Party, 1945-1967* (Stirling, 2013); and Peter Lynch, *SNP: The History of the Scottish National Party* (Cardiff, 2013).
29. Somerville, *Through the Maelstrom*, 49–55.
30. His main pamphlets are *Scotland and Westminster: An Exposure of London Domination and a Plea for a Scottish Socialist Government* (Glasgow, 1939); *Scotland Nation or a Desert* (Glasgow, 1943); *Hitler in the Highlands* (Glasgow, 1944); and *Stepmother Britain* (Glasgow, 1945). The quote is an apocryphal one from the 1980s.
31. J. M. MacCormick, quoted in Alexander M. MacEwen, *The Thistle and the Rose: Scotland's Problems Today* (London, 1932), 7.
32. 'The Caledonian Antisyzygy and the Gaelic Idea, (1931–32)', in Duncan Glen (ed.), *Selected Essays of Hugh MacDiarmid* (London, 1969), 73.

33. NLS, Acc. 6058, box 1, June 1924, Gibson Memorandum on the Scottish Home Rule Association.
34. This was the view of the prominent journalist George Malcolm Thomson who was quite sympathetic to the movement. NLS, Acc. 5927, Dott collection, G. M. Thomson to Dott, 19 July 1929.
35. Angus Clark, 'Scotland's Fundamental Need', *Scots Independent*, June 1932, 117.
36. Writing as C. M. Grieve in *Scots Independent*, May 1929, 90.
37. Ian Kershaw, *To Hell and Back, Europe 1914–1949* (London, 2016), 197–208.
38. NLS, McIntyre Collection, Minutes of the National Council Meeting of the Scottish National Party 4 May 1934, 90.
39. Giovani Capoccia, *Defending Democracy: Reactions to Extremism in Interwar Europe* (Baltimore MD, 2007); Martin Blinkhorn, *Fascism and the Right in Europe, 1919–1945* (London, 2000); Peter Davies, *The Extreme Right in France, 1789 to the Present* (London, 2002), 79–100; Adam Holm, '"Opposing the Past": Danish Radical Conservatism and Right-Wing Authoritarianism in the Inter-War Years', *Politics, Religion & Ideology*, vol. 2, 3 (2001), 1–24; Lena Berggren, 'Swedish Fascism: Why Bother?', *Journal of Contemporary History*, vol. 37, 3 (2002), 395–417; Erik Hansen, 'Fascism and Nazism in the Netherlands, 1929–39', *European Studies Review*, 11 (1981), 355–85; and Martin Conway, 'The Extreme Right in Interwar Francophone Belgium: Explanations of a Failure', *European History Quarterly*, vol. 26 (1996), 267–94.
40. *Scots Independent*, April 1934, 87.
41. *Scots Independent*, December 1934, 213.
42. See Finlay, *Independent and Free*, 162–206, for the party's electoral performance.
43. The plethora of Liberal policy concerns was described as 'Faddism' and was associated with the lack of direction experienced by the Liberal Party following the departure of William Gladstone as leader in 1894; see Thomas William Heyck, 'Home Rule, Radicalism and the Liberal Party, 1886–1895', *Journal of British Studies*, vol. 13, 2 (1974), 66–91; and D. A. Hamer, *The Politics of Electoral Pressure: A Study in the History of Victorian Reform Agitation* (London, 1977).
44. *Scots Independent*, March 1933, 71.
45. *Policy of the National Party* (Stirling, 1963), 6.
46. House of Commons Debates, 24 November 1932, vol. 272, 262.
47. *Scots Independent*, January 1934, 34.
48. Finlay, *Independent and Free*, 206–13.
49. For a chronologically based discussion of the evolution of SNP policy, see Peter Lynch, 'From Social Democracy Back to No Ideology? The Scottish National Party and Ideological Change in a Multi-level Electoral Setting', *Regional and Federal Studies*, vol. 19, 4–5 (2009), 619–37.
50. As Iain Hutchison points out these were the key departments of the Scottish Office and reflected their relative greater importance than that for the United Kingdom as a whole; I. G. C. Hutchison, 'Government', in T. M. Devine and R. J. Finlay (eds), *Scotland in the Twentieth Century* (Edinburgh, 1996), 46–53.
51. Lynch, *SNP: The History of the Scottish National Party*, 166–8.
52. On the intellectual continuity between the pre-war Liberal Party and the post-war Labour Party, see I. G. C. Hutchison, *A Political History of Scotland, 1832–1924: Parties, Elections and Issues* (Edinburgh, 1986); and Catriona M. M. MacDonald, *The Radical Thread: Political Change in Scotland, Paisley Politics, 1885–1924* (East Linton, 2000).

53. On the Scottish Conservative Party, see David Torrance, *We in Scotland: Thatcherism in a Cold Climate* (Edinburgh, 2009).
54. The London Scots Self-Government Committee were influential in the Labour Party in the 1930s and included noted individuals such as Rev. James Barr and Tom Johnston in the late 1940s.
55. NLS, Tom Gibson Papers, Acc. 6058, box 1, Roland Muirhead to Tom Gibson, 23 December 1926.
56. NLS, Tom Gibson Papers, Acc. 6058; Tom Gibson, 'Memorandum on Scottish Home Rule Association', June 1924.
57. Somerville, *Through the Maelstrom*.
58. *Scots Independent*, February 1936, 2.
59. NLS, Dep. 217, Gibb Papers, box 2, Resignation letter, 2 March 1939.
60. D. H. McNeil, *Scots Independent*, April 1937, 3.
61. J. M. MacCormick, *The Flag in the Wind: The Story of the National Movement in Scotland* (London, 1955).
62. *Outlook*, December 1936, 55.
63. M. C. Dyer, 'A Nationalist in the Churchillian Sense: John MacCormick, the Paisley By-Election of 18th February 1948, Home Rule, and the Crisis in Scottish Liberalism', *Parliamentary History*, vol. 22, 3 (2003), 285–307.
64. James Mitchell, 'The Breakthrough to Mainstream: The Politics of Potential and Blackmail', in Gerry Hassan (ed.), *The Modern SNP: From Protest to Power* (Edinburgh, 2009), 31–41; and James Mitchell, 'The Evolution of Devolution: Labour's Home Rule Strategy in Opposition', *Government and Opposition*, vol. 33, 4 (1998), 479–96.
65. Richard J. Finlay, 'Thomas Hill Gibson', *Oxford Dictionary of National Biography*.
66. NLS, Acc. 6058, box 1, 5 March 1926, 'Plans for the Scots Independent', which sets out Gibson's ideas where the national movement should be heading and a central place should be allocated to 'such matters as economic and social problems facing Scotland'.
67. 'Our Industrial Future: The Clash with England's Interests', *Scots Independent*, March 1928, 65.
68. 'Scottish National Finance: A Further Examination of the White Paper', *Scots Independent*, March 1933, 74.
69. *Scots Independent*, April 1931, 84.
70. 'Shipping and Trade', *Scots Independent*, November 1930, 7.
71. NLS, Acc. 3721, box 80, file 100, 27 June 1928, 'Note on Question of Taxes'.
72. 'But What of London: The Burden of Its Upkeep', *Scots Independent*, December 1927, 23.
73. *Scots Independent*, January 1928, 34.
74. *Scots Independent*, June 1931, 117.
75. 'Economics and Policy: Scotland's Problem', *Scots Independent*, September 1933, 183.
76. Catherine P. Snodgrass, *Scotland in the Modern World: A Plea for Freedom, Self-Government and Full Participation* (Stirling, n.d.), 9.
77. W. A. Hunter, *The Financial Relations of England and Scotland* (Edinburgh, 1892).
78. The term was invented by the *London Evening Standard* and Donald Dewar quoted from the newspaper during the debate on the closure of Ravenscraig Steel Works, House of Commons Debates, 21 May 1990, vol. 173, col. 28: 'The Scots, who have become subsidy junkies as successive Governments ... have tried to bribe them with ever larger handouts at the expense of the comparatively little-subsidised English

taxpayer, will no doubt wail like a trampled bagpipe at the removal of British Steel's financial support for Ravenscraig.'
79. On the issue of subsidies, see George Rosie, *Scotching the Myth: An Investigation*, Scottish Centre for Social and Economic Research (1992).
80. https://www.taxresearch.org.uk/Blog/2019/08/21/whatever-gers-reports-today-its-important-to-remember-its-still-crap-or-a-completely-rubbish-app.
81. It is worth bringing up the fact that the Czechs complained about subsidizing the Slovaks when they were united, but since the 'Velvet Divorce' Slovak GDP is now more or less the same as Czeckia.
82. David Cannadine, *Class in Britain* (London, 2000), 106–63.
83. Given the importance of the issue, there has been remarkably little in the way of an endeavour to actually measure the size of the Scottish working class in the twentieth century. David McCrone estimated it to be between three-quarters and two-thirds of the population, and in 1961, 52 per cent of workers were classed as 'manual labour'. David McCrone, 'We're a' Jock Thamson's Bairns: Social Class in Twentieth Century Scotland', in T. M. Devine and R. J. Finlay (eds), *Scotland in the Twentieth Century* (Edinburgh, 1996), 106–10.
84. Quoted in Walter Murray, *Scottish Home Rule: The Case in 90 Points* (Glasgow, 1922), 21.
85. Labour MP David Kirkwood in *Scottish Home Rule*, May 1928, 239.
86. NLS, Dep. 209, Papers of Neil M. Gunn, box 15, File 2, letter of J. M. MacCormick to D. H. MacNeill, 8 February 1932.
87. *Scots Independent*, June 1936, 2.
88. NLS, Dep. 207, Papers of Neil M. Gunn, letter to John MacCormick, 2 July 1936.
89. It is often forgotten that the Conservative Party was the most successful political organization in interwar Scotland. The party won most seats between 1918 and 1922, in the general election of 1923 Labour won most seats and again in 1929. From 1931, the Tories dominated until 1945. See Iain G. C. Hutchison, *Scottish Politics in the Twentieth Century* (Basingstoke, 2001), 41–53, 70–9.
90. Finlay, *Independent and Free*, 22–4.
91. *Scots Independent*, July 1934, 135.
92. NLS, Dep. 209, box 15, Neil Gunn to John M. MacCormick, 21 October 1934, list the top three targets seats as Inverness, Ross and Cromarty and the Western Isles.
93. SNP, *Self-Government in Practice* (Glasgow, n.d.), 19–21; on Irish economic performance, see J. Peter Neary and Cormac O'Grada, 'Protection, Economic War and Structural Change: The 1930s in Ireland', *Irish Historical Studies*, vol. 27, 107 (1991), 250–66.
94. *Scots Independent*, July 1934, 135.
95. Patricia Clavin, *The Great Depression in Europe, 1929–31* (London, 2000); Jan Kofman, *Economic Nationalism and Development: Central and Eastern Europe between the Two World Wars* (London, 1997); Tim Rooth, *British Protectionism and the International Economy: Overseas Commercial Policy in the 1930s* (Cambridge, 1993).
96. Martin Daunton, *Wealth and Welfare: An Economic and Social History of Britain, 1851–1951* (Oxford, 2007), 17–19.
97. Roger Middleton, *The British Economy since 1945* (London, 2000), 25–60.
98. Jim Tomlinson, *Employment Policy: The Crucial Years, 1939–1955* (Oxford, 1987).
99. Arthur Donaldson, *Scotland's Tomorrow* (Glasgow, n.d.), 12.
100. Morgan, *Britain since 1945*, 70; and Peter Hennessay, *Never Again: Britain, 1945–51* (London, 2006), 2.

101. Robert D. McIntyre, *Some Principles for Scottish Reconstruction* (Glasgow, 1944), 1–2.
102. NLS, Acc. 10090, McIntyre Collection, undated draft speech.
103. Donaldson, *Scotland's Tomorrow*, 20.
104. David Dutton, *British Politics since 1945: The Rise and Fall of Consensus* (London, 1991), 53–86.
105. T. M. Devine, 'The Break-Up of Britain: Scotland and the End of Empire, the Prothero Lecture', *Transactions of the Royal Historical Society*, vol. 16 (2006), 163–80.
106. Richard J. Finlay, *Modern Scotland, 1914–2000* (London, 2004), 256–72.
107. House of Commons Debates, 12 June 1945, vol. 411, col. 1574.
108. Archie Lamont, *Scotland's Wealth and Poverty* (Glasgow, 1953), 4.
109. See Thomas Burns, *Plan for Scotland* (Glasgow, 1939), 19.
110. R. H. Campbell, 'The Committee of Ex-Secretaries of State and Industrial Policy', *Scottish Industrial History*, vol. 2 (1979), 1–10.
111. Graham Walker, *Thomas Johnston* (Manchester, 1988), 151–79.
112. James G. Kellas, *The Scottish Political System* (Cambridge, 1975), 62–7.
113. Patrick Abercrombie and Robert H. Matthew, *Clyde Valley Regional Plan* (London, 1949).
114. Speech, 20 May 1949.
115. MacCormick, *Flag in the Wind*, 139–40.
116. *Report of the Committee on Scottish Financial and Trade Statistics*, Cmd. 8609 (1952).
117. House of Lords Debate, 20 November 1951, vol. 174, col. 397.
118. Richard Rodger, *Scottish Housing in the Twentieth Century* (Leicester, 1989), 195–203.
119. SNP, *Policy of the Scottish National Party* (Stirling, 1963) 14–15.
120. N. F. R. Crafts, 'The Golden Age of Economic Growth in Western Europe, 1950–1973', *Economic History Review*, new series, vol. 48, 3 (1995), 429–47.
121. Donald Bain, *Scotland: Facts and Comparisons* (West Calder, 1969).
122. Billy Wolfe, *Scotland Lives: The Quest for Independence* (Edinburgh, 1973), 133.
123. Gordon Wilson, *SNP; The Turbulent Years 1960–1990* (Stirling, 2000), 119–55, 166.
124. Ibid., 201.
125. For an in-depth discussion on the growth of neo-nationalism and its association with the left, see Ben Jackson, *The Case for Independence: A History of Nationalist Political Thought in Modern Scotland* (Cambridge, 2020), 123–73.
126. See, in particular, Stephen Maxwell, edited by Jamie Maxwell, *The Case for Left Wing Nationalism and Other Essays* (Edinburgh, 2013).
127. Edited by Alan Lawson and started in 1983.
128. See T. M. Devine, *Independence or Union: Scotland's Past and Scotland's Present* (London, 2016), 184–204.
129. David McCrone, *Understanding Scotland: The Sociology of a Nation* (2001 edn), 104–27.
130. Devine, *Independence or Union*, 167–83.
131. James Mitchell, 'Factions, Tendencies and Consensus in the SNP in the 1980s', in Alice Brown and Richard Parry (eds), *The Scottish Government Yearbook 1990*, Unit for the Study of Government in Scotland (Edinburgh, 1990), 49–6.
132. It is worth pointing out that in that in the past decade not only has the SNP in European terms been one of the most successful political parties in terms of elections, but it has bucked the international trend while being firmly committed to a left-of-centre agenda.
133. C. M. Grieve, 'Neo Gaelic Economics II', *Scots Independent*, February 1928, 54.

134. Christopher Harvie, 'MacDiarmid the Socialist', *Scottish Labour History Society Journal*, vol. 15 (1981), 4–11.
135. The idea featured prominently in Angus Clark's journal *The Free Man: New Scotland* (1933–46) which was associated with the fundamentalist wing of the movement.
136. H. J. Hanham, *Scottish Nationalism* (London, 1969), 173.
137. Editorial 'The Aims and Policy of the Scottish National Party', *Scots Independent*, January 1947, 1–2.
138. Ibid.
139. For a discussion of the wider issues surrounding this, see Malcolm R. Petrie, 'Anti-Socialism, Liberalism and Individualism: Rethinking the Realignment of Scottish Politics, 1945–1970', *Transactions of the Royal Historical Society*, vol. 28 (2018), 197–217.
140. Ibid.
141. Donaldson, *Scotland's Tomorrow*, 10–14.
142. 'Aims and Policy of the Scottish National Party', 1.
143. Archie Lamont, *Scotland: A Wealthy Nation* (Glasgow, 1945), 1–5.
144. Christopher Harvie, *The Lights of Liberalism: University Liberals and the Challenge of Democracy, 1860–1886* (London, 1976), is worth close reading for the role of Scots in the origins of the New Liberalism.
145. Michael Freeden, *The New Liberalism: An Ideology of Social Reform* (Oxford, 1986), remains the standard work.
146. See Ewen A. Cameron, 'The Young Scots Society', *Oxford Dictionary of National Biography*, https://www.oxforddnb.com/view/10.1093/ref:odnb/9780198614 128.001.0001/odnb-9780198614128-e-100417.
147. 'How the SNP See Politics', *Glasgow Herald*, 25 July 1968.
148. NLS, Acc. 10090, McIntyre Collection, 199, undated draft speech.
149. For a biography that contains a lot of McIntyre's thoughts and writings, see Dick Douglas, *At the Helm: The Life and Times of Dr Robert D. McIntyre* (Stirling, 1996).

Conclusion

1. Tom Nairn, *The Break-Up of Britain: Crisis and Neo Nationalism* (London, 1981) 104; and 'The Three Dreams of Scottish Nationalism', *New Left Review*, May/June 1968, 4–11.
2. Edwin Muir, *Scott and Scotland* (London, 1938).
3. William Bell, *Rip Van Scotland* (Oxford, 1930), 38–9.
4. https://www.washingtonpost.com/opinions/global-opinions/scotlands-post-national-nationalism/2016/08/27/ce607152-6afb-11e6-ba32-5a4bf5aad4fa_story.html.
5. Fintan O'Toole, *Heroic Failure: Brexit and the Politics of Pain* (London, 2019).
6. Philip Dodd and Robert Colls (eds), *Englishness Politics and Culture, 1880–1920* (London, 1987); Robert Colls, *The Identity of England* (Oxford, 2002); Krishan Kumar, *The Making of English National Identity* (Cambridge, 2010); and Jeremy Black, *English Nationalism: A Short History* (London, 2018).
7. Norman Davies, *Vanished Kingdoms: The History of Half-Forgotten Europe* (London, 2012).
8. On France, see Eugen Weber, *Peasants into Frenchmen: The Modernization of Rural France, 1870–1914* (Stanford, 1976). In the nineteenth century the local press,

provincial urban city culture, military recruitment, provincial societies and clubs and distinctive regional economies all add up to a highly decentralized picture of British society. In the mid-nineteenth century the print run of the *Times* was only fifty thousand.

9. See Gavin Essler, *How Britain Ends: English Nationalism and the Rebirth of Four Nations* (London, 2021).

Select bibliography

Acherson, Neal, 'Scotland, Brexit and the Persistence of Empire', in Stuart Ward and Astrid Rasch (eds), *Embers of Empire in Brexit Britain*, 71–9 (London, 2019).
Anderson, Benedict, *Imagined Communities: Reflections on the Origins and Spread of Nationalism* (London, 2016, rev. edn).
Ash, Marinell, *The Strange Death of Scottish History* (Edinburgh, 1980).
Bell, Henry, *John Maclean: Hero of Red Clydeside* (London, 2018).
Berger, Stefan, with Conrad, Chris, *The Past as History: National Identity and Historical Consciousness in Modern Europe* (Basingstoke, 2014).
Berger, Stefan, Donovan, Mark, and Passmore, Kevin (eds), *Writing National Histories: Western Europe since 1800* (London, 1998).
Berger, Stefan, and Lorenz, Chris (eds), *Nationalizing the Past: Historians as Nation Builders in Europe* (Basingstoke, 2010).
Bew, Paul, *Ideology and the Irish Question: Ulster Unionism and Irish Nationalism, 1912–1916* (Oxford, 1994).
Billig, Michael, *Banal Nationalism* (London, 1995).
Bold, Alan, *MacDiarmid: A Critical Biography* (London, 1988).
Boyce, D. George, *Nationalism in Ireland* (Baltimore, 1982).
Boyce, D. George, and O'Day, Alan (eds), *The Making of Modern Irish History: Revisionism and the Revisionist Controversy* (London, 1996).
Bracher, Karl Dietrich, *The Age of Ideologies: A History of Political Thought in the Twentieth Century* (London, 1984).
Brand, Jack, *The National Movement in Scotland* (London, 1978).
Breuilly, John, *Nationalism and the State* (Manchester, 1993).
Breuilly, John (ed.), *The Oxford Handbook of the History of Nationalism* (Oxford, 2016).
Brotherstone, Terry (ed.), *Covenant, Charter and Party: Traditions of Revolt and Protest in Modern Scotland* (Aberdeen, 1989).
Broun, Dauvit, *Scottish Independence and the Idea of Britain: From the Picts to Alexander III* (Edinburgh, 2013).
Buckland, Patrick, *The Factory of Grievance: Devolved Government in Northern Ireland, 1921–39* (Dublin, 1979).
Burgess, Thomas Paul (ed.), *The Contested Identities of Ulster Protestants* (London, 2015).
Cairns, Gerard, *No Language, No Nation: The Life and Times of The Honourable Ruaraidh Erskine of Mar* (Perth, 2021).
Cameron, Ewen A., *Land for the People? The British Government and the Scottish Highland, 1880–1925* (East Linton, 2001).
Cannadine, David, *Class in Britain* (London, 2000).
Capoccia, Giovani, *Defending Democracy: Reactions to Extremism in Interwar Europe* (Baltimore, 2007).
Clarke, Peter, *The Keynesian Revolution in the Making, 1924–36* (Oxford, 1988).
Clavin, Patricia, *The Great Depression in Europe, 1929–31* (London, 2000).

Coleman, James, *Remembering the Past in Nineteenth-Century Scotland: Commemoration, Nationality, Memory* (Edinburgh, 2014).
Colls, Robert, *The Identity of England* (Oxford, 2002).
Cowan, Edward J. (ed.), *The Wallace Book* (Edinburgh, 2007).
Cowan, Edward J., and Finlay, Richard J. (eds), *Scottish History: The Power of the Past* (Edinburgh, 2002).
Cragoe, Matthew, '"We Like Local Patriotism": The Conservative Party and the Discourse of Decentralisation, 1947–51', *English Historical Review*, vol. 122, 498 (2007), 965–85.
Dalyell, Tam, *Devolution: The End of Britain* (London, 1977).
Daunton, Martin, *Wealth and Welfare: An Economic and Social History of Britain, 1851–1951* (Oxford, 2007).
Davie, George Elder, *The Democratic Intellect: Scotland and Her Universities in the Nineteenth Century* (Edinburgh, 1964).
Denver, David, Mitchell, James, Pattie, Charles and Bochel, Hugh, *Scotland Decides: The Devolution Issue and the Referendum of 1997* (London, 2000).
Devine, T. M., 'The Break-Up of Britain: Scotland and the End of Empire, The Prothero Lecture', *Transactions of the Royal Historical Society*, vol. 16 (2006), 163–80.
Devine, T. M., *Independence or Union? Scotland's Past and Scotland's Present* (London, 2017).
Devine, T. M., *The Scottish Nation: A Modern History* (London, 2012).
Devine, T. M., *To the Ends of the Earth: Scotland's Global Diaspora, 1750–2010* (London, 2012).
Devine, T. M., 'The Union of 1707 and Scottish Development', *Scottish Economic and Social History*, vol. 5, 1 (1985), 23–40.
Devine, Tom M., and Finlay, R. J. (eds), *Scotland in the Twentieth Century* (Edinburgh, 1996).
Douglas, Dick, *At the Helm: The Life and Times of Dr Robert D. McIntyre* (Stirling, 1996).
Dyer, Michael C., 'A Nationalist in the Churchillian Sense: John MacCormick, the Paisley By-election of 18th February, Home Rule, and the Crisis in Scottish Liberalism', *Parliamentary History*, vol. 2, 3 (2003), 285–307.
Edwards, Owen Dudley, *A Claim of Right for Scotland* (Edinburgh, 1989).
Essler, Gavin, *How Britain Ends: English Nationalism and the Rebirth of Four Nations* (London, 2021).
Fanning, Ronan, *Fatal Path: British Government and the Irish Revolution, 1910–1922* (London, 2013).
Ferguson, William, *The Identity of the Scottish Nation: An Historic Quest* (Edinburgh, 1998).
Ferriter, Diarmid, *The Border: The Legacy of a Century of Anglo Irish Politics* (London, 2019).
Ferriter, Diarmid, *A Nation and Not a Rabble: The Irish Revolution, 1913–23* (London, 2015).
Ferriter, Diarmid, *The Transformation of Ireland* (Woodstock, 2007).
Finlay, Richard J., *Independent and Free: Scottish Politics and the Origins of the Scottish National Party, 1918–1945* (Edinburgh, 1994).
Finlay, Richard J., *Modern Scotland, 1914–2000* (London, 2004).
Finlay, Richard J., 'National Identity in Crisis: Politicians, Intellectuals and "The End of Scotland?", 1920–1939', *History*, vol. 79, 256 (1994).
Frank, Tibor, and Hadler, Frank (eds), *Disputed Territories and Shared Pasts: Overlapping National Histories in Modern Europe* (Basingstoke, 2015).

Freeden, Michael, *Ideology: A Very Short Introduction* (Oxford, 2003).
Freeden, Michael, *The New Liberalism: An Ideology of Social Reform* (Oxford, 1986).
Fry, Michael, *The Union: England, Scotland and the Treaty of 1707* (Edinburgh, 2006).
Garvin, Tom, *Nationalist Revolutionaries in Ireland, 1858-1928* (Oxford, 1987).
Gellner, Ernest, *Nations and Nationalism* (London 2nd edn, 2006).
Gibson, Cory, *The Voice of the People: Hamish Henderson and Scottish Cultural Politics* (Edinburgh, 2017).
Grosby, Steven, *Nationalism: A Very Short Introduction* (Oxford, 2005).
Halliday, James, *Scotland: A Concise History* (Edinburgh, 1996).
Hamer, D. A., *The Politics of Electoral Pressure: A Study in Victorian Reform Agitation* (London, 1977).
Hames, Scott, *The Literary Politics of Scottish Devolution: Voice, Class and Nation* (Edinburgh, 2019).
Hanham, Harry J. *Scottish Nationalism* (London, 1969).
Harvie, Chris, *Scotland and Nationalism: Scottish Society and Politics, 1707 to the Present* (London, 1998).
Hassan, Gerry (ed.), *The Modern SNP: From Protest to Power* (Edinburgh, 2009).
Hastings, Derek, *Nationalism in Modern Europe* (2017).
Heater, Derek, *National Self-Determination: Woodrow Wilson and His Legacy* (2014).
Henderson, Ailsa, and Wyn Jones, Richard, *Englishness: The Political Force That Is Transforming Britain* (Oxford, 2021).
Hennessy, Peter, *Never Again: Britain, 1945-51* (London, 2006).
Holmes, Martin, *The Labour Government, 1974-79: Political Aims and Economic Reality* (London, 1987).
Howell, David, *A Lost Left: Three Studies in Socialism and Nationalism* (Manchester, 1986).
Hroch, Miroslav, *European Nations: Explaining Their Formation* (London, 2015).
Hutchison, Iain G. C., *A Political History of Scotland, 1832-1924: Parties, Elections and Issues* (Edinburgh, 1986).
Hutchison, Iain G. C., *Scottish Politics in the Twentieth Century* (Basingstoke, 2000).
Ichijo, Atsuko, *Scottish Nationalism and the Idea of Europe, Concepts of Europe and the Nation* (London, 2004).
Jackson, Alvin, *Home Rule: An Irish History* (Oxford, 2004).
Jackson, Alvin, *The Two Unions: Ireland, Scotland and the Survival of the United Kingdom, 1707-2007* (Oxford, 2011).
Jackson, Ben, *The Case for Independence: A History of Nationalist Political Thought in Modern Scotland* (Cambridge, 2020).
Jackson, Ben, *Equality and the British Left: A Study in Progressive Political Thought, 1900-64* (Manchester, 2011).
Jalland, Patricia, 'United Kingdom Devolution 1910-14: Political Panacea or Tactical Diversion?', *English Historical Review*, vol. 114, 373 (1979), 757-85.
Johns, Rob, and Mitchell, James, *Takeover: Explaining the Extraordinary Rise of the SNP* (London, 2016).
Jones, Richard Wyn, 'Ever Looser Union: The Future of the UK', *British Academy Review*, vol. 22 (2013), 8-11.
Kaye, Harvey J., and Kiernan, Victor, *History, Classes and Nation States* (Cambridge, 1988).
Keating, Michael, and Bleiman, David, *Labour and Scottish Nationalism* (London, 1978).
Keir, Sir David Lindsay, *The Constitutional History of Modern Britain* (London, 1961).
Kellas, James G., *The Scottish Political System* (Cambridge, 1975).

Kendle, John, *Ireland and the Federal Solution: The Debate over the United Kingdom Constitution, 1870–1920* (Montreal, 1989).
Kershaw, Ian, *To Hell and Back: Europe 1914–1949* (London, 2016).
Kidd, Colin, *British Identities before Nationalism: Ethnicity and Nationhood in the Atlantic World, 1600–1800* (Cambridge, 1999).
Kidd, Colin, *Subverting Scotland's Past: Scottish Whig Historians and the Creation of an Anglo-British Identity, 1689–1830* (Cambridge, 1993).
Kidd, Colin, *Union and Unionisms: Political Thought in Scotland, 1500–2000* (Cambridge, 2008).
Kitchen, Martin, *British Policy towards the Soviet Union during the Second World War* (Basingstoke, 2014).
Kofman, Jan, *Economic Nationalism and Development: Central and Eastern Europe between the Two World Wars* (London, 1997).
Korman, Sharon, *The Right of Conquest: The Acquisition of Territory by Force in International Law and Practice* (Oxford, 1996).
Laffin, Michael, *The Resurrection of Ireland: The Sinn Fein Party 1916–23* (Cambridge, 1999).
Leith, Murray Stuart, and Soule, Daniel P. J., *Political Discourse and National Identity in Scotland* (Edinburgh, 2012).
Lloyd-Jones, Naomi, 'Liberalism, Scottish Nationalism and the Home Rule Crisis, c. 1886–1893', *English Historical Review*, vol. 129, 538 (2014), 862–87.
Lynch, Michael, *Scotland: A New History* (London, 1991).
Lynch, Peter, *SNP: A History of the Scottish National Party* (Cardiff, 2013).
Lynch, Robert, *The Partition of Ireland, 1918–25* (Cambridge, 2019).
MacCormick, John M., *The Flag in the Wind: The Story of the National Movement in Scotland* (London, 1955).
MacCormick, Neil (ed.), *The Scottish Debate: Essays on Scottish Nationalism* (Oxford, 1970).
MacDonald, Catriona M. M., *The Radical Thread: Political Change in Scotland, Paisley Politics, 1885–1924* (East Linton, 2000).
MacDonald, Catriona M. M., *Whaur Extremes Meet: Scotland's Twentieth Century* (Edinburgh, 2009).
Macinnes, Allan I., *A History of Scotland* (Basingstoke, 2015).
Macinnes, Allan I., *Union and Empire: The Making of the United Kingdom in 1707* (Cambridge, 2007).
Mackenzie, Compton, *The Four Winds of Love*: Book Four, *The North Wind of Love*, Volume One (London, 1944).
MacQueen, Hector L., 'Legal Nationalism: Lord Cooper, Legal History and Comparative Law', *Edinburgh Law Review*, vol. 9, 3 (2005), 395–406.
Macwhirter, Iain, *Tsunami: Scotland's Democratic Revolution* (Glasgow, 2015).
Martin, Francis X., and Byme, Francis J. (eds), *The Scholar Revolutionary: Eoin MacNeill, 1867–1945 and the Making of the New Ireland* (Shannon, 1973).
Maxwell, Stephen, *The Case for Left Wing Nationalism and Other Essays*, ed. Jamie Maxwell (Edinburgh, 2013).
McCrone, David, *The Sociology of Nationalism: Tomorrow's Ancestors* (London, 1998).
McCrone, David, *Understanding Scotland: The Sociology of a Stateless Nation* (London, 1992).
McCulloch, Marjory, *The Novels of Neil M. Gunn: A Critical Study* (Edinburgh, 1987).

McKibbin, Ross, *The Ideologies of Class: Social Relations in Britain, 1880–1950* (Oxford, 1994).
McLean, Iain, 'The Rise and Fall of the Scottish National Party', *Political Studies*, vol. 18, 3 (1970), 357–72.
McNeill, Duncan H., *The Historical Scottish Constitution* (Edinburgh, 1971).
Middleton, Roger, *The British Economy since 1945* (London, 2000).
Miller, William L., *The End of British Politics? Scots and English Political Behaviour in the Seventies* (Oxford, 1981).
Mitchell, James, *Conservatives and the Union: A Study of Conservative Party Attitudes to Scotland* (Edinburgh, 1990).
Mitchell, James, *Devolution in the United Kingdom* (Manchester, 2012).
Mitchell, James, *The Scottish Question* (Oxford, 2014).
Mitchell, James, *Strategies for Self-Government: The Campaign for a Scottish Parliament* (Edinburgh, 2001).
Mitchell, James, Bennie, Lynne, and Johns, Rob, *The Scottish National Party: Transition to Power* (Oxford, 2011).
Mitchell, James, and Hassan, Gerry (eds), *Scottish National Party Leaders* (London, 2016).
Morton, Graeme, *Unionists Nationalism: Governing Urban Scotland, 1830–1860* (East Linton, 1999).
Muir, Edwin, *Scott and Scotland* (London, 1938).
Muller, Klaus Peter (ed.), *Scotland and Arbroath, 1320–2020: 700 Years of Fighting for Freedom, Sovereignty and Independence* (Leck, 2020).
Murkens, Jo E., Jones, Peter, and Keating, Michael, *Scottish Independence: Legal and Constitutional Issues* (Edinburgh, 2002).
Nairn, Tom, *The Break-Up of Britain: Crisis and Neo-nationalism* (London, 1981).
O'Day, Alan, *Irish Home Rule, 1867–1921* (Manchester, 1998).
O'Toole, Fintan, *Heroic Failure: Brexit and the Politics of Pain* (London, 2019).
Ozkirimli, Umut, *Theories of Nationalism: A Critical Introduction* (London, 2000).
Paterson, Lindsay, *The Autonomy of Modern Scotland* (Edinburgh, 1994).
Paton, Herbert J., *The Claim of Scotland* (London, 1968).
Pederson, Susan, *The Guardians: The League of Nations and the Crisis of Empire* (Oxford, 2015).
Pentland, Gordon, 'Edward Heath, the Declaration of Perth and the Scottish Conservative and Unionist Party, 1966–70', *20th Century British History*, vol. 26, 2 (2015), 249–73.
Petrie, Malcolm, 'Anti-Socialism, Liberalism and Individualism: Rethinking the Realignment of Scottish Politics, 1945–1970', *Transactions of the Royal Historical Society*, vol. 28 (2018), 197–217.
Pittock, Murray G. H., *The Invention of Scotland: the Stuart Myth and Scottish Identity, 1639 to the Present* (London, 1991).
Pittock, Murray G. H., *Scottish Nationality* (Basingstoke, 2001).
Porter, Bernard, *Britain before Brexit: Historical Essay on Britain and Europe* (London, 2021).
Prott, Volker, *The Politics of Self-Determination: Remaking Territories and National Identities in Europe, 1917–1923* (Oxford, 2016).
Pugh, Martin, *The Tories and the People, 1885–1935* (London, 1985).
Raffe, Alastair, '1707, 2007, and the Unionist Turn in Scottish History', *Historical Journal*, vol. 53, 4 (2010), 1071–83.
Ramsden, John, *The Age of Balfour and Baldwin* (London, 1978).

Reid, J. M., *Scotland: Past and Present* (Oxford, 1959).
Ripley, Brian, and McHugh, John, *John Maclean* (Manchester, 1989).
Rose, Sonya A., *Which People's War: National Identity and Citizenship in Wartime Britain, 1939-1945* (Oxford, 2003).
Roshwald, Aviel, *Ethnic Nationalism and the Fall of Empires: Central Europe, Russia and the Middle East, 1914-23* (London, 2000).
Russell, Michael (ed.), *Stop the World: The Autobiography of Winnie Ewing* (Edinburgh, 2004).
Saville, Richard, *The Economic Development of Modern Scotland* (Edinburgh, 1985).
Schulze, Hagen, *States, Nations and Nationalism: From the Middle Ages to the Present* (London, 1998).
Searle, G. R., *The Liberal Party: Triumph and Disintegration, 1886-1929* (Basingstoke, 1992).
Seawright, David, *An Important Matter of Principle: The Decline of the Conservative and Unionist Party* (London, 2018 edn).
Seton-Watson, Hugh, *Nations and States* (London, 1977).
Sharp, Alan, *The Consequence of the Peace: The Versailles Settlement, Its Aftermath and Its Legacy, 1919-2015* (London, 2015).
Sillars, Jim, *Scotland: The Case for Optimism* (Edinburgh, 1986).
Smith, Anthony D., *The Ethnic Origins of Nations* (Oxford, 1999 edn).
Smith, Anthony D., *Nationalism* (Cambridge, 2010).
Smith, Malcolm, *Britain 1940: History, Myth and Popular Memory* (London, 2000).
Somerville, Paula, *Through the Maelstrom: A History of the Scottish National Party, 1945-1967* (Stirling, 2013).
Stern, Ludmila, *Western Intellectuals and the Soviet Union, 1920-1940: From Red Square to the Left Bank* (London, 2006).
Stewart, Anthony T. Q., *The Narrow Ground: The Roots of Conflict in Ulster*, (London, 1989).
Stewart, Anthony T. Q., *The Ulster Crisis: Resistance to Home Rule, 1912-14* (London, 1969).
Tomlinson, Jim, *Employment Policy: The Crucial Years, 1939-1955* (Oxford, 1987).
Torrance, David, *Noel Skelton and the Property Owning Democracy* (London, 2010).
Torrance, David, *We in Scotland: Thatcherism in a Cold Climate* (Edinburgh, 2009).
Townsend, Charles, *Easter 1916: The Irish Rebellion* (London, 2015).
Townsend, Charles, *Political Violence in Ireland: Government and Resistance since 1848* (Oxford, 1985).
Udy, Giles, *Labour and the Gulag, Russia and the Seduction of the British Left* (London, 2017).
Walker, Graham, 'The Scotland Is British Campaign 1976-78', *Scottish Affairs*, vol. 61 (2007), 74-100.
Walker, Graham, *Thomas Johnston* (Manchester, 1988).
Walker, Neil (ed.), *MacCormick's Scotland* (Edinburgh, 2012).
Webb, Keith, *The Growth of Nationalism in Scotland* (Glasgow, 1978).
Weight, Richard, *Patriots: National Identity in Britain, 1940-2000* (London, 2002).
Whatley, Christopher A., *Bought and Sold for English Gold? Explaining the Union of 1707* (Edinburgh, 2001).
Wheare, K. C., *The Statute of Westminster and Dominion Status* (London, 1949).
Williams, Gwyn A., *When Was Wales? The History, People and Culture of an Ancient Country* (London, 1985).

Wilson, Gordon, *SNP: The Turbulent Years 1960–1990* (Stirling, 2000).
Wolfe, Billy, *Scotland Lives: The Quest for Independence* (Edinburgh, 1973).
Wolff, Larry, *Woodrow Wilson and the Reimagining of Eastern Europe* (Stanford, 2020).
Young, James D., 'Nationalism, Marxism and Scottish History', *Journal of Contemporary History*, vol. 20 (1985), 337–55.
Zimmer, Oliver, *Nationalism in Europe, 1890–1940* (Basingstoke, 2003).

Index

1320 Club 115
1820 Rising 16, 103

Abercrombie, Sir Patrick 182
Aberdeen 140, 149
Act of Settlement 99
Adams, William G. S. 74
agriculture 20, 21, 82, 83, 84, 102, 167, 169, 177, 182, 183, 188–9, 190
Alison, Sir Archibald 111
Alston, Dr James 96
Ancram, Michael 126
Anderson, John 99
Anglicization 191–2
Anglo-Saxon 30, 36, 58, 78, 102, 141
Anglo-Scots 31, 35, 153
anglophobia 78, 153–4
Anne I 97
anti-conscription 113, 168
Argyll and Sutherland Highlanders 67
aristocracy 34, 37, 44, 46, 59, 95, 130, 153–4
Attwood, William 99
Austro-Hungarian Empire 7, 11, 26, 62, 77, 79, 80
autarky 178–9, 188

Bagehot, Walter 93
Balfour Commission 123
Balfour of Burleigh, Alexander Bruce 6th Lord 99
Baltic States 14, 78, 80, 92
Bartlett, Robert 25
Belgium 71
Bell, William 73
Blair, Tony 129
Boothby, Robert 150
Bracher, Karl Dietrich 157
Brexit 2, 5, 125, 192
Bright, John 175

British empire 4, 5, 10, 14, 27, 30, 35, 43, 44, 48, 49, 51, 63, 68, 70, 75, 77, 84, 105, 115, 121, 126, 136, 138, 142, 147–8, 149, 150, 152, 156, 173
British global decline 5, 107, 179
'British Group of Nations' 135–8
British state 2, 3, 10, 15–16, 18, 20, 27, 33, 37, 41, 47, 56, 57, 65, 69, 80, 81, 89, 105, 106, 107, 111, 113, 116, 118, 123, 127, 128, 129, 132, 140, 143, 145, 146, 148, 152, 153, 154, 158, 160, 178–9, 184, 185, 192
Brown, Oliver 163
Buchan, John 150, 167
Buchanan, George 32, 152
bureaucracy 20, 178, 179, 187
Burke, Edmund 129
Burns, Robert 37, 40, 44, 45, 191
business 154, 172, 179, 187, 188

Cameron, David 118
Campaign for a Scottish Assembly 116
Campbell, Elma 172
Campbell, Roy 29
capitalism 4, 7, 27, 37, 61, 75, 80, 82, 84, 121, 159, 163, 176, 179, 185, 187
Carlyle, Thomas 28, 38
Carr, E. H. 81
Carson, Edward 145
Carvour, Camillo Benso 74
Catholicism 30, 37, 59, 142, 151
Catto Committee Report on the Financial Relations between Scotland and England (1951) 183
celticism 30–4, 35, 36, 39–41, 46, 75, 78, 102, 155, 186
centre ground 157, 168, 175–81, 189, 190
Chamberlain, Neville 14
Charles II 99, 109
Church of England 94–5, 109

Church of Scotland 12, 34, 94–5, 99, 100–1, 109, 115
Churchill, Winston 134, 182, 183
Cinead mac Ailpin (Kenneth MacAlpin)
civil disobedience 112–15
Claim of Right 1689 16, 97
  1989 127
Clann Alban 105
class 4, 20, 151–2, 153, 158–9, 160, 161, 164, 165–6, 168, 172, 175, 176, 177, 180, 184, 190
Clyde Valley Plan 182
Cold War 79, 92
Cole, George D. H. 78
Collins, Sir Godfrey 171
colonialism 12, 26, 28, 30–4, 43, 53, 61, 73, 80, 114, 135, 192
communism 75, 159, 167, 168, 178, 187
concentric circles 150
Connelly, James 162
conquest 42–4, 46, 48, 63, 91, 103, 112, 141
conscripted female labour 113
consensus politics 20, 157, 159, 176–7, 178, 179, 184, 185
Conservative Party and government 7, 18, 19, 20, 21, 60, 69, 75, 90, 91, 100, 105, 110, 115, 116, 117, 122, 126, 127, 129=130, 134, 135, 137, 139, 144, 148, 151, 153, 155, 156, 161, 166, 167, 169, 170, 171, 172, 178, 180, 183, 184, 185, 188, 189, 190
Constitution and constitutionalism 3, 7, 15–17, 18, 41, 47, 105, 107, 108, 109, 111, 112, 116, 128, 129, 161, 192
Cooper, Thomas Lord Baron of Culross 93–4, 97, 110
Coronation of Edward (1903) 98, 99, 114
Coronation of Elizabeth (1953) 114–15
Coupland, Sir Reginald 5
covenanters 37, 109
Cowan, William 127–8
Craik, Sir Henry 149, 150
Crawford, Lindsay 108
crofting 84, 184
culture 25, 50, 52, 53, 58, 60, 61, 64, 68, 80, 83, 123, 191
Cunninghame-Graham, Robert B. 70
Czechoslovakia 58, 80

Dalyell, Tam 128
Dante, Alighieri 140, 144
Darien Scheme 29
Davies, Norman 192
Daunton, Martin 178
Davie, George Elder 101
Declaration of Arbroath 15, 16, 44, 52, 109, 110, 114
'Declaration of Perth' (1968) 135
decolonization 76
democracy 79, 81, 104–5, 109, 116, 117, 121, 125, 132, 135, 140, 157, 158, 164, 165, 167, 170, 184, 188
democratic deficit 105, 110, 129
democratic intellect 101
demographics 1, 50, 84, 172, 192
Devine, T. M. 29
Devolution 7, 10, 11, 17, 43, 47, 48, 49, 68, 90, 107, 116, 118, 122, 123–4, 125, 128, 129–35, 136, 148, 156, 183
  administrative 123, 128, 182, 192
Dewar, Donald 125
Dicey, Albert Venn 93, 98
Dickinson, Harry 8
Disruption of 1843 95, 100, 109
dominion nations of the British Empire 5, 10, 11, 17, 30, 50, 63, 68, 75, 76, 105, 122, 136, 137, 147–8, 152, 154, 187
Donaldson, Arthur 179
Dott, George 76
Dott, Mary 76
Douglas-Home, Alexander 183
Douglas Social Credit Scheme 21, 186, 187
Dublin 18–19, 145, 152
Dundee 49, 133, 134
Dunfermline 69

Economics 14, 20, 21, 28, 43, 44, 48, 49, 50, 51, 66, 67, 72, 75, 80, 82, 85, 108, 123, 128, 129, 137, 140, 151–2, 154, 157, 158, 162, 163, 164, 168, 172–3, 176, 178–81, 182, 183, 184, 186–8
  Keynesian 140, 159, 178, 180
Edinburgh 18, 35, 128, 134, 148, 149, 150, 152, 163
Edward I 'Hammer of the Scots' 32, 37, 43, 48, 99, 106, 114, 141, 153, 154
Einstein, Albert 74

Elections and electoral system 6, 10, 20, 60, 66, 67, 72, 90, 92, 104, 106, 108, 116, 124, 129, 132, 134, 148, 151, 157, 161, 164, 165, 166, 167, 170, 171, 175, 176–7, 180, 184, 185
electoral mandate 2, 67, 104, 105, 106, 107, 109, 110, 116, 130, 135, 148, 165, 166, 175, 186
Elizabeth II 53, 91, 99, 114
Elliot, Walter 9, 150, 169
emigration 50, 138
England 4, 11, 15, 18–20, 26, 29, 34, 35, 36, 40, 42, 43, 45, 46–8, 52, 65, 69, 70, 73, 75, 77, 84, 92, 101, 102, 107, 108, 109, 111, 118, 123, 129, 134, 135, 138, 141, 143, 145, 146, 147–8, 149, 150, 153–6, 172–3, 185–6, 192, 193
Erskine of Mar, Ruaraidh 31, 64, 154
'Establishment' 154
ethnicity 16, 21, 25, 30–4, 37, 39–40, 58–9, 60, 102
Europe 11, 12, 13, 16, 20, 21, 23, 25, 26, 30, 45, 48, 50, 51, 55, 57, 61, 71, 76, 77, 80, 83, 101, 105, 137, 141, 143, 158, 159, 160, 161, 163, 164–5, 173, 177, 179, 184, 189, 192
European Union 76–7, 144, 189, 193
extremism 14, 164

fascism 56, 72, 75, 85, 86, 105, 115, 163, 164–5, 178, 187
federalism 5, 48, 123–4, 128, 131, 134, 136, 137
Festival of Britain 114
feudalism 35, 37, 46, 48, 59, 83, 111, 185
First World War *see* World War One
Fisher, Herbert A. L. 77
fishing 69, 102, 169, 177, 182, 188–9
Fletcher of Saltoun, Andrew 42
Foreign Office 77, 121
Forsyth, Michael 169
France 26, 29, 56, 70, 77, 79, 129, 192
Fry, Michael 110

Gaelic 30, 34, 35, 36, 75, 83, 84, 141, 187
Garibaldi, Giuseppe 59, 74
gender 21
geography 80
George, Henry 51

Germany 26, 56, 58, 62, 70, 79, 92, 143, 157, 164
Gibb, Andrew Dewar 73, 111, 171
Gibson, Robert 171
Gibson, Tom 171–4, 189
Gillies, Iain 162
Gillies, William 32
Gilmour Inquiry into Scottish Administration (1937) 182
Gladstone, William, E. 145, 148
Glasgow 51, 149
Glasgow Herald 91
Glasgow University 13, 47, 89, 145, 172
government spending 20, 172–3, 174–5, 180
Great Crash (1929) and depression 66, 82, 137, 140, 151, 159, 164–5, 178, 186
Greece 7, 79
Greenock 171
grievance 168, 169–75
Grieve, Christopher Murray *see* MacDiarmid, Hugh
Gunn, Neil 9, 72, 85, 176

Hague Conference 1948 76
Hames, Scott 5
Hamilton, James 4th duke 95
Hanham, Harry 187
Hanoverians 34, 35, 99
Harvie, Christopher 187
Henderson, Hamish 160
Highland Clearances 83–4
Highlands 34, 35, 36, 40, 50, 51, 53, 61, 67, 82, 95, 141, 167, 178, 187
  Clearances 153
history 3, 4, 7, 11, 12, 15, 23, 26, 39, 40–1, 48, 51, 53, 61, 63, 68, 91, 103, 143, 153, 192
  constitutional 89, 98, 107–8, 109–10
  early modern 27, 29
  medieval 25, 28, 30, 32, 34–7, 46, 55, 61, 141, 146
  whig school 140
home rule 5, 8, 10, 11, 15, 17–19, 49, 54, 60, 64, 66, 68, 76, 80, 90, 103, 105, 106, 116, 121, 123, 124, 125, 127, 129–35, 137, 139, 146, 148, 150, 152, 154, 156, 165, 167, 169, 170, 177, 182, 183, 185

Horne, Sir Robert 61, 151
Horsburgh, Florence 49
House of Commons 106, 111, 133, 147, 152, 182, 184
House of Lords 95-6, 97, 111, 130
housing 169, 180, 181-2, 183, 184
Hroch, Miroslav 55
Hume Brown, Peter 61
Hutchison, Iain, G. C. 130

identity politics 161
ideology 3, 4, 7, 8-9, 12, 20, 24, 26, 28, 37, 46, 56-7, 58, 59, 60, 68, 70-2, 75, 104, 115, 130, 135, 139, 140, 143, 144, 157, 160, 162-3, 166, 168-9, 170, 171, 172-3, 175, 176, 179, 183, 185, 186, 187, 189
immigration 39, 61, 192
imperialism 14, 26, 27, 28, 30, 48, 55, 61, 65, 76, 80, 111, 142, 153, 155, 157, 161, 163, 164
India 14, 137, 152, 153, 155-6
individualism 21, 75, 79-80, 111, 159, 187, 188, 189-90
industry 50-1, 82, 154, 165, 167, 172-4, 177, 181, 184
infant mortality 173
intellectuals 59, 159, 190
international relations 10, 11, 15, 25, 29, 37, 63, 70, 73, 76, 77, 78, 91, 129, 137, 150, 154
internationalism 64, 74, 179
Inverness 149
Ireland 4, 7, 12, 15, 16, 17, 18-19, 23, 26, 28, 29, 35-7, 40-1, 44, 58, 59, 61, 64, 66, 76, 77, 78, 82, 92, 102, 103-4, 105, 107, 115, 123, 126, 132, 134, 135, 136, 137, 139, 143, 147, 152, 153, 155, 160, 161, 193
  Bank of Ireland 136
  Easter Rising 1916 59, 104
  Great Famine 160
  home rule 145, 148
  partition 25
  Union 28, 91, 92, 94, 97, 98, 144, 145
  Revolution 29, 30, 37, 39, 40, 104, 105, 118
Irish Free State 147, 178
Irish in Scotland 50

Irish Self-Determination League of Great Britain 40
irredentism 25
Italy 59, 164

Jackson, Ben 5
Jacobites 33-4, 42, 43, 94, 95, 103, 112
James VI 32, 35, 44, 144
James VII 16, 109
Jews 58
Johnston, Thomas 37, 64, 150, 182

Keane, Sir John 136
Keir, Sir David L. 89
Kershaw, Ian 14
Kidd, James 146
Kilbrandon Report 123, 128
Kinloch, John L. 177, 189
Kirkcaldy 113
Kirkwood, David 64
Knox, John 27, 37, 191
Kossuth, Lajos 7, 59

Labour Party and government 10, 19, 20, 21, 53, 64, 69, 75, 90, 107, 113, 115, 116, 117, 124, 131, 134, 135, 152, 153, 155, 161, 166, 169, 170, 171, 176, 177, 178, 180, 182, 183, 184, 185, 187, 188, 189
Lamont, Archie 74, 182
land ownership 83, 153, 162, 166-7, 176
landscape 83-7
Latvia 23
League of Nations 11, 62-5, 68, 76, 77, 154
left/right political axis 4, 20, 54, 57, 60, 72, 127, 157-9, 160, 162, 166, 169, 171, 176, 185, 186, 189-90
left wing 4, 13, 78, 115, 127, 157, 158, 160, 162, 168, 169, 172, 175, 176, 184, 185-6, 189
legalism 90-4, 103, 106, 112, 116
Liberal Democrats 128
Liberal Party and liberalism 2, 21, 37, 69, 75, 107, 130, 134, 148-9, 161, 166, 169, 171, 172, 175-6, 177, 178, 183, 185, 188, 189, 190
  National Liberals 171
  New Liberalism 21, 189-90
Liberal Unionists 148

Lindsay, Isobel 139
Lithgow, Sir James 169
Lithuania 97
Liverpool 131
Livingstone, David 40, 145
Lloyd-Jones, Naomi 5
local government 20, 47, 67, 69, 109, 110, 131
localism 144, 148, 150
Lockhart of Carnwath, George 34
London 19, 39, 66, 70, 102, 106, 128, 129, 131, 142, 152, 156, 183
Lord Advocate 96
Lowlands 40, 53, 61, 141
Lynch, Peter 169

MacCormick, John M. 47, 96, 109, 113, 139, 171, 176, 183
MacCormick, Neil 128
MacDiarmid, Hugh 9, 31, 53, 75, 78, 85, 105, 112, 160, 163, 164, 165, 172, 186-7, 181
MacDiarmid, J. M. 124
Macdonald, Ramsay 75
MacEwen, Sir Alexander 165
Macinnes, Allan I. 29
Mackenzie, Sir Compton 1, 75, 79, 80-1, 84, 86, 112, 113-14, 165, 172
MacKinnon, David 121
Mackinnon, James 91, 97
Maclay, John P. 19
Maclean, John 37, 39, 81, 162
MacLean, Neil 64
MacNaecail, H. C. 36
Mair, John 144
Major, John 118
Manchester 149
Marxism 62, 160
Mary, Queen of Scots 16, 37, 109
Massie, Alex 1
Maxton, James 64, 150
Maxwell, Sir Herbert 146
Mazzini, Giuseppe 71, 74
McAllion, John 117
McIntyre, Robert D. 57, 106-7, 109, 113, 179, 181, 187-8, 189
McLean, Iain 7
McLeish, Henry 125
Mitchell, James 7, 186

monarchy 25, 32, 34, 42, 47, 52, 91, 95, 111, 114, 136, 137, 141, 155
Montrose, James Graham, 6th Duke of 136
Motherwell 106, 113
Movement to Oppose the Agitation for a Scottish National Parliament 154
Muir, Edwin 191
Muirhead, Robert F. 73, 138
Muirhead, Roland 57, 66, 134, 170, 177, 189
Murphy, Richard 175
Murray, Walter Rev. 177

Nairn, Tom 53, 160, 185, 191
National Association for the Vindication of Scottish Rights (1853) 5, 96
National Covenant 1638 16, 34, 52, 100-1, 109
National Covenant 1948 113, 116, 134-5, 170, 171, 183
'national efficiency' 132
national identity 5, 7, 17, 19, 45, 47, 50, 60, 74, 80, 85, 100, 121, 123, 131, 141-2, 143, 145, 146, 148, 150, 152, 191, 192
National Party of Scotland (NPS) 112, 124, 135, 137-8, 162, 165, 170-1, 172
nationalism 2, 3, 5, 7, 8, 12, 13-14, 23, 26, 29-30, 37, 40, 50, 53, 55-64, 67, 70-7, 78, 87, 92, 102, 105, 115, 117, 121, 131-2, 133, 140, 142, 143, 150, 155, 156, 157, 160, 163, 167, 175, 177-8, 187, 192
  authoritarian nationalism 58, 61-2, 71, 73, 79, 165, 178
  big nation nationalism 149-53, 155, 193
  civic nationalism 59-60, 72, 74
  expedient or instrumental nationalism 57-8, 71-2, 190
  liberal nationalism 59
  small 'n' nationalism 126, 183, 193
nationhood 3, 11
Nazis 58, 85
Netherlands 23, 77
New Liberalism 21
Newcastle 149
Northern Ireland 2, 16, 19, 23, 32, 34, 59, 102, 123, 134, 145, 146, 148, 156, 193

Norway 147
nuclear disarmament 82

O'Brien, Art 40
O'Casey, Sean 78
O'Grada, Cormic 160
opinion polls 126
Orr, Christine 75
Orwell, George 78
Ottoman Empire 7, 11, 62, 77, 80
Oxford 140, 141

pacifism 105, 113
Paisley 171, 183
Palmerston, Henry John Temple, 3rd viscount 145
Paris Peace Conference 1919 see Treaty of Versailles
'parliamentary congestion' 132–3
Parnell, Charles 17, 34, 139
Paton, Herbert J. 92
Pearce, Patrick 59
Petrie, Malcolm 5
Picts 11, 61
planning 151, 159, 181, 182, 187
plebiscite 110, 116
Pocock, John G. A. 144
Poland 7, 26, 77, 80, 97, 143
Poll Tax 110
pragmatism 190
Presbyterianism 95, 99, 100, 165
Pressure groups 10, 72, 116, 171
propaganda 79, 104
Protestantism 30, 37, 142, 151
public expenditure 129
public health 181

race 21, 25, 30, 32, 34, 36–7, 39, 49, 50, 58, 61, 78, 141, 142, 150, 164
Radical Scotland 185
radicalism 174–6
Raffe, Alastair 143
Ragman's Roll 154
Rait, Robert 98
Ramsay, William Mitchell 140–3
Redmond, John 107
referendum
   1979 126, 130, 148
   1997 126
   2014 1, 4, 128
Reformation 1560 26, 27, 37, 52, 109, 191
religious sectarianism 27, 42
Renan, Ernest 11
republicanism 30, 32, 34, 37, 42, 45, 59, 126
revolution 15, 30, 39, 41, 52, 91, 102–3, 112, 115, 157, 192
Rifkind, Malcolm 131, 169
right of resistance 92, 104
right of self-determination 11, 13, 18, 57, 62, 69, 72, 74, 108, 118, 138
right-wing 14, 65, 78, 115, 129, 158, 161, 162, 165, 168, 169, 176, 186, 192
Robert the Bruce 16, 37, 52, 103, 111, 114, 146
Robertson, George 126
Roebuck, John 18
Romania 80
Rosebery, Archibald Primrose, 5th Earl of 29, 52, 103, 145, 146
rural society 50, 82, 85, 166, 178, 184, 187, 188, 190
Russia 7, 11, 26, 70, 79, 143

Salamis 79
Salisbury, Robert Cascoyne-Cecil, 3rd Marquess 145
Saltire Society 48
'Scotland is British' campaign 148
Scots 11
Scots Independent 9, 168, 171
Scots National League (SNL) 33, 192
Scott, Sir Walter 36
Scottish Civil Society 100–6
Scottish Constitutional Convention 54, 170
Scottish Crown and Regalia 98–9
Scottish education 12, 45, 52, 100, 101, 102, 169, 174, 191
Scottish Enlightenment 28, 49
Scottish Government 2, 7
Scottish Grand Committee 182
Scottish History Society 146
Scottish Home Rule Association 169–70
Scottish independence 2, 3, 4, 5, 7, 8, 13, 15, 17, 19, 27, 40, 43, 46, 51, 54, 55, 57, 64, 66, 68, 72, 76, 79, 87, 80, 93, 105, 117–18, 121, 124,

126, 128, 129, 132, 133, 136, 153, 154, 156, 160, 162–3, 164, 165–6, 168, 169, 173, 175, 179, 185, 187, 192
  'stepping stone to' 17, 124, 128, 131, 139, 156
Scottish Office 68, 123, 127, 182
Scottish law (*see also* legalism) 12, 16, 24–5, 41, 42, 45, 47, 60, 63, 89, 93, 95, 96, 100, 101–2, 109, 110–11, 154, 189
Scottish Liberation Army 115
Scottish literature 10, 31, 85–6
Scottish National Congress 163
Scottish National Convention (1989) 127
Scottish National Movement (SNM) 39
Scottish National Party (SNP) 2, 7, 9, 20, 33, 56, 57, 59, 65, 67–8, 72, 76, 85, 90, 104, 106, 109, 112, 113, 116, 117, 118, 128, 129, 132, 135, 137, 157, 161, 162–3, 164–5, 168, 171, 175, 177, 178, 179, 181, 184, 185, 186, 188, 189–90, 192
Scottish parliament 4, 12, 17, 42, 54, 60, 80, 105, 109, 117, 121, 124, 125, 127, 128, 135, 138, 150, 151, 152, 156, 181, 182
Scottish Party 171
Scottish renaissance 53, 85, 191
Scottish Secretary of State 9, 171, 182
Scottish Socialist Party 163
Scottish Unionist Party *see also* Conservative Party 148
Scrymgeour, Edwin 96
Second World War *see* World War Two
self-government 5, 10, 12, 14, 19, 30, 49, 64, 66, 68, 109, 122, 125, 129, 135, 136–40, 152, 156, 165–6, 168, 169, 170, 176, 183, 185
Shaw, Alexander 44
Shinwell, Manny 64
Sillars, Jim 76
Sinn Fein 30, 34, 92, 106, 107
Skelton, Noel 147–8
small nations 13–14, 26, 65, 71, 75, 76, 77–83, 87, 122, 146, 149–50, 155, 173, 187, 189, 192
Smith Commission 118
Snodgrass, Catherine 174

social Darwinism 50, 58, 77
social democratic 21, 184, 187, 192
social theorist 8
socialism 7, 37, 75, 78, 115, 121, 153, 162, 164, 176, 179, 187
Solemn League and Covenant 16, 34
Somers, Lord John 97
Soviet Union 14, 39, 56, 78, 81, 151, 159, 161, 179
sovereignty 15–16, 18, 37, 47, 54, 89, 90, 92, 96, 98, 99, 108, 109, 117, 138, 139
  of parliament 93–4, 97, 99, 103, 108, 109, 116, 118
  of the people 105, 106–18, 124, 125, 127
Spence, Lewis 39, 67
St. Giles Cathedral 114
state intervention 20, 139–40, 152, 157–60, 165, 172, 178, 180, 181–6, 187
Statute of Westminster 105, 137
Stevenson, Robert Louis 53, 145
Stewart, Anthony Q. 23
Stirling 112
Stone of Destiny 113–14
subsidies 129, 151, 174
Sudaten crisis (1938) 14, 58, 78
Sweden 147

tactical voting 185
'Tartan Monster' 191
'Tartan Tories' 185
taxation 29, 41
technology 28, 48, 50, 157
Thatcher, Margaret 2, 53, 59, 117, 130, 131, 182
trade unions 158, 182, 187
Treaty of Union 1707 2, 3, 12, 15–16, 18, 23, 25, 28–9, 33, 35, 40–1, 43, 45, 47, 48, 91, 94, 95, 96, 97, 101, 103, 108, 109, 110, 113, 114, 128, 140, 142, 146, 191, 192
Tudors 11
Turner, Arthur 79

unemployment 84, 151, 167, 178, 180
Union (*see also* Treaty of Union 1707) 1, 3, 4, 5, 42–8, 49, 50, 66, 67, 83, 89, 91, 93–100, 103, 104, 108, 112, 118, 125, 130, 147, 168

Union of the Crowns 1603 11, 27, 32, 41, 142, 144
Unionism 7, 12, 16, 17–19, 28–30, 49, 52, 53, 68, 102, 108, 121, 123, 126, 127, 129, 139, 140–6, 147, 151, 153, 155, 156, 192
Unionist nationalism 7, 143–4
Unitarism 145, 146
United Nation 76, 77, 92, 174
United States 30, 37, 81, 96, 153, 158, 179

Versailles Treaty 1919 11, 14, 25, 62–3, 64, 65, 76, 77, 78, 82, 136

Wales 5, 12, 25, 61, 77, 78, 123, 135, 146, 151, 155, 193
Wallace, William 24, 30, 37, 45, 48, 52, 103, 106, 146
Wapenshaw 111
War of Spanish Succession (1702–1713) 95
Welfare State 59, 114, 179, 180, 186
Westminster 15–16, 20, 33, 34, 45, 49, 66, 67, 68, 69, 72, 89, 93, 94, 96, 97, 101, 102, 105, 111, 116, 121, 125, 126, 132, 133, 134, 135, 136, 155, 156, 157, 162, 163, 165, 169, 172, 173–4, 176, 178, 181, 183, 188
Wilkie, Alexander 64
Williams, Gwyn 18
Wilson, Gordon 185
Wilson, Harold 180
Wolfe, William 184
Wood, Wendy 112
Woodburn, Arthur 134, 152
World War One 2, 10, 11, 44, 51, 57, 62, 65, 70, 72, 78, 80, 96, 105, 118, 133, 136, 137, 143, 147, 158, 164, 169, 175, 189
World War Two 14, 58, 61, 67, 71, 79, 84, 91, 106, 113, 137, 139, 150, 152, 159, 161, 168, 176, 178

Yorkshire 70
Young, Douglas 106, 113, 139
Young Scots Society 189
Younger George (1851–1929) 148, 149
Younger, George (1931–2003) 130
Yugoslavia 59, 79, 80

www.ingramcontent.com/pod-product-compliance
Lightning Source LLC
Chambersburg PA
CBHW062132300426
44115CB00012BA/1892